3rd edition
REVISED & EXPANDED

LAN TUTORIAL
WITH GLOSSARY OF TERMS

A COMPLETE INTRODUCTION TO LOCAL AREA NETWORKS
BY THE EDITORS OF LAN MAGAZINE

MILLER FREEMAN BOOKS
LAN Networking Library
San Francisco

Third Edition
Miller Freeman Books, 600 Harrison Street,
San Francisco, California 94107
Publishers of *LAN Magazine*
A member of the United Newspapers Group

un Miller Freeman

Cover Photo: Jeff Berkowitz, Lifesmith Classic Fractals
Editor, First and Second Editions: Patricia Schnaidt
Editor, Third Edition: Steve Steinke
Illustrations: Rick Eberly

ISBN 0-87930-379-4
Printed in USA
95 96 97 98   5 4 3 2 1

Contents

Acknowledgments

The third edition of the LAN tutorial includes each installment of an ongoing series of articles that originally appeared in *LAN Magazine* through December 1995. These tutorials were written by Rebecca J. Campbell, Lee Chae, Dave Fogle, Alan Frank, Melanie McMullen, Steve Steinke, Aaron Brenner, Jim Carr, Ken Mackin, Thomas Peltier, Patricia Schnaidt, and Bonny Hinners. Melanie McMullen and Steve Steinke expanded and upgraded the glossary to provide an even more comprehensive quick reference for unfamiliar terms.

This third edition was edited by Steve Steinke, building on the editorial framework created by Patricia Schnaidt from the first and second editions.

The Editors of *LAN: The Network Solutions Magazine*

Section I

Network Basics

Buying a LAN

A local area network (LAN) is a data communications network spanning a limited geographical area, a few miles at most. A LAN allows users to share information and computer resources, including mass storage devices, backup facilities, applications software, data files, printers, plotters, and processors.

A LAN is made up of network interface cards that fit inside the connected computers, cable (or an equivalent wireless connection) to connect these computers together, protocol software to move data from computer to computer, user interface software to connect the user and the network, and operating system software to actually service users' needs for resources like files and printers. Finally, a LAN runs end-user applications.

Once a network spans more than a few miles, such as a campus environment, it can be referred to as a metropolitan area network (MAN). A MAN spans a region such as a city. A wide area network (WAN) brings companies into the sphere of networking by connecting computers in the entire enterprise, which may span over several cities, states, and countries.

WHY A LAN?

Although LANs were originally designed to share expensive printers and mass storage devices, networks have evolved into essential communications media. In addition to staple applications such as file and print sharing, electronic mail (e-mail) and shared databases have become essential. Companies are using networks for their mission-critical applications, such as airline reservation systems, inventory systems, point-of-sale systems, and order-entry systems. Applications are being redesigned to take advantage of the client-server architecture inherent in networks.

Networks may contain the pantheon of computer devices, including personal computers such as Macintoshes and IBM compatibles, engineering workstations such as Suns and HPs, minicomputers such as the VAX or AS/400, and mainframes. Printers, plotters, scanners, and fax machines are also standard LAN fare.

Data is a corporation's major asset. Networks are a way for companies to leverage that asset and distribute it to the proper people. For example, the marketing department can access mainframe data from their Macintoshes. From their familiar Mac interfaces, they can make projections and create attractive presentations. The accounting department can use its favorite workstations and software, as can engineering, purchasing, and sales. Although each department needs a different type of computer, they all need access to corporate data. With the proper software, the different departments can share access and share information.

Connectivity is the first goal of networks. With simple connectivity, different types of computers can communicate. Today's goal is interoperability, which enables these computers to communicate in a meaningful way.

LANs require a certain mindset, one that is different from the traditional MIS (Management Information Systems) way of thinking. Whereas MIS tightly controls the data and programs that reside on the mainframe, a network brings accessibility.

If you have the right mindset, LANs bring communication, democracy, productivity, and savings to a corporation. A LAN connects the people in your company and makes every form of discourse possible, from electronic messages to lengthy documents. Second, a network is democratic. A LAN distributes your company's informational resources to everyone connected. Once the LAN is installed, everyone from the mail clerk to the CEO will want (and should have) access to the information. A network increases productivity. A LAN's ability to share computer resources and information easily helps people do their jobs more quickly, efficiently, and with less hassle than standalone PCs or minicomputers. A network brings savings. A LAN saves money by allowing users to share expensive computer resources—printers, plotters, large disks, optical drives, software, and above all, information.

WHICH LAN SHOULD I BUY?

Buying and installing a LAN is not simple. A network is more complicated than choosing, installing, and maintaining a minicomputer or mainframe, simply because so many combinations of hardware and software exist.

The type of LAN you buy depends on the work your business does. Before you evaluate different vendors' options, vigorously assess your company's computer needs and resources, both present and future. Plan for expansion; a network never shrinks, it only grows.

What business problem do you want to solve? What is the primary application for the network? Is a LAN indeed the best method? If occasional file and printer sharing is the main application, then you will do best with one of the so-called entry-level or peer-to-peer LANs—ones that boast low-cost and easy maintenance, but may be slower and less featured than full-fledged networks. If database access is the primary motive, then make sure you choose fast hardware and software. If the network will be used for communications and electronic mail, then compatibility with a wide range of standards should be the deciding factor.

Other considerations include the computer and network literacy of the users, the types of computers to be connected, the time you want to spend on administration, and your budget.

Usually, a company wants the network to do everything: share files, printers, databases, electronic mail, and connect to remote resources. Unfortunately, no network does everything. Vendors must make compromises. They may sacrifice ease of use for performance. They may exchange high performance for compatibility with multiple systems. Extensive research and an understanding of the possibilities before you buy is essential to a successful LAN system.

LAN Protocols

A LAN *protocol* is a set of rules for communicating between computers. Protocols govern format, timing, sequencing, and error control. Without these rules, the computer cannot make sense of the stream of incoming bits.

But there is more than just basic communication. Suppose you plan to send a file from one computer to another. You could simply send it all in one single string of data. Unfortunately, that would stop others from using the LAN for the entire time it takes to send the message. This would not be appreciated by the other users. Additionally, if an error occurred during the transmission, the entire file would have to be sent again. To resolve both of these problems, the file is broken into small pieces called packets and the packets are grouped in a certain fashion. This means that information must be added to tell the receiver where each group belongs in relation to others, but this is a minor issue. To further improve transmission reliability, timing information and error correcting information are added.

Because of this complexity, computer communication is broken down into steps. Each step has its own rules of operation and, consequently, its own protocol. These steps must be executed in a certain order, from the top down on transmission and from the bottom up on reception. Because of this hierarchical arrangement, the term *protocol stack* is often used to describe these steps. A protocol stack, therefore, is a set of rules for communication, and each step in the sequence has its own subset of rules.

What is a protocol, really? It is software that resides either in a computer's memory or in the memory of a transmission device, like a network interface card. When data is ready for transmission, this software is executed. The software prepares data for transmission and sets the transmission in motion. At the receiving end, the software takes the data off the wire and prepares it for the computer by taking off all the information added by the transmitting end.

There are a lot of protocols, and this often leads to confusion. A Novell network communicates through its own set of rules (its own protocol called IPX/SPX), Microsoft does it another way (NetBEUI) DEC does it a third way (DECnet), and IBM does it yet a fourth (NetBIOS). Since the transmitter and the receiver have to "speak" the same protocol, these four systems cannot talk directly to each other. And even if they could directly communicate, there is no guarantee the data would be usable once it was communicated.

Anyone who's ever wanted to transfer data from an IBM-compatible personal computer to an Apple Macintosh computer realizes that what should be a simple procedure is anything but. These two popular computers use widely differing—and incompatible—file systems. That makes exchanging information between them impossible, unless you have translation software or a LAN. Even with a network, file transfer between these two types of computers isn't always transparent.

If two types of personal computers can't communicate easily, imagine the problems occurring between PCs and mainframe computers, which operate in vastly different environments and usually under their own proprietary operating software and protocols. For example, the original IBM PC's peripheral interface—known as a bus—transmits data eight bits at a time. The newer 386 and 486 PCs have 32-bit buses, and mainframes have even wider buses. This means that peripherals designed to operate with one bus are incompatible with another bus, and this includes network interface cards (NICs). Similar incompatibilities also exist with software. For instance, Unix-based applications (and data generated with them) cannot be used on PCs operating under MS-DOS. Resolving some of these incompatibilities is where protocol standards fit in.

A protocol standard is a set of rules for computer communication that has been widely agreed upon and implemented by many vendors, users, and standards bodies. Ideally, a protocol standard should allow computers to talk to each other, even if they are from different vendors. Computers don't have to use an industry-standard protocol to communicate, but if they use a proprietary protocol then they can only communicate with equipment of their own kind.

There are many standard protocols, none of which could be called universal, but the successful ones are moving towards full compliance with something called the OSI model. The standards and protocols associated with the OSI reference model are the cornerstone of the open systems concept for linking the literally dozens of dissimilar computers found in offices throughout the world.

THE OSI MODEL

The Open System Interconnection (OSI) model is a set of protocols that attempt to define and standardize the data communications process. The OSI model is set by the International Standards Organization (ISO). The OSI model has the support of most major computer and network vendors, many large customers, and most governments, including the United States.

The OSI model is a concept that describes how data communications should take place. It divides the process into seven groups, called layers. Into these layers are fitted the protocol standards developed by the ISO and other standards bodies, including the Institute of Electrical and Electronic Engineers (IEEE), American National Standards Institute (ANSI), and the International Telecommunications Union (ITU), formerly known as the CCITT (Comite Consultatif Internationale de Telegraphique et Telephone).

The OSI model is not a single definition of how data communications actually takes place in the real world. Numerous protocols may exist at each layer. The OSI model states how the process should be divided and what protocols should be used at each layer. If a network vendor implements one of the protocols at each layer, its network components should work with other vendors' offerings.

The OSI model is modular. Each successive layer of the OSI model works with the one above and below it. At least in theory, you may substitute one protocol for another at the same layer without affecting the operation of layers above or below. For example, Token Ring or Ethernet hardware should operate with multiple upper-layer services, including the transport protocols, network operating system, internetwork protocols, and applications interfaces. However, for this interoperability to work, vendors must create products to meet the OSI model's specifications.

MYRIAD PROTOCOL STACKS

Layer	ISO	TCP/IP	IBM
7. Application	FTAM X.400 JTAM X.500 VT CASE	SMTP FTP NFS Telnet SNMP	
6. Presentation	8923		
5. Session	8327		NetBIOS APPC
4. Transport	8073 (TPO) 8602 (CONS)	UDP TCP	NetBEUI APPC
3. Network	8208 (X.25) 8473 (CLNS) 9542 (ES-IS) 8348 (CONS)	IP	APPC
2. Data-Link	8802.2 LLC 8802.3/4/5	LLC Ethernet	LLC HDLC SDLC MAC
1. Physical	8802.3 Ethernet 8802.4 Token Bus 8802.5 Token Ring	Ethernet FDDI Token Ring	Token Ring Ethernet FDDI

The OSI model is not a single definition of how data communications takes place. It states how the processes should be divided and offers several options. In addition to the OSI protocols, as defined by ISO, networks can use the TCP/IP protocol suite, the IBM Systems Network Architecture (SNA) suite, and others. TCP/IP and SNA roughly follow the OSI structure.

Although each layer of the OSI model provides its own set of functions, it is possible to group the layers into two distinct categories. The first four layers—physical, data link, network, and transport—provide the end-to-end services necessary for the transfer of data between two systems. These layers provide the protocols associated with the communications network used to link two computers together.

The top three layers—the application, presentation, and session layers—provide the application services required for the exchange of information. That is, they allow two applications, each running on a different node of the network, to interact with each other through the services provided by their respective operating systems.

A graphical illustration of the OSI model is shown on page 9. The following is a description of just what each layer does.

1. The *Physical* layer provides the electrical and mechanical interface to the network medium (the cable). This layer gives the data-link layer (layer 2) its ability to transport a stream of serial data bits between two communicating systems; it conveys the bits that move along the cable. It is responsible for making sure that the raw bits get from one place to another, no matter what shape they are in, and deals with the mechanical and electrical characteristics of the cable.

2. *The Data-Link* layer handles the physical transfer, framing (the assembly of data into a single unit or block), flow control and error-control functions (and retransmission in the event of an error) over a single transmission link; it is responsible for getting the data packaged and onto the network cable. The data link layer provides the network layer (layer 3) reliable information-transfer capabilities. The data-link layer is often subdivided into two parts—Logical Link Control (LLC) and Medium Access Control (MAC)—depending on the implementation.

3. The *Network layer* establishes, maintains, and terminates logical and/or physical connections. The network layer is responsible for translating logical addresses, or names, into physical addresses. It provides network routing and flow-control functions across the computer-network interface.

4. The *Transport layer* ensures data is successfully sent and received between the two computers. If data is sent incorrectly, this layer has the responsibility to ask for retransmission of the data. Specifically, it provides a network-independent, reliable message-independent, reliable message-interchange service to the top three application-oriented lay-

ers. This layer acts as an interface between the bottom and top three layers. By providing the session layer (layer 5) with a reliable message-transfer service, it hides the detailed operation of the underlying network from the session layer.

5. The *Session layer* decides when to turn communication on and off between two computers—it provides the mechanisms that control the data-exchange process and coordinates the interaction between them. It sets up and clears communication channels between two communicating components. Unlike the network layer (layer 3), it deals with the programs running in each machine to establish conversations between them.

6. The *Presentation layer* performs code conversion and data reformatting (syntax translation). It is the translator of the network, making sure the data is in the correct form for the receiving application. Of course, both the sending and receiving applications must be able to use data subscribing to one of the available abstract data syntax forms.

7. The *Application layer* provides the user interface between the software running in the computer and the network. It provides functions to the user's software, including file transfer access and management (FTAM) and electronic mail.

Unfortunately, protocols in the real world do not conform precisely to these neat definitions. Some network products and architectures combine layers. Others leave layers out. Still others break the layers apart. But no matter how they do it, all working network products achieve the same result—getting data from here to there. The question is, do they do it in a way that is compatible with networks in the rest of the world?

WHAT OSI IS AND IS NOT

While discussing the OSI reference model it is important to understand what the model does not specify as well as what it actually spells out. The ISO created the OSI reference model solely to describe the external behavior of electronics systems, not their internal functions.

The reference model does not determine programming or operating sys-

THE OSI PROTOCOLS

Layer									
7	X.400	FTAM	VT	X.500	CMP	ROSE	ODA	EDIFACT	RDA
6		ACSE							
		Presentation							
5	Session								
4	Transport Class 0-4								
3	Connection-Oriented, Connectionless								
2	CSMA/CD (Ethernet)	Token Bus	Token Ring	FDDI	X.25			ISDN	
1	8802/3	8802/4	8802/5	XT3.9	HDLC LAPB			ISDN	
					114A	EIA 232			

ISO has specified many different protocols at each layer of the OSI model. Some of the options are shown above.

tem functions, nor does it specify an application programming interface (API). Neither does it dictate the end-user interface—that is, the command-line and/or icon-based prompts a user uses to interact with a computer system.

OSI merely describes what is placed on a network cable and when it will be placed there. It does not state how vendors must build their computers, only the kinds of behavior these systems may exhibit while performing certain communications operations.

The OSI standards can be grouped into pairs—one defines the services offered by a network component, while the second specifies the protocol used by that component to provide the defined service. This concept permits a vendor to develop network elements that are more or less ignorant of the other components on the network. They are said to be ignorant in that they may need to know that other network components exist, but not the specific details about their operating systems or interface buses. One of the primary benefits of this concept is that vendors can change the internal design of their network components without affecting their network functionality, as long as they maintain the OSI-prescribed external attributes. The figure on the preceding page shows the protocols in the OSI model.

CONNECTION TYPES

The OSI model is inherently connection-oriented, but the services each OSI layer provides can either be connection-oriented, or connectionless. In the three-step connection-oriented mode operation (the steps are connection establishment, data transfer, and connection release), an explicit binding between two systems takes place.

In connectionless operation, no such explicit link occurs; data transfer takes place with no specified connection and disconnection function occurring between the two communicating systems. Connectionless communication is also known as datagram communication.

AT THE PHYSICAL LAYER

Let's compare some real protocols to the OSI model. The best known physical layer standards of the OSI model are those from the IEEE. That is, the ISO adopted some of the IEEE's physical network standards as part of its OSI model, including IEEE 802.3 or Ethernet, IEEE 802.4 or token-passing bus, and IEEE 802.5 or Token Ring. ISO has changed the numbering scheme, however, so 802.3 networks are referred to as ISO 8802-3, 802.4 networks are ISO 8802-4, and 802.5 networks are ISO 8802-5.

Each physical layer standard defines the network's physical characteristics and how to get raw data from one place to another. They also define how multiple computers can simultaneously use the network without interfering with each other. (Technically, this last part is a job for the data-link layer, but we'll deal with that later.)

IEEE 802.3 defines a network that can transmit data at 10Mbps and uses a logical bus (or a straight line) layout. (Physically, the network can be configured as a bus or a star.) Data is simultaneously broadcast to all machines on the network and is non-directional on the cable. All machines receive every broadcast, but only those meant to receive the data will respond with an acknowledgment. Network access is determined by a protocol called Carrier Sense Multiple Access/Collision Detection (CSMA/CD). CSMA/CD lets all computers send data whenever the cable is free of traffic. If the data collides with another data packet, both computers "back off," or wait, then try again to send the data until receipt is acknowledged. Thus, once there is a high level of traffic, the more users there are, the more crowded and slower the network will become. Ethernet has found wide acceptance in office automation networks.

IEEE 802.4 defines a physical network that has a bus layout. Like 802.3, Token Bus is a broadcast network. All machines receive all data but do not respond unless data is addressed to them. But unlike 802.3, network access is determined by a token that moves around the network. The token is broadcast to every device but only the device that is next in line for the token gets it. Once a device has the token it may transmit data. The Manufacturing Automation Protocol (MAP) and Technical Office Protocol (TOP) standards use an 802.4 physical layer. Token Bus has had little success outside of factory automation networks.

IEEE 802.5 defines a network that transmits data at 4Mbps or 16Mbps and uses a logical ring layout, but is physically configured as a star. Data moves around the ring from station to station, and each station regenerates the signal. It is not a broadcast network. The network access protocol is token-passing. The token and data move about in a ring, rather than over a bus as it does in Token Bus. Token Ring has found moderate acceptance in office automation networks.

There are other physical and data-link layer standards, some that conform to the OSI model and others that don't. Arcnet is a well known one that does not conform to any standard but its own. It uses a token-passing bus access method, but not the same as does IEEE 802.4. LocalTalk is Apple's proprietary network that transmits data at 230.4Kbps and uses CSMA/CA (Collision Avoidance). Fiber Distributed Data Interface (FDDI) is an ANSI and OSI standard for a fiber-optic LAN that uses a token-passing protocol to transmit data at 100Mbps on a ring.

WHEN IT BEGAN

The International Standards Organization, based in Geneva, Switzerland, is a multinational body of representatives from the standards-setting agencies of about 30 countries. These agencies include the American National Standards Institute (ANSI) and British Standards Institute (BSI).

Because of the multinational nature of Europe, and their critical need for intersystem communication, the market for OSI-based products is particularly strong there. As a result, the European Computer Manufacturers' Association (ECMA) has played a major role in developing the OSI standards. In fact, European networking vendors and users are generally further advanced in their OSI implementations than are their American counterparts, who rely principally on proprietary solutions such as IBM's Systems Network Architecture (SNA) or the Internet's Transmission Control Protocol/Internet Protocol (TCP/IP).

Creating the OSI standards has been a long, drawn-out process: The ISO began work on OSI protocols in the late 1970s, finally releasing its seven-layer architecture in 1984. It wasn't until 1988 that the five-step standards-setting process finally resulted in stabilized protocols for the upper layers of the OSI reference model. As the OSI protocols continue to stabilize, the marketplace will encourage vendors to become more compliant. In turn, OSI will continue its evolution—incorporating the technological advances that inevitably occur in the electronics marketplace.

WHERE OSI IS NOW

As noted, the OSI-ratification process progresses slowly; only after many years have vendors brought OSI-compatible applications to the market. Among the first of these have been X.400-based electronic mail packages; Retix (Santa Monica, Calif.) and Touch Communications (Campbell, Calif.) offer X.400 e-mail products. In real-world application, these X.400 e-mail packages allow incompatible end-user e-mail programs, such as Lotus' (Cambridge, Mass.), cc:Mail and IBM's PROFS, to communicate with each other.

Retix is also at the forefront of providing an OSI-compliant X.500 directory service application. This protocol specifies a global network addressing scheme that simplifies sending electronic messages across large, multi-segment networks.

A third OSI application, File Transfer, Access, and Management (FTAM), is also in use. This provides the protocols for the exchange of files between two incompatible systems.

In Europe, vendors and users are implementing what is known as EDIFACT, for Electronic Data Interchange for Administration, Commerce, and Transport. EDIFACT, which became ISO international standard 9735 in 1988, provides a syntax that allows international trading partners to define the format and structure of business-related documents such as purchase orders and invoices.

EDIFACT allows one company to create order-entry forms online, then exchange the data added to those forms with computers in another company. The receiving company's computers then use the EDIFACT structural syntax to interpret and process the received document.

When fully implemented, EDIFACT, X.400, and X.500 will allow quick and easy transmittance of forms-based data across a wide variety of incompatible computer systems and large, enterprisewide networks, thus fulfilling the original "open systems communications" promise of OSI.

LAN Protocols, Part II

The Data-Link layer (the second OSI layer) is often divided into two sublayers; the Logical Link Control (LLC) and the Medium Access Control (MAC). The IEEE also defines standards at the data-link layer. The ISO standards for the MAC, or lower half of the data-link layer, were taken directly from the IEEE 802.x standards.

Medium Access Control, as its name suggests, is the protocol that determines which computer gets to use the cable (the transmission medium) when several computers are trying. For example, 802.3 allows packets to collide with each other, forcing the computers to retry a transmission until it is received. 802.4 and 802.5 limit conversation to the computer with the token. Remember, this is done in fractions of a second, so even when the network is busy, users don't wait very long for access on any of these three network types.

The upper half of the data-link layer, the LLC, provides reliable data transfer over the physical link. In essence, it manages the physical link.

The IEEE splits the data-link layer in half because the layer has two jobs to do. The first is to coordinate the physical transfer of data. The second is to manage access to the physical medium. Dividing the layer allows for more modularity and therefore more flexibility. The type of medium access control has more to do with the physical requirements of the network than the actual management of data transfer. In other words, the MAC layer is closer to the physical layer than the LLC layer. By dividing the layer, a number of MAC layers can be created, each corresponding to a different physical layer, but just one LLC layer can handle them all. This increases flexibility and gives the LLC an important role in providing an interface between the various MAC layers and the higher-layer protocols. The role of the data-link's upper layer is so crucial, the IEEE gave it a standard of its own: 802.2 LLC.

Besides 802.2, other protocols can perform the LLC functions. High-level Data-Link Control (HDLC) is a protocol from ISO, which also conforms to the

17

OSI model. IBM's Synchronous Data-Link Control (SDLC) does not conform to the OSI model but performs functions similar to the data-link layer. Digital Equipment's DDCMP or Digital Data Communications Protocol provides similar functions.

THREE TRANSPORT PROTOCOLS

The ISO has established protocol standards for the middle layers of the OSI model. The transport layer, at layer four, ensures that data is reliably transferred among transport services and users. Layer five, the session layer, is responsible for process-to-process communication. The line between the session and transport layers is often blurred.

As of yet, no ISO transport or session layer has been implemented on a widespread basis, nor has the complete OSI protocol stack been established. To make matters more confusing, most middle-layer protocols on the market today do not fit neatly into the OSI model's of transport and session layers, since many were created before the ISO began work on the OSI model.

The good news is many existing protocols are being incorporated into the OSI model. Where existing protocols are not incorporated, interfaces to the OSI model are being implemented. This is the case for TCP/IP, and IPX, which are the major middle-layer protocols available today.

In the PC LAN environment, NetBIOS has been an important protocol. IBM developed NetBIOS (or Network Basic Input/Output System) as an input/output system for networks. NetBIOS can be considered a session-layer protocol that acts as an application interface to the network. It provides the tools for a program to establish a session with another program over the network. Many programs have been written to this interface.

NetBIOS does not obey the rules of the OSI model in that it does not talk only to the layers above and below it. Programs can talk directly to NetBIOS, skipping the application and presentation layers. This doesn't keep NetBIOS from doing its job; it just makes it incompatible with the OSI model. The main drawback of NetBIOS is it is limited to working on a single network.

TCP/IP or Transmission Control Protocol/Internet Protocol is actually several protocols. TCP is a transport protocol. IP operates on the network

THE TCP/IP PROTOCOL STACK

5-7	File Transfer Protocol (FTP)	Trivial File Transfer Protocol (TFTP)	Simple Mail Transfer Protocol (SMTP)	Telnet	Simple Network Management Protocol (SNMP)
4	Transmission Control Protocol (TCP)		User Datagram Protocol (UDP)		
3	Internet Protocol (IP)				
2	Logical Link Control (LLC)				
	Medium Access Control (MAC)				
1	Ethernet	Token Ring	FDDI	X.25	

The TCP/IP stack includes protocols that provide services equivalent to the OSI stack.

layer. TCP/IP enjoys enormous support in government, scientific, and academic internetworks. These environments use Unix and other large-computer operating systems. Recently, corporate networks have begun to approach the size of networks found in the government and in universities, which has driven them to look for internetworking protocol standards. They have found that TCP/IP is useful and it has become a de facto standard. Many people view TCP/IP as an interim solution until OSI is deployed in the next 10 years (and beyond).

Often when TCP/IP is discussed, SMTP, FTP, Telnet, and SNMP are discussed. These are applications written specifically for TCP/IP. SMTP or the Simple Mail Transfer Protocol is electronic mail. FTP stands for File Transfer Protocol and is used to exchange files among computers running TCP/IP. Telnet is remote log-in and terminal emulation software. SNMP or the Simple

Network Management Protocol has enjoyed a recent surge as the favored network management protocol. The figure on the preceding page shows the protocols of TCP/IP.

Advanced Program-to-Program Communications (APPC) is one of IBM's newest transport protocols. Like NetBIOS, APPC provides an interface to the network for programs to communicate, but it is not limited to one network as is NetBIOS. APPC also is part of IBM's System Application Architecture (SAA), which NetBIOS is not. IBM offers APPC on its range of operating systems, from mainframe operating systems to OS/2. However, APPC is a significant break from the hierarchical, mainframe mentality because all computers running APPC communicate as peers. That means a PC can communicate directly with a mainframe. Previously in the IBM world, PCs were forced to emulate terminals when communicating with mainframes.

APPC has received much publicity; unfortunately, few applications for APPC exist. Nevertheless, IBM is promoting APPC as a protocol standard for the future. Its robustness, flexibility, and reliability make APPC worth the extra effort when developing applications for the SAA environment.

Novell uses IPX/SPX as its native transport protocol, though the company has announced its intention to permit "native" implementation of TCP/IP in place of IPX/SPX. Internetwork Packet Exchange (IPX) and Sequenced Packet Exchange (SPX) are both variants of Xerox's XNS protocol. IPX provides network layer services, while SPX is somewhat rarely employed by applications that need transport layer services. Because IPX implementations prior to the introduction of NetWare Link Services Protocol (NLSP) in NetWare 4 cause a great deal of broadcast traffic and require frequent transmission acknowledgements which can cause problems in a WAN, Novell also supports TCP/IP.

Other popular transport layer protocols include XNS and NetBEUI. XNS or Xerox Network System was one of the first local area network protocols used on a wide basis, mainly for Ethernet networks. 3Com's 3+ uses a version of it. NetBEUI is IBM's transport protocol for its PC networking products. (The legacy of IBM's long-deceased partnership with Microsoft lives on in Microsoft's default implementations of NetBEUI in Windows for Workgroups and Windows NT Server.)

PROTOCOL BABEL

If the number of available protocols seems like senseless confusion, it is and it isn't. Certain protocols have different advantages in specific environments. No single protocol stack will work better than every other in every setting. NetBIOS works well in small PC networks but is practically useless for communicating with WANs; APPC works well in peer-to-peer mainframe environments; TCP/IP excels in internetworks and heterogenous environments.

On the other hand, much more is made about the differences in protocols than is warranted. Proprietary protocols can be perfect solutions in many cases. Besides, if proprietary protocols are sufficiently widespread, they become de facto standards, and gateways to other protocols are built. These include DEC's protocol suite, Sun Microsystems' Network Filing System and other protocols, and Apple's AppleTalk protocols. While these enjoy widespread use, that use is based on the computers these companies sell and not the proliferation of the protocols throughout the networking industry.

Whether it's proprietary or standard protocol, users are faced with the dilemma of choice. This choice is made slightly easier by the shakeout and standardization that has occurred at the physical and data-link layers. There are three choices: Token Ring, Ethernet, or FDDI. At the transport layers, IPX/SPX and TCP/IP are emerging as the dominant protocols.

The AppleTalk Protocols

The Apple Macintosh operating system, as its many supporters will tell you, is extremely easy to learn and use. Apple's AppleTalk network system brings the same kind of simplicity of use to Macintosh connectivity.

Although not an official LAN standard, AppleTalk can be considered a de facto standard: With AppleTalk connectivity options built into every Macintosh, millions of Macs possess ready-made networking capabilities. This has not been lost on Mac aficionados, who have used AppleTalk to link thousands of Macs into efficient, cost-effective LANs.

NETWORKING THE MAC

When you consider the kind of work performed by the typical Macintosh user, it's not surprising that Mac users have readily accepted networking. For example, take the desktop publishing environment where the Mac prevails: Few writers are good artists, and vice versa. The nature of their jobs, however, demands that they combine their diverse efforts into a single product.

The ability to share and combine files online means those producing documents with PCs can easily merge graphics and other images with text without having to swap diskettes or "cut and paste" hard-copy images. This means the job gets done faster and more efficiently. Networked Macs are thus the rule rather than the exception in these situations, and AppleTalk is Apple's solution to Mac connectivity.

Apple calls AppleTalk "a comprehensive network system" made up of hardware and software components. An AppleTalk network can consist of many different kinds of computer systems and servers and a variety of cabling and connectivity products. Because it was designed to support a variety of machines, Apple developed a suite of proprietary protocols that permits communication between the varying devices that users might need to attach to an AppleTalk network.

However, AppleTalk is not a network operating system, a media-access control (MAC) method such as Ethernet, or a cabling system (LocalTalk is a trade name of Apple's cabling system). Rather, AppleTalk is a nonstandard suite of protocols that while not fully compliant, still provides most of the functions spelled out by the International Standards Organization's Open Systems Interconnection (OSI) reference model.

As the next page illustrates, the six-layer suite of AppleTalk protocols supports numerous connectivity options, including LocalTalk, Ethernet, and Token Ring. AppleTalk also supports Northern Telecom's Meridian, a 2.5Mbps twisted-pair network. This set of protocols allows connections of virtually any computing device to an AppleTalk network. Here's how it works.

AT THE PHYSICAL LAYER

To many network users, the media (or cabling system) that connects PCs into a network is the network—that's all they ever see of it. Their NOS software operates transparently, having been set up by their network administrator, and their network interface card (NIC) is installed inside their computer, out of sight and mind. In the case of AppleTalk, the original (and only) media users see are Apple's own LocalTalk products.

This scheme, driven by Apple's data-link layer, LocalTalk Link Access Protocol (LLAP), uses proprietary modular plugs and wiring to link Macs and LaserWriter printers into a network.

Since AppleTalk's 1984 release, Apple and other third-party vendors have developed data-link protocols to support Ethernet, Token Ring, and Arcnet networks, which exchange data at 10Mbps, 4Mbps, and 2.5Mbps respectively, all faster than LocalTalk's 230.4Kbps rate.

Despite its relative lack of performance, LocalTalk offers one major benefit these technologies lack: Every Macintosh computer that Apple has manufactured contains the built-in LocalTalk connection; Apple LaserWriters and Apple IIgs computers, as well as many other Apple peripherals, also contain this built-in connection. Apple's Quadra computers come with Ethernet built in.

APPLETALK PROTOCOL ARCHITECTURE AND
THE ISO-OSI REFERENCE MODEL

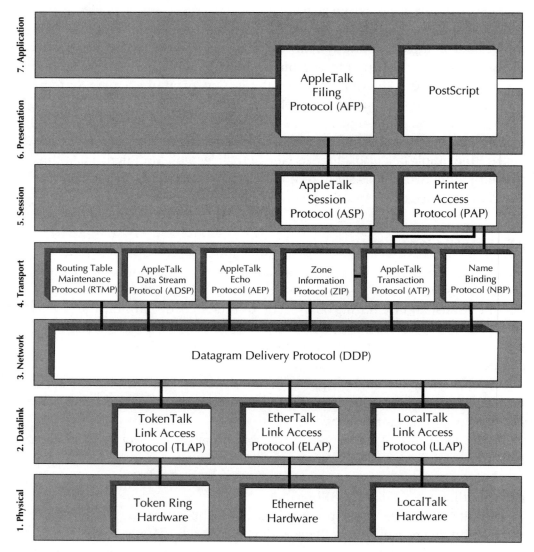

Apple Computer's six-layer AppleTalk protocol suite, although not fully compliant with the seven-layer OSI reference model, provides many of the capabilities and functions defined by OSI. Here, the two protocol suites are compared side-by-side.

This ready-made networking option makes LocalTalk an ideal connectivity option for Mac users, particularly those who don't require the better data-exchange performance delivered by Ethernet, Token Ring, or Arcnet. LocalTalk users get most of the benefits of networking—that is, file and printer sharing, access to electronic mail, and other shared resources—without the added costs associated with a network adapter board.

LOCALTALK'S ACCESS METHOD

LocalTalk, like Ethernet, uses a Carrier-Sense, Multiple-Access (CSMA), media-access scheme to place data packets on the network wire. It does not rely on collision detection (CSMA/CD), as does Ethernet. It uses CSMA/CA, for Carrier-Sense, Multiple-Access with Collision Avoidance.

Stations on a CSMA/CA network, rather than sensing collisions between data packets sent by multiple stations, send out a small (three-byte) packet that signals their intent to place data on the wire. This packet tells all other stations on the wire to wait until the signalling node's data has been sent before they attempt to send data. If collisions between packets are going to occur, they will occur between the preliminary packets, not the actual data packets.

This best effort packet-delivery system, managed by LLAP, does not guarantee that the packet reaches its destination, but it does ensure that all packets delivered are free of errors. The LLAP provides the data-link access specifications and uses a dynamic address-acquisition method that enables AppleTalk's plug-and-play capabilities over twisted-pair wiring.

LOCALTALK'S LIMITATIONS

LocalTalk, though convenient, suffers from other limitations besides its slow data-transfer rate. For example, LocalTalk workgroups are limited to 32 nodes over a 1,000-foot cable run. Ethernet and Token Ring both support substantially greater numbers of nodes.

The EtherTalk, TokenTalk, and Arcnet Link Access Protocols (ELAP, TLAP, and ALAP, respectively) manage AppleTalk network access to Ethernet, Token Ring and Arcnet networks. Apple developed EtherTalk and TokenTalk as extensions of the two protocols' industry-standard data-link processes. Standard Microsystems developed ALAP. One of the key responsibilities of ELAP, TLAP, and ALAP is mapping AppleTalk addresses into the standard data-link Ethernet, Token Ring, or Arcnet address required for proper routing of data.

Because the Ethernet, Token Ring, and Arcnet addressing schemes are incompatible with LLAP, AppleTalk node addresses must be translated into the appropriate format; the AppleTalk Address Resolution Protocol (AARP) handles this translation.

One layer up in the AppleTalk stack is the Datagram Delivery Protocol (DDP). The DDP works with the Routing Table Maintenance Protocol (RTMP) and AppleTalk Echo Protocol (AEP) to ensure data transmission across an Internet.

END-TO-END SERVICES

The DDP exchanges data packets called datagrams. Datagram delivery is the basis for building other value-added AppleTalk services, such as electronic mail. The DDP permits running AppleTalk as a process-to-process, best-effort delivery system, in which the processes running in the nodes of an interconnected network can exchange packets with each other.

The DDP provides these processes with addressable entitles called sockets, and processes can attach themselves to one or more sockets in their nodes. Once associated with a socket, a process can exchange packets with other nodes via these sockets. Once linked to a socket, the process becomes accessible from any point on the AppleTalk network. It is then called a network-visible entity.

The RTMP provides the logic that routes datagrams through router ports to other networks; it permits routers to dynamically learn routes to other AppleTalk networks in an Internet. The AEP lets nodes send datagrams to any other nodes and to receive a copy, or "echo," of the datagram sent. This confirms the existence of a node and helps measure round-trip delays.

RELIABLE DATA DELIVERY

The data-delivery group of protocols—the AppleTalk Transaction Protocol

(ATP), Printer Access Protocol (PAP), AppleTalk Session Protocol (ASP), and the AppleTalk Data Stream Protocol (ADSP)—guarantee the delivery of data. These protocols can be further broken into two groups, one offering transaction-based services, the other data-stream-based faculties.

Transaction-based protocols use the request-response model typically found in server-workstation interactions. Data stream protocols deliver bi-directional data flow between two communicating nodes.

The ATP directs the AppleTalk transaction processes, in which sockets issue requests that require response (typically, status reports). ATP binds the request and response to guarantee a reliable exchange. The PAP sets up a connection-oriented service that sends print requests to AppleTalk-compatible printers.

ASP opens, maintains, and closes transactions during a session, while ADSP provides a full-duplex, byte-stream service between any two sockets on an AppleTalk Internet.

At the highest level of AppleTalk are the AppleTalk Filing Protocol (AFP) and the PostScript protocol. The AFP, built on top of ASP, permits users to share data files and applications on a shared server, while PostScript, a programming language understood by Apple's LaserWriter and numerous other output devices, provides a standard way of describing graphics and text data.

The AFP, which conducts the dialog between a user's computer and an AppleShare server, is one of the key AppleTalk protocols. AFP was designed to provide the tools that allow supporting different types of computers—that is, Macs and IBM PCs—over an AppleTalk network.

The AFP is also important because any network operating system that is fully compatible with it can operate transparently on any AppleTalk network. In turn, this means that such an NOS can support all AppleTalk-compatible applications.

Topologies

Understanding the topology of LAN technologies can tell you a lot about your alternatives when installing or expanding a LAN. At its basic level, the topology of a network refers to the way in which all of its pieces have been connected. That is, it refers to the layout of the computers, printers, and other equipment hooked to the network in your building.

Because cable connects these scattered computing resources together into a network, your network's topology is also a function of the way in which the cabling is organized, whether it is arrayed in a bus, ring, or star (which are the three basic physical topologies available to LAN designers). Although recent technological advances have blurred the distinctions between the physical and logical arrangements, the topology you select (or are forced to select) may also dictate the media-access control method (that is, Ethernet or Token Ring) under which your network will operate.

A network's logical layout may differ from its physical layout. The logical topology defines the electrical path; the physical path defines how the cables, concentrators, and nodes are arranged. For example, Ethernet must be a logical bus network; however, it can be physically configured as a bus or star. Token Ring is a logical ring, but is physically configured as a star. FDDI, a logical ring, is physically configured either as a ring or a star.

THE STAR ROUTE

Until recently, the star topology has been found mostly in minicomputer and mainframe environments. These typically consist of a system of terminals or PCs, each wired to a central processor. It is also used by AT&T in both its Starlan network and its Private Branch Exchange (PBX) based network. The star topology is ideal for wide area network (WAN) applications in which outlying offices must communicate with a central office.

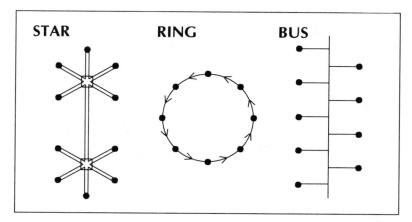

The three basic physical network topologies are the star, ring, and bus. The star is most often used in minicomputer networks. The ring was popularized by Token Ring, and the bus is used in Ethernet.

A principle advantage of the star topology is that it not only allows centralizing key networking resources—concentrators or line conditioning equipment—but also gives the network administrator a focal point for network management. When something goes wrong with the network, the administrator can troubleshoot it from one place, usually a wiring closet, but possibly from a remote management console.

The star-based network requires a substantial investment in cable, however. Each workstation is connected to the central concentrator by its own dedicated line. In some star-based network technologies (Arcnet, for example) this line is coax cable that runs from an active hub to a workstation. (Arcnet can also operate as a bus.)

The 10Base-T Ethernet standard permits operating traditionally bus-based Ethernet in a star-wired configuration using unshielded twisted-pair (or high grade telephone) wiring.

CASCADED STARS

The use of a modular multiport repeater (also known as a hub or concentrator) with Ethernet allows creating large networks made of what can be called cascaded stars. In this arrangement, one centralized multiport repeater serves as

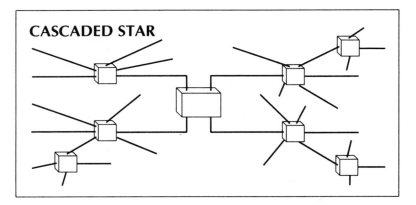

Twisted-pair Ethernets are often composed of cascaded stars, in which multiple multi-port repeaters (represented by boxes) are connected to one another and to a central repeater.

the focal point for many other multiport repeaters, in effect creating a series of star-based Ethernets.

Using modular multiport repeaters also permits mixing star- and bus-based Ethernet workgroups into a single large network. In this instance, the modular repeater must only be able to accept modules that support the many Ethernet-compatible cable types.

THE RING

IBM popularized the ring topology with its Token Ring technology. Like the bus, a Token Ring network uses a single cable. Unlike the bus, the cable's ends are looped to form a complete logical circle or ring. Physically, Token Ring is a star-wired network. Each workstation is connected directly to a central device called a Media Access Unit (MAU). Logically (or electronically), however, the Token Ring remains a true ring.

Unlike the bus, Token Ring uses a deterministic, rather than a contention-based, access method. In the Token Ring access method, an electronic signal called a token is passed from station to station on the ring, with each station regenerating the token as it passes by.

When a station wishes to transmit data over the network, it must wait until the token is passed to it by its neighboring station. It takes control of the sta-

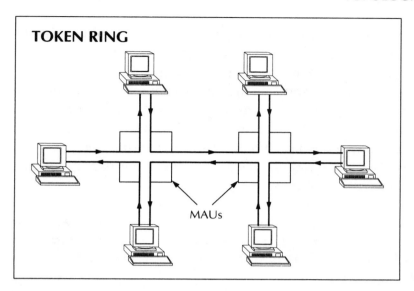

TOKEN RING

MAUs

Although a physical star, IBM's Token Ring implementation is logically (or electronically) a ring. The arrows represent a data packet as it moves from one station to another around the ring.

tion and then places a data packet on the network. Only after the data packet has made a full circuit of the ring, returning to its originator, does the station release the token for the next workstation.

Token Ring can also be expanded by linking multiple rings together, just like Ethernet. In these arrangements, one Token Ring, usually a 16Mbps ring, is dedicated as an internetwork loop, with work group or departmental rings connecting to the company-wide ring via a PC running bridging software.

TAKING THE BUS

In a bus topology, all workstations on the network are attached to a single cable, which is terminated at each end with a special signal-damping device. Ethernet, AppleTalk, and IBM's PC Network are examples of bus-based networks. This sharing of the transmission media (or cable) has several important ramifications. Most importantly, it means that the cable can carry only one message at a time, and each workstation on the network must be capable of knowing when it can and cannot use this shared media.

Ethernet employs what is called a Carrier Sense Multiple Access/Collision Detection (CSMA/CD) access method to arbitrate use of the cable and to maximize its throughput. In this method, each station on the bus is always listening on the cable for transmission for other stations. It only transmits when the cable is not busy with another transmission. It is able to sense the collision that occurs when it and another station on the bus transmit at the same moment. Having sensed that a collision has occurred—and that the transmission has miscarried—each workstation waits a random time period (usually several microseconds) before retransmitting.

Naturally, frequent retransmission can slow down an Ethernet LAN; this limits the number of workstations that can be placed on any network segment. Fortunately, network managers have access to numerous devices, such as switches, bridges, and routers, that divide Ethernets in small segments to mitigate this problem.

One common arrangement is to run numerous secondary segments off a backbone bus. In a typical installation, thick Ethernet coaxial cabling running between a building's floors would serve as the backbone. PCs on each floor would be connected to each other and the backbone via thin coaxial or twisted-pair cable.

These secondary buses can be linked to the primary bus via a transceiver, a repeater, a bridge, or a router. Each of these devices has its own benefits and disadvantages, principally in the amount of traffic control and administration they require.

Two major shortcomings of the bus topology are that it requires lots of cable, and troubleshooting the length of several thousand feet of cable can be time-consuming and frustrating. The bus topology is, however, highly expandable—installers can tap into the cable at almost any point along the bus.

REALITY INJECTION

Unfortunately, reality often dictates the choice of network topology and access method. For example, organizations with a large installed base of IBM equipment must generally opt for an IBM Token Ring network because IBM heavily endorses Token Ring. Or it may be physically or financially impossible to install a particular cable type. For example, cable raceways may be jammed full with cable, dictating that you use a cable with a narrow diameter, such as fiber, or even a wireless, radio-based transmission method.

More likely, an organization's LAN installation will contain variations on all three topologies. In these situations, just as when you are out in the back country hiking, it pays to be flexible. After all, having several alternative routes can mean the difference between an easy climb and struggling uphill.

Access Methods

Access method is the term given to the set of rules by which networks arbitrate the use of a common medium. It is the way the LAN keeps different streams of data from crashing into each other as they share the network.

Networks need access methods for the same reason streets need traffic lights—to keep people from hitting each other. Think of the access method as traffic law. The network cable is the street. Traffic law (or the access method) regulates the use of the street (or cable), determining who can drive (or send data) where and at what time. On a network, if two or more people try to send data at exactly the same time, their signals will interfere with each other, ruining the data being transmitted. The access method prevents this.

The access method works at the data-link layer (layer 2) because it is concerned with the use of the medium that connects users. The access method doesn't care what is being sent over the network, just like the traffic law doesn't stipulate what you can carry. It just says you have to drive on the right side of the road and obey the traffic lights and signs.

Three traditional access methods are used today, although others exist and may become increasingly important. They are Ethernet, token ring, and ARCnet. Actually, these technologies encompass wider-ranging standards than their access methods. They also define other features of network transmission, such as the electrical characteristics of signals, and the size of data packets sent. Nevertheless, these standards are best known by the access methods they employ.

ETHERNET

Ethernet is the most common network access method. It was developed by Xerox in the mid-1970s. It describes data transmission at 10Mbps and other throughput rates using the CSMA/CD protocol. Ethernet gained its popularity

34

in engineering, scientific, and university environments. According to the market research firm Dataquest, the shipments of Ethernet interface adapters have grown substantially faster than those of token ring through the mid-1990s. ARCnet unit shipments have declined, and little new development of ARCnet-based solutions should be expected.

The Ethernet access method is Carrier Sense Multiple Access/Collision Detection (CSMA/CD). This is a broadcast access method, which means every computer "hears" every transmission, but not every computer "listens" to every transmission.

Here's how CSMA/CD works. When a computer wants to send a message it does, as long as the cable isn't in use by another transmitting node. (This is the carrier sense part.) The signal it sends moves up and down the cable in every direction, passing every computer on the network segment. (This is multiple access.) Every computer can hear the message, but unless the message is addressed to it, the computer ignores it. Only the computer to which the message is addressed receives the message. The message is recognized because it contains the address of the destination computer. An acknowledgment can be correctly addressed because the original message also contains the address of the sending computer.

A "collision" occurs if two computers send at the same time (because there is a narrow window of time in which the second computer may have begun transmitting but the "busy signal" has not yet reached the first computer, which blithely begins to transmit). A collision doesn't make any noise, but the signals become garbled and the messages can't be understood. In fact, nodes that detect a collision automatically transmit a special "jam" signal, which unambiguously destroys the colliding transmissions. When this happens, each of the colliding computers "backs off" or waits for a random amount of time, then tries to retransmit. This wait/retransmission sequence can repeat until both messages are transmitted successfully. The whole process takes a small fraction of a second.

Ethernet's detractors characterize it as an inefficient access method because frames are prone to collisions. But while collisions occur, they don't consume very much throughput capacity in most cases. Since the whole process of transmitting, colliding, and retransmitting takes place so quickly, the delay a collision causes is normally minuscule. Of course, as the traffic on a network approaches the total throughput capacity, the number of collisions will mount and the network will slow considerably. This happens with some large-scale imaging or engineering applications, or network segments with too many nodes. As long as an Ethernet network has a low traffic load, traditionally the most common environment, delay caused by collisions is seldom noticeable.

TOKEN RING

When token ring was introduced in 1984, it was not the first token-passing, ring network, but because it was endorsed by IBM, it has had a tremendous impact on the network industry. Token ring has become part of IBM's connectivity solution for all its computers—personal, midrange, and mainframe. IBM's specifications match those of the IEEE 802.5 standard.

Token ring unit shipments are still increasing in 1995, though this growth is unlikely to continue for long. IBM has had a stranglehold on the token ring market, though it no longer supplies the 90 percent share of token ring network interface cards that characterized this market in the 1980s.

The original token ring transmits data at 4Mbps; the newer specification calls for 16Mbps transmission. In token ring, the computers are arranged in a logical ring, but all data passing between work stations is routed through a hub. A multi-station access unit (MSAU or MAU) acts as the hub, and each work station is connected to it. Token ring uses a token-passing access method to prevent data collisions—a token being a series of data bits created by one of the computers. The token moves around the ring, giving successive computers the right to transmit. If a computer receives the token, it may transmit a message of any length as long as the time to send does not exceed the token-holding timer (this combination of token and data is called a frame). As this message (frame) moves around the network, each computer regenerates the signal. Only the receiving computer copies the message into its memory, then marks the message as received. The sending computer removes the message from the token and recirculates it.

Token ring's advantages include reliability and ease of maintenance. It uses a star-wired ring topology in which all computers are directly wired to a MAU. The MAU allows malfunctioning computers to be disconnected from the network. This overcomes one disadvantage of token-passing, which is that one malfunctioning computer can bring down the network since all computers are actively passing signals around the ring.

ARCNET

Arcnet was developed by Datapoint in the early 1970s. It is especially popular in very small networks, since it is inexpensive and easy to maintain. Arcnet uses a token-passing access method that works on a star-bus topology. Data is transmitted at 2.5Mbps. The network cable is laid out as a series of stars. Each computer is attached to a hub at the center of a star and the hubs are connected in a bus or line. ArcnetPlus is designed as a backbone technology and can transmit data at 20Mbps.

When a computer wants to send data on an Arcnet network, it must have the token. The token moves around the network in a given pattern, which in Arcnet's case is a logical ring. All computers on the network are numbered with an address from 0 to 255. (The maximum number of computers on each Arcnet segment is thus 256.) The token moves from computer to computer in numerical order, even if adjacent numbers are at physically opposite ends of the network. When the token reaches the highest number on the network it moves to the lowest, thus creating a logical ring.

Once a computer has the token it can send one 512-byte packet. A packet is composed of the destination address, its own address, up to 508 bytes of data, and other information. The packet moves from node to node in sequential order until it reaches the destination node. At the destination, the data is removed and the token released to the next node. Since one packet is often too small for an entire message, the token may need to make several rounds to complete a data transfer.

The advantage of token passing is predictability. Because the token moves through the network in a determined path, it is possible to calculate the best and worst cases for data transmission. This makes network performance predictable. It also means introduction of new network nodes will have a predictable effect. This differs from Ethernet, where the addition of new nodes may or may not seriously effect performance. However, a predictable network can be misleading—for example, lost tokens will affect worst-case delivery times.

A disadvantage of the token-passing access method is the fact that each node acts as a repeater, accepting and regenerating the token as it passes around the network in a specific pattern. If there is a malfunctioning node, the token may be destroyed or simply lost, bringing down the whole network. The token must then be regenerated.

Section II

Network Hardware

Cabling

Cable is the medium that ordinarily connects network devices. Cable's ability to transmit encoded signals enables it to carry data from one place to another. These signals may be electrical as in copper cable or light pulses as in fiber-optic cable.

A few networks don't use cable at all. Instead, data is carried through the air as microwave, infrared, radio frequency, or laser-produced visible light signals. These wireless networks are often expensive, and may require licenses from the Federal Communications Commission. When the cost of running cable is prohibitively high or a network must be mobile or temporary, a wireless LAN can make sense.

THREE CHOICES

LAN users have three basic cable choices: coaxial, twisted-pair, and fiber-optic. Coaxial and twisted-pair cables both use copper wire to conduct the signals; fiber-optic cable uses a glass or plastic conductor. Before the Ethernet standards for unshielded twisted pair installations were approved in 1992, the majority of LANs used coaxial cable, but a high proportion of subsequent installations have used the more flexible and less costly unshielded twisted pair medium. The use of fiber-optics is growing, albeit slowly. Fiber is most often used on the backbone network and is not commonly run to the desktop.

Originally, access protocols were tied to cable type. Ethernet and Arcnet ran on coaxial cable only. (Most of the installed coaxial cable is there because Ethernet and Arcnet have been around for so long.) However, these protocols have since been modified to run on shielded and unshielded twisted-pair, and fiber-optic cable. Cable type is no longer tied to the access method. Arcnet and Ethernet run on coaxial cable, unshielded twisted-pair, and fiber-optic cabling. Token Ring runs on unshielded and shielded twisted-pair and fiber-optic cabling.

A tradeoff between speed and distance exists, especially with copper cable. It is possible to increase the speed of data transmission, but this reduces the distance that data can travel without regeneration. Signal regenerating products like repeaters and amplifiers can help, but the physical properties of cable impose certain limitations.

COAXIAL CABLE

Coaxial cable, or coax, has a long history. If you have cable television in your home, you have coaxial cable. Broadband transmission, a type of LAN transmission, uses the same principles as cable TV and runs on coax. Broadband and cable TV take advantage of coax's ability to transmit many signals at the same time. Each signal is called a channel. Each channel travels along at a different frequency, so it does not interfere with other channels.

Coax has a large bandwidth, which means it can handle plenty of traffic at high speeds. Other advantages include its relative immunity to electromagnetic interference (as compared to twisted-pair), its ability to carry signals over a significant distance, and its familiarity to many cable installers.

Coax cable has four parts. The inner conductor is a solid metal wire surrounded by insulation. A thin, tubular piece of metal screen surrounds the insulation. Its axis of curvature coincides with that of the inner conductor, hence the name coaxial. Finally, an outer plastic cover surrounds the rest.

Coax comes in several sizes. Standard Ethernet cable, the yellow stuff called thick Ethernet, is about the diameter of a man's thumb. Thin Ethernet, the black cable, is about a thick as a woman's pinky finger. Arcnet uses RG/68 coax cable. Thicker coax is more robust, harder to damage, and transmits data over longer distances. It's also more difficult to connect.

Standard Ethernet requires a "vampire tap" and drop cable to connect a LAN device. This combination is bulky and expensive. Thin Ethernet uses a biconic (or BNC) connector, which is easier to install than vampire taps.

TWISTED-PAIR

Twisted-pair cable has been around a lot longer than coaxial, but it has been carrying voice, not data. Unshielded twisted-pair is used extensively in the nationwide telephone system. Every building and home that has telephones is wired with twisted-pair cable.

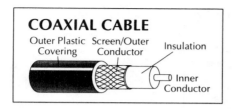

Coaxial cable, also called coax, is the oldest network cable. It is proven, easy to use, has a large bandwidth, and can support transmission over long distances.

In the past few years, vendors have been able to transmit data over twisted-pair at reasonable speeds and distances. Some of the first PC LANs, such as Omninet or 10Net, used twisted-pair cable but could only transmit data at 1Mbps. Token Ring, when it was introduced in 1984, was able to transmit data at 4Mbps over shielded twisted-pair. In 1987, several vendors announced Ethernet that can transmit data over unshielded twisted-pair, but computers can only be about 300 feet apart, not the 2,000 feet allowed by thick coax. Recent developments in technology make it possible to run even 16Mbps Token Ring and 100Mbps FDDI traffic over unshielded twisted-pair.

Twisted-pair offers some significant benefits. It's lighter, thinner, more flexible, and easier to install than coax or fiber-optic cable. It's also inexpensive. It is therefore ideal in offices or work groups that are free of severe electromagnetic interference.

Although there are a variety of types of twisted-pair cable types, shielded and unshielded are the two most important. Shielded twisted-pair has an RF-insulating material wrapped around the two twisted wires. Unshielded twisted-pair (or ordinary telephone wire) does not. Shielded twisted-pair is more immune to interference, which usually translates into higher transmission speeds over longer distance—it is more expensive, however.

Unshielded twisted-pair is fast becoming the media of choice. By 1993, the market research firm Dataquest projected that 78 percent of Ethernet connections will be made via twisted-pair cables. Unshielded twisted-pair is also gaining in popularity for Token Ring networks, which were traditionally wired with shielded twisted-pair.

The most important result of the telephone industry's use of twisted-pair is modular cabling. A modular cabling system, built with patch panels, wiring

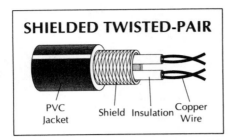

Shielded twisted-pair's shield increases its immunity to electromagnetic interference, which allows it to transmit data over longer distances than unshielded twisted-pair.

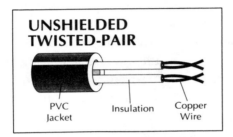

Unshielded twisted-pair is installed nearly everywhere. Besides being inexpensive and readily available, it is flexible and familiar to cable installers. It has become the cable of choice for departmental networks.

closets, and connector jacks, makes it easier to move computers from one place to another without rewiring the LAN. A modular cabling system allows a company to pre-wire a building for its phone and data services. Once the wire is in place, people can move from office to office, and new cabling does not have to be run.

FIBROUS DIET

Fiber-optics has been touted as the answer to all the problems of copper cable. It can carry voice, video, and data. It has enormous bandwidth and can carry signals for extremely long distances. Because it uses light pulses, not electricity to carry data, it is immune to electromagnetic interference. It is also more secure than copper cable, because an intruder cannot eavesdrop on the signals, but must physically tap into the cable. To get at the information inside, a device must be attached, and the light level will subsequently decrease.

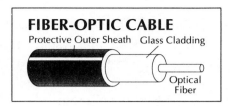

FIBER-OPTIC CABLE
Protective Outer Sheath   Glass Cladding
Optical Fiber

Fiber-optic cable offers tremendous bandwidth, tight security, immunity to electro-magnetic interference, and can carry data over very long distances. It is mostly used in backbones.

Despite its many advantages, fiber-optic's deployment has been slow. According to Dataquest figures, by 1993, fiber-optics held only 1.4 percent of the LAN market. Cable installer's experience and fiber's high cost is holding back its widespread installation. Very simply, installing fiber-optic cable is very difficult. Splicing fiber-optic cables together is even more difficult. Putting connectors on the fiber-optic cable is also harder than for copper cable. The expense of diagnostic tools is another problem. Time domain reflectometers, ohmeters, voltmeters, and oscilloscopes can be easily connected to any type of copper cable. But such tools must be specifically designed for fiber-optics use—there are no fiber-optic adapters for copper-based tools.

Fiber-optics has enjoyed its greatest success as a backbone medium for connecting sub-networks. Its properties make it ideal for the heavy traffic, hostile environments, and great distances that characterize backbone networks. Its immunity to electrical interference makes it ideal for the factory floor, another popular application.

Fiber-optic cable itself is a core fiber surrounded by cladding. A protective covering surrounds both. LEDs or light emitting diodes send the signals down the cable. A detector receives the signals and converts them back to the electrical impulses that computers can understand. While the bits are encoded into light in a number of ways, the most popular method is to vary the intensity of the light.

Fiber-optic cable can be multimode or single-mode. In single-mode cable, the light travels straight down the fiber, which means data can travel greater distances. But since single-mode cable has a larger diameter than multimode cable, it is harder (more expensive) to manufacture. In multimode cable, the light bounces off the cable's walls as it travels down, which causes the signals to weaken sooner, and therefore data cannot travel great distances. Single-mode cable is most often used in the nationwide telephone system, and multimode cable is most used in LANs, since data is not required to travel across the country.

Standards for fiber-optic LANs have been developed. ANSI's Fiber Distributed Data Interface (FDDI) describes a network that can transmit data at 100Mbps. It also specifies a dual, counter-rotating ring, which makes it fault tolerant. The IEEE has also developed standards for fiber-optic Ethernet.

Imaging applications and the proliferation of networks will force installation of high capacity LANs. Fiber-optics has enormous potential. Its capacities are tremendous. When wiring a new building, the best strategy is to run fiber-optic backbones, with twisted-pair to the desktops.

Interface Cards

The Network Interface Card (NIC) provides the physical connection to the network. Every computer attached to a LAN uses some sort of network interface card or chip. In most cases, the card fits into the expansion slot of the computer, although some cards are external units that attach to the computer through a serial or parallel port. Internal cards are generally used for PCs, Macs, and some workstations. Internal interface cards can also be used in minicomputers and mainframes. External boxes are often used for laptops. In some cases, the network circuitry is integrated onto the computer's motherboard.

The interface card takes data from the PC, puts it into the appropriate format, and sends it over the cable to another LAN interface card. This card receives the data, puts it into a form the PC understands, and sends it to the PC.

The interface card's role can be broken into eight tasks: host-to-card communications; buffering, frame formation; parallel-to-serial conversion; encoding and decoding; cable access; handshaking; and transmission and reception. These steps get the data from the memory of one computer onto the cable, and reversing the steps gets the data off the cable and into the memory of another computer.

BEFORE TRANSMISSION

The first step in transmission is the communication between the personal computer and the network interface card. There are three ways to move data between the PC's memory to the network interface card: I/O, direct memory access, and shared memory.

I/O is the simplest method. The most important types are memory-mapped I/O and program I/O. In a memory-mapped I/O transfer, the host CPU assigns some of its memory space to the I/O device, in this case the network interface card. Out of the possible 640KB of RAM that is available for DOS PCs, a few KB are allocated to the network card. This memory is then treated as if it were the PC's main memory. No special instructions in the CPU are needed to get data from the card since it is like taking data from one part of main memory to another.

With program I/O, the CPU is given a set of special instructions to handle the input/output functions. These instructions can be built into the chip or come with software. To send data, a request is sent from the network interface card to the CPU. The CPU then moves the data from the card over the bus to main memory. Because the CPU is required to handle the I/O process, it cannot perform other tasks while data is being transferred. This makes it slow. Also, I/O takes up PC memory.

Direct Memory Access (DMA) is another method. All Intel-based computers come with a DMA controller chip that takes care of transferring data from an input/output device to the PC's main memory so the PC's CPU does not have to get involved in the transfer. For DMA transfer, the controller or processor on the interface card sends a signal to the CPU indicating it wants to transfer information. The CPU then relinquishes control of the PC bus to the DMA controller.

Once the DMA controller has command of the bus, it takes the data from the card and places it directly in memory. The CPU had told it the appropriate memory address at which to begin putting data in memory. After all the data is in memory, the DMA controller returns control of the bus to the CPU and tells it how much data has been put in memory.

DMA is generally faster than I/O because the DMA controller removes work from the CPU, so the CPU can perform other functions while data transfer is taking place. The disadvantage is the CPU cannot access memory while the DMA controller is working.

In shared memory, part of host PC's memory is shared by the network interface card's processor. Shared memory is a very fast transfer method, since no buffering on the card is required. Because the card and the PC do their work on the data in the same place, no transfer is necessary. Although shared memory is the fastest method of moving data between the network interface card and the PC, it is more difficult to build than DMA or I/O. Shared memory takes more PC RAM than the other methods.

The second component of PC-to-NIC communication is buffering. The buffer is a storage place that holds data as it is moving into and out of the NIC.

A buffer is necessary because some parts of data transfer are slower than others. For example, data comes into the card faster than it can be converted from a serial or parallel format, depacketized, read, and sent. This is true in both directions. To compensate for delays inherent in transmission, a buffer temporarily holds data either for transmission onto the cable or for transfer into the PC. While in the buffer, data may be acted on, such as put into frames, or it may simply wait while the NIC handles other things.

An alternative to buffering is to use PC RAM. This can be less expensive, but is usually slower and it requires memory.

The NIC's most important job is frame formation. Frames are the basic units of transmission. Files and messages are broken into frames for transmission. At the other end the frames are reassembled to form the file or message. A frame has three sections: header, data, and trailer. The header includes an alert to signal that the frame is on its way, the frame's source address, destination address, and clock information to synchronize transmission. In some networks, headers also have preamble bits used for various purposes, like setting up parameters for transmission. They can also have a control field to direct the frame through the network, a byte count, and a message type field.

The data section contains the data being sent, for example, the numbers in a spreadsheet or words in a document. On some networks, the data section of a frame can be as large as 12KB. On Ethernet, it is 1,500 bytes. Most networks fall between 1KB and 4KB.

The trailer contains error checking information called a cyclical redundancy check (CRC). It is a number that is the result of a mathematical calculation the sending NIC does on the frame. When the frame arrives at its destination, the mathematical calculation is repeated. If the result is the same—all the ones and zeros are in the right place—no errors occurred in transmission. If the numbers don't match, an error has occurred and the frame must be retransmitted.

TRANSMISSION

Parallel-to-serial conversion is the next step in transmission. Data comes from the PC in parallel form, 8, 16, or 32 bits at a time, depending on the bus width. But it must travel over the cable in serial form, which is one bit at a time. Thus, the network interface card must convert between the two. A parallel-to-serial controller is responsible for this task. Once a frame is formed and changed from parallel to serial, it is nearly ready to be sent over the line. First it must be encoded, which means it must be converted into a series of electrical pulses that convey information.

Most network interface cards use Manchester encoding. Serial data is divided into bit periods. Each of these periods (or fractions of seconds) is divided in half, and the halves together represent a bit. From the first half to the second half of each bit period there is a change in the signal's polarity, from positive to negative, or vice versa. The change during each bit period represents the data. A change from negative to positive represents a one. A change from positive to negative represents a zero. Or vice versa depending on the network. Ethernet uses Manchester encoding. Token Ring uses a another version called Differential Manchester encoding, in which the mid-bit transmission is used for clocking information. Either way, these ones and zeroes represent data.

Before data can be sent, however, the network interface card must have access to the cable. Token Ring and Arcnet use a token to grant network access. Ethernet lets any workstation transmit at will if it finds the cable unoccupied and senses collisions if two senders inadvertently transmit simultaneously. The access method protocol, circuitry, and firmware reside on the network access card.

After getting data from the PC, formatting it, encoding it, and getting access to the cable, the interface card for some types of networks has one more task before it can send data: handshaking. In order to send data successfully, a second NIC must be waiting to receive it. A short period of communication between two cards ensues before data is sent. During this period, the NICs negotiate the parameters for the upcoming communication. The transmitting card sends the parameters it wants to use. The receiving card answers with its parameters. Parameters include the maximum frame size, how many frames should be sent before an answer, timer values, how long to wait for an answer, and buffer sizes. The card with the slower, smaller, less complicated parameters always wins because more sophisticated cards can "lower" themselves while less sophisticated cards can't "raise" themselves.

Finally, everything is set. The only thing left is for the NIC's transceiver to put the data on the cable. The transceiver gives the data power to make it down the line. It actually puts the electrical signal out over the cable, making sure the data can get to the next NIC, repeater, amplifier, or bridge.

At the other end, a transceiver waits to accept the signal and begin the whole process in reverse, from modulated signal through decoding, serial-to-parallel conversion, and depacketizing the information into a format readable by the receiving device.

PICK A CARD

More than any other LAN component, the network interface card determines the performance of the LAN. The speed of the disk drives, file servers, and network operating system are important, but the speed of the interface card and its software driver determine the network speed.

Choosing network cards is a difficult process. Nearly every vendor claims to have the fastest cards. Benchmarking, even when done by independent sources, measures a myriad of parameters. Look at the bus width (a card using a 32-bit bus is normally faster than one that uses an 8-bit bus), the bus type (Extended Industry Standard Architecture bus or Micro Channel is faster than Industry Standard Architecture bus), the type of memory transfer (shared memory is faster than I/O and DMA), and whether the card can perform bus mastering. But most important, test the speed of the network card driver.

Performance is one, albeit critical, factor. Reliability is essential. Speed is irrelevant if the card causes errors, loses frames, drops the line, or just doesn't work. Nothing is more frustrating than having to isolate network hardware problems. Evaluate the vendor's reputation, longevity in the business, and technical support services.

File Servers

A file server is a combination of computer, internal hardware, and software that allows LAN users to share computer programs and data. A file server usually has a significantly faster processor, faster network interface card, more memory, and more data storage than most PCs. It may also have a tape back-up unit, modems, and several printers attached.

SERVER HARDWARE

Server software is that portion of the network operating system that "serves" a computer's resources to other LAN users. This software accepts incoming requests from LAN users and gives back files and other resources. Users achieve this connection by mapping a local logical drive, drive F: for instance, to the server's physical drive. That is, using a designated drive letter from A to Z, users access the server's physical drive as if it were one of their own local drives. Application programs do the same. The network operating system takes care of routing traffic across the network to the proper file server hard disk and back.

A file server must find data quickly and get to the requesting workstation with minimal delay. Factors affecting the server's performance include the CPU's speed, the network interface card's speed, the amount of RAM available, the type of disk and controller, the cable type and length, the network software's efficiency, the application type being run, and the number of users on the network.

Most high-performance file servers include a very fast, very large hard disk. Access time is the time required to get data off the disk and it is broken into seek and rotation times. Average *seek time*, which accounts for the bulk of the time, is the time the disk head takes to move to the correct track on the platter. Average *rotation time* is the time taken for the platter to turn to the sector where the data is stored. Most of the time, the average access time is all you need to know when buying a server hard disk.

One overlooked aspect of the hard disk is its controller. Standard ST, Enhanced Small Device Interface (ESDI), Small Computer System Interface (SCSI), and Integrated Drive Electronics (IDE) are four types. ST drives are inexpensive and practically obsolete, ESDI drives are faster, but less common with each passing month, SCSI drives are easily expandable, and IDE drives are often the default on workstations and low-end server models. The tradeoff depends on your application and financial situation. Today, most LAN drives are SCSI.

Disk capacity is crucial. A rule of thumb is to figure out how much disk space you will need, and then double it. LANs always grow so expandability is important. The file server should be able to accommodate more disk drives as needed. A file server (and a NOS) should permit you to add storage into the multiple gigabyte range. Disk arrays, which are composed of multiple drives and controllers, will provide fault tolerance but won't necessarily improve performance.

MEMORY NEEDS

A *cache* can make the hard disk appear to work faster than it actually does. Cache is space in high speed memory that is set aside to hold the last data read from the disk. The server software and the disk controller take more data off the disk than the user actually requested. This adjacent data, stored in the cache, is available when the next request is made, saving the file server from going to the disk to get it. It doesn't speed the work of the disk, but it eliminates some disk access, which moves data faster.

Caching is effective because a file server usually makes several accesses to disk when retrieving or writing data. Caching works because the next information a user requests is generally stored sectors adjacent to the data just requested. Caching also works because the disk controller usually can't get all the data with a single access to disk. So the disk controller reads the next couple of sectors after what the user requested, because chances are that the data the user wants next will be in those blocks.

Some server software caches only disk reads. This way, if the file server crashes, no data is lost because the data in the cache is identical to what is on the disk. Other file server software caches both read and write.

The amount of RAM necessary for disk caching varies from vendor to vendor. In general, a bigger cache is better, although a point of diminishing returns sets in. Moreover, the more data kept in a cache the more it is vulnerable to server failure. A power loss will wipe out data in the cache, although data written to disk will not be lost. Most vendors take precautions for this, writing and verifying data at specified intervals, thereby protecting as much data as possible while still increasing performance.

PROCESSOR, CLOCK, AND PORTS

File servers should be more powerful than workstations for the shared services they provide. In some small networks with nondedicated servers, a last-generation processor will perform fine. However, once data sharing passes beyond a handful of users or light word processing, more powerful file servers are a necessity. Servers that provide only file and print services are likely to be more dependent on the amount of RAM, the disk subsystem performance, and the performance of the system bus than they are on the processor itself. Applications servers , on the other hand, can often absorb all the CPU processing power they can get.

Every server should have plenty of expansion slots as well as multiple serial and parallel ports. More than one or two locally connected printers can take up all available ports, since few PCs have more than one of each type of interface on the motherboard. Keep this in mind if you are using the file server as a router or switch. Two or three network interface cards, one or two drive controllers, and extra serial or parallel ports may occupy more ports than are available in the file server.

After performance, the main concerns when choosing a file server are reliability and compatibility. A PC file server needs to have a good power supply so it does not experience power drops or outages. It must work with standard software drivers such as network drivers, disk drivers, and video drivers, which means its BIOS must be compatible with those of other major vendors. Most cheap IBM clones do not work well as file servers.

Multiprocessor Servers

The very nature of LANs places tremendous demands on servers. These central repositories of data and application files literally serve the needs of the many users on the LAN. This means they're usually interacting with more than one client at a time. Unfortunately, this isn't the job that most computers acting as servers were designed for.

The typical first-generation network server was basically a souped-up version of an IBM-compatible personal computer with an Intel microprocessor. These very personal computers were created to deliver computing resources to individuals, not groups. As such, they contain a single CPU, or microprocessor, designed to do one thing at a time.

As single-user systems, single-CPU computers perform admirably. As multiuser servers on a network, however, they have performed less admirably. Their single-processor architecture can't always keep up with multiple users' demands.

The earlier, smaller networks primarily provided disk input/output and printer access. Users remained content despite delays in network service because of the benefits they derived (for example, improved company communications and shared resources).

But as LANs grow larger and the processing burden placed on servers becomes more complex, the single-CPU architecture has become less viable, especially with specialized applications that require the server to do much of the processing now performed by PCs at the desktop (for example, SQL database front ends). Hence, the development of a host of multiprocessor servers designed specifically for use with LANs. These computers—most notably NetFrame's NetFrame and Compaq's Systempro, and the clones they have spawned—are dramatically changing the way network servers are implemented in a typical network.

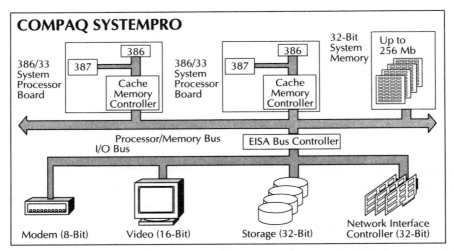

Compaq's Systempro super server relies on two buses to maintain compatibility with existing adapters, such as network interface cards, video boards, and disk controllers. This architecture allows Compaq to update the processor-memory bus as new technology develops without altering the I/O bus.

IT'S NOTHING NEW

Multiprocessor computers aren't new—they've existed since the early 1960s. Of course, their creators called them mainframes and/or minicomputers and designed them for large-scale, centralized data processing departments, not the sort of distributed processing found in LANs. And while many networks use these, they actually make poor server alternatives: They cost too much, pose many connectivity problems, and PC-oriented users often find them hard to understand.

Enter the multiprocessor server designed for integration into LANs. These use many of the same concepts found in mainframes. For example, the NetFrame provides the redundancy and memory error detection and correction facilities found on mainframes.

In designing multiprocessor systems, computer engineers have generally taken two tacks: one known as a *tightly coupled system;* the second, a *loosely coupled system.* In the first, two or more CPUs share a common communications path (or bus) and system memory; Compaq took this approach with its Systempro. In the loosely coupled system, two or more CPUs have their own separate memory and communications channels but communicate over a shared bus; with modifications, this is NetFrame's approach.

Both the NetFrame and the Systempro feature what NetFrame calls a main data path or primary data highway and a centralized main memory (8MB to 64MB on the NetFrame, up to 256MB on the Systempro). The main data path is 32 bits wide on the Systempro (Compaq calls this its processor/memory bus), and 64 bits wide on the NetFrame. From there, the two architectures vary substantially, both using proprietary designs.

THE SYSTEMPRO DESIGN

The Compaq Systempro's design—which Compaq calls its Flexible Advanced Systems Architecture/Multiprocessor (Flex/MP)—relies on the Extended Industry Standard Architecture (EISA) bus structure promulgated by Compaq and others. The Systempro deviates from the classical tightly coupled approach in that it features two buses—one for the CPUs, a second (EISA) for the I/O channels. An EISA bus controller manages communication between the two.

The Systempro can operate with two processors—any combination of 386 and 486 CPUs—which are added to the processor memory bus via plug-in system processor boards, with the 486 version providing a range of 8 to 40 MIPS. (MIPS, for millions of instructions per second, are a key metric of a computer's processing capabilities.) Compaq says adding a second 386/33 (for 33MHz processor) almost doubles the computing performance to support processor-intensive applications, such as a database server in a LAN environment.

Compaq teams each processor with its own cache memory controller. This substantially increases execution performance by allowing each processor to store and fetch certain often used instructions and data from its own area of dedicated cache memory. In the Flex/MP system, bus master and direct memory access (DMA) activities, which slow a processor down by impeding its access to the system bus, take place on the EISA I/O bus, independently of the processor bus. This separation of the processor/memory subsystems from the expansion bus is important to end users with large investments in ISA/EISA-compatible expansion products (such as network interface cards, disk con-

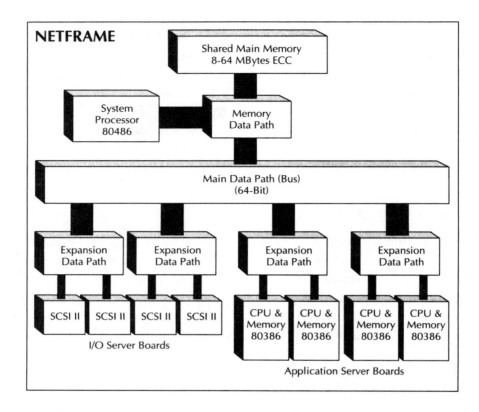

The NetFrame uses a loosely coupled system. Its hierarchical I/O structure works with plug-in I/O and application servers. Each application server has its own processor and memory and is capable of running database servers, network operating systems, etc.

trollers, and video adapters). Compaq says this separation allows it to optimize high-speed processor and 486 processor technology without sacrificing compatibility with thousands of existing expansion boards.

Compaq's Systempro super server relies on two buses to maintain compatibility with existing adapters, such as network interface cards, video boards, and disk controllers. This architecture allows Compaq to update the processor-memory bus as new technology develops without altering the I/O bus.

Compaq offers this example to show the performance benefits of its multiprocessor system: As Compaq's 32-bit intelligent drive array controller, working in concert with two processors, loads data into the system memory via bus master transfers, one CPU manages request from NICs while the second sorts a database. This balanced approach—with the CPUs acting as dual partners—means no single subsystem limits overall system performance.

THE NETFRAME DESIGN

The NetFrame relies on a hierarchical I/O structure with a central system processor, which works with what NetFrame calls plug-in I/O and application servers. Depending on specific options, the system processor can be a 386 or 486, both operating at 25MHz.

Each application server contains its own processor and dedicated memory (from 4MB to 32MB), thus creating a standalone computer that can be dedicated to a specific application. For example, one application server could run a database, a second the LAN Manager network operating system, a third Novell's NetWare 386. Various models of the NetFrame accommodate from three to eight of each add-on server board. The NetFrame's I/O server boards can support several types of I/O devices through SCSI II, Ethernet and Token Ring adapters, and RS-232 serial or RS-422 LocalTalk connections. With industry standard interfaces like these, users can continue using the network interface adapters they know. They can also use any hard disk and controller subsystem compatible with the SCSI II standard.

In addition, because the application servers share access to the main memory, they can communicate with each other over the memory bus—that is, pass data packets back and forth across RAM. This means that individual application server boards running different network operating systems and/or under different physical-access methods could communicate directly across the RAM, bypassing slower cable communications.

The NetFrame operates at eight times the throughput of a high-end PC or workstation, according to NetFrame.

Network Wiring Hubs

It's no surprise that network administrators responded to the passage of the IEEE's 10BaseT Ethernet standard with a sigh of relief. The 10BaseT standard spells out the exact ways in which Ethernet data signals can be sent over telephone wire, and that should make those professionals' daily lives a good deal more pleasant than heretofore possible.

Ostensibly, 10BaseT gives them a low-cost cabling alternative—unshielded twisted-pair wiring (UTP), better known as telephone wire—for transmitting Ethernet data signals. Millions of miles of telephone wire installed in buildings worldwide can now be safely used for Ethernet data transmission. The ability to use existing UTP and its resulting savings from not having to pull new cable may be a superficial benefit of 10BaseT. Not all UTP hidden behind walls can support Ethernet, so they often need new cables, anyway.

10BaseT's real benefits promise to overshadow the economics of not pulling new cabling. The true benefits of 10BaseT will be derived through increased control of Ethernet networks in general and network cabling plants specifically. The 10BaseT standard's most important feature might very well be that it gives Ethernet topological parity with IBM's Token Ring scheme, the industry's other popular networking technology.

The 10BaseT standard calls for connecting Ethernet workgroups in a star topology that focuses all network cabling in a single wiring concentrator, or hub, as shown in the figure on the next page. Token Ring's physical star topology, with its centralized wiring hub, has been one of the major reasons it has made substantial popularity gains against Ethernet in recent years.

AT THE LAN'S CENTER

Why would Ethernet managers want to concentrate the wiring at the center of their networks? Token Ring's centralized architecture makes its LAN cabling systems, which are in reality electrical rings, easy to manage—and that's a distinct selling point to overworked network managers.

A description of a traditional Ethernet bus-style network explains the whys of centralized networks: in a standard Ethernet, the network cabling runs from one node (e.g., computer or printer) to another, in essence meandering from desk to desk in a continuous single strand. This is a simplified bus network, which can also contain cable branches running off the main, or backbone, cable; in such branching cable systems, however, the problems described here are virtually identical to those affecting non-branching buses.

Imagine the headache of troubleshooting this seemingly never-ending stretch of cable on a bus: When workstations on a bus-based LAN experience network-related trouble, a technician may have to inspect the entire cable segment, which can be several kilometers long, before finding the problem. This can be time-consuming, frustrating, and costly.

Troubleshooting a hub-based network entails no such run-arounds: Each workstation is attached directly to the hub via its own unshared cable. This means the technician troubleshooting a particular network node has to worry about only the cable segment running from the hub to that node, not the entire network wiring system. This can represent substantial time savings in diagnosing network failures.

A LOOK AT A HUB

Although each of the network hubs on the market are similar to each other, they're also dramatically different. All of the network hubs contain two basic components—a chassis and topology-specific modules—that allow creating easily reconfigurable networks. But each vendor has elected to work within its own design philosophy that makes for significant physical differences among those available.

A chassis is the hub's most visible component. It acts as the hub enclosure and serves as the interface between each of the individual modules. Individual vendor's hubs contain varying numbers of accessory slots, each of which accepts a single module.

TYPICAL HUB LAYOUT

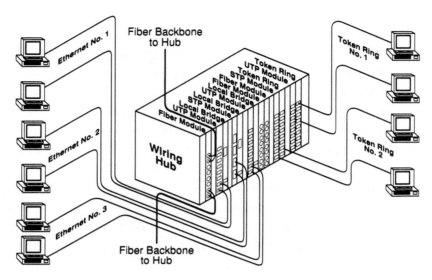

A wiring concentrator focuses the cable for multiple LAN topologies—for example, UTP and thin coaxial Ethernet, Token Ring, and FDDI—into a single unit.

The hubs usually contain an integral power supply and/or primary controller unit. Depending on a vendor's design philosophy, the controller unit may perform network management functions, serve as a repeater for all modules in the chassis, or act as the connection point to hubs located in other parts of a building or office of campus complex.

The modules serve as the link between the chassis and the network cabling and are thus cable-specific. That means they contain connectors that accept only certain types of connectors, each of which is associated with a specific type of cable. For example, a vendor may support IBM's Type 3 (IBM-certified UTP) Token Ring wiring and its associated connector with one module, thick and thin Ethernet coaxial cable with another, the UTP wire used in 10BaseT Ethernets with a third module, and Arcnet coax or fiber-optical cable with still other modules.

Each module usually contains connectors for multiple workstations. Placing two, four, or six connectors is common, depending of the intended use and type of cable to be attached to the module. For instance, thick coax connections require what is called a DIX connector, which is substantially larger that the RJ-45 used with UTP.

Some vendors offer modules that combine connector types, but only within a single type of network technology. For example, most hub manufacturers sell modules that support connections to both thick or thin Ethernet coax and 10BaseT UTP.

THEIR PHYSICAL DIFFERENCES

As is often the case in free enterprise, various network product vendors have applied their own proprietary sets of design rules to their hubs. For instance, some hubs are six to eight inches high, while others are 12 to 18 inches, and the physical and/or electrical junctions that connect the module to the chassis generally differ in each vendors' implementations.

The reasons for these differences range from the complex, such as needing to cram sufficient functionality onto a product, to the simple, such as merely ensuring that the hub is physically compatible with the vendor's existing products. These design differences mean, of course, that a module designed for one vendor's wiring concentrators generally will neither fit in nor operate with another vendor's hub.

Fortunately, these physical incompatibilities don't carry over to the hubs' abilities to communicate with each other. Although the modules themselves may be physically and/or electrically incompatible, the cable-specific jacks on them provide industry-standard connections.

For instance, the 10BaseT connectors (known as eight-pin modular connectors and sometimes called RJ-45 connectors, which are physically similar but electrically dissimilar) on one vendor's hubs are identical to those on another's. This is also true for the thin and thick coax, fiber-optic, Token Ring, and Arcnet connectors.

Because these connectors are identical, it's possible to connect one vendor's hubs to another's. In fact, 14 vendors demonstrated this type of interoperability between their hubs at the Interop show in San Jose, Calif., in October of 1989.

A WEALTH OF OTHER BENEFITS

The wiring hub's modular design allows vendors to integrate a wealth of other features and cabling options into them. As already noted, this architecture permits mixing the different cabling media—that is, fiber-optic, thick and thin cable, and UTP—into one wiring center. Without such hubs, expensive internetwork devices such as bridges and routers are required.

Just as importantly, the modular approach also allows mixing different media-access technologies, such as Token Ring and Ethernet or Ethernet and Fiber Distributed Data Interface (FDDI), in a single hub. This permits merging and managing the several different types of network technologies at a single point.

This capability is especially valuable to the growing number of large corporations where small clusters of Token Rings and Ethernets have sprung up independently. Again, it often means an organization does not have to purchase an internetworking device to connect and manage a variety of workgroups.

Vendors have also moved hubs out of the local workgroup and into so-called enterprise networks. Hubs can be daisy chained together—that is, connected one after another—to form large networks made up of multiple workgroups connected to separate-but-interlinked hubs.

On a more complex level, vendors are developing modules—usually in conjunction with non-hub vendors—that provide internetwork bridging and routing capabilities. These modules route and filter network traffic between the modules in hubs, whether the hubs are in a local or remote site. Filtering allows a network manager to improve internetwork performance and security by restricting the flow of specified types of data packets across internetwork borders.

BOON TO MANAGEMENT

Network hubs are ideal for centralizing network management capabilities. Numerous vendors have announced "intelligent" network hubs. Intelligence in this context refers to the hub's ability to accept management and configuration commands over the network cabling from a remote workstation.

Putting intelligence into a hub allows these devices to perform many functions that normally require an on-site technician's presence. For instance, network managers sitting at a centrally located network management station can not only turn remote hubs on or off, they can turn off individual modules and even individual ports within a module. They then can reroute traffic from the failed module or port to a working one.

This ability is vital in large, enterprisewide networks, where a single manager may be in charge of a WAN spanning several cities or states. In such situations, it's not always economically feasible to maintain a technician on-site to troubleshoot occasional problems. The ability to reconfigure the hub from a remote site can thus mean the difference between keeping a network segment online or shutting it down until a technician can make the trip to repair the failed unit.

Wireless Networking

Dealing with cabling problems is one of a network manager's primary jobs. Troubleshooting cables for breaks and bad connections and overseeing the relocation of computers are not only time-consuming tasks, but frustrating as well.

Installing new cable can be an expensive proposition, costing hundreds or even thousands of dollars per network connection. The cable itself is not that expensive—unshielded twisted-pair wire, for example, costs only a few cents per inch. But paying union technicians to pull new cable is costly, especially in old buildings that may contain asbestos or other hazardous materials.

As a result, some network managers turn to wireless networking, rather than cable, when they expand existing LANs or build new ones. Wireless LANs give network designers a level of flexibility unavailable to wire-based systems.

Wireless networks—which send and receive data through a transmission and reception device attached directly to the network adapter card—make moving PCs connected to wireless networks a much simpler process than with wire-based systems. Network managers can merely move the PC, without adding cable or testing its associated connections. This capability makes wireless networks a tempting alternative to cable-based ones.

GOING WIRELESS—PROS AND CONS

Wireless LANs offer network managers a host of advantages over traditional hard-wired network technologies. In addition to simplifying the move of networked PCs, they can also be less expensive to buy and build—over the lifetime of the LAN—than cabled LANs. The most obvious cost savings come from not needing to remove and install and test the cable. Their initial installation costs, however, are higher, since you must purchase the wireless transmission and reception electronics.

Some wireless connections won't require building permits, as can be the case with large-scale cable installations. This feature can save additional time and money.

66

There are tradeoffs, however. By nature of the medium, wireless networks transmit at slower data rates than wire-based networks. They also impose limitations on the number of connected nodes and how far apart those nodes can be placed from each other.

Some wireless networks—infrared ones—require line-of-sight communications. This limitation restricts their usefulness in many situations, such as in so-called hard-walled offices and multi-story buildings.

Manufacturers use three basic technologies to carry data over their wireless networking products: infrared light signals, narrow-band Radio Frequency (RF) signals, and spread-spectrum RF signals. Here's a look at the basics of how each operates and what their operational characteristics mean to network managers and users.

MAKING LIGHT OF DATA

Infrared networking products transport data via light waves that are invisible to humans. Infrared light, falling in the 1,000 gigahertz (GHz) and higher range, shares all the properties of visible light: It can be reflected off, but cannot penetrate, solid objects such as walls.

The primary advantage of infrared technology is its great bandwidth, allowing it to carry hundreds of megabits of data per second. In addition, because no government body regulates use of light frequencies, infrared data transmission is unlicensed.

Infrared networks share the technology used with the remote-control units that come with home electronics equipment, such as TVs and stereos. Receivers for wireless networks, like the channel changer and TV, must be visible to the transmitter, either directly or via reflection.

Infrared-based networks can be implemented with mirrors that focus the light signal to an extremely tight beam. Because focusing delivers essentially all of the transmitted signal to the receiver, it permits high-speed communication that can equal or surpass that of 16Mbps Token Ring networks. Mirror-based systems are well suited for point-to-point applications, such as building-to-building connections where transceivers are seldom moved. They are less satisfactory for in-building networks, however: The receiver must have a direct, unobscured view of the sending unit, and any movement in either unit can break the connection.

To work around this line-of-sight requirement, some infrared networks spread, or "flood" light around an area, which allows a single transmitter to reach multiple receivers, while reducing the effects of the transmitter or receiver being moved. A more diffused signal, however, reduces data rates and shortens the distance over which the signal can be reliably sent.

Another disadvantage of infrared networks is their susceptibility to interference from other light sources, including the sun and some lighting fixtures. Focused systems, because they produce a stronger light beam, offer greater immunity to light interference than unfocused ones.

UP IN THE AIR

Radio frequency transmission, while not limited to line-of-sight environments, offers its own set of thorny technical issues, including available bandwidth, signal reflections and interference, and Federal Communications Commission (FCC) regulations.

Manufacturers have taken two tacks in developing RF network products. Narrow-band transmission, requires licensing by the FCC because it needs a "clear" communications channel—one that is uninterrupted by other narrow-band transmitters. Spread-spectrum transmission uses special unregulated frequencies that require no FCC licensing.

Narrow-band networking products transmit data directly on a center frequency, much like a radio broadcast, so the transmitter and receiver must be tuned to the same bandwidth. Like the signals from radio and TV stations, narrow-band signals are subject to interference from signal reflections. This interference is caused when signals reflected off walls and other objects arrive at an antenna at different intervals.

Such "ghosts" make data communication unreliable. Unlike the human eye, communications equipment is not sophisticated or intelligent enough to discern the difference between reflections and the "real" transmission.

Vendors of narrow-band wireless products must thus be able to guarantee their customers a clear channel. A clear channel can only be ensured by carefully allocating each available frequency band to make sure that two nearby networks do not share the same frequency.

SPREADING DATA AROUND

Wireless networks using the spread-spectrum technique transmit in the 902MHz to 928MHz frequency range, which has been set aside by the FCC for wireless data communications. Combining spread-spectrum transmission's characteristics with an extremely low power output (250 milliwatts) means it is highly unlikely that one spread-spectrum network user will interfere with another.

Spread-spectrum transmission distributes, or "spreads," a radio signal over a broad frequency range. To do this, spread-spectrum networks use what is called a *predetermined pseudo-random sequence* to transmit data. This pseudo-random sequence is actually a predetermined digital signal pattern that places data on a combination of frequencies from across the entire spread-spectrum band.

A receiving device must thus know the specific signal pattern used by the transmitting device to decode data. This technique makes spread-spectrum LANs secure and reliable. In fact, the spread-spectrum technology was developed by the U.S. military during World War II for secure voice communications.

One of spread-spectrum's main benefits is that it allows multiple networks to share a single frequency as long as different pseudo-random sequences transfer data. In these situations, the signals from one network are interpreted by another as random noise and are ignored. Another advantage of spread-spectrum networks: They don't require line-of-sight communications, making them suitable for hard-wall offices as well as open office environments.

On the down side is spread-spectrum's relatively low data rate of 2Mbps. While this rate is sufficient for some network environments, it's inadequate for many applications, particularly data- or graphics-intensive uses.

WIRELESS TOPOLOGY ISSUES

Like their cable-based counterparts, wireless networks must provide clearly defined methods of accessing the transmission channel. Vendors use two basic techniques for granting this access: One, called a *peer-level system,* lets every node on the network communicate directly with every other node. The second uses a dedicated server architecture, with all network devices communicating through a central control station.

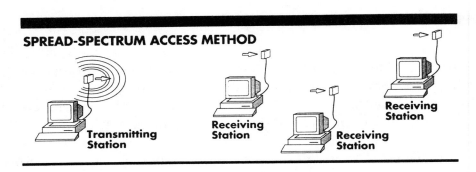

SPREAD-SPECTRUM ACCESS METHOD

Transmitting Station

Receiving Station

Receiving Station

Receiving Station

Although every device in a spread-spectrum network can "hear" every data transmission, only the specified nodes will accept a particular message. That's because each transmission contains an address that tells the destination station to copy and respond to that message. The remaining nodes on the network simply ignore the transmission.

Peer-level wireless networks typically cost less to build than those with central control units, primarily because they don't require the central hardware. But because there is no central point of control in peer-level systems, managing the network, including providing security, collecting network statistics, and performing network management and diagnostics, can be difficult.

Because they do feature a dedicated server environment, controller-based wireless networks permit centralized management, security, and maintenance capabilities. The central control unit also provides access to other services, including local and wide area networks.

THE WIRELESS MARKETPLACE

A number of vendors, including NCR, Motorola, Windata, and Photonics, market wireless networking products. These offer a variety of features and benefits, including varying degrees of performance, transmission characteristics, and network operating system support. Additionally, the IEEE has formed a committee, 802.11, to study and standardize wireless networks.

Many of the new pen-based, hand-held PCs include wireless networking capabilities as an option. These products can give end users even greater flexibility in their networking choices.

Twisted-Pair FDDI

Dick is nailing down the last-minute details of the biggest deal his company has closed. He doesn't have time to jump on a plane, but he wants to see the faces of the other dealmakers. He establishes a videoconference with them—some powerbrokers reside in his building, and some work across the country—but he never leaves his desk.

Jane electronically routes a document that contains the three-dimensional drawings and specifications for the new turbine that she's designing to Sally in marketing. Sally writes the marketing collateral, scans in the color photographs, writes the copy, packages it with an e-mail message, and sends it over the network to her vice president. Her boss, not being the type to use a keyboard, adds a voice message to the file, noting his approval or disapproval, and routes the document back.

Scenarios from the future? Yes. But if the computer and software manufacturers have their way, you will be the beneficiary of multimedia applications at your desktop. Apple, Microsoft, IBM, and Intel are serious about making multimedia sell. From the Newton to Kaleida to full-motion video demonstrations, vendors plan to serve you a full plate of multimedia applications.

One bottleneck is the speed of existing networks. While some people contend that an ordinary Ethernet or Token Ring network can handle small- to medium-size loads of multimedia traffic—say five or six people using an Ethernet-based videoconferencing application—others prophesy the great famine of bandwidth and propose cultivating FDDI instead.

With its 100Mbps of bandwidth, support for thousands of user devices, built-in redundancy, and expansive geographic coverage, FDDI appears to be perfect.

Except it hasn't sold. Despite manufacturers' enthusiasm, FDDI's market share can be measured in single-digit numbers. Dataquest says 3,100 FDDI adapters were sold in 1991. FDDI is expensive. Although manufacturers have dropped their prices on the network interface cards, it hasn't been sufficient—

the cost of the opto-electronics used in the adapters and the price of installing fiber-optic cable is still prohibitively high. The solution? Take the "F" out of FDDI.

Instead of running FDDI over fiber-optic cable, run it over copper—specifically twisted-pair. Shielded twisted-pair is less expensive than fiber-optics, and unshielded twisted-pair is even cheaper. Plus, a large number of LAN installers and managers are familiar with the cable: You've removed the fear factor.

Now you have to deal with the electronics. At 100Mbps, the electrical signals that comprise the packets emit too much radiation to be contained by the twisted-pair, cladding, or any shielding. Without modification, running FDDI over twisted pair would not pass FCC radiation emissions standards. Nor could data be reliably delivered over 100 meters of twisted-pair, the distance from the hub to the farthest workstation required by the ANSI and IEEE for all LAN standards.

A TRIAD FOR A SOLUTION

In June, 1992, ANSI approved a scheme for running FDDI over twisted-pair. Reliably and safely running FDDI transmissions over both shielded and unshielded twisted pair calls for a triad of technologies: *scrambling*, a *multilevel encoding* scheme, and *equalization* techniques.

When no data is being sent over an FDDI network, an idle signal of binary ones is sent. Once this repetitive pattern is encoded and transmitted over a copper wire, some of the signal is emitted as electromagnetic interference (EMI). This emission's particular frequency, at the signal strength required to allow proper reception of the data, causes radiated interference that makes it difficult to conform to the FCC's regulations.

To meet FCC regulations, manufacturers must either shorten the distance between the hub and the workstation (which makes the solution less applicable and less useful) or scramble the data. Scrambling is preferred. The FDDI data is scrambled with a pseudo-random sequence that eliminates the repetitive patterns. This causes the "spectral peak" of the emissions to be more evenly distributed over the spectrum of the transmitted signal. Ultimately, the peak electromagnetic interference lowers, and it meets FCC emission regulations.

Running FDDI over twisted-pair also involves multilevel encoding. Twisted-pair wire carries lower frequency signals better than higher frequency because of the lower attenuation, less EMI, and less near-end crosstalk. Near-end crosstalk is one of the most deadly interferences; it is the part of the transmitted signal that is electromagnetically coupled back into the signal being received. Reflections can cause interference with the "real" signal, causing packet damage and retransmissions. Yet lower frequencies usually mean lower data rates.

ANSI has decided on a multilevel encoding scheme that reduces the frequency of the transmitted signal while it maintains a 100Mbps data rate. This scheme, called MLT-3, was developed by Crescendo Communications and allows three possible voltage levels, rather than the usual two. Instead of changing back and forth between two "states" on every one or zero, it rotates among three states. Specifically, when the encoded data is a 1, it transitions to the next state, rather than back to the original.

With the MLT-3 scheme, the peak power is 20 MHz; with FDDI's usual NRZI (Non-Return to Zero, Invert on Ones) encoding scheme, the peak power is 62.5 MHz. With MLT-3, the frequency spectrum has less power in the higher frequencies and more power in the lower frequencies, where twisted-pair transmission fares better.

Equalization is the third panel of the technology triptych. Because of its physical properties, twisted pair conducts lower frequencies better than higher frequencies and so tends to distort the overall signal. By compensating for the distortion after the signal has been received by the device, the receiver can better accommodate different lengths of cable. Equalization at the receiving end is part of ANSI's recommendation.

TO SHIELD OR NOT TO SHIELD?

Much of 1992's debate on copper FDDI has focused around whether to use shielded or unshielded twisted-pair. STP has better electrical and transmission characteristics, but UTP is far more widely installed and costs less. Another point of contention was whether one copper FDDI scheme should accommodate both cable types, or if separate schemes should be used for each.

The camp calling for one scheme for both UTP and STP included Crescendo Communications, AT&T, British Telecom, Fibronics, Hewlett-Packard, and

Ungermann-Bass. The Crescendo *et. al.* solution allows lower levels of electromagnetic radiation, which will cost more and be more difficult to design up front but will make adoption easier in the end. A tribe of the single-scheme team, Cabletron and National Semiconductor, proposed a way that would be simpler to implement but would not allow higher levels of EMI.

The competing specification, which was advocated by AMD, Chipcom, Digital Equipment, IBM, Motorola, and SynOptics, proposed a method for running FDDI over STP. By default, UTP would have to be accommodated in a different manner. Having two solutions would require manufacturers to develop completely different products and create unnecessary confusion for users.

The Crescendo approach—and the one adopted by ANSI—should be able to meet FCC Class B and the European Economic Community specifications for emissions. Products that meet lower EMI levels can be installed more universally, particularly in Europe. This approach, which will be implemented in an integrated circuit, is a bit more expensive than the others proposed; however, it delivers a greater utility and a lower long-term cost to the user.

Copper FDDI is the same as fiber-optic FDDI in every respect except the cable type. It uses the same Medium Access Control, Physical Layer, and Station Management protocols. Only the transceiver—the "Physical Layer Medium Dependent," in the obfuscated language of standards committees—changes. Copper FDDI allows users to run the same NOS drivers, applications, and management software as with fiber-optic FDDI.

Despite the software compatibility, you can't run copper FDDI on just any UTP. You can't use the same telephone wire your PBX uses or your 10BaseT network probably uses. You need special, high-quality cable designed for data, not voice. Specifically, copper FDDI needs Category 5 UTP.

The installed base of UTP is largely voice-grade, although if you're lucky or prescient, when you installed your new 10BaseT network, you ran data-grade UTP rather than using the existing phone wire. If that cable is Category 5, then you can use the wire for FDDI. Otherwise, call the cable installer. The amortization schedule of copper FDDI won't be nearly as attractive as it is with 10BaseT.

For those who use STP, copper FDDI can run over that cable as is. The bulk of this market will be IBM customers, present or past.

WHAT DOES THIS MEAN?

FDDI vendors are eyeballing the installed base of 10BaseT (and to some extent, Token Ring) and hoping to lure them to FDDI with promises of multimedia applications and speedy response times.

Should you be lured? Multimedia, imaging, and conferencing applications are coming but many experts say that FDDI will not be able to support their widespread usage. But do your users really need 100Mbps to the desktop? While some say yes, other multimedia fans envision a world where users have their own Ethernet or Token Ring segments.

If each user had a 10Mbps pipe to himself, then he could participate in most multimedia applications. This configuration is generally used for high-powered Sun and Hewlett-Packard workstations; expect to see more manufacturers push this solution for PC users.

A more instantly gratifying application is a high-speed backbone of servers, where the file and application servers are attached directly to the 100Mbps copper backbone or concentrator. Although users are still attached to the slower Token Ring and Ethernet segments, they at least benefit partially from speedier networking. This configuration is not new, but with the high cost of fiber-optic FDDI, it has not been widely implemented. Instead, companies have built their networks around high-speed routers in the "inverted backbone" configuration.

Others agree with the need for high-speed, copper-based networks, but point out that FDDI's token-passing access method is optimized for large backbones. For a peer-to-peer network, the latency (the time it takes for the token to go around the ring) will be too long. Latency will be especially important in bridged or routed FDDI networks, whether copper or fiber-optic.

ANSI's acceptance of the Crescendo encoding scheme is just the beginning of this technology. The specification must be finalized, products must be engineered, and compatibility must be ensured.

ATM
(Asynchronous Transfer Mode)

Stick your card into the ATM slot, and:

  A. Several crisp new $20 bills pop out of the cash machine.

  B. Gigabits of bandwidth shoot out of your workstation.

  C. Nothing happens. And if this is another network acronym, I'm not interested.

ATM has nothing to do with automated teller machines, although Asynchronous Transfer Mode promises to deliver vast amounts of bandwidth to LAN users. While ATM was envisioned as technology for public network carriers, its application has been recast, and you can expect to see ATM deployed in private as well as public networks over the next decade.

ATM is the purported solution to the LAN/WAN integration quandary. Companies are looking for an efficient and cost-effective method of integrating their dispersed multiprotocol LANs, and frame relay, SMDS, and T-3 are vying as contenders. So far, none has been wholly successful. LAN technologies, with their ability to carry large amounts of data over limited distances, are inherently unsuitable in a geographically large network. WAN services, although able to efficiently carry voice and to a lesser extent data over long distances, offer limited bandwidth. ATM, however, can effectively integrate the benefits of LAN and WAN technologies while minimizing the side effects of both.

ATM offers a high bandwidth service that is capable of carrying data, voice, and video over great distances. ATM can provide interfaces to transmission speeds ranging from 1Mbps to 1Gbps. It offers low latency, making it suitable for time-sensitive or isochronous services such as video and voice. Plus, it is protocol- and distance-independent.

WHAT'S WRONG WITH LANS

There's nothing wrong with LANs, as long as their users are local to their server and their applications don't require vast amounts of bandwidth. But beyond that, LANs are shared media that don't scale gracefully.

Most LANs are relatively low speed. Ethernet and Token Ring were designed many years ago when LANs were primarily occupied with file transfer. LANs stand to be the delivery mechanism of a whole host of distributed, client-server applications, but these applications must be viable over a wide area network. While 10Mbps may have once seemed extravagant, MIPS and RAM are inexpensive, and workstations and PCs are pumping vast amounts of data onto the network. Five users on an Ethernet aren't uncommon; some Ethernets have just one user.

FDDI, designed as a 100Mbps backbone technology and rescaled into a high-speed workgroup technology, can accommodate the high bandwidth needs of workstations. Adapter cards and hubs are costly to purchase, and fiber is expensive to install, although twisted-pair FDDI will bring down the pricing to be competitive with the more expensive Token Ring products. But at 100Mbps, FDDI is inherently a LAN technology and limited to transmitting information a few kilometers, not cross country.

LANs don't scale well. When traffic becomes overwhelming, network managers segment the network with bridges and routers, thereby reducing overall traffic. Segmentation increases delay—as anyone sitting on the other side of a router from the desired server can attest.

LANs don't scale well because they are a shared media. All users on the same LAN must share the available bandwidth, whether it is a 10Mbps or 100Mbps pipe. When a station transmits, it occupies the entire bandwidth, and all other stations that want to transmit must wait until the sender has finished. Even on a high-speed LAN such as FDDI, only one station may use the bandwidth at any given time. Two stations that want to transmit 50Mbps each cannot transmit in parallel.

THE KILLER APPLICATION

The next "killer" application may do more than spur product sales, as killer applications are supposed to do; it may kill the network. The multimedia applications looming on the horizon will consume every spare Kbps on the LAN but will not be sated. Apple, Microsoft, IBM, and many other developers are writing applications that will integrate voice, video, and data. Image-enabled software, such as Lotus Notes, is only the beginning. Novell is integrating image capability into NetWare. E-mail will come equipped so users can make voice annotations. Imagine having workers improve their job skills or students expand their knowledge by downloading video clips from video servers that reside in different cities. Consider the possibilities of interactive video. Now ruminate on these applications' effects on the LAN and WAN.

FDDI was once supposed to be the medium for multimedia applications, but because of its hard-to-expand bandwidth and insensitivity to time delays, FDDI is suitable in only limited applications. Whereas data can tolerate some delays in transmissions, video and voice cannot. FDDI, like all LAN technologies, cannot guarantee that quality of service.

The proposed FDDI-II is sensitive to the needs of voice and video; however, the specification is still under development and is completely incompatible with FDDI-I (or what we think of as FDDI). Before writing off FDDI, however, consider that compression techniques will reduce the bandwidth needed to transmit real-time data and increase FDDI's applicability as a local medium for multimedia and bandwidth-intensive applications.

THE TECHNICAL DETAILS

ATM can be used to integrate disparate LANs across the WAN as well as on the LAN. ATM is a switch technology, not a shared media technology, which diverges from traditional LAN architecture, but is quite common in telecommunications.

Specifically, ATM is a CCITT and ANSI standard for cell switching that operates at speeds from 1.544Mbps to 1.2Gbps, with several specified interim speeds. Cells are short fixed-length packets, and in ATM, the cells consist of 48 bytes of user information plus five bytes for the header. Because the cell size is fixed, network delays and latencies can be predicted, making ATM suitable for carrying real-time information. LANs use variable length packets, which makes delays unpredictable and unsuitable for carrying voice and video. With the fixed cell size, large packet switches can be built rather inexpensively.

With an ATM network or any switched network, any one user can directly connect to any other user. Contrast this with a LAN internetwork, where a user may have to go over several segments to reach another user. The architecture is simplified, although the components are more difficult and costly to design.

ATM is scalable. With ATM, additional switches can be added to increase the network capacity. In a switched-based architecture, the aggregate capacity of the network goes up as more ports or lines are added. With a shared medium such as LANs, the aggregate capacity remains the same.

Logical connections between users are made via virtual circuits and virtual paths. Virtual circuits can be permanently established, thereby guaranteeing a level of access, or set up dynamically, allowing for the network service to adjust itself to the demand. For each call, the user specifies the average and peak traffic rates, peak traffic duration, and burstiness of the traffic. By setting these parameters, network designers can ensure that the voice, video, and data traffic get the required quality of service. For example, the network can respond to a traffic burst by automatically allocating additional bandwidth to a particular virtual circuit. Or, certain types of traffic or calls can be prioritized according to their importance or sensitivity to time delay.

Cell relay separates the relaying of data cells from the management of logical connections. Hardware will process the cells, while software will establish the virtual circuits, manage the resources, route calls, and handle billing. This separation into layers enables you to upgrade the hardware and software separately, thereby allowing a longer life for the network infrastructure.

ATM is independent of the upper-layer network protocols. On the physical layer, it is based on the Synchronous Digital Hierarchy, which is similar to SONET. ATM can use a variety of transmission speeds and protocols at the physical layer. For example, Adaptive's ATM adapter cards will use the FDDI interface.

WHERE ATM FITS

ATM may make its appearance in several places on your network: hubs, routers, to the desktop, and eventually, as a publicly offered service over the next several years.

ATM will also make its appearance on the desktop. Workstation vendors will equip their machines with ATM interfaces in the same way Ethernet or FDDI are used today. Multimedia and other bandwidth intensive applications suitable for ATM to the desktop include engineering, financial analysis, medical imaging, and multimedia. Initially, prices of ATM adapter cards will be high—in the $1,500 to $2,000 range, but if ATM is widely deployed, then prices will decrease. Adaptive and 3Com have announced product or their intentions to build ATM adapter cards. Router vendors are incorporating ATM into their products, primarily to enable the construction of ATM workgroups.

The network hub manufacturers are evolving their products from using a bus-based architecture (usually several Ethernets, Token Rings and/ or FDDIs) to a switch. This change enables them to achieve higher throughput and support new applications and larger networks.

NOT JUST ANOTHER ACRONYM

It seems like every time you turn around, there's another LAN or WAN technology claiming to be the ultimate solution. A barrage of standards and a slew of acronyms assail network planners and administrators. ISDN didn't work, then there was frame relay and SMDS. Why should ATM be any different?

ATM is designed to handle the needs of both voice and data, thereby reintegrating the communication that was disjointed by computers and telephones. ATM has strong support from manufacturers, telephone companies, and users, both domestically and internationally. Whereas the U.S. and Europe use different speed T-1, ISDN, and other WAN services, ATM—at 155Mbps— provides a common ground for a single global infrastructure. Also ATM is at the beginning of its lifecycle. ATM supports speeds up to 1.2Gbps but also accommodates slower speeds. You can install it today, and with the advent of SONET, the infrastructure and transmission system should be viable for the next decade.

Broadband LANs

Networks can be classified as *baseband* and *broadband*. Baseband LANs, such as Ethernet, Arcnet, and Token Ring, are much more common in the office environment. Broadband LANs are popular where multiple services, such as closed circuit TV, data, and voice, are needed. Broadband is also popular in factory environments.

Broadband LANs work in much the same way that cable television works. Broadband LANs transmit multiple radio frequency signals on the same cable, usually coaxial but sometimes fiber. This ability to send many types of communication simultaneously over the same cable, including voice, video, and data, distinguishes broadband LANs from the far more common baseband LANs. To accomplish this feat, broadband LANs use a technique called frequency division multiplexing.

Frequency division multiplexing is used to put several channels on the same cable simultaneously. To understand frequency division multiplexing, think of the cable as a highway. A highway has a width, which determines how many lanes are possible; the cable has bandwidth, which also determines its capacity. Highway width is measured in feet; LAN bandwidth is measured in Hertz or cycles per second. It is the difference between a higher and a lower frequency—the greater the spread between the upper and lower frequency, the more information can be transported.

Each "lane" or channel on a cable uses a different set of frequencies. Just as cars travelling in different lanes of a highway do not collide, information occupying one frequency band or channel on a cable does not interfere with information on another band. Thus, frequency division multiplexing sends its different types of information at unique frequencies.

Frequency-division-multiplexed information is generally sent in analog, not digital, form. Digital signals are discrete—one or zero. Analog is continuous, like a wave. To reconcile this difference, digital computer data must be converted into analog form for transmission over a broadband cable. The con-

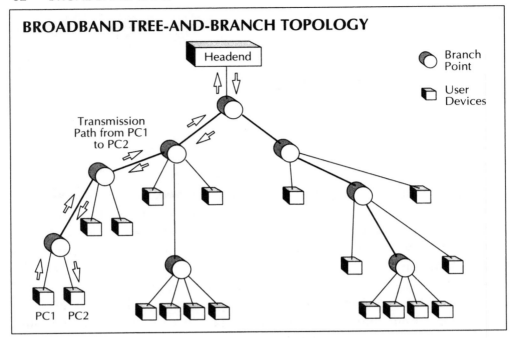

BROADBAND TREE-AND-BRANCH TOPOLOGY

Broadband LANs use a tree-and-branch topology. All transmissions travel up through the tree to the headend, where the signal's frequency is altered so it can travel to its destination. In this illustration, even though PC1 and PC2 are adjacent, their messages must travel through the headend.

version device is called a *broadband modem*. Once the broadband modem converts the data to analog form, it puts the data on the correct channel.

A TREE TOPOLOGY

Broadband LANs use a tree-and-branch topology. The root of the tree is the *headend,* or *central retransmission facility.* The trunk cable is attached to this root. Various branch cables are attached to the trunk cable. From there, user devices may be connected. Although most broadband networks use a single cable, some use a dual cable system, one for each direction to and from the headend. A dual cabling system has twice the bandwidth of a single cable system. The figure on the following page shows the layout of a broadband network.

A headend is essential. All transmissions must pass through the headend, because each device transmits on one frequency and receives on another. The headend is responsible for translating the device's transmit frequency to the receive frequency of another device. This frequency translation is called *remodulation.*

To illustrate how a broadband LAN works, let's follow a transmission, say a file transfer, from one PC to another PC. The PC sends the file to its broadband modem, where it is modulated into analog form. The modem sends data at one frequency, called the *return frequency* and receives at another called the *forward frequency.* These terms sound reversed because they are named from the headend's point of view.

Before getting to the headend, the signal probably passes through several splitters and couplers, where the signal loses strength. It also passes through amplifiers, where the signal gains strength. According to the principle of *unity gain*, the signal must arrive at the headend with the correct strength, usually at a level lower than the transmission strength.

At the headend, the packet is translated from the return frequency to the forward frequency then sent back onto the cable to the receiving PC. The trip to the receiving PC is just like the trip to the headend, except in reverse. Once at the receiving PC, the receiving modem translates the file back to digital form so the PC can understand it.

Forward and return frequencies make a pair. The headend can handle more than one pair of frequencies, although it cannot mix and match them. One complex part of designing a broadband LAN is deciding which information will travel on which frequencies. In many designs, the bandwidth is divided into 6MHz slices, which is the same bandwidth a television channel uses. Each type of communication takes one or more slices. Thus, an Ungermann-Bass Net/One broadband network might run over two channels, a television security system runs over another channel, and voice communications take up other channels. In general, higher speed communication services, such as Ethernet and data services, take up larger chunks of bandwidth than slower services, such as security and voice communications.

UNITY GAIN

All components of a broadband system either amplify or weaken the signal strength. As radio frequency signals travel down a cable, they deteriorate or experience signal loss. Devices on the broadband network, such as splitters, couplers, power inserters, and equalizers, also cause loss. The amount of loss experienced by a particular signal depends on many factors, including the diameter of the cable, the components it encounters, the distance it has travelled, and its frequency.

Broadband LANs are equipped with devices called amplifiers to counteract this unavoidable loss. Amplifiers attach to the cable in certain places and regenerate signals to a level determined by the system design. Any distortion the signal has picked up is also amplified.

The goal in designing a broadband system is to reach *unity gain*. Unity gain means that the amount of loss caused by the components in the system is equal to the amount of gain caused by amplifiers in the system. Achieving unity gains is complicated since the amount of loss imposed by a component depends on the signal frequency. Thus, amplifiers and other components are placed strategically to keep signal conditions uniform as signals move from device to device.

Since different frequencies are affected differently by various components on the network, achieving and maintaining unity gain is an arduous task. Consequently, broadband LANs—far more so than baseband LANs—require trained professionals for design and installation. Also, broadband systems are best suited for large installations with large staffs of networking professionals, although smaller installations that require multiple service types can also benefit from broadband.

UPS AND DOWNS

Broadband shines in campus environments, especially if several different types of communication must travel to the same locations. Support for multiple services saves cable costs and provides the ability to add services as needed. For example, a company might start with a data network and later add voice, security, a building management system, environmental controls, process management, and closed-circuit television.

A centralized tree-and-branch wiring scheme makes more sense than stringing together multiple baseband LANs in different buildings. Another advantage is broadband's immunity to electrical noise. Broadband LANs typically use frequencies above most machine-generated electrical noise, which is in the low frequency range. Baseband LANs, except those using fiber, are not so fortunate.

The price for this flexibility is complexity. Designing, planning, and installing broadband LANs is extremely time consuming and difficult. Along with deciding where cables and devices go, a LAN planner must evaluate the radio frequency requirements. Hundreds, and possibly thousands, of calculations can be necessary for the design and installation of a broadband LAN cable plant.

Maintaining a broadband LAN is also more difficult than maintaining a baseband LAN. Over time, the radio frequency settings of the components will drift (literally going out of tune) and cause transmission problems. The components require periodic tuning, which is more tedious than difficult.

Most end-user companies are not prepared to install a broadband LAN unaided. Installations require the resources and expertise of a broadband design and installation company. Experienced network planners can guide an end-user company through the process of creating the network, deciding which services will be used, where different devices will be placed, and so on.

Speedier Token Ring

While Ethernet enjoys the lion's share of methods to speed up a congested local network, Token Ring finally gets its turn with full-duplex transmission and switching hubs.

Unlike Ethernet, a myriad of ways to speed up Token Ring has been late to materialize. First, at 16Mbps, Token Ring is already faster than 10Mbps Ethernet. And its token-passing nature makes it more resilient under heavy loads, so the need for speed isn't as great. Second, the installed base of Token Ring is smaller, so fewer MIS shops are clamoring to manufacturers for a solution. Third, because Token Ring is largely a follow-IBM's-lead technology, until IBM pushes speedier Token Ring, only few adventurous shops will try it.

Both IBM and the IEEE 802.5 committee are working to define a standard for full-duplex transmission from the station to the hub that will bring Token Ring to 32Mbps. This bandwidth remedy has another part: replace the shared-media hub with a switch.

Like Ethernet switching, Token Ring switching is targeted at the problem of localized congestion. Typically, the servers will be placed on the 32Mbps full-duplex switched ports, while the end users' machines will be on the 16Mbps ports, either as dedicated machines or on shared segments. Additionally, full-duplex transmission will be useful for interconnecting Token Ring switches in a workgroup.

WHAT'S FULL DUPLEX?

Normal LAN transmission is half-duplex, meaning stations can either send or receive, but they cannot do both simultaneously. If a station can send and receive at the same time, the process is called full-duplex transmission.

Full-duplex Token Ring advocates point out that with a switched hub and full-duplex transmission, the users' machines are guaranteed consistent access to 32Mbps of bandwidth. With any shared-media LAN—even the

86

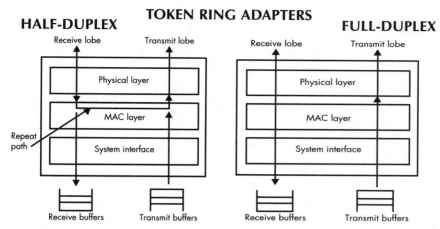

In current Token Ring, the repeat path carries the token and error information. When a station wants to transmit a frame, the media-access control layer must queue the frame until it can possess the token.

Because a full-duplex Token Ring link is point-to-point, a token isn't required. The repeat path is used to carry data, not the token. When a packet is ready for transmission, it's immediately placed upon the wire.

100Mbps varieties of Fiber Distributed Data Interface (FDDI), 100Mbps Ethernet, and VG-AnyLAN—access to bandwidth must be shared among all of the stations that are on the network. Performance degrades with the addition of more users. With a switched network, that bandwidth is dedicated to each station.

So how does full-duplex Token Ring work? It's actually pretty simple. Token Ring already supports full-duplex transmission. The "forward" path transmission is used for data, and the "return" path transmission is used for the token and for error control. If you have a switch and dedicated machines to each port, then each link is a point-to-point connection. Because each station has dedicated access to the switch, there is no need to mediate access to the link, and hence the network doesn't need a medium access protocol. In other words, a point-to-point Token Ring doesn't need its token. Figures 1 and 2 show half- and full-duplex transmission.

Making full duplex work requires some changes to the Token Ring protocols. First, the token access and token recovery protocols are eliminated. Remember, you don't need a token in a point-to-point link. Also, the frame repeating, frame stripping, and end-of-frame status update protocols are removed. In their place, that link can be used to carry data.

With no token, one may wonder if this is still Token Ring. "It's not a ring anymore; it's not a token anymore," says Norm Strole, senior engineer, local network development at IBM (Raleigh, NC). "From an architectural perspective, full-duplex Token Ring is using the same frame format, the same header, and the same trailer, so the end-to-end protocols don't know that anything changed at the MAC level."

Preserving the Token Ring frame format is important so full-duplex Token Ring can work with existing applications software and network equipment for Token Ring. The frame control field, priority bits, destination and source address fields, and source routing subfields are all maintained. The source routing subfields aren't needed in a switched environment, but they are retained to ensure backward compatibility with shared-media hubs and source routing bridges.

One tricky point with full duplex is clocking. In half-duplex Token Ring, the active monitor station determines the system clock for the entire network. Since the active monitor does not exist in full-duplex Token Ring, each station or switch port must transmit frames using its own timing crystal. Stations receive the incoming frames via the acquired clock of the incoming link.

BANDWIDTH IMPROVEMENTS

Being able to transmit on both the send and receive wires, thereby effectively doubling throughput, isn't the only benefit of full-duplex transmission, say its promoters. Stations will also gain a slight performance increase from not having to wait for the token before they can transmit. When a station has data to send, it transmits it immediately.

In half-duplex Token Ring, the amount of time a station has to wait to transmit depends on how many upstream stations also have data ready to transmit. On a heavily used half-duplex Token Ring, the token wait time could be several milliseconds, but on a full-duplex Token Ring, the access delay is nearly zero. Advocates say that full-duplex Token Ring will actually be more stable than the half-duplex variety. For example, link errors will affect only that particular segment, instead of being propagated throughout the network. Also, all of the errors associated with maintaining token flow are not a concern.

MAKE THE SWITCH?

The switch is a key piece in revving up Token Ring. Full-duplex transmission uses a switch with full-duplex ports instead of a shared-media hub or concentrator. With a switch, either a single station or a segment with multiple stations can be attached to each switch port. For full duplex to be possible, the port can have only one station attached. You must have this point-to-point link, so that you don't need the medium access method. Although currently being debated in the 802.5 committee, switches most likely will be able to support full-duplex and half-duplex transmission on a port-by-port basis.

Switches can be designed as either store-and-forward or cut-through. A cut-through switch receives the data from the incoming port, looks up the appropriate outgoing port in its address table, and moves the data to that port even before the entire frame is fully received. A store-and-forward switch, which is really a MAC-layer bridge, buffers the entire incoming frame before it looks up the outgoing port in its address table and transmits the data.

Cut-through switches offer the lowest end-to-end delay, or latency, when the traffic loads are low, but they have their tradeoffs. When traffic bursts—as LAN traffic is wont to do—a cut-through switch may not be able to handle the load unless it can revert to store-and-forward. Also, cut-through packets can propagate bad packets throughout the network, since they do not wait to see if the frame is good before passing it along.

Store-and-forward switches have higher latency. They are necessary when going from a higher speed network to a lower speed one, such as from 100Mbps to 16Mbps.

WHAT IT'S GOING TO TAKE?

Full-duplex Token Ring and switching solves the problem of congestion on the local network by speeding up access, either to selective machines or to every machine. Most commonly, servers will be placed on the switch's full-duplex ports, while the users' computers reside on the shared or dedicated 16Mbps segments. The 32Mbps links will speedily transport requests and responses from the clients and servers, and eventually, the 32Mbps bandwidth will become key as multiprocessing network operating systems, such as Windows NT and OS/2, come to market.

If you implement full-duplex Token Ring and switching in your network, you can preserve the existing architecture. You replace the shared-media hubs with the switch, and replace the adapters of the machines you want to speed up—presumably the servers. Cabling remains the same. Since replacing workstation adapters with new ones will probably be prohibitively expensive, implementation of full-duplex Token Ring is most economically limited to the servers. Most Token Ring adapters will be able to support full-duplex transmission with the addition of new driver software or a programmable ROM, although the implementation will vary from one manufacturer to another.

Note that protocol analyzers and other MAC-level tools will need to be revamped to work in a switched environment. Management tools rely on being able to see all of the frames that pass on the network wire; however, in a switched environment, packets are sent only between the computer and its port. Network management functions will have to migrate to the hub as well as the adapter cards.

Full-duplex Token Ring throws another entry into the fray of speeding up your local networks. Like full-duplex Ethernet, it is designed to solve the very specific problem of congestion on local networks, mostly at the servers. Multiple full-duplex adapters can be placed in the hub, and with the addition of software, the load can be balanced across the segments.

Other high-speed solutions abound. FDDI is time tested, but requires you to replace your hubs and adapters. Down the road, 802.3 100Mbps Ethernet, 802.12 VG-AnyLAN, and low-speed ATM are your options. Using VG-Any LAN will enable you to preserve your Token Ring frames, but all three are brand-new technologies.

Which Fast LAN?

Local networks have hit the performance wall. The growing sophistication of network usage, including client-server applications, as well as the increasing number of users on networks, has resulted in far more network traffic than ever before. If your network mainly serves the file and print needs of your users, perhaps you haven't noticed the problem. But if your users are involved with client-server applications, mainframes, distributed enterprise networks, or Lotus Notes, then you've probably heard the chorus: "The network is too slow!"

You can make the biggest performance difference by concentrating your efforts on the server. The server is shared by all, and changing the media to the servers is a less-monumental task than trying to change all the adapters in all the workstations on all the networks. First, make sure that the server is up to snuff—that it has a sufficiently speedy disk, enough memory, and a network interface card that's designed for a server. If the network is still too slow, closely consider the media. Maybe it needs improving.

The revenue opportunity hasn't been lost on the network product manufacturers, and they are proffering all sorts of solutions to the crunch. Some or many of the products may pan out as real-world solutions for your network. But you will probably find that keeping track of the pantheon of proposed solutions is harder than trying to memorize the Greek gods when you were in grade school. With that in mind, here's a cheat sheet to speeding up your LAN.

SEGMENT AND SPEED

The most common way to increase network performance is to reduce the number of users per network in a process called segmentation. While a year ago an Ethernet may have had 20 users per segment, that number has dropped rapidly—to about 10. Traditionally, network managers have used bridges or routers to segment their networks.

91

Many people have discovered that, for a local network, the difficulty of installing and managing routers is not worth the effort, and they've made the jump to switches. A few network managers have gone so far as to give each user a dedicated Ethernet segment, although such special treatment is usually reserved for the servers. Most switches are new and improved store-and-forward Media Access Control-layer bridges now sporting multiple processors, although some switches process packets without first buffering them.

Another solution to the bandwidth crunch is to increase the speed of the media. Instead of transmitting at 10Mbps or 16Mbps, the network transmits at 20Mbps, 32Mbps, or 100Mbps. This strategy has had historical success: When Token Ring moved from 4Mbps to 16Mbps, it alleviated many traffic clots. And, going from 234Kbps LocalTalk to 10Mbps EtherTalk vastly improved the performance of many Macintosh networks. Two basic approaches are proffered: Add full-duplex transmission to an existing media type, or change the media type.

DOUBLE THE SPEED

Full-duplex transmission is teaching the old Ethernet and Token Ring dogs a new trick. Ethernet is inherently half-duplex in that one wire in the 10BaseT pair is used to transmit data and the other is used to receive data. Packets travelling on both wire pairs at the same time indicate a collision. However, if there is only one user per Ethernet segment, then collision arbitration does not need to occur, since that user "owns" the Ethernet. The collision-detection circuitry becomes unnecessary, and data can travel on that wire.

Full-duplex is also suitable for Token Ring, although Token Ring networks don't suffer the same performance bottlenecks as Ethernets do. Token Ring is already a full-duplex scheme: One wire pair carries data and the second pair carries the token and error-correction information. As with Ethernet, when you dedicate one user per segment, the media-access method—the token—is unnecessary and therefore can be eliminated. That second wire pair can be used to carry data.

To get your Ethernet into full-duplex mode, you'll need a switch that's capable of full-duplex, one user per switch port, and full-duplex Ethernet cards. The more advanced Ethernet cards already operate in full-duplex mode

TABLE 1: HIGH-SPEED NETWORKS COMPARED

	Full-Duplex Ethernet	Full-Duplex Token Ring	FDDI	Fast Ethernet	VG-AnyLAN
Speed	20Mbps	32Mbps	100Mbps	100Mbps	100Mbps
Standard	IEEE 802.3 1995 or later	IEEE 802.5 1995 or later	ANSI X.3T9 1989	IEEE 802.3 draft 1994 standard 1995	IEEE 802.12 1995
Frame type	Ethernet	Token Ring	FDDI	Ethernet	Ethernet Token Ring
Equipment needed	Full-duplex NIC and switch	Full-duplex NIC and switch	Card and hub or switch	Card and hub or switch	Card and hub or switch
Cable type	Category 3, 4,5	Category 5, STP	Category 5 STP, fiber	Category 3, 4, 5 STP, fiber	Category 3, 4, 5 STP, fiber
Cost	$250	$400	$800	$500	$500

for behind-the-scenes management, and their manufacturers can modify that hardware and software to support full-duplex for the user. Users of older or less-sophisticated Ethernet cards aren't as fortunate. Most Token Ring cards can be upgraded either via new driver software or a ROM. Vendors are charging little or no premium for full-duplex transmission.

SPEED THE MEDIA

Critics of full-duplex say that doubling the bandwidth is hardly worth the cost and effort—the cost of buying a switch and dedicating one port per user and the effort of changing server NICs.

These critics say you can invest the same effort, but get a five- or 10-time improvement in the theoretical throughput, by moving to one of the new 100Mbps options: Fiber Distributed Data Interface (FDDI), 100Mbps Ethernet, or VG-AnyLAN.

With more than five years under its belt, FDDI is the most proven of the 100Mbps technologies, although its success has been limited to the backbone. As a local segment, FDDI hasn't taken off except for high-powered engineering applications. Attaching servers to the FDDI backbone, however, is a more popular application. Couple FDDI with a switch, and your users can get 100Mbps dedicated access to their servers.

FDDI and its copper brethren, CDDI, cards are being priced more aggressively to get within range of the pricing on 100BaseT and 100VG, but the switch and hub ports tend to be sold at a premium. If you need high bandwidth today, FDDI is the best proven choice.

802.3 Fast Ethernet and 802.12 VG-AnyLAN are challengers to FDDI. The manufacturers target pricing at twice the cost of 10BaseT, about $250 a card. Both types can operate with a plain old hub, but most people will probably implement them in conjunction with a switch.

802.3 Fast Ethernet uses the Ethernet frame format—but don't be fooled by manufacturers' claims. Technically, Fast Ethernet is not really Ethernet. But if all your software continues to work, do you really care about the internals of the network cards? No—well, not until you get to network-analysis tools, then the internals become very important. Management tools will have to be modified or made anew.

Fast Ethernet has received vast amounts of media attention, and the bulk of the Ethernet vendors stand behind 100Mbps Ethernet.

IN THE WORKS

The 802.12 committee is working on VG-AnyLAN, which is largely backed by Hewlett-Packard (Roseville, CA) and IBM. 802.12 also offers 100Mbps transmission and operates with Category 3, shielded twisted-pair, and fiber optic cable.

802.12 accommodates both Ethernet and Token Ring frame formats (although not in the same physical hub). As with Fast Ethernet, low-level network-analysis tools will need to be updated to operate with 802.12 networks. The technology uses a round-robin access method, which its inventors say is better for multimedia traffic.

Hewlett-Packard has started to ship prestandard VG-AnyLAN products. Like 802.3 Fast Ethernet, 802.12 VG-AnyLAN is slated to cost about twice the price of 10BaseT. With both technologies, the cards and hubs (or switches) will have to be replaced.

Both VG-AnyLAN and Fast Ethernet are nascent technologies that are shipping in prestandard implementations this year. Implementing them with a switched hub makes more sense than does implementing them with a traditional shared-media hub. And, until product prices drop significantly, you can offset the high cost of dedicating a segment per user by placing only the server on a high-speed port.

Basic Electricity Boot Camp

This crash course in electricity will help you with some of the terms and technology.

The circuitry in computer systems is powered by direct current (DC), the type of electricity produced by batteries. A battery produces a voltage at a constant level. Electric utilities, however, supply power with alternating current (AC), in which voltage constantly varies. To power a computer system, the computer's circuitry converts AC into DC of the proper voltage.

GENERATOR X

When an electrical current flows through a conductor, a magnetic field (or "flux") develops around the conductor. The highest flux density occurs when the conductor is formed into a coil having many turns. In electronics and electricity, a coil is usually known as an inductor. If a steady DC current is run through the coil, you would have an electromagnet—a device with the properties of a conventional magnet, except you can turn it on or off by placing a switch in the circuit.

There's reciprocity in the interaction between electron flow and magnetism. If you sweep one pole of a magnet quickly past an electrical conductor (at a right angle to it), a voltage will be momentarily "induced" in the conductor. The polarity of the voltage will depend upon which pole of the magnet you're using, and in which direction it sweeps past the conductor.

This phenomenon becomes more apparent when the conductor is formed into a coil of many turns. Figure 1 shows a coil mounted close to a magnet that is spinning on a shaft. As the north pole of the magnet sweeps past the coil, a voltage is induced in the coil, and, if there is a "complete" circuit, current will flow. As the south pole of the magnet sweeps past, a voltage of opposite polarity is induced, and current flows in the opposite direction.

96

A GENERATOR

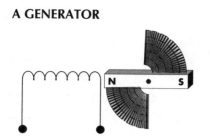

Figure 1. To generate electrical power, a coil is mounted close to a magnet that is spinning on a shaft. As the poles of the magnet sweep past the coil, voltages of alternating polarity are induced in the coil.

A SINE WAVE

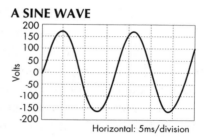

Figure 2. A 120-volt, 60-Hz generator produces power output that cyclically varies from 169.7V to -169.7V.

This relationship is the fundamental operating principle of a generator. The output, known as alternating current, is the type of power that electric utility companies supply to businesses and homes. A practical generator would likely have two coils mounted on opposite sides of the spinning magnet and wired together in a series connection. Because the coils are in a series, the voltages combine, and the voltage output of the generator will be twice that of each coil.

Figure 2 is a graph of the voltage produced by such a generator as a function of time. Let's assume that this happens to be a 120-volt, 60-Hz generator. The voltage at one point in the cycle momentarily passes through 0 volts, but it's headed for a maximum of 169.7 volts. After that point, the voltage declines, passing through 0 volts, then reverses its polarity, and has a negative "peak" of -169.7 volts.

This curve is known as a sine wave since the voltage at any point is proportional to the sine of the angle of rotation. The magnet is rotating 60 times a second, so the sine wave repeats at the same frequency, making the period of a single cycle one-sixtieth of a second.

CURRENT EVENTS

In a direct-current system, it's easy to determine voltage because it is non-varying or varies slowly over time. You can simply make a measurement with a DC voltmeter. But in an AC circuit, the voltage is constantly changing.

Electrical engineers state the voltage of an AC sine wave as the RMS (root-mean-square), a value equal to the peak value of the sine wave divided by the square root of two, which is approximately 1.414. If you know the RMS voltage, you can multiply it by the square root of two to calculate the peak voltage of the curve. If you were to power a light bulb from 120V(RMS) AC, you would get the same amount of light from the bulb as you would by powering it from 120V DC.

Yet another device uses electromagnetic induction: the transformer. Remember that a coil (inductor) develops a magnetic field when current flows through it. If alternating current is sent through the coil, it will produce an undulating magnetic field that reverses its polarity whenever the current reverses direction. If a second coil is wound around the first (but the two are electrically insulated from each other), the magnetic field of the first coil will induce a voltage in the second coil. In effect, the first coil sets up the same type of alternating magnetic field that is produced by the spinning magnet of a generator.

Just as an iron core improves the inductance of a coil, it has the same positive effect in a transformer, and most power transformers are wound on iron cores. As Figure 3 shows, a transformer is made up of two coils (usually referred to as windings) that are electrically insulated from each other. The two parallel lines separating the windings indicate that this is an iron-core transformer. The winding on the left, termed the primary, is connected to the electric utility's AC power grid. On the right is the secondary winding, in which the magnetic flux induces an AC voltage.

The "turns ratio" of the transformer describes how many turns are on the primary and secondary winding relative to each other. A turns ratio of 5-to-1 means that there are five times as many turns in the primary winding as there are in the secondary winding.

A transformer "transforms" AC voltages in direct proportion to the turns ratio. With a 5-to-1 turns ratio, the voltage on the secondary will be one-fifth that on the primary. This would be a "step-down" transformer, since it steps down (reduces) the voltage. A transformer with a 1-to-3 turns ratio, on the other hand, would be a "step-up" transformer, with the voltage on the sec-

A TRANSFORMER

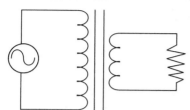

Figure 3. In a transformer, two coils (usually referred to as windings) are electrically insulated from each other. The left-hand winding, which is connected to the utility AC power grid, is called the primary winding. The secondary winding, on the right is connected to a load.

CONNECTING DEVICES TO GROUND

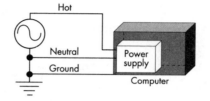

Figure 4. Power-using devices such as computers are connected to "ground" through the facility wiring.

ondary being three times that on the primary. The current, however, will be reduced by the same factor; the current on the secondary will be one-third that on the primary.

Step-up transformers at utility power plants increase the voltage for transmission over long distances. Then, nearer the delivery points, utility substations use step-down transformers to bring the voltage down to a lower level for distribution through neighborhoods. Finally, numerous transformers on utility poles step the power down again before it goes to commercial and residential customers. Energy losses in power distribution are caused by the resistance of the conductors, and forcing large currents through a resistance produces high power losses. By stepping up the voltage in long distance transmission lines, then, utilities are able to minimize the current, and thereby minimize transmission losses.

The world's earliest commercial electric power systems were DC, but AC eventually won out, primarily because transformers, which only work with AC, could easily step voltages up or down, as needed.

WELL-GROUNDED

One further point we need to address: How is voltage measured? What is the frame of reference? On virtually all computers (and many other devices), the chassis is connected to "ground." This means that the chassis is at the earth's potential, and that is the reference point for measuring the voltages in the system's various circuits.

The block diagram in Figure 4 shows how grounding works. The symbol of a sine wave in a circle represents the power source. For our purposes, this is the building's main switch panel. Below the power source, the stacked series of lines represents ground. This normally consists of a heavy-gauge wire or cable that connects the switch panel to a thick copper ground rod driven into the earth. (In large, steel-framed buildings, one of the building's steel columns will serve as the ground point.)

Note that one side of the AC power wires is also connected to ground at the switch panel. This line is known as the "neutral" line, because it is at essentially earth potential. The other power-carrying wire is usually referred to as the "hot" line. It is this line that will rise and fall in voltage over the 360-degree cycle of a complete sine wave. (The neutral line can't vary significantly from 0 volts, because it is grounded at the main switch panel.)

On the right side of the figure is a block diagram of the computer, including its power supply. The computer is connected to the main switch panel via the building's wiring, with its three-wire power cord plugged into a wall outlet. Of the three wires, the two power-carrying wires (hot and neutral) go into the power supply—and nowhere else. The computer's chassis is connected to the grounding wire. The grounding wire serves two purposes: safety and signal reference. Grounding the chassis ensures that it will be at the same potential as the earth, which eliminates any possibility of electrocution if someone should happen to touch the chassis. The second function performed by grounding the chassis is to set up a reference (of 0 volts) to which all other voltages in the system can be compared.

Fiber Optics for Networks

In networking applications, fiber optic cable offers several advantages over copper wiring. For a given length of cable, fiber has far less signal attenuation than copper, which allows you to use longer cable runs. A copper circuit can pick up unwanted electrical "noise" (spurious signals unrelated to the desired source signal). This noise is electrically induced into the circuit by virtue of the cable running close to AC power wires, fluorescent lights, or other noise sources.

A copper circuit can also pick up stray signals from adjacent data circuits. What's more, if the circuit is close enough to be picking up outside data signals, it's also likely to be inducing its own signals into the other circuits. This problem is known as "crosstalk."

A further disadvantage of copper data links is that they are susceptible to transient overvoltages (or impulses), which can momentarily reach hundreds or thousands of volts. Transient overvoltages can damage computers and networking equipment and, at the very least, they can be erroneously interpreted as data, leading to problems similar to those caused by electrical noise contamination.

Finally, the numerous copper-wire network links between computers can potentially cause electrical ground loops that interfere with signal reception.

With optical fiber networks, these types of problems can be avoided. Fiber optic links use light as the medium for data signaling. An optically clear glass fiber functions as a light guide, carrying a light signal from source to destination. The fact that the fiber does not use or carry electrical signals makes it immune to induced electrical signals and impulses. And since glass is an electrical insulator, using fiber optic links is the best way to avoid network ground loops.

Even with these advantages, fiber optics is still a new technology to the LAN world, and it may seem foreign to many network managers. This

Figure 1. Lan travels along a fiber optic light guide (or cable) from a special LED light source to a photoreceptor. The cladding layer reflects back any stray light waves traveling along the core.

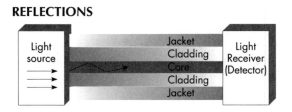

REFLECTIONS

CABLE CROSS-SECTION

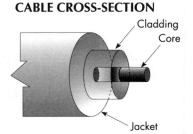

Figure 2. A fiber optic cable consists of several layers—an inner glass core of extremely high optical clarity, a wider glass cladding layer, and an encasing jacket.

"Tutorial," then, is aimed at enlightening you (if you'll pardon the pun) about this relatively new medium.

BOUNCING ALONG

Figure 1 shows how light travels along a fiber optic light guide. The light source could be almost any type of light, but for networking applications where very-high-frequency signaling is desired, a specialized LED is typically used. At the other end of the light guide is some type of light receptor—often a photodiode.

A fiber optic cable consists of several layers (see Figure 2). The "core" is glass of extremely high optical clarity—a tiny filament typically 62.5 microns in diameter. The core is surrounded by another layer of glass, known as the cladding, which typically has an outer diameter of 125 microns. The entire fiber (core and cladding) is usually encased in a plastic jacket, for mechanical protection. The material used for the jacket will depend on building codes and other mechanical requirements of a particular network installation.

Only the core and cladding are involved in the light transmission. Cables are typically specified according to the diameters (in microns) of these two layers. Thus, the cable just described would be listed as 62.5/125 micron optical fiber.

Physicists classify light-passing media according to their index of refraction, a measurement that correlates with the speed at which light travels through it. The kinds of glass used for the fiber's core and cladding have slightly different optical indices of refraction. As a result, light rays are reflected at the boundary between the two layers. As shown in Figure 1, light rays traveling along the core will be reflected back inside, should they stray toward the cladding. Thus light can't get out of the core, and that makes the core an excellent light guide.

A COMMON THREAD

One type of fiber optic cable can serve virtually all local area networking needs, says N. D'Arcy Roche, president and CEO of Raylan (Palo Alto, CA). This is the 62.5/125 micron multimode fiber that's specified for Fiber Distributed Data Interface (FDDI). "It is a dual-fiber cable that can be either a two-fiber duplex cable (like an electrical lamp cord) or two fibers in a round jacket," Roche says. "This cable can accommodate 10Mbps Ethernet, up through OC-12 (622Mbps) speeds. This eliminates the question of what fiber to choose for a given installation."

Roche says that this fiber can serve for either of two commonly used transmission wavelengths—1,300nm and 850nm. FDDI, as currently specified by the IEEE, uses the 1,300nm transmission window, but Roche says that several vendors (Raylan included) have introduced 850nm options for FDDI. The LED light sources and photodiode receivers for 1,300nm operation are expensive, while 850nm devices are substantially lower in cost.

The one drawback of transceivers using the 850nm window for FDDI is that there's no standard for that window. Acceptance by ANSI's X3T9.5 committee (the committee that oversees FDDI standards) is still pending. This means there are no guarantees of interoperability between the various vendors' products.

The 62.5/125 micron multimode fiber has a bandwidth of 160MHz over a length of 1km, with 3.75dB of signal attenuation (light reduction) when operating in the 850nm band. At 1,300nm, the same fiber has a bandwidth of 500MHz, over a distance of 1km, with 1.5dB of attenuation. Over shorter distances, bandwidth increases and attenuation decreases, but you can see that fiber cable can comfortably accommodate cable lengths approximately an order of magnitude greater than UTP copper wiring—with greater bandwidth and far less attenuation.

GOING THE DISTANCE

Telephone companies and other long-distance carriers typically use single-mode optical cable, which has a much smaller core—in the range of 8 microns. It offers a wider bandwidth than multimode fiber, and substantially lower attenuation per kilometer. These factors make it the ultimate medium for city-to-city communications, as signal repeaters can be spaced many kilometers apart, reducing costs and maintenance requirements proportionately. But taking advantage of single-mode fiber, typically, also means using rather exotic (and expensive) laser light sources and photo receivers. For in-building networking (as well as campus cable runs of less than 1km), multimode fiber is the cable of choice.

Thomas-Conrad (Austin, TX) is another major player in optical fiber-based networking, with its Thomas-Conrad Networking System (TCNS), a 100Mbps network that competes with FDDI. (Unlike FDDI, TCNS is proprietary.)

Peter Rauch, director of product marketing for TCNS, says that Thomas-Conrad specifies multimode cable with core diameters of 50 microns to 140 microns, but that 62.5-micron cable is the most frequently used. TCNS uses the straight tip (ST) connector developed by AT&T. This bayonet-type connector fastens with a quarter-turn and looks similar to the BNC connector commonly used with thin Ethernet cabling.

LIGHT STANDARDS

It's common to associate fiber optic cabling with high data rate applications such as FDDI and TCNS, but optical fiber can also be used for Ethernet and Token Ring. The Fiber Optic Inter-Repeater Link (FOIRL) standard is used to connect Ethernet hubs. FOIRL doesn't boost the data rate for Ethernet—it's still 10Mbps—but it does allow you to connect hubs with cable runs of up to 1km. More recently, the IEEE has come out with a 10BaseFL specification that's comparable to FOIRL, but allows 2km cable runs.

The IEEE's 802.5j standard addresses Token Ring over fiber optic cable, but this specification only covers "drops" (hub-to-end-node). There is no standard covering the use of fiber for the connections between hubs (using the Ring Out and Ring In ports). While various vendors offer solutions for fiber connections between hubs, these are proprietary, so you can't count on interoperability among them.

The fact that all commonly used networking technologies can use 62.5/125 micron multimode fiber means you can install fiber now, run Ethernet or Token Ring initially, then move up to higher speeds—100Mbps FDDI or TCNS, or 155Mbps Asynchronous Transfer Mode (ATM)—in the future.

You can't count on all systems using the same termination at the ends of the cables, however. The ST connector is perhaps the most commonly used. If you should move from one type of network to another, you may have to change connectors accordingly, but both Roche and Rauch say that this is seldom a problem. For example, if you have in-the-wall cabling that uses ST connectors, and network adapters that use a different connector, you can use patch cords with the appropriate connectors at each end to make the transition.

Who are the major suppliers of fiber optic cable and connectors, and how do you choose the specific type you need? Rauch recommends that you seek the advice of your local cable installation contractor, who will know the local building codes and which cable is best for specific applications.

Fiber optic cabling is gaining popularity as its cost comes closer to parity with copper. Its transmission properties are unquestionably desirable, particularly for high-speed networks or in cases where long distances must be spanned. If you're looking for more illumination on the subject, consult vendors of fiber optic systems for background materials. I'd also recommend *The Technician's Guide to Fiber Optics* by Donald J. Sterling (Albany, NY: Delmar Publishers, 1987 and 1993; ISBN 0827358350). The first edition lacks the latest information—on Ethernet 10BaseFL, for example—but it offers an excellent discourse on the physics of optical cabling, light sources, and detectors. I haven't had the opportunity to review the second edition, but it should be considerably more up-to-date on the latest standards.

Lay of the LAN—Cabling Basics

If you're on a network, your machine has to be connected to at least one other machine, whether through metal cabling, fiber optic light guides, or radio waves. Even as new technologies, such as radio wave-based networks and infrared light-based networks, produce new ways for connecting nodes to each other, the least expensive and most popular medium for networking computers is still copper wire.

Networks based on copper cabling generally use one of two main cable types: coaxial or twisted-pair. ARCnet started with RG-62/U and RG-59/U coaxial cable, but now includes twisted-pair and even fiber optic cabling. Likewise, Ethernet, which was defined in the IEEE 802.3 standard, was originally implemented only on thick coaxial baseband cabling. But the Ethernet standard has expanded to include broadband coaxial, fiber optic cabling, and twisted-pair.

ETHERNET CABLING

The thick Ethernet cabling standard was designed to serve as a network backbone. In this design, machines are connected to a thick, 0.4-inch double-shielded coaxial segment, or bus, through transceiver cables, using 15-pin transceiver or AUI cables. Each AUI cable can be up to 50 meters long—which is a blessing given the difficulty of maneuvering the thick, trunk cabling.

The thick Ethernet cabling system has been standardized by the IEEE as 10Base5. The "10" in 10Base5 refers to its 10Mbps transmission rate, while the term "Base" refers to baseband cabling and the "5" refers to the maximum length for a segment in hundreds of meters. The coaxial transceivers are connected directly into the coaxial trunk either by piercing the cabling (called a vampire tap, appropriately enough) or by in-line connection with N connectors. From there, an AUI cable connects each transceiver to a network interface card on a node. Each end of the 10Base5 segment must have a 50-Ohm terminating resistor installed, and only one terminator should be grounded.

106

ETHERNET SLIMS DOWN

10Base2, also known as thin Ethernet—or in slang as cheapernet, was developed to lower the cost of installing an Ethernet network. In fact, this thin coaxial cabling can still be the most cost-effective solution for companies that want to connect a few PCs within a relatively small area.

However, with 10Base2, the Ethernet bus connects directly to a T connector on the back of each node. Consequently, the design is much more prone to disaster: If any user breaks the chain (for example, by accidentally disconnecting the wrong part of the T connector), either the entire network will go down or, at the very least, the side of the network that doesn't have a server will be isolated.

The 10Base2 standard has a 10Mbps transmission speed, and it uses thin, flexible RG-58A/U coaxial cable, typically 0.2 inches in diameter, with a stranded conductor. Like 10Base5, the coaxial bus must be terminated at each end, and one end must be grounded. The maximum length of a 10Base2 segment is 185 meters, which is not the 200 meter limit you might expect based on its name.

WITH A TWIST

Partly in response to complaints about the difficulty of troubleshooting coaxial Ethernet and partly to take advantage of the existing wiring in many offices, the 10BaseT standard was developed to work with Category 3 twisted-pair copper cabling. (The "T" in 10BaseT stands for twisted pair.)

Common in newer buildings, Category 3 cabling is often used as phone wiring. But because it has low noise and crosstalk characteristics, it can be used to support a network installation that can deliver 10Mbps performance.

In some older buildings, the cabling may not be up to Category 3 specifications, and subsequently, may not be able to support a network installation. In this situation, you may still want to install twisted-pair cabling rather than coaxial despite its higher price, because it has an easier installation.

The 10BaseT specification calls for unshielded twisted-pair cabling, commonly called UTP, to use two of the four pairs of conductors in a typical Category 3 cable (see Figure 1). One pair transmits data, while the other is meant to receive data. The standard doesn't specify exactly what the remaining

10BASET WIRING CONFIGURATION

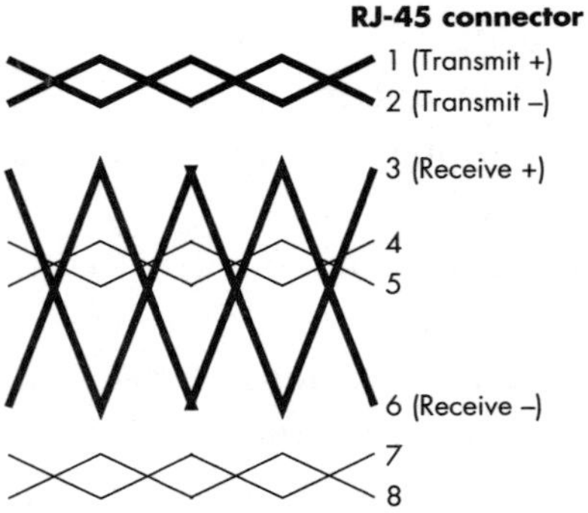

RJ-45 connector

1 (Transmit +)
2 (Transmit –)

3 (Receive +)

4
5

6 (Receive –)

7
8

Figure 1. UTP cabling typically has four pairs of wire in one sheath, which connects to an RJ-45 modular jack. For 10BaseT, only the 1-2 pair and the 3-6 pair are wired, but not used with Ethernet.

TOKEN RING PHYSICAL TOPOLOGY

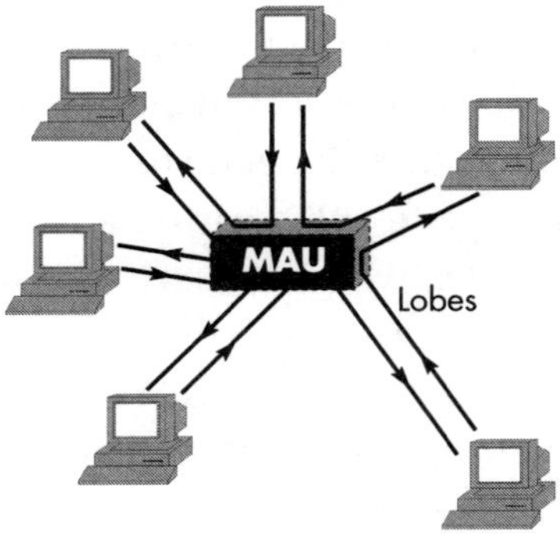

MAU

Lobes

Figure 2. In Token Ring networks, packets are forwarded from station to station until they arrive at the correct address. Although Token Ring uses a star configuration, each station is still connected, via the MAU, to the next station on the ring.

two pairs of conductors can be used for, so many cable installers use them to create a second 10BaseT data connection. However, this practice may complicate future conversion to faster transmission speeds, because the emerging standards for 100Mbps transmission over Category 3 cabling will require the use of all four pairs of cable.

Like 10Base2 and 10Base5, 10BaseT uses a star topology in which each node connects to a central concentrator or multiport repeater, which is typically located in a central equipment room or wiring closet. This topology meshes well with the existing cabling layout in most buildings.

FAST ETHERNET CABLING

With many users outgrowing the 10Mbps data rate of 10BaseT, vendors are responding with new products and standards to wring more speed from copper cabling. Two physical cabling strategies are emerging: using all four pairs of conductors in existing Category 3 cabling, or using two pairs of conductors in the faster and more noise resistant Category 5 cabling. Category 5 specifications permit signaling rates of up to 100MHz, compared to Category 3 which allows rates of up to 16MHz.

Two emerging standards, 100BaseTX and 100BaseT4, conform to the IEEE 802.3 standard, while a third, 100VG-AnyLAN conforms to the new IEEE 802.12

TOKEN RING WIRING CONFIGURATION

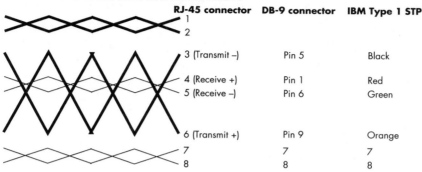

	RJ-45 connector	DB-9 connector	IBM Type 1 STP
	1		
	2		
	3 (Transmit –)	Pin 5	Black
	4 (Receive +)	Pin 1	Red
	5 (Receive –)	Pin 6	Green
	6 (Transmit +)	Pin 9	Orange
	7	7	7
	8	8	8

Figure 3. Token Ring initially used IBM Type 1 STP wiring. Now it typically uses a 9-pin D-subminiature (DB-9) connector, although it also has been implemented over UTP using RJ-45 connectors. As shown, wiring configurations depend on which type of cabling you're using.

specification. 100BaseTX uses two-pair Category 5 cabling, and 100BaseT4 uses four-pair Category 3, 4, or 5 cabling. 100VG-AnyLAN can use either cabling strategy.

TOKEN RING CABLING

Based on a token-passing logical ring topology, Token Ring networks tend to show predictable performance degradation curves when under heavy loads, as opposed to Ethernet networks, which degrade less predictably when stressed.

Although it's based on a logical ring topology, a Token Ring network looks more like a star, with each node connected directly to a central MAU. Think of this cabling arrangement as being a collapsed star, in which the middle of each segment of the ring has been pulled back to the central hub (see Figure 2, page 25). The internal circuitry of the MAU is configured as a ring. As a node is inserted into the ring and activated, a relay in the MAU closes to include the node (called a lobe) in the electrical ring.

Token Ring networks come in two "flavors": 4Mbps and 16Mbps. Telephone-grade UTP cabling can be used for 4Mbps Token Ring equipment. IBM calls this cabling Type 3, and it is roughly equivalent to Category 2 cabling. Connecting a 4Mbps Token Ring adapter to Type 3 cabling requires a media filter to reduce electrical noise. Like 10BaseT, Token Ring networks use two pairs of conductors, but in a different configuration (see Figure 3).

IBM Type 1 cabling is required for 16Mbps Token Ring networks. This requires the same wiring configuration as UTP cabling, but with solid, thicker, and heavier conductors. Each pair of wires is shielded with foil, and the resulting four-pair cable is further protected with braided shielding. IBM developed special hermaphroditic connectors to allow Type 1 cables to attach to either workstation patch cords or to other Type 1 cables as extensions.

PLAN FOR SUCCESS

Whether you're using Token Ring or Ethernet, or if you're just starting to network your company, the cabling you choose and how you install it can make a big impact on network performance. So take the time to carefully plan your wiring layout. For example, make sure your cable distances don't exceed the recommended standard length, and double check the cabling and connections to ensure they meet established specifications.

Such steps can do more than make your network faster and more reliable; it can free you from the chore of constantly reacting to problems caused by the physical wiring plant, which are generally hard to trace. Additionally, if you plan right, you can use the same wiring when you upgrade to a faster network, saving your company money.

PCI: New Bus on the Block

The PCI bus may have arrived just in time to carry the load that faster networks and multimedia put on the I/O subsystem.

As computer CPUs and memory subsystems advance in performance, the I/O subsystems are challenged to keep up. Video graphics controllers, network adapters, and hard disk controllers demand high levels of data throughput.

The Peripheral Component Interconnect (PCI) bus was developed to address these needs for higher I/O transfer rates. Like EISA, PCI is a 32-bit-wide bus, allowing data to be transferred four bytes at a time. But, while EISA has an 8.33MHz bus clock rate, the PCI 2.0 specification allows for a clock rate of up to 33MHz. The product of the four-byte bus width and 33MHz clock frequency gives PCI a 132MBps theoretical maximum throughput, compared to EISA's 33MBps.

Although PCI was largely developed by Intel, a company known for its 80x86 family of microprocessors, it was conceived as a processor-independent I/O bus. As an example of this processor independence, Apple Computer's newest PowerPC-based Macintoshes use the PCI bus.

LOADING UP

If you've shopped around for PCI-based systems, you've probably noticed that most of today's offerings have three or fewer PCI slots. This is problematic if you are planning to use a PCI-based system as a network file server; servers need lots of slots to handle multiple NICs and disk controllers.

According to Robert McNair, applications engineering manager for Intel's PCI components division (Santa Clara, CA), part of the reason for the relatively low PCI slot-count on today's machines is a bus-loading limitation. A second reason involves the large installed base of ISA and EISA adapter cards, which users will no doubt be reluctant to replace immediately. A system that also contains several EISA or ISA slots—in addition to PCI—can take advantage of this installed base.

As for the bus-loading issue, no matter what device is "driving" the bus (putting electrical signals onto the bus), it will only be capable of driving a limited number of devices. If there are too many electrical loads, signal voltages may not quite meet their required tolerances, resulting in signal errors. In extreme cases, circuits may be damaged if they are supplied with more current than they can handle.

PCI can drive a maximum of 10 loads, says McNair. In determining bus loading, the PCI chipset that drives the PCI bus itself counts as one load. Any PCI components (such as an embedded PCI graphics or SCSI controller, mounted on the motherboard) count as one load each.

PCI slots are counted as one and one-half to two loads each. Why not one load? If each slot could support only one load, it would create quite a hardship for the designers of PCI add-in boards. This is because you could only have a single PCI device on each card. By allowing cards to present a load equivalent to two PCI loads, the designers of the PCI specification gave board designers more freedom in the types of products they can design.

What these bus-loading rules mean is that a PCI bus will, in most cases, be limited to a maximum of four slots. (As an example, if the PCI chipset is taking one load and a PCI- based graphics controller is taking another, a system designer would have eight loads left to apportion among the slots, which equates to four slots).

System designers can get past the limitations outlined above by using PCI "bridges"—integrated circuits that serve as signal amplifiers and repeaters. Through the use of a bridge, a system designer can hang a second PCI bus off of another one. (But bear in mind that the PCI bridge itself presents a load to the primary bus; it usually counts as one load.)

Other types of bridges may connect either an EISA bus or an ISA bus to a PCI bus. The manner in which bridges are employed can have a significant impact on overall system performance. For example, consider Figure 1, which illustrates two different ways in which to bridge several buses together. In this figure, Approach A represents a cascaded configuration, in which PCI bus 2 is connected (via a PCI-to-PCI bridge) to PCI bus 1. The EISA bus, too, is cascad-

A BRIDGE TOO FAR?

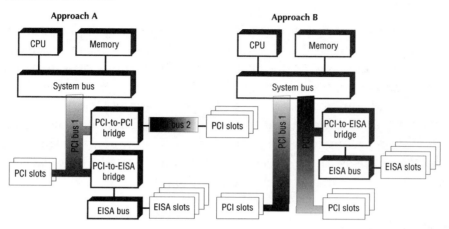

Figure 1. Bridges can be used to connect one PCI bus to another. Other bridges can link a PCI bus to an EISA or ISA bus. But how systems designers use these bridges can impact overall performance. In this example, Approach B offers higher total I/O throughput than Approach A, due to the peer-level arrangement of the two PCI buses in Approach B.

ed from PCI bus 1. Because of this cascaded arrangement, all data flowing to or from any adapters plugged in to any of the PCI or EISA slots must cross PCI bus 1—putting an upper limit of 132MBps on total I/O.

Approach B in Figure 1 shows a second arrangement, which I'll refer to as a peer arrangement because both PCI bus 1 and PCI bus 2 are bridged directly off the system bus. Neither one depends on the other to get or send data. In this case, total system I/O can go as high as 264MBps—twice that of Approach A.

Figure 1 doesn't represent any specific computer system. Rather, it illustrates, in a general way, the difference between cascaded and peer-level PCI bus arrangements. Hewlett-Packard (HP, Palo Alto, CA) has begun using these two approaches in the company's NetServer line of network servers. Larry Shintaku, advanced development manager for HP's NetServer division (Santa Clara, CA), says that the company's entry-level NetServers use the cascaded-bus configuration (similar to Approach A, Figure 1)—as do most of the other PCI-based servers from other vendors. HP's high-end NetServers use the peer arrangement, for higher total I/O throughput capability.

On the PCI slot-count issue, Shintaku takes much the same perspective as Intel's McNair, saying that bus-loading constraints are one reason that most of today's PCI systems have relatively few PCI slots, but that there's also a need to have enough ISA (or EISA) slots to accommodate older boards.

In terms of mechanical arrangements, PCI uses a multiplexed data and address bus. This means that the same electrical conductor paths are used to carry data and addresses. (It doesn't carry them both at the same time, however; it alternates as necessary, with one signal line indicating whether the information currently on the bus represents data or an address.)

By multiplexing the data and address information onto one set of conductors, PCI's designers managed to get a fairly low pin-count, with respect to EISA or other 32-bit buses. This reduces cost by allowing a smaller physical connector and takes up less "real estate" on motherboards.

YOU'RE IN MY SLOT

PCI's specifiers also came up with a clever way to conserve back-panel space on computers. Because PCI won't replace ISA or EISA overnight, most systems will carry two types of I/O slots, usually a mixture of PCI and EISA or PCI and ISA. There may not be enough physical slots on the back panel to accommodate as many I/O boards as a customer may want (network server applications, in particular, often demand lots of slots), therefore, PCI's designers came up with the concept of "shared" slots. A shared slot, for example, may (depending on its design) be used for either a PCI board/EISA board or a PCI board/ISA board.

Figure 2 shows the layout of a typical shared slot. It is a top view, looking down on the motherboard. EISA cards have their printed circuit boards on one side of the metal mounting bracket that is used to secure the board to the computer's back panel. With PCI, the circuit board is mounted on the other side of the bracket. Looking at the diagram, you can see that this allows two connectors (PCI and EISA, in this example) to be placed side-by-side in the space occupied by one physical slot.

Shared slots don't increase the total number of slots—a five-slot system, for example, is still a five-slot system—but by sharing slots, a designer could come up with a system that has three PCI slots and three ISA slots. One of the slots would have to be a shared slot. This arrangement gives users the flexibility to

A PCI/EISA SHARED SLOT (TOP VIEW)

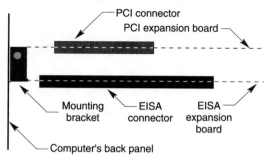

Figure 2. System designers can create "shared" I/O slots, which can be used for either of two types of expansion boards. The shared slot illustrated here will accept either a PCI or EISA card.

use a combination of three PCI boards and two ISA, or two PCI boards and three ISA.

Intel's McNair notes that PCI's interrupt scheme is different from ISA's. PCI permits several devices to share a single interrupt, provided that all of the devices are capable of sharing interrupts. With the ISA bus, only one device is allowed to use a particular interrupt.

PCI can allow shared interrupts because it uses "level-triggered" interrupts, while the ISA bus uses "edge-triggered" interrupts (EISA can use either). "Level-triggered" means that the computer is sensitive to the voltage level that is on each interrupt line. For example, an interrupt line may be at a 5-volt level when there are no interrupts. When an interrupt occurs, it is signaled by the interrupt line going to 0 volts. (The voltages may vary or the logic inverted from this example, depending on your computer's design; the principle still holds true, however.)

With edge-triggered interrupts, the computer only responds to the transition between one state and the next. In other words, it only pays attention to the leading edge of the voltage waveform on the interrupt line.

When a PCI-based system receives an interrupt on one of the PCI interrupt lines (there are four of them), it knows that one—and possibly more—of the devices using that interrupt line needs attention. It then begins polling each device in turn, to find out which one sent the interrupt. Once the correct device is located, the system will immediately jump to the interrupt handler (also known as an interrupt service routine, or ISR) for that device.

When the ISR is complete, the system returns to the activity it was performing prior to the interruption. But, if the interrupt line previously mentioned is still indicating an interrupt (if the interrupt line is still being held low, in our example), the system will once again poll devices to find out which one is calling for an interrupt, then service that interrupt.

By using a combination of interrupt-driven and polling techniques, PCI can be much more flexible in its interrupt scheme than ISA. Although ISA supports more individual interrupts, the fact that each device must have its own interrupt line means you're more likely to run out of interrupts with ISA.

PCI's ability to have multiple devices sharing a single interrupt line is made possible by its use of level-triggered interrupts. If interrupts were edge-triggered, it is possible that some of the incoming interrupts might be lost. For example, if a second interrupt were to come in while the processor was still in the midst of processing a previous one, the processor would return from servicing the first interrupt but not be aware that a second interrupt had been asserted. With level-triggered interrupts, by contrast, any device assigned to that interrupt line can bring the line low to assert an interrupt. This line will continue to stay low until all pending interrupts have been serviced, ensuring that the processor doesn't miss any incoming interrupts.

PCI should offer enough I/O throughput to satisfy most of today's needs—especially if a dual, peer-level PCI arrangement is used. But PCI's developers have already made plans for expansion, by supporting a future 64-bit bus, and clock rates up to 66MHz. The compact pinout of PCI's multiplexed bus allows a second connector to be placed right behind the first, without taking up too much real estate on the motherboard. McNair says the 66MHz bus may not be needed for a long time—at least on PC-class machines. While high-powered engineering workstations may be able to take advantage of it, bottlenecks in other parts of PC systems may mean they can't effectively make use of the doubled clock rate.

Fast Ethernet: 100BaseT

The idea of Fast Ethernet was first proposed in 1992. In August 1993, a group of vendors came together to form the Fast Ethernet Alliance (FEA). The goal of the FEA was to speed Fast Ethernet through the Institute of Electrical and Electronic Engineers (IEEE) 802.3 body, the committee that controls the standards for Ethernet. Fast Ethernet and the FEA succeeded, and in June 1995, the technology passed a full review and was formally assigned the name 802.3u.

The IEEE's name for Fast Ethernet is 100BaseT, and the reason for this name is simple: 100BaseT is an extension of the 10BaseT standard, designed to raise the data transmission capacity of 10BaseT from 10Mbps to 100Mbps. An important strategy incorporated by 100BaseT is its use of the Carrier Sense Multiple Access with Collision Detection (CSMA/CD) protocol—which is the same protocol that 10BaseT uses—because of its ability to work with several different types of cable, including basic twisted-pair wiring. Both of these features play an important role in business considerations, and they make 100BaseT an attractive migration path for those networks based on 10BaseT.

The basic business argument for 100BaseT resides in the fact that Fast Ethernet is a legacy technology. Because it uses the same transmission protocol as older versions of Ethernet and is compatible with the same types of cable, less capital investment will be needed to convert an Ethernet-based network to Fast Ethernet than to other forms of high-speed networking. Also, because 100BaseT is a continuation of the old Ethernet standard, many of the same network analysis tools, procedures, and applications that run over the old Ethernet network work with 100BaseT. Consequently, managers experienced at running an Ethernet network should find the 100BaseT environment familiar, meaning less time and money must be spent by the company on training.

PROTOCOL PRESERVATION

Perhaps the shrewdest strategy taken with Fast Ethernet was the decision to leave the transmission protocol intact. The transmission protocol, in this case CSMA/CD, is the method a network uses to transmit data from one node to another, over the cable. In the OSI model, CSMA/CD is part of the Media Access Control, or MAC, layer. The MAC layer specifies how information is formatted for transmission and the way in which a network device gains access to, or control of, a network for transmission.

The name CSMA/CD can be broken down into two parts: Carrier Sense Multiple Access and Collision Detection. The first part of the name describes how a node equipped with a network adapter determines the appropriate time to send a transmission. In CSMA, a network node first "listens" to the wire to find out if any other transmission is currently being broadcast over the network. If the node receives a carrier tone, which implies that the network is busy with another transmission, it holds onto its transmission and waits until the network is clear. When it does sense a quiet network, it begins its transmission. The broadcast is actually sent to all nodes on the network segment, but only the node with the correct address accepts the transmission.

The Collision Detection feature is meant to remedy situations in which two or more nodes inadvertently broadcast a transmission at the same time. Under the CSMA structure, any node that is ready to transmit first listens to determine whether the network is free. If two nodes were to listen at the exact same moment, however, both would perceive the network to be free and both would transmit their packets simultaneously. In this situation, the transmissions would interfere with each other (network engineers call this a collision) and neither would reach its destination intact. Thanks to Collision Detection, a node will listen to the line again after it has broadcast its packet. If it detects a collision, it waits a random period of time and rebroadcasts the transmission, again listening for a collision.

THREE KINDS OF FAST

Another important consideration, along with the adoption of the CSMA/CD protocol, was the decision to design 100BaseT so it uses many basic forms of cabling—those used by older versions of Ethernet and newer forms of cabling, as well. To accommodate the different types of cables, Fast Ethernet comes in three forms: 100BaseTX, 100BaseT4, and 100BaseFX. Both 100BaseTX and 100BaseT4 work with twisted-pair cabling standards, while 100BaseFX was created to work with fiber optic cabling.

MAXIMUM NETWORK DIAMETER FOR 10BASE5

Figure 1. In traditional 10Mbps Ethernet networks, the maximum distance between two end stations is 2,500 meters.

The 100BaseTX standard is compatible with two pairs of UTP or STP. One pair is designated for reception and the other for transmission. The two basic cabling standards that meet this requirement are EIA/TIA-568 Category 5 UTP and IBM's Type 1 STP. The attractiveness of 100BaseTX lies in its ability to provide full-duplex performance with network servers and the fact that it uses only two of the four pairs of wiring, leaving two pairs free for future enhancements to your network.

However, if you plan on using Category 5 cabling with 100BaseTX, be forewarned of the drawbacks related to Category 5. The cable is more expensive than other types of four-pair cabling, such as Category 3, and it requires the installation of punchdown blocks, connectors, and patch panels that are all Category 5-compliant.

The 100BaseT4 standard requires a less sophisticated cable than Category 5. The reason is that 100BaseT4 uses four pairs of wiring: one for transmission, one for reception, and two that can either transmit or receive data. Therefore, 100BaseT4 has the use of three pairs of wiring to either transmit or receive data. By dividing up the 100Mbps data signal among the three pairs of wiring, 100BaseT4 reduces the average frequency of signals on the cable, allowing lower-quality cable to handle the signal successfully. Categories 3 and 4 UTP cabling, as well as Category 5 UTP and Type 1 STP, can all work in 100BaseT4 implementations.

The advantage of 100BaseT4 is its flexible cable requirements. Category 3 and 4 cabling is more prevalent in current networks, and if they aren't already

LENGTH LIMITATIONS FOR 100 BASET

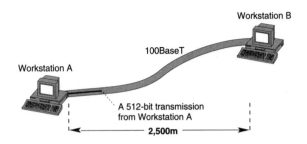

Figure 2. The maximum length limitation for 100BaseT is 250 meters, only 10 percent of the 2,500-meter maximum theoretical size of Ethernet.

being used in your network, they cost less than Category 5 cabling. The downside is that 100BaseT4 uses all four pairs of wiring, and it does not support full-duplex operation.

Fast Ethernet also offers a standard for operation over multimode fiber with a 62.5 micron core and 125 micron cladding. The 100BaseFX standard is designed mainly for backbone use, connecting Fast Ethernet repeaters scattered about the building. The traditional benefits of fiber optic cabling are still valid with 100BaseFX: protection from electromagnetic noise, increased security, and longer distances allowed between network devices.

THE SHORT RUN

Although Fast Ethernet is a continuation of the Ethernet standard, the migration from a 10BaseT network to a 100BaseT network isn't a straight, one-to-one conversion of hardware—some changes to the network topology may be required.

Theoretically, Fast Ethernet limits the end- to-end network diameter or the network segment diameter to 250 meters; only 10 percent of the 2,500-meter maximum theoretical size of Ethernet. Fast Ethernet's restriction is based on the speed of 100Mbps transmission and the nature of the CSMA/CD protocol.

Figures 1, 2, and 3 illustrate why a 100BaseT network can't be longer than 250 meters. In the figures, Workstations A and B represent the farthest ends of the network or network segment.

For Ethernet to work, a workstation transmitting data must listen long

MAXIMUM NETWORK DIAMETER FOR 100BASET

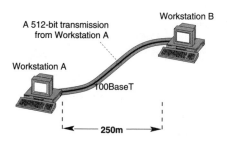

Figure 3. Because of the increased throughput capabilities of 100BaseT, workstations A and B can be no farther than 250 meters apart.

enough to make sure the data has reached its destination safely. In a 10Mbps Ethernet network, such as 10Base5, the length of time a workstation listens for a collision is equivalent to how far a 512-bit frame (the frame size is specified in the Ethernet standard) travels before the workstation is finished processing it. In a 10Mbps Ethernet network, that distance is 2,500 meters (see Figure 1).

However, a 512-bit frame (the 802.3u standard specifies the same frame size, 512 bit, as the 802.3 standard) being transmitted by a workstation in the faster 100Mbps Ethernet network travels only about 250 meters before the workstation is finished processing it (see Figure 2). If the receiving workstation was located farther than 250 meters from the transmitting workstation, the frame may collide with another frame down the line, and the transmitting workstation, having finished processing the transmission already, would not be listening for the collision. For this reason, the maximum network diameter for a 100BaseT network is 250 meters (see Figure 3).

To take advantage of the 250 meters, though, you will need to install two repeaters to connect all of the nodes. And, a node cannot be located farther than 100 meters away from a repeater—Fast Ethernet adopted the 10BaseT rule that determines 100 meters to be the farthest allowable distance a workstation can be from a hub. Due to latency introduced by connection devices such as repeaters, the actual operational distances between nodes will probably prove to be less than those stated. So, it would be prudent to measure distances on the short side.

To incorporate longer runs in your network, you'll have to invest in fiber cabling. For example, you can use 100BaseFX in half- duplex mode to connect a switch to either another switch or an end station located up to 450 meters away. A full-duplex 100BaseFX installation will allow two network devices up to two kilometers apart to communicate.

A SIMPLE SETUP

Aside from the cabling, you'll need to deal with network adapters in workstations and servers, 100BaseT hubs, and possibly some 100BaseT switches.

The adapters you'll need for a Fast Ethernet network are called 10/100Mbps Ethernet adapters. These adapters take advantage of an autosensing feature—provided for in the 100BaseT standard—that allows the adapters to automatically sense 10Mbps and 100Mbps speed capabilities. You'll also need to install a 100BaseT hub to service the group of workstations and servers you've converted to 100BaseT.

When a PC or server equipped with a 10/100 adapter is turned on, it will emit a signal that broadcasts its 100Mbps capabilities. If the receiving station, most likely a hub, is similarly suited for 100BaseT operation, it will return a signal that automatically places both the hub and PC or server in 100BaseT mode. If the hub is only 10BaseT-capable, it won't return the signal and the PC or server will automatically go into 10BaseT mode.

For a small-scale 100BaseT setup, you can use a 10/100 bridge or switch to allow the 100BaseT part of your network to operate with the 10BaseT installed base.

DECEPTIVE SPEED

As a last piece of advice, Fast Ethernet's capabilities seem best suited for peak traffic problems. For example, if you have some users running CAD or imaging applications who need to have a higher peak throughput, Fast Ethernet can help you out. But, if your problem is caused by an overload of users, 100BaseT starts to drag at about the 50-percent utilization rate—in other words, at the same traditional threshold as 10BaseT. After all, it is an extension of 10BaseT.

Section III

Network Software

LAN Applications

In its most generic sense, the term *application* applies to a task. For example, a widget maker needs to take orders and transmit these orders to a warehouse where the widgets are shipped to customers. The widget factory and warehouse must exchange inventory information. This whole procedure might be called an order entry and inventory control application. In this sense, other applications include list management, accounting, design, marketing, and sales—the tasks of any enterprise.

More specifically, the term *application* refers to the computer software used to get a job done. Thus, database management packages such as dBase IV, Paradox, and Oracle are called application software, as are other types of software such as WordPerfect, Co/Session, and 1-2-3. In this sense, application software is distinguished from system software, which is the software that makes computers and LANs operate. Think of the application software running on top and taking advantage of the system software and hardware.

Finally, *application* refers to programs written to perform a specific task. For example, many users have written applications in the dBase language. These customized applications are written by and for end-users, not by software vendors. This can get tricky, because some value-added resellers and system integrators write such customized programs to sell. The difference is they are not selling generic applications software as Microsoft, Borland and Lotus do. They, like the end-users themselves, are creating customized programs using the software of developers such as Borland and Microsoft.

Network operating system software, such as NetWare, LAN Manager, and VINES, provide some applications. This presents some complications and indicates some changing directions for the PC LAN industry.

LANs exist for applications. That is, users install LANs to get a job done. Users can have computers, cable, interface cards, file servers, and protocols, but without applications software users can't do much but copy files from disk to disk. LAN application software is what people use. The network is just the substrate upon which they use it.

APPLICATION TYPES

There are three types of applications—*LAN-ignorant, LAN-aware,* and *LAN-intrinsic.*

LAN-ignorant applications are written for use on one computer by one person. These programs often run on a network. That is, they may be stored on a file server and LAN users may run them at their workstations. Most of the time there are severe limitations on what these applications can do. Moreover, if two people try to use the program at the same time, data can be lost or corrupted.

For example, if two people try to work on the same 1-2-3 spreadsheet, the person making the last change to the spreadsheet will write over all the changes made by the user who first saved his work. The program has no way of keeping the users from destroying each other's work. It lacks *concurrency control.* On the other hand, 1-2-3 can be used safely by several people at the same time, as long they are using different spreadsheets (and if they have a license to do so). But the standalone version of 1-2-3 does not provide functions to take advantage of the network.

LAN-aware applications are a step above LAN-ignorant applications. Usually, they are LAN-ignorant programs modified to run on a network. These programs recognize they will be used by several users at a time. They have concurrency control features such as file and record locking to coordinate usage by multiple users. For example, when a Paradox user begins to modify an address in a mailing list database, other users who are also looking at the same database table are prevented from changing that particular address record. This is called *record locking.* When the change is complete, the change is displayed on the screen of every other user looking at the table.

Another LAN-aware feature is *file locking.* This is a less sophisticated and less used form of concurrency control. Instead of keeping users out of a particular record, they are kept out of the entire file altogether while another user has it open. Word processing programs are the primary users of this type of concurrency control.

Communications software and electronic mail are also LAN-aware applications. They use the LAN to extend the abilities of a PC and share network resources.

At the same time, even these LAN-aware applications use the LAN as little more than a peripheral sharing device. The file server holds the data and the program but does not do any processing. Users access the program as if it were local, but all the work is being done by their PC, including all concurrency control. This is changing.

LAN-aware programs make up the vast majority of programs written for networks. They are a big improvement over LAN-ignorant applications and have gone a long way to spur the growth of networking. As they become more sophisticated, the distinction between LAN-aware and LAN-intrinsic is blurring.

LAN-INTRINSIC APPLICATIONS

LAN-intrinsic applications actually share the processing power of several computers. Usually, although not always, this is done by dividing the application program into pieces. One piece is the server, which does data processing; the other piece is the client, which talks to the user. A database server is a good example of this application type. Its principles can be generalized for other LAN-intrinsic applications.

A database server is composed of front and back ends. The front end is responsible for formulating requests and displaying formatted data to the user. At the front end, users make queries, write reports, create new databases—all the tasks they do with any other database management program. The back end is responsible for managing and searching for data, concurrency control, and security. When a user asks for all the employees in the company database that make more than $50,000, this request is transmitted to the database server or back end. The database server then looks for all the employees making over $50,000 and sends these records to the front end.

In the LAN-aware method, one program, not two, runs in the user's machine. When the request for middle-income employees is made, the server downloads the entire file over the network to the user program. The user's PC then searches through the file to find the employees with the requested salaries. This takes up much more network bandwidth because the whole file is transferred, instead of just a few records. Other traffic includes concurrency control commands to lock various files and records as needed.

With a database server, concurrency control traffic is eliminated because

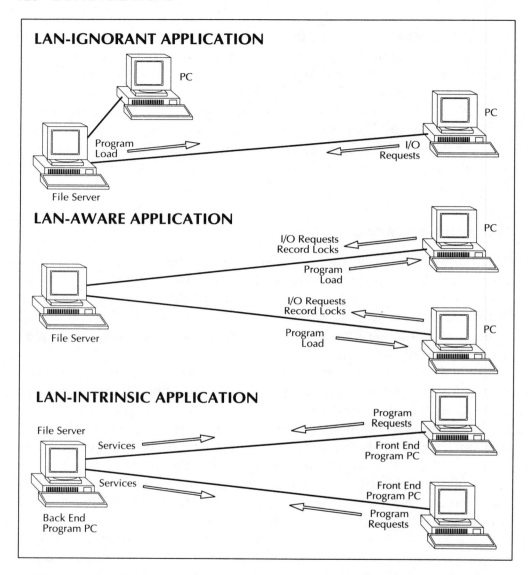

LAN-ignorant applications use the network in the simplest ways—trading I/O requests. LAN-aware applications take advantage of the LAN by establishing concurrency control and communications features such as record locking or electronic mail. LAN-intrinsic applications, the grail of the network computing industry, share processing power across the network, distributing data and computing power to open up a whole new range of LAN uses.

the server takes care of it. Even more important, only the requested records are sent over the network. The result is a more efficient, safer, and better performing program and network. The two programs are working together to create one application—a true LAN-intrinsic application.

By implication, LAN-intrinsic applications have the ability to distribute data over the entire network. They can also distribute processes. This makes for distributed databases, compile servers, compute servers, multitasking communications servers, and many other applications in which programs cooperate across the LAN to get a job done.

Only a few LAN-intrinsic applications are available now. New LAN environments created by operating systems like OS/2 and network operating systems like LAN Manager will help their development by providing multitasking, more memory, faster processors, and programming interfaces that make writing LAN-intrinsic programs easier. It will take time.

UTILITIES AND APPLICATIONS

A category of applications we have not discussed is LAN utilities. Usually, utilities are programs written for LAN administration and management. One example is NetWare's SYSCON. Others include printer and disk management utilities.

Increasingly, utilities are included in network operating systems. For example, NetWare comes with numerous programs to administer and manage the network. But, even more striking than this development, is the way in which application software and system software are coming together.

Client-Server Computing

The term "client-server computing" has meant many things to many people. In the mainframe or minicomputer environment, it has been used to refer to the relationship between the host computer and its associated dumb terminals. In traditional local area networking terminology, it has also described the association between a personal computer acting as a "server" of data and applications files and the "client" PCs that request those files via a network operating system over LAN cabling.

In the newly emerging distributed network environments, however, *client-server computing* takes on a more specific definition: It refers to a relationship in which the server plays a more sophisticated role on the network, performing much of the processing formerly handled by its client PCs while still retaining its requester-server (i.e., data storage) responsibilities.

We'll focus on this definition of the client-server model here.

CLIENT-SERVER BASICS

As client-server computing systems have evolved, their creators have taken some parts from the centralized host world, and other parts from the decentralized PC environment. As such, client-server systems also combine benefits from both. From the host world, for instance, comes centralized data storage that can be centrally secured against unauthorized access. From the PC environment comes the standalone computing power needed to run powerful and easy-to-use applications and graphics packages unavailable with dumb terminals connected to a host.

In understanding client-server computing, it thus helps to understand how the traditional computing environments—that is, the host/terminal and file-server/PC—process data and application files: They do so in a totally one-sided fashion. In the former instance, all data manipulation takes place on the

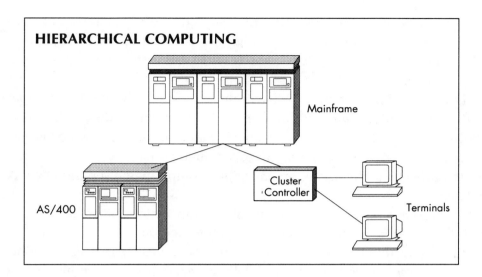

HIERARCHICAL COMPUTING

Mainframe

AS/400

Cluster Controller

Terminals

In the hierarchical computing environment, all data manipulation takes place on the host mainframe or minicomputer. The terminals merely display the results.

host; the terminals merely display the results of the mainframe's computation. Because the terminal is incapable of data manipulation, its functionality is thus limited; in particular, it offers almost no graphics capabilities. The figures in this chapter show hierarchical and client-server computing models.

In the standard file-server/PC relationship, the client PCs perform virtually all of the data processing. The server responds to data (and application) requests from the client, thus playing the role of an intelligent high-speed disk system by forwarding stored information to the appropriate client. This means that the server must first locate the requested files on its disk subsystem, then transfer them through its own memory and over the network cabling to the end-user PC.

When a user wants to access a database on the server, for example, the server first downloads the application software to memory in the user's PC. When the user queries the data-base for a particular data record, the server sends entire groups of data associated with it.

While this method does give users the data they need, it does so at the expense of efficiency: First, entire files rather than just needed data are sent across the LAN, unnecessarily using too much of the LAN bandwidth. And because the user's PC does the processing, each end user whose work requires heavy and frequent database access needs a high-performance computer with plenty of memory.

In the client-server computing environment, conversely, developers separate their applications into two components, a "front end" and a "back end," with the elements sharing the processing demands according to which is best suited for the task. This separation of responsibilities allows client-server systems to more efficiently use an organization's computing power and network bandwidth.

The *front end,* or client-based part of the application, provides the end-user interface—that is, the onscreen images the user follows while interacting with the application—as well as processing capabilities. As in the traditional LAN client-server model, the *back end* delivers server-based functions such as data lookup and retrieval.

In the client-server computing architecture, however, only the front end of the applications—not the entire application—is loaded into users' PCs when they start the program. Now, when a user's front-end application queries a database for a particular record, the back-end server-based software searches for the specific record and sends it—not entire masses of data—to the user.

This significantly reduces the volume of data moving across the LAN because entire databases are not continually being sent back and forth between server and client. This offers secondary benefits in that reduced traffic can also lower the risk of electrical or mechanical malfunctions compromising the integrity of data.

Another benefit of client-server computing: Because the server rather than the client handles much of the manipulation of data, it eliminates the need to give each employee who accesses the database a high-performance PC. Only the database server needs a large, fast hard disk, high-performance controller hardware, or multiple high-powered processor chips.

Although the most widely employed server in the client-server realm is the database server, a server in a distributed computing environment can be, among other things, an image or audio processor or an expert system.

In these situations, the database server, which usually resides on a dedi-

A CLIENT-SERVER SYSTEM

In the client-server computing environment, a single networked personal computer can access multiple services—stock market look-up quotes, a database, or an order-entry system—that previously required two or three terminals or PCs.

cated computer, acts as an "engine" to drive the system. The applications in turn can request/update data in the database, using the database server's capabilities and benefits—for instance, improved security and centralized access—in the process.

A 'SEQUEL' IN THE WORKS

Because PC software applications seldom "talk" the same language and thus do not readily exchange data, software developers have had to agree on a common language for handling this data interchange. This language, called a Structured Query Language (or SQL, and pronounced sequel, as in another "Rocky" or "Star Wars" sequel), acts as the translator between applications. SQL is a high-level language that allows distributed databases to exchange information. Virtually every popular relational databases running on IBM PCs, Macintoshes, mini, and mainframe computers, supports SQL.

Developed in the 1970s by IBM, SQL is an English-like query-type language that most database vendors have standardized on. SQL has become the standard for retrieving data from a relational database, and any database that supports SQL can theoretically exchange data with any other SQL-compatible database.

THE GOOD NEWS

The good news about SQL is that end users usually don't have to learn or even know about it. The application program should hide the SQL language commands (principally, these commands come in the form of verbs such as DELETE, SELECT, and UPDATE) from the user interface. A front-end e-mail application, for instance, could use SQL as a tool to locate a recipient's network address and determine the optimum way to "mail" a message. The database server operates in conjunction with a communications server to actually deliver the mail—all without the e-mail end user knowing about it.

The front-end component of a database server does not necessarily have to be a database application; this opens an amazing variety of possibilities. Any application that can make use of a database of information, including spreadsheets, point-of-sale software, and computer-aided drafting/engineering (CAD/CAE), can be incorporated into the database-server environment.

Take the example of a stock broker. It is not atypical for securities salespeople to have two or three computers and/or terminals in their office, each one connected to a different computer system. A networked PC might provide access to a server-based database of the broker's important customers, showing their holdings, priorities, etc. A terminal might provide up-to-the minute stock prices from an online timesharing host via a modem connection. And another PC might offer access to an order-entry system so the broker can process customer orders on the spot.

With a client-server system, the securities firm could deliver all those capabilities via a single client personal computer connected to a distributed database server. In this scenario, the database server acts as a transparent network manager, tracking down the requested services without questioning the end user for network address information.

When the broker's front-end application asks for stock quotes, the database server could automatically open a link through a communications gateway, retrieve information from the online host, and report back to the user's PC with only the specific data requested.

Similarly, the database server could also use the order-entry application's front-end instructions to provide an onscreen sales form. Or the database could display the customer's preferences—not to buy stock of companies with facilities in South Africa, for instance, to sell IBM stock when it reaches $110 a share, or to buy Microsoft when it drops below $90.

And the database server would provide all this information without the broker specifying where any of it is located.

Defining Downsizing

Large corporations, faced with increasingly competitive markets that require immediate response to customer needs, have sometimes turned to *downsizing* to become more efficient. But this type of downsizing, unlike the more traditional one, doesn't set off alarms in economists' minds.

Instead, the updated definition of downsizing describes the process of migrating mission-critical computer applications, such as customer databases and manufacturing-control software, "down" from a mainframe or minicomputer "to" personal computers that are connected via LANs. This kind of downsizing brings about productivity gains without negatively affecting the size of an organization's workforce, as the earlier form does.

Downsizing in both its forms, whether it's employee layoffs, especially within middle management, or moving critical computing capabilities away from a centralized host, can lead to increased profits. However, the layoffs version does so at the expense of human resources, while the computer version takes advantage of improved networking technology to add efficiency.

Organizations benefit from both kinds of downsizing. Both can help an organization become more responsive to its customers. For instance, when a company downsizes by eliminating one or two levels of middle management, it streamlines its operations. This new structure puts decision-makers, not clerks without authority, in direct contact with customers, for example. Because decision-makers are then front-line workers, they can take immediate action to resolve customers' problems or to expedite orders.

INCREASING PRODUCTIVITY

Downsizing a company's computer resources can produce similar productivity gains. In traditional mainframe-based environments, the MIS department controls access to the company's computing resources, specifically the mainframe or minicomputer and the data stored on it.

In these situations, only corporate MIS employees have direct access to the mainframe and its storehouse of valuable information. A number of factors may necessitate such a setup. First, mainframe applications are difficult to learn and to run, and few people have the time or inclination to become proficient at manipulating the data on the mainframe. Security issues, as well, prohibit widespread access to the system.

In such situations, non-MIS business workers must request reports from MIS, which acts as an intermediary between employees and the data they need to do their jobs. If the MIS department is understaffed, as many are, it can take several days or longer to deliver a report to the worker who asked for it.

Because delays can mean the difference in keeping customers satisfied, keeping data only on mainframes isn't a particularly efficient way of dealing with time-critical problems, even though many large organizations rely on mainframes for their computing resources.

Moving the company's data from a mainframe to LAN-based applications eliminates the MIS middleman. Downsizing computer resources makes front-line employees more productive by giving them direct access to the crucial data and applications they need. Direct access to pertinent information enables them to make decisions more rapidly.

Let's look at some forces making network-based downsizing possible.

DESKTOP-BASED POWER

The introduction and subsequent widespread acceptance of the personal computer and PC-based LANs in the early 1980s are key factors that started many large companies on the road to downsizing. The PC put computing power on workers' desks, allowing them to perform complex data calculations previously possible for only a few MIS personnel.

The growth of networking in the late 1980s permitted PC users to share the results of the desktop computing power. For instance, several workers could access the same database at one time or move data between their workstations.

What the growth of networks did not significantly impact was the use of mainframes and minicomputers for key, compute-intensive applications, especially in Fortune 1000 companies. These corporations continued to run accounting, payroll, and inventory control-type applications on hosts.

There were several reasons for this decision, including corporate politics. For instance, many organizations simply had no corporate networking policies that assured upper management that LANs were viable resources the company could rely on. Without these policies and procedures, management perceived LANs as e-mail networks, suitable for exchanging messages but little else.

More important was the fact that while mainframes and minis are secure from unauthorized access, PCs and PC networks are not so secure. And security is vital to running mission-critical applications on a LAN.

Mainframes are housed in climate- and access-controlled environments that maximize security. Mainframe-based applications also enforce a variety of security measures that require large-scale computing power to implement.

Until recently, however, LAN-based servers generally were found out in the open, where everyone in the department could access them. Moreover, many were merely high-powered PCs, complete with keyboards and monitors, adapted to act as servers. Such easy access poses an additional security threat, and the applications running on them seldom implemented any form of special security or data-protection measures.

In these kinds of situations, it's difficult to guarantee that the applications and the data on them are secure. For instance, an unauthorized person could accidentally turn the server off or reboot it, disrupting network services while users manipulated or entered critical data. Or a disgruntled employee could cause mischief by deleting important files and applications.

Also, few adapted PC servers offer redundant capabilities that provide on-the-fly backup computing resources in the event of a system breakdown. These capabilities, such as redundant power supplies and disks, are crucial to providing the reliability that's required in transaction-processing and accounting environments.

Now, however, vendors of LAN products are delivering more reliable and powerful PC-based hardware and software products. For instance, many file server vendors equip their products with locking front panels that restrict access to the machine's controls and internal components. Some offer remote-control software management capabilities similar to those found in mainframe environments.

Network operating system vendors have also responded to the need for increased reliability, building fault-tolerant disk and server mirroring capabilities into their products. And distributed-computing applications, in which a database server controls access to a variety of information resources spread throughout an organization, are now emerging in the market, adding another key tool for the movement toward downsizing.

EFFICIENCY FROM DOWNSIZING

Downsizing computer applications to LAN-based systems can make an organization more efficient, but improving user access to data is only one benefit.

In addition, downsizing gives a company more computing power per dollar and at a significantly lower cost than with mainframes. PCs and workstations, especially those based on Reduced Instruction Set Computing (RISC) technology, now provide computing power almost equal to that of many mainframes and at much lower cost per MIPS.

Downsizing can also improve network performance by allowing network managers to segment their LANs into functional workgroups, with data and applications distributed among the workgroups. This segmentation reduces overall network traffic, which can be a major problem when a single host computer interacts repeatedly with a large number of other computers on a network.

Not surprisingly, organizations find that they must make tradeoffs for these benefits. They must begin thinking of their PCs and networks as being part of a system rather than individual units, as many do now.

THE DOWNSIZING TRADEOFFS

In particular, downsizing requires the implementation of mainframe-like security measures on LAN-based resources. Such steps include incorporating fault-tolerant systems, including CPUs and memory subsystems, into network hardware and software. Fault-tolerant measures such as server and disk-mirroring systems provide access to data when a primary device fails. Security issues include using uninterruptable power supplies that guarantee electricity during disruptive power outages.

Key hardware and software, such as servers and the applications running on them, also require protection from unauthorized physical access. Many organizations now enclose servers and other important network equipment in computer rooms locked to keep casual contact to a minimum.

Downsizing also requires maintenance services similar to those needed for mainframes. Fast, competent technical response when a system fails is vital to ensuring that network users can access a customer database or information when they need it to make important decisions.

A CAUTIOUS FIRST STEP

Because downsizing is a complex process, many organizations move into downsizing step by step. For example, they downsize only certain applications or even just parts of applications. This cautious approach can help minimize potential problems.

For example, it does not always make sense to use a PC-based computer as a corporate-wide database repository. In particular, the disk storage systems shipped with mainframes and minicomputers are generally faster and can hold considerably more data than those for PCs.

But it does make sense to use a distributed-processing application to give PC users access to that mainframe-resident data. In this arrangement, the end-user application, or *front end,* runs on the user's PC. The distributed-processing, or application, engine running on a PC-based server handles the necessary user-host transaction processing. Or, a PC database server may be used for a departmental application.

The database engine and end-user front end have thus been downsized to PCs. Between them, the front- and back-end applications give users direct access to important data without jeopardizing the integrity or security of the organization's mainframe database.

Whether a particular application, such as statistical analysis, three-dimensional graphics modeling, order entry, or customer support, is a candidate for downsizing depends on a variety of factors, including the organization's structure as well as strictly technical problems.

But more and more companies, intent on becoming more efficient without losing key workers, are turning to downsizing—the "good" kind, that is.

Network Operating Systems

A network operating system (NOS) causes a collection of independent computers to act as one system. A network operating system is analogous to a desktop operating system like DOS or OS/2, except it operates over more than one computer. Like DOS, a network operating system works behind the scenes to provide services for users and application programs. But instead of controlling the pieces of a single computer, a network operating system controls the operation of the network system, including who uses it, when they can use it, what they have access to, and which network resources are available.

At a basic level, the NOS allows LAN users to share files and peripherals such as disks and printers. Most NOSs do much more. They provide data integrity and security by keeping people out of certain resources and files. They have administrative tools to add, change, and remove users, computers, and peripherals from the network. They have troubleshooting tools to tell LAN managers what is happening on the network. They have internetworking support to tie multiple networks together.

REDIRECTION

At the heart of the NOS is redirection. *Redirection* is taking something headed in one direction and making it go in a different direction. With redirection, an operating program does not know or care where its output is going.

You are probably familiar with DOS redirection. For example, the DOS command DIR > FILENAME will redirect a directory listing to a file instead of to the screen. The ">" tells DOS to give the results of the command to the entity on the right.

Network operating systems depend heavily on redirection, only in this case data is being redirected from one computer to another over the network cable, not over the PC's bus to local files or printers. Nevertheless, the operation is similar. If you type "COPY C: FILEA F:", FILEA will be copied from your local drive C: to the network drive F:. The NOS makes it appear to the COPY command that drive F: is local, when it really resides on another computer that is attached to the same network. The COPY command doesn't know or care that drive F: is across the network. It sends the file to DOS and the NOS reroutes the file across the LAN to drive F:.

Redirection can be done with printers and other peripherals. Thus, LPT1: or COM1: can be a network printer instead of a local printer and the NOS redirects file to these devices. With a NOS, users don't need to know about redirection; they just type the drive designator or print from their word processors as always.

SERVER SOFTWARE

The computer with drive F: must expect data, if the output from the user's PC can be redirected successfully. To do this, it must make its drive available to network users. This is part of the NOS's function at the server.

A NOS is made of a redirector and a server. Not all machines need to run the server software, because not all computers need to share their resources. But all LAN workstations must run redirector software because every client has to be able to put data onto the network.

With some NOSs, the computer running the server software cannot be used as a workstation. This is called a *dedicated server*. Novell's NetWare uses this kind of setup almost exclusively (although the low-end NetWare Lite can use nondedicated servers). With some other NOSs, all workstations on the network can also be servers. This a *nondedicated server* setup. This approach is used by Sitka and Artisoft, among others.

The two server approaches have advantages and disadvantages. Nondedicated servers allow for more flexibility, since users can make resources available on their computers as necessary. However, a nondedicated server approach requires that the users are willing to take some administrative responsibility for their computers and it necessitates that they be somewhat LAN-literate. Backing up the shared data, setting up security, and setting up access rights become more complicated and often become the responsibility of the user, not the administrator. Another drawback is that non-dedicated servers often suffer some performance degradation when being used simultaneously as a workstation and as a server.

Dedicated servers have the opposite advantages and disadvantages. They are easier to administer since all data is in one place. They are faster because they don't have a local user to serve. On the other hand, it is harder to make resources available on an ad hoc basis, since setting up a server is more difficult and time-consuming. If a dedicated server fails, all users are forced to stop working because all resources are centralized. Your choice of dedicated or non-dedicated operation will depend on the work your network is doing.

FILE SERVICE

A file server's primary task is to make files available to users, although it also makes other resources available, including printers and plotters. File service allows users to share the files on a server. The server PC can make its whole disk, certain directories, or certain files available. The file server's hard disk becomes an extension of each user's PC.

The NOS can let the LAN administrator determine which users are allowed to use which files, for example, keeping the mail clerk out of the payroll file. Suppose a user wants to use a file residing on the file server's hard disk. Drive F: is set to correspond with the file server's hard disk. The actual process of setting up virtual drives has several names, including *mapping, mounting,* and *publishing.*

Now, suppose a user wants to run WordPerfect. At the F: prompt, the user types "WP" to load WordPerfect. WordPerfect is loaded from the server over the network, and into the user's PC's memory. Meanwhile, other people can use WordPerfect from the file server (assuming there is a license for multiple users). WordPerfect makes sure no other user can get the document file being used by "locking" the file. With many applications, file locking allows other users to read the document but not edit it.

File service is an extension of the local PC. Applications work just as they would on a local PC. Some programs, however, have been designed to take advantage of the network, rather than just run on one. For example, some databases allow two users to edit the same table but not the same record and each user can see the other's changes.

The NOS provides much more than just file service; it provides security, administration, printer sharing, backup, and fault tolerance.

SERVER OPERATION

The server software makes a single-user computer into a multi-user machine. Instead of just one user, a server has many users. But we must qualify what we mean by "many users." A NOS allows many users to share the server's peripherals, printers, disks, and plotters, but it does not allow multiple users to share its processor. For now let's see how the file server allows users to share its peripherals.

In many cases, the file server is running the PC's native operating system (such as DOS or the Macintosh OS) as well as the NOS. When users' requests come in, the NOS receives and interprets them, then hands them to the operating system for execution. So if a request comes in to open a file, DOS opens the file and gives it to the NOS, which gives it to the user. If many users make requests at the same time, the NOS queues them and hands them to DOS one at a time.

High-performance NOSs, including Novell NetWare, Banyan VINES, and Microsoft LAN Manager, do not run DOS in the file server. DOS is replaced with a multitasking operating system, thereby gaining a performance advantage; however, they lose some compatibility and require dedicated file servers. In NetWare's case, it is a proprietary OS. VINES runs Unix; LAN Manager currently runs OS/2 but eventually will use Windows NT.

THE OS/2 NOS

File service is a tremendous improvement over single-user operation, it pales in significance to the enhancements that come with the new NOSs based on multitasking operating systems such as IBM/Microsoft OS/2.

The biggest advantage of a multitasking operating system is a server can offer a task. That is, the server can offer its processor to other users while it is serving requests for files and printers. A fast server can be used to do onerous chores like program compiling, calculations, and database sorting. It also means new types of programs can take advantage of the server processor.

Instead of just getting files from the server, the server can run programs that work with the programs users are running. The best example is a database server. A database server does things like sorting, searching, and indexing so the user's program and PC don't have to. This cuts down on network traffic since fewer items are travelling between the user and server. It also improves security, since all data is stored centrally.

Printing

One of the most basic reasons to install a network is to share peripherals, including hard disks and printers. Sharing printers means only a few PCs need have printers attached, instead of each user having his own printer. Users send their documents, spreadsheets, and reports to the print server. Because the print server handles all the printing requirements for the group, the number of expensive printers can be reduced, and printing may be faster.

Once at the print server, the jobs are entered into a queue, where they wait for the printer to become available. Queues are just what they sound like—waiting lines for access to the printer. Jobs are normally serviced in a first-in-first-out order, although most print servers allow users to prioritize print jobs so they can be moved up or skipped to the top of the queue.

PRINTING IN ACTION

For a print server to handle multiple jobs at the same time, it must have a print spool. (Spool is reportedly an acronym for Simultaneous Peripheral Operation On Line.) A spool is hardware and software that controls a buffer. The buffer is memory that holds data. One or more print jobs may wait in the buffer while the printer is working on another job. Often, print jobs are spooled to the print server's hard disk.

When printing from a standalone application, the path from the PC to the printer is fairly direct. Using networked printers requires a more circuitous path. More opportunity for glitches exists, and they frequently occur.

Like retrieving files from network drives, using networked printers requires redirection. Software in the user's computer captures the print job and sends it over the network. The application, a word processor for example, thinks it is printing to the local printer port, but the network client software redirects the output over the network.

146

Printer redirection is a common occurrence, locally as well as over a network. For example, using a serial printer requires that output bound for a parallel port (LPT1, for instance) be redirected out the serial port (COM1, for instance). DOS allows you to do this with the MODE command.

Similar redirection takes place over the network, but the network operating system, not the PC operating system, is redirecting the output. The user's application tells the network operating system to redirect all output headed for the local LPT1 port over the network to, say, the print server's LPT3 port. The network operating system gets the job to the print server.

At the print server, the file is spooled to disk. Spooling may be done because the printer is busy. Spooling is necessary if the printer is not fast enough to take the whole file at once.

The print server's software handles the incoming job. If the printer is free, the document can be printed immediately. If the printer is busy, the document is spooled in a print file on the print server's hard disk. The file joins the queue, waiting its turn to be sent to the printer.

The print server's buffer feeds print jobs to the printer at the correct pace. Data waiting to be printed is stored in the buffer before it is sent. The larger the buffer, the faster the printing, since fewer disk accesses are necessary to feed the file to the printer.

In principal, redirection, spooling, and buffering and LAN printing should be easy; however, problems occur frequently. Although printer sharing was an original impetus for installing a network, LANs still don't always share printers gracefully and easily.

PRINTING PROBLEMS

Problems crop up when trying to print on a network, including applications talking directly to the printer port, conflicting print spools, multiple print buffers, and multiple users. Some problems are inherent in having multiple people use the same printer.

A common problem is the conflict between the application and network. Some applications try to talk directly to the printer port and the network operating system does not have the opportunity to redirect the output. This problem occurs more often when printing to serial ports rather than parallel ports,

STANDALONE PRINTING

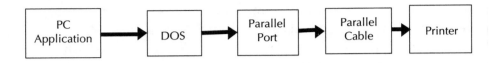

LAN PRINTING

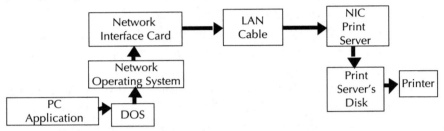

When printing from a standalone application, the path from the PC to the printer is fairly direct. Using networked printers requires a more circuitous path. More opportunity for glitches exists, and they frequently occur.

because it is easier to handle a serial port than a parallel port. Therefore, more applications leave parallel operations to DOS. One solution is to configure the application to use the parallel port, where possible.

Another problem occurs when an application has its own print spool. The application will check the hardware directly to see when to send data, thereby causing problems for the network spool. The solution is to disable the application's spool.

Multiple print buffers cause problems. Print servers are not the only devices with print buffers. The application, PC, network, and printer may also have buffers. Usually, all these buffers will work together, but sometimes disruptions happen while one buffer waits for another. The solution is to use only one of these buffers. Performance will not be hurt significantly and memory resources may be conserved.

A fourth LAN printing problem arises when multiple users share one printer. Each user sets the printer differently, different fonts, character widths, line spacing, etc. Often, the printer retains these settings. And while some applications, network operating systems, and print utilities allow users to send control codes to the printer, others don't. Where supported, these codes can reset a printer after every print job. This way, all users know the printer is starting with particular settings, no matter who has used it previously.

In some cases, the application's printer control codes may interfere with network operations or network printer control codes. For example, a printer control code from the application may be misinterpreted by the network operating system as a release printer code, leaving the user disconnected from the printer. Another symptom of such conflicts is garbled printing. Most likely, the application will have to be reconfigured not to use the printer control code commands, leaving the network operating system or print utility in charge.

The last set of LAN printing problems is inherent in the process. Multiple users have different requirements for paper, but most printers can only hold one type of paper at a time. The classic problem is a user prints his file, only to discover someone took out the letterhead he just put in the tray. Or that someone left green paper in the tray. One solution is to have multiple printers, each configured with a different type of paper. Some companies now manufacture printers with several paper trays and allow users to specify the paper tray. Electronic mail or some type of notification may be effective as well.

PRINT UTILITIES

Ironically, while an early reason to buy a network was to share peripherals, today network operating systems still do not share printers adeptly. All network operating systems support some kind of LAN printing, but functionality varies widely. Some network operating systems require the user to leave the application before setting up the print process. The user must explicitly tell the network operating system to look for a print job and then tell it when the job is over. Others require that all shared printers are attached to a file server. This, too, is inconvenient, especially when file servers should be locked in a closet for security purposes. Finally, many network operating systems will not allow users to send printer control codes to network printers.

Print utilities exist to solve these problems. Such utilities allow users to control the printer and print server from their PCs, without exiting their application. Users may manipulate the print queue, check which files are spooled, choose print codes, send jobs, reconfigure the printer, and perform other tasks.

Print utilities are usually terminate-and-stay resident programs so they can operate from within any application.

One feature of many printing utilities is the ability to automate printer configuration. For example, a printing utility will send printer control codes to reset the printer to default configuration after every print job. This way, every user knows how the printer is set before using it.

Another helpful feature is print notification. Users are notified when their print jobs have finished printing, a terrific convenience if the printer is out of earshot. Another useful feature is the ability to standardize line and form feeds so users don't have to do this manually. This reduces the chance users will go to the printer and change it, or leave it off line.

Many print utilities allow any PC on the network to act as a print server. When any PC can act as a print server, printers may be placed conveniently throughout the office. Such a print server can be dedicated to its purpose or it may double as a workstation. While a nondedicated print server allows you to place printers easily and inexpensively around the network, it has some drawbacks. If many people need that printer, the owner of the print server/PC will be constantly interrupted when users pick up their print jobs and want to chat. Besides user distractions, the user may reboot or turn off the PC, thereby killing all print jobs in the queue. Some print servers are dedicated boxes, which sit on the network. These devices have a CPU and memory for spooling and buffering; however, without an on/off switch, a user cannot accidentally turn them off.

SMALL ADVICE

While printing on a network should be easy, it's not. Most problems arise because printing in general is not as easy as it should be. Pinouts, cables, and ports on the printers themselves create an endless stream of problems. Add the network, and printers become even more of a hassle. Fortunately, many network operating system vendors now recognize the need for easier LAN printing, and have incorporated features into the NOS that once could only be obtained through a third-party utility.

OS/2 LANs

OS/2, the operating system from IBM, is special for several reasons. The operating system has several features that improve networking significantly. These features are not necessarily unique—other operating systems such as Unix and VMS also have them—but OS/2 was the first PC operating system to include them. The most relevant features of OS/2 are multitasking and interprocess communications.

With these two features, OS/2 provides a much better platform upon which to build powerful multiuser, distributed applications—the kind that run on networks—than DOS. These LAN-intrinsic applications take advantage of the network to provide services and performance simply unavailable under DOS. For example, a distributed database, which allows a user to pull data from two different machines and combine it into one report, is a LAN-intrinsic application. It must run on a network. While it is conceivable to build such an application using DOS-based machines, the amount of work necessary is significantly greater and the performance is significantly lower.

OS/2 provides a better platform upon which to build these applications because of its Application Programming Interfaces (APIs), particularly for multitasking and interprocess communications. These APIs provide services to applications that other PC operating systems can't match. Crucially, they provide the basic mechanisms by which geographically separate programs can exchange commands and information. That is, OS/2 APIs have networking in mind. This becomes even more the case when OS/2 is combined with an OS/2-based network operating system such as Microsoft's LAN Manager or IBM's LAN Server.

VIRTUAL OS/2

Before delving into the intricacies of OS/2's multitasking and interprocess

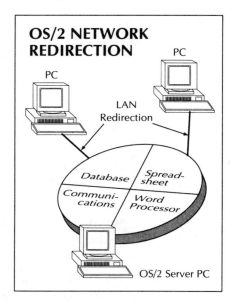

With a network operating system, output from an OS/2 application on one PC can be redirected over a network to another PC. Combining redirection with OS/2's multi-tasking, multiple users can share the same processor. With this combination, powerful new applications can be built.

communication, we need to lay the foundations upon which they are built. The two most important pillars are OS/2's memory model and virtual device support.

OS/2 is a protected-mode operating system, which means it requires a microprocessor that uses *protected mode,* such as an 286, 386 or 486 chip, or one of IBM's new RISC-processor based PCs. Protected mode is best understood by comparing it to real mode. The 8086 and 8088 run in real mode. Under *real mode,* programs have direct access to a PC's hardware devices, including memory, disk drives, serial ports, keyboard, and screen. That means programs can bypass the operating system, in this case DOS, and do what they like with the hardware. For example, a word processing program may decide to send something to a printer port. It can take over that port and DOS can't stop it, even if the program is going to interfere with another program that is already using the port.

Multitasking is impossible under real mode because there is no way to keep programs from interfering with each other as they use the PC's various components. The most acute form of this occurs when programs overwrite each other in memory. For example, a database program may use extra memory for sorting a database. In real mode, there is nothing to prevent another program, say, a spreadsheet, using this memory for a recalculation. When both programs try to put data in the same place, whichever program gets there first loses, since the second program writes over the data of the first. If the second program writes over some of the executing code of the first program, then not only is data corrupted but the computer may hang since it can't continue with the first program.

Under protected mode, programs generally do not have direct access to the PC's hardware devices. The devices are protected from application programs, which is where the name "protected" comes from. But because they don't have direct access to devices, programs need some method to use them. That's where OS/2 comes in. OS/2 sits between the programs and the hardware, regulating access to the latter. OS/2's intermediary position between programs and hardware forms the basis of multitasking, which is the ability to run several programs at the same time.

How does OS/2 give programs access to hardware while keeping them from colliding with each other? The answer is twofold: *virtual memory* and *virtual devices.* Actually virtual memory is a special case of a virtual device, but memory is so crucial to the workings of a computer it is a device that deserves special attention.

Virtual memory works as follows: Virtual memory introduces an additional step in a program's access to memory. Instead of simply asking for a physical memory address, as it does under DOS, programs ask for a virtual memory address. OS/2 then converts that virtual address into a physical address. This process is called mapping. In this way, OS/2 keeps track of where everything is, preventing one program from taking the memory of another by preventing it from directly accessing memory in the first place.

In addition, because OS/2 is handling their placement, program data and code need not always reside in memory. OS/2 may map a virtual address to a hard disk. It may decide it is better to put a piece of program code or data onto the hard disk rather than in memory. The program using the code or data still asks for the same virtual address. OS/2 just fills the request from another place. This process is called *segment swapping.*

OS/2 uses segment swapping when not enough RAM is available. OS/2 divides memory into 64KB chunks called segments. If there isn't room for a program to load completely, segments of program already in memory may be swapped to disk to make room for the new program. When the swapped-out data is needed, OS/2 swaps it back in and swaps another program out. The result is the amount of memory available is no longer equivalent to the amount of physical memory. Original versions of OS/2 use up to 48MB of memory, either on disk or in RAM, which is about 50 times the limit of DOS.

OS/2 handles devices similarly. Instead of directly accessing physical devices like parallel ports and video screens, programs are presented with virtual ports and screens. Applications write to or read from these virtual devices and OS/2 takes or sends the data. Each device has the appearance of its own keyboard, screen, and printer, but OS/2 is really just presenting each program with a virtual device, which it then maps to the real device as necessary.

OS/2's virtual memory and device management makes it possible to run many programs at the same time. Key roadblocks of DOS are eliminated. Programs can use more memory and they can no longer interfere with each other. But not only are virtual memory and device management the basis for multitasking, they are the basis for multiuser operation.

OS/2 MULTITASKING

No PC can actually do two things simultaneously, because a single processor can only perform one operation at a time. Processors can, however, do things so quickly the user thinks the processor is doing many things at once. And since they are doing things so quickly, processors often sit around and do nothing. Multitasking takes advantage of this idle time.

Suppose you are typing a letter using a word processing program like WordPerfect. The computer captures the letters you type and puts them on the screen. The time it takes to do this is a fraction of the time it takes for you to type the letter. Therefore, the computer is spending most of its time waiting for your next keystroke. But suppose it could do something else while waiting?

This is exactly what a PC running OS/2 does. The computer's idle time can be used by other tasks. While you are typing, the computer may download a file from another computer, recalculate a spreadsheet, sort a database, or draw a graph. To accomplish all these things at once, OS/2 divides the computer's time up into pieces called time slices. These last no longer than a fraction of a second. For one time slice, the computer works on the letter you are typing. During the next time slice, it stops working on your word processing, and starts downloading a file that you requested. Then this task is suspended while the spreadsheet recalculation takes place. Thus it goes, around and around from one task to the next. Of course, the time slices are so small that you don't notice the machine is working on other things while you are typing.

The results are manifold. The ability to allocate a computer's time increases its efficiency, which in turn increases the user's productivity because time is not wasted moving among applications. Multitasking can also make multiuser operation possible. Because the operating system is automatically multitasking, less work is needed to make it do many things at once for many people. It is better able to handle many simultaneous requests from many users.

MULTIUSER OS/2

Multiuser operation does not, strictly speaking, require multitasking, however. A computer could work for many people one at a time. When one is finished working the next could start, and so on. Obviously, this process is not what users expect of a computer system.

True multiuser operation requires the ability to accept input from numerous sources and redirect various output to multiple devices. Neither DOS nor OS/2 can do this alone. (DOS is single-user and single-tasking; OS/2 is multitasking but single-user; Unix is both multitasking and multiuser.) However, with the help of a network operating system, any of the three can provide services for multiple users. The difference is in the types of service they provide.

On a DOS-based PC network, the network operating system handles the multiple users for DOS. As the requests come in from the users, the network operating system feeds them to DOS one at a time. DOS then fulfills the requests. Then the network operating system ensures that the answers are returned to the users. There are limitations, however, to the type of requests DOS can fulfill. DOS can only do the simple input/output tasks for multiple people, such as reads and writes to a hard disk. It can't handle multiple programs in memory.

OS/2, on the other hand, allows users also to share processors, which is the basis for LAN-intrinsic applications. This is accomplished through multitasking, redirection, and interprocess communication.

OS/2 is multitasking. A way to assign different tasks to different users is needed to make it multiuser. This way is virtual devices and network redirection. Network redirection, as provided by a network operating system, tricks OS/2 into thinking it is mapping a virtual device to a local physical device, when in reality it is mapping that device to a remote physical device. For example, during one of its time slices, OS/2 can draw a graph for a remote user. The network operating system redirects the output from the OS/2 virtual screen over the LAN to the remote user's physical screen. In another time slice, OS/2 can accept keystrokes from another user, mapping them to a virtual keyboard. In this way, virtual devices and multitasking help OS/2 provide the basis for multi-user operation. But the network operating system is necessary to complete the multi-user picture.

The result is OS/2 allows multi-user operation. It allows multiple users to share a processor whereas DOS only allows multiple users to share peripheral devices. This is extremely important for networking. It is OS/2's multitasking abilities and its support for virtual devices that make it such a good foundation for LAN-intrinsic applications.

Multiuser OS/2 LANs

OS/2 is not a multiuser operating system, but its multitasking ability provides the basis of support for multiuser client-server and distributed applications—the real LAN-intrinsic applications—especially once a tightly integrated network operating system is added. To make this transition, a mechanism by which the processes communicate is needed. This mechanism is an *interprocess communication* (IPC).

IPC OVERVIEW

There are many forms of interprocess communication. Microsoft Windows and Apple Macintosh users are familiar with one of the simpler types. Cutting and pasting data from one program into another using the clipboard is interprocess communication. OS/2 supports this type of data exchange, and much more, since it has more sophisticated interprocess communication capabilities.

OS/2 has a set of APIs that allow programmers to write applications that communicate while running concurrently on an OS/2 PC. More importantly, OS/2 APIs allow programmers to divide one program into multiple parts called processes or *threads*. These threads can communicate with each other. The advantage is increased speed and specialization. Different processes of a program may be tailored to fit particular tasks. Then, by running the processes simultaneously, instead of sequentially, each will complete its task more quickly.

A bigger advantage, OS/2's APIs allow one process to be shared by many others. This forms the basis of a client-server application. Imagine starting a program that sorts and stores raw data, like names, company names, addresses, and telephone numbers. We'll call this the database server application. Then start two more programs: a report writer and an address book. With OS/2

157

APIs, it is possible for the report writer and address book to get all their data from the database server at the same time. They don't have to handle sorting and storing the data; they just ask for and receive the data.

The advantages are tremendous. Because they don't have to handle data, the report writer and address book are much easier to program. Second, because each program has less to do, it can be more specialized. Third, because both use the database server, they can share information. For example, information added into the address book may be used in the report. Fourth, the programs can run concurrently, allowing a report to be run while the address book finds and displays addresses. Finally, data is not the only shared element. The address book might signal the database server to perform some task (other than a data transfer). This revolutionized what can be done on a PC.

Now imagine putting the address book on one machine, the report writer on another, and the database server on a third, and having them all work as if they resided in the same machine. Such a LAN-intrinsic application changes the face of computing.

OS/2'S IPC

An understanding of the tools of interprocess communication is essential. There are five mechanisms: shared memory, flags, semaphores, queues, and pipes.

Shared memory is a portion of memory that multiple processes can access. Process A puts data into the shared memory space. Then Process B gets it out. OS/2 ensures the two don't collide.

Flags are signals that processes give to each other. One process issues a flag and the others look out for that flag. When it is received, a particular action is taken.

Semaphores are similar to flags, except semaphores are used to exchange data, rather than for alerts. Semaphores might be used to coordinate the use of shared memory, for example.

Queues are a place for one process to put data in and another process to take data from. In OS/2, queues are not necessarily first-in, first-out. The receiving program may take data out of the queue in any order.

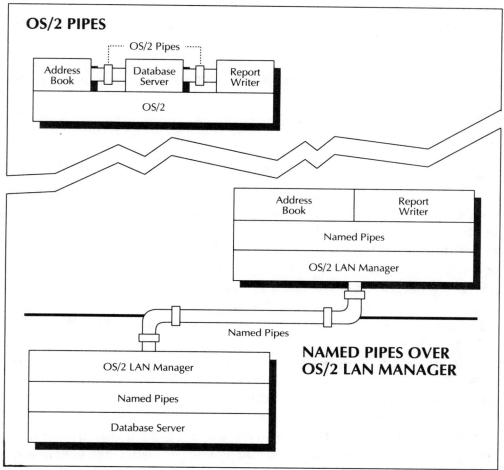

OS/2 processes communicate using pipes, which are opened, read, and written like files. Pipes make it easy for applications to be developed that share processes, saving memory and boosting performance. Named Pipes, an API that is part of LAN Manager, extend the concept of pipes over the network. It provides interprocess communication between programs on different computers. The result is distributed, client-server applications.

Pipes are like queues except they are first-in, first-out. One process opens the pipe and sends data through it to the receiving process.

In regard to the network, queues and pipes are the most important IPC. OS/2 queues and pipes are easier to use than many IPCs. A programmer can open, read, and write to pipes as if they were files, which are very familiar operations. OS/2 handles all the tasks behind setting up the pipes and queues. This is a tremendous boon for the programmer.

So far, all these IPCs work only within one OS/2 machine. With the addition of a network operating system, OS/2's IPC and multitasking features can be extended over a LAN.

NETWORK IPC

The key to extending OS/2's features over a network is an API for IPC. Many are available, but NetBIOS, APPC, and Named Pipes are the most important. None is exclusive to OS/2, but Named Pipes was developed for OS/2. The three have similar goals, but accomplish them differently.

NetBIOS is the basis of IBM's PC LAN Program and Microsoft's MS-Net. IBM originally developed APPC for communications among mainframes and midranges, but it has extended it to include PCs. Named Pipes was developed by Microsoft as an extension to OS/2's pipes. Because of the volume of programs in existence, more programmers are familiar with NetBIOS than APPC or Named Pipes.

The differences between the three IPC APIs are their sizes and ease of use. APPC is more sophisticated than Named Pipes and NetBIOS, but it requires much more memory. APPC and NetBIOS are more difficult to write to than Named Pipes. Named Pipes contains much of the logic necessary to set up communication between two processes, which makes it easier to develop client-server and distributed applications. With so much network logic already embedded in the API, using Named Pipes can increase the application's performance since fewer messages need to be passed between processes.

By combining multitasking and interprocess communication, OS/2 provides a platform upon which to build multiuser, distributed LAN-intrinsic application. Add a tightly coupled LAN operating system and OS/2 LANs can do things never done before on a PC.

Application Servers

One of the quiet revolutions changing the nature of computer networking is the growing use of special-purpose, or *application servers*. Whether they offer network users online access to facsimile capabilities, a mainframe gateway, or any of a variety of other sophisticated features, application servers add significant value to a network.

Unlike traditional network file servers, which act as intelligent, high-capacity data-storage and input/output systems, application servers perform specialized roles within a network environment. These may encompass managing printing queues, storing and routing electronic mail, or providing access to a database.

Application servers also reduce the demands placed on traditional file servers. Without having to handle special responsibilities, file servers can focus their processing resources on their primary jobs, network I/O and storing network data.

APPLICATION SERVER TYPES

Like many areas in the continually evolving electronics industry, compiling a comprehensive list of application server types is probably impossible. Still, we can pinpoint at least nine distinct types of application servers: asynchronous communications servers, backup servers, database servers, e-mail servers, fax servers, image servers, optical disk servers, print servers, and directory servers.

Briefly, communications servers provide dial in and dial out access to networks; backup servers manage the archiving of a network's data-storage systems; database servers allow accessing data stored on a variety of computers; e-mail servers act as electronic post offices; and fax servers allow multiple network users to send and receive faxes online. Image-processing servers permit entering and maintaining digitally processed images, such as cancelled checks, into a database; optical disc servers grant access to the huge amounts of data stored on CD-ROMs, and print servers manage the printing process, including changing fonts and forms.

We'll describe the operation of four application servers—fax, print, management, and backup—in more detail shortly. Other application servers are described elsewhere in this book.

THEY WORK TOGETHER

Before continuing, it's important to clarify one point: With the exception of a traditional file server, application servers generally require the services of another server to operate properly. This means a network would contain several types of application servers, all working in tandem and relying on each other.

For example, a fax server requires access to a file server and the word-processing files contained thereon, before it can transmit data. And it might require using the resources of a print server for access to a laser printer. A database server requires access to data stored on a variety of other application servers, and hosts, especially those where corporate databases are located.

Similarly, a key trend in the development of e-mail servers is to allow the e-mail "post office" machine to use the naming or directory service maintained by the network operating system, which is generally found on a file server. This simplifies managing the network because the administrator must keep track of and update only one naming service, not two.

TRANSPARENT OPERATION

One of the major strengths of application servers is their "transparent" operation to end users. That is, other than invoking an e-mail program, fax menu, or similar start-up program, most network users aren't even aware they're using an application server.

For instance, users of fax servers don't need to know they're accessing a device dedicated to sending and receiving faxes online. When they want to send a fax, they merely respond to onscreen prompts from the server software program by typing a destination fax machine's telephone number, the name of the file they want sent, the name of the recipient, and a short cover letter.

The fax server takes care of the rest automatically. It dials the phone number, transmits the fax via an internal modem, even redials the number should it get a busy signal. It also retrieves and stores incoming faxes without user intervention.

SERVING PRINTING NEEDS

Print servers were among the first of the special-purpose devices to appear on the network scene. Originally, they acted much like "traffic cops," starting and stopping print jobs or redirecting them to a specific printer, leaving functions such as font and forms management to the user.

Now, however, a print server can be configured so it lets one user print in Helvetica, a second in Times Roman, without either user worrying about changing fonts. Print servers must be aware of which hard and soft fonts are available, which page description languages are installed, and the like. (Hard fonts are those provided by the printer itself; soft fonts are those downloaded from a PC application to the printer.)

Intelligent print servers know which printers are capable of certain tasks or have certain size paper trays, and direct output accordingly. Some advanced print servers can balance loads among multiple printers. Some also offer management and accounting features, enabling a network administrator to charge back users for the printers' services.

PUBLISHING THE FAX

A fax server can turn anyone with the correct destination phone numbers and the willingness to pay the associated line costs into an electronic publisher. In many ways, fax servers can replace both regular mail and electronic-mail systems. And they certainly reduce the time spent manually feeding sheets of paper into a standard fax machine.

A fax server is a hardware-software combination with connections to both the network—this can be any of the commonly used Ethernet, Arcnet, or Token

Ring connectors—and the telephone system (via a standard RJ-11 modular jack). The fax server works in conjunction with a file server to let users send copies of their network-based electronic files—they can be word processing documents, spreadsheet forms, or graphics images—directly across the phone system to another fax machine.

In this application, users specify which files they want faxed, and the fax server accesses the correct file server to retrieve the needed files. It sends the fax out over the telephone system via its internal modem.

Obviously, this process eliminates several steps, including printing the original file on paper, then feeding it to a fax machine for transmission. It also holds more far-reaching ramifications, especially for organizations that need to fax out multiple copies of a single document.

With a fax server, the fax-sending process can be automated, much like a mail merge operation. This means, for example, that a company could use a fax server to "publish" dozens or even hundreds of personalized copies of a newsletter electronically, without requiring someone to manually perform the chore.

BACKING UP THE LAN

Several vendors have taken a similar approach to providing backup capabilities. Backup servers, as the name implies, are dedicated to providing centralized data archival (and recovery) facilities.

Legato Systems (Palo Alto, CA) has moved the backup-and-recovery process into the client-server environment with its NetWorker product. NetWorker is made up of client and server software, with the latter running on one or more backup servers. The client software, which runs on each PC on the network, determines which files to back up and routes them across the network to the right backup server. The server software manages the backup media—generally, tapes—and maintains an index of previous backups and their associated media volumes.

This system lets servers back up files on any network client. The online file backup history index also simplifies recovery operations—as users browse the index, they see historical views of the network file system at specified times. A lost file can thus be quickly identified and recovered.

ON THE DOWNSIDE

Naturally, there's a downside to using application servers. The most obvious, of course, is the cost of the additional hardware for each special-purpose server. And compatibility issues often create problems—that is, one application server may not operate on the same network with another. Placing numerous application servers on a network also adds complexity.

Because of these kinds of issues, application servers are more apt to be found in large corporate networks, where technical personnel are readily available, than in small, departmental workgroups. Still, many network users have discovered that the value added by application servers makes them well worth the expenses they entail.

Database Servers

Structured Query Language (SQL) is IBM's English-like database query language. It was developed to provide a relatively simple method for entering, retrieving, and changing data in an IBM database. Because IBM used it, SQL quickly became a standard other database vendors wanted to support. ANSI has standardized SQL as well. Using a common database language makes it easier to develop network database applications.

A database server is software that manages data in a database. It updates, deletes, adds, changes, and protects data, which is usually stored on a powerful computer with a large disk to which many users have access.

The database server software also protects data. Since network data can be accessed by many people, it must be protected from several potential problems. First, when two or more people work on the same database record at a time, they could overwrite each other's changes and cause data to be corrupted. Database server software must establish rules to regulate access to multiple simultaneous users. These rules are called *concurrency control*. Second, not every company employee needs access to every piece of data in the shared database. Therefore, a database server must also provide rules to regulate access, including passwords, access rights, and data encryption. These rules are called *access control*.

THE FRONT END

The database server does not contain the software needed for user interfaces, writing reports, generating applications, and other software associated with databases. The database server or *back-end* only manipulates data. Presenting, entering, and updating data is handled by the *front-end*. The front-end application usually runs on a different machine from the database server software.

Front-end software takes many forms because data can be manipulated and used differently. For example, Acme Widget Company has a database that contains customer information and inventory data. Different front-ends allow sales people to do promotional mailings to Acme's customer list. Outside distributors and salespeople on the road can dial into the database to learn which products are in stock. The service department can call up a customer's file when he calls and access all past ordering information. The accounting department can prevent customers from ordering more products if they are delinquent on their payments. Each group has a front-end tailored to their jobs, but they access the same database.

Different front-ends use a common access method—SQL—to communicate with the back-end. While the front and back ends communicate relatively easily, SQL is not a good language for nontechnical users. While programmers are not fazed by its syntax, salespeople, accountants, and technical support people do not want to type SQL commands.

In most applications, SQL will run "behind the scenes." Query-By-Example (QBE) is a simple front-end application. A QBE program asks users to provide an example of the type of data they want to get. A spreadsheet talks SQL to the back-end server, but the user continues to work with a familiar interface. If the user wishes, most front-end applications also permit users to execute SQL commands.

SERVER ADVANTAGES

A database server has several advantages over the traditional file server model of databases. In the file server model, there is only one program. Although this program is stored on the file server, it executes in the workstation. The one piece of software performs both front- and back-end functions. When a user loads the database, the program file is downloaded to his or her workstation. When data is requested, the software gets the database file from the server, searches through the file, finds the requested records, and then downloads the information to the workstation and displays it on the screen. The whole database travels across the network from the file server to the workstation.

In a database server, the tasks are divided. The front-end requests the data, the request is translated into SQL, and it is sent over the network to the server. The database server executes the search on the machine where the data exists.

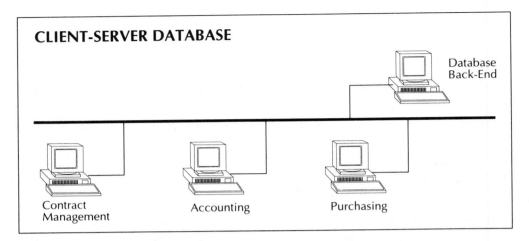

CLIENT-SERVER DATABASE

Database Back-End

Contract Management

Accounting

Purchasing

The back end of a database server manipulates, stores, and protects data. The front ends interface with the users, dealing with requests and displaying the results. Different front ends may access the same back-end server, as the example shows.

Only the requested records are returned to the front-end using SQL and a network transport mechanism. This cuts down on network traffic and makes execution faster, especially when many people are using the same data.

Data is not the only traffic that is eliminated. In the file server model, concurrency control information must be handled by the workstation. With a database server, these commands do not have to be transmitted over the network, since they are handled locally. A database server provides better data integrity.

As mentioned, another advantage is that different front-ends can access the same back-end. This is not possible with the file server model.

Because a database server is intelligent, it can shorten the application development cycle and allow applications to execute faster. One method is *stored procedures*. Stored procedures are short programs that reside on the server, waiting to be executed. Any front-end can call the stored procedures. This saves programmers from including redundant code segments in every application. It also saves memory in the workstation. *Triggers* are similar to stored procedures; however, stored procedures are compiled code, and triggers are uncompiled code.

Despite the usage of SQL, no standard method exists by which all front-ends can talk to back-ends from different vendors. Each database server has its own access methods that the front-ends must use because of different types of SQL used as well as differences in transport protocols. The result is applications written to work on one database server will not work on another. Although this is inconvenient for developers, it is a less serious problem for end users. When users choose a database management system, those choose a set of unique programming environments.

Database servers are an enormous improvement over other database management systems. They are faster, more powerful, more secure, more reliable, and easier to use. Their ability to accommodate a myriad of front-ends will make data sharing much easier. Their client-server design make them the next step in LAN databases.

SQL Front Ends

Much of what has been written about client-server computing has focused primarily on the "hows" of this new technology. That is, it has dealt mostly with the server database engine and how the client application communicates with the server via a Structured Query Language, or SQL.

Very little has been written about the front-end applications, however. For the most part, this has been because very few truly front-end applications have been available commercially. Developers have discovered that these applications, which give end users transparent access to data on server-based databases scattered around a network, are difficult to create, and thus have been slow getting them to market.

In addition, of the few front-end applications that have been available, most were developed for use by *developers* of front-end packages. These front-end development tools, which are intended to help developers create user friendly SQL front ends for less-technical users, require considerable knowledge about databases in general and SQL in particular. Now, finally, the first production-quality products in the second tier of the SQL front ends—those designs for nonprogrammers—are beginning to come to market. These new products promise to bring true distributed database functionality and capabilities to what have been, until now, nondatabase users.

THE CLIENT-SERVER MODEL

Client-server computing brings together three primary components: a back-end database program, an Application Programming Interface (API)—which is a standardized SQL application—and a front-end client application. In this environment, the client application initiates the communication process across a network by issuing a request to the SQL-API. The SQL database server responds by querying the back-end database application, which performs the necessary manipulations to find the data requested, and returns the answer to the end user.

In the client-server model, the database server can offer access to a variety of data, not just those based on text and/or numbers. For instance, the data could be standard row-and-column data or the information stored in an image-processing system—such as digitized images of cancelled checks in a check-processing application at a bank.

Some of the benefits of this architecture are obvious: For one, neither the end user nor front-end application needs to know where the data it wants has been stored; this is handled by the SQL API. And, because the front and back ends are separate programs, they can be specialized applications—for example, the front end can be designed for ease of use, the back end for performance.

A CHANGEABLE MODEL

Client-server computing also means that either the front- or back-end program can be exchanged for another without upsetting the system. This is because the well-defined interface (the SQL programming language) acts as a shield that separates the characteristics of one end from the other. It means that a SQL database server can respond to multiple front end applications simultaneously, too.

A SQL front-end application can communicate with SQL-compatible databases residing on various types of systems, including those running MS-DOS, OS/2, VMS, or Unix. Similarly, a wide variety of front-end programs can utilize data from a single database or multiple databases, all without requiring the end user to know where the data is located.

Another benefit of the client-server architecture: It permits maintaining a single centralized database accessible to everyone on a network. This means that the database is always up-to-date—network users share access to the database, working with just one copy of it (multiuser databases contain security features that keep track of multiple updates that could jeopardize the integrity of data).

When a user queries such a central database via a SQL front end, the resulting data is thus always accurate. And because SQL front ends "hide" database

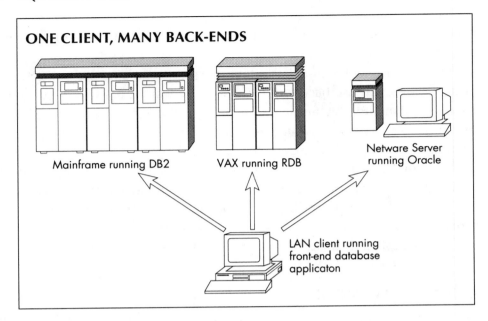

ONE CLIENT, MANY BACK-ENDS

Mainframe running DB2   VAX running RDB

Netware Server
running Oracle

LAN client running
front-end database
applicaton

Under the client-server model, one client can access many different back-end databases.

transactions from users, the client-server model makes accessing the database quick and easy.

DATABASE PUBLISHING

Database publishing consumes substantial resources at many companies. For example, many organizations regularly publish updated employee phone lists or need to tabulate weekly or monthly totals for outside sales personnel, then incorporate them into a formal report or presentation. Others use desktop publishing packages with databases to produce quarterly catalogs and price lists.

In a typical office, an administrative assistant or secretary would use several applications—a word processor, a database application, and a desktop publishing package or presentation graphics program—to generate such a report or catalog. This process can entail several steps: typing text into a file, querying a database to generate the sales totals or phone list, cutting and pasting or retyping the database figure into the word processing document, then using a desktop publishing program such as Aldus PageMaker to create the final report.

Two SQL-based front-end applications, Marc Software's (Palo Alto, Calif.) WordMarc-Oracle Connection and PageAhead Software's (Seattle, Wash.) PageAhead teamed with PageMaker, can eliminate several of these steps.

WordMarc Oracle Connection is a full-featured word processing program that allows Oracle database users to retrieve and incorporate information in an Oracle database into a WordMarc document. This process uses an on-screen menu. WordMarc users can incorporate "snapshot" reports that don't change as the Oracle data is changed or "live-linked" reports that are automatically updated when changes are made in Oracle. (These live links are preserved across nodes of a network.)

With WordMarc, Oracle-based data can be merged directly with WordMarc mail-merge documents to produce desktop-publishing quality letters and reports, according to the company. WordMarc also lets users create a WordMarc mail-merge database from Oracle data or send entries from the WordMarc database to an Oracle database.

The ability to incorporate the live-linked data into word-processing files means users don't have to retype or cut and past database files for use in reports generated with text-based applications.

ANOTHER APPROACH

PageAhead takes the database-publishing process a step further. PageAhead is a Microsoft Windows front-end tool that links Aldus' PageMaker (and eventually other desktop publishing software) to Oracle's RDBMS database. This capability allows creating what PageAhead calls "professional-quality directories, catalogs, and other data-intensive publications" from Oracle databases.

PageAhead lets users create macros that run inside PageMaker. Macros are programming statements that combine instructions to perform a series of operations within one command. When embedded within a PageMaker file, a PageAhead macro tells PageMaker how to retrieve data from an Oracle database, which can reside on a mainframe or mini- or microcomputer. The macro also provides the instructions to turn the data into a publishable document.

In this arrangement, the database information is never really an integral part of the original PageMaker text file, as is typically done now. Rather, the PageAhead macro acts as a pointer to the database. This means that whenever the original PageMaker document is subsequently reprinted, all the updates that have been made to the database since the last printing will automatically be included in the new edition.

For example, a company that sends out quarterly product catalogs or price list updates could simply create a master file containing the standard information you would find in a catalog or price list—for example, company name, address, and purchase order policies. Also included in the file would be a PageAhead macro pointing to the correct database information. When PageMaker is used to format the file, the macro automatically creates the final document, with updated prices.

When it comes time to reissue the catalog or price list, the company simply would have to run the original file through PageMaker again. The macro will automatically retrieve and print new information from the database, not the outdated prices or parts numbers, which have been removed from the database.

GUPTA'S SQL WINDOWS

Many of the available SQL front ends, including Gupta's SQLWindows and JYACC's JAM, are application-development tools and not truly end-user products.

SQLWindows looks like a drawing tool but works like an applications generator, automatically generating SQL code as its user draws visual items in the program's "design window." Its graphical report writer, called Report Windows, lets less-sophisticated programmers build Windows-based database applications without programming in Gupta SQLWindows Application Language.

Gupta says SQL Report Windows is a WYSIWYG (What You See Is What You Get) graphical report designer. It allows developers to create applications that make full use of Windows' font and graphics support features. Developers can write user interfaces with scroll bars, "radio" buttons, pop-up menus, and dialog boxes without having to program.

Gupta also says that SQLWindows is compatible with databases other than its own SQLBase Server, including DB2 and Oracle's RDBMS. Future releases of SQLWindows will support gateways to IBM's OS/2 Extended Edition Database Manager, Microsoft's SQL Server, Novell's NetWare SQL, and Informix.

IN A JAM

JYACC's JAM (JYACC Application Manager) version 5.0 is the core of what the company says is an integrated product "family that allows developers to proto-type and deliver database and LAN-based applications that are hardware, soft-ware, operating system, and network independent."

In essence, JAM is a user-interface manager that lets developers produce "sophisticated applications quickly and easily," according to the company. JAM/DBi (Database Interface) links JAM's front-end development tools to sev-eral databases, including Oracle, Gupta's SQLBase, and Microsoft's SQL Server.

JAM's screen-editing functions include clipboards for clipping and merg-ing sections of forms, block moves and copies for manipulating data objects in a form, and a line-drawing facility. Its use of virtual screens, viewports, "radio" buttons, checklists, and scroll bars gives character-based applications a "graphical look and feel," according to JYACC.

Mail-Enabled Applications

Token Ring, Ethernet, FDDI. It's all basically plumbing, and once it works, you give the network-access method about as much thought as you give to the copper pipes that bring hot and cold water when you turn on the tap. TCP/IP, IPX/SPX, and NetBEUI are the valves that control the flow of data. Copper pipes and flow-control valves interest only plumbers and architects. What the average person really needs is the end result of the plumbing system—the dishwasher, the showerhead, the lawn sprinkler system.

There's a new appliance on the horizon that is going to change how we view networking and networked applications, and that's *mail-enabled applications*. Mail-enabled applications will deliver a new type of network appliance and new level of functionality. Mail will evolve from messaging to a complete communications medium.

Mail-enabled applications will deliver the infrastructure for e-mail management applications, work-flow automation applications, document distribution, and forms processing. The groundwork is beginning to be laid, with mail engines from Novell, Lotus, Microsoft, and others.

Applications that take advantage of these mail engines are in their earliest stages. And from the looks of applications such as Beyond's BeyondMail for rules-based mail management and Reach Software's MailMan for work-flow automation and eventually forms processing, the progress of mail-enabled applications seems quite promising.

TODAY'S E-MAIL IS MESSAGING

Right now, electronic mail is little more than an elaborate messaging scheme. Users on a network can send and receive messages, which are usually short and text-based, and sometimes have files attached. Users can ask for return receipts, send registered mail, forward messages to other users using the same e-mail program, and find out what time the recipient has read the mail. They can construct mailing lists from an address book or directory of e-mail users. With the right software, users on dissimilar computers, say a Macintosh user and an IBM PC user, can exchange messages with relative ease.

Despite the sophistication, e-mail systems remain fundamentally interpersonal communication. One person sends mail to another or to a group of people. The recipient or recipients read the e-mail, perhaps with a file attached, and respond to the message, usually by sending another e-mail message.

This isn't to disparage e-mail's power. E-mail can significantly increase an individual's productivity. It allows people to work offline, as it were, responding to messages on their time and their terms, rather than answering a phone call or having a face-to-face meeting. E-mail has been proven to increase workers' productivity, at least until the onslaught of messages becomes so great that any time savings is eroded by the time taken to manage the volume of messages.

MAIL BONDING

E-mail has the potential for becoming more than a method of interpersonal communication. It can become the platform upon which many other forms of communication occur and can serve as the skeleton for other applications. Mail-enabled applications are the merging of messaging with other application software.

The problem lies in the fact that most people do their work in one set of applications—WordPerfect, 1-2-3, and Paradox—and then want to communicate their ideas and share that work with their coworkers. However, messaging is not inherently part of a word processor, a spreadsheet, a database, or most other applications. Messaging is not even a part of most applications that could easily accommodate messaging, such as purchasing systems or contact management systems.

Most applications do not include mail or messaging capabilities for some very simple reasons. First, when these packages were conceived of and written, the concept of mail-enabling didn't exist or make sense. Many of these packages were written before networks became widespread.

Second, for those software publishers who do want to move toward mail-enabling, some roadblocks are in the way. There's no standard, de facto or otherwise. Each e-mail vendor implements a different scheme for mail-enabling, requiring applications vendors to choose among the options. This setup requires the application developers to choose correctly, or potentially lose business.

Also, many companies use more than one electronic mail system. For example, the mainframe terminal users may use PROFS, the VAX users may use All-In-One, and the PC LAN users may use any one of dozens of packages, but probably use cc:Mail, Microsoft Mail (formerly Network Courier), or DaVinci's eMail. To use a mail-enabled application, the interface must be able to work with all of the company's existing mail systems.

Any application that uses document routing or communication can become a mail-enabled application. Whether mail-enabled applications become widespread is a matter of how easily the problems can be solved, how easily existing applications can be adapted, and how easily new applications can be written. And that's a function of the available tools.

MAKING IT HAPPEN

Mail-enabled applications, although in their embryonic stages, have great potential. Take for instance, a consulting engineer whose client, a hospital, wants to purchase a boiler. Maybe the engineering firm has an old catalog lying around from one of their suppliers. Maybe an administrative assistant has to call the supplier's salesperson to send a new catalog to both them and their client. Either way, the engineers have to leaf through the catalog, looking for the specifications they need. Then they have to call the salesperson and ask for more detailed spec sheets on the various models and manufacturers.

Now consider the boiler manufacturer, who has to handle inquiry calls from customers across the country. The manufacturer is using a lot of resources in pre-sale and post-sale support calls. The company probably has an entire department set up to deal with simple calls, preventing their employees from resolving the more complex issues.

If customers could dial into the manufacturer's computer system, search the documents for answers to simple queries, and download the right specifications sheets and other documentation, then the sales support desk wouldn't have to spend its time manually sending out these packages, and they could spend their time on more meaningful calls. Once at the customer site or even at the manufacturer, the electronic documents could simply be forwarded from one person to another.

While it would seem that this scenario calls for an ordinary document management system, the key is document transport, which can be done via electronic messaging. Put the spec sheet—or any other type of file—in an envelope, and send it. But the forms and routing aspects that simple e-mail systems lack must be solved. The forms can be merely another user interface talking to a mail engine, and the routing can be a rules-based system directing messages to the right people.

Such mail-enabling is appropriate for any application that requires forms distribution. A purchasing system is another example, where one group of managers must approve a requisition if the purchase is below a certain dollar amount, and another set of managers must sign off if the purchase is over a certain amount.

If the requisitions were in the form of e-mail messages and the system had the built-in intelligence to route the documents to the proper people, a mail-enabled application would be born. Ideally the people wouldn't even have to use the same front-end mail applications as long as they subscribed to a standard back-end engine or a common interface.

POWER IN THE BACK END

Like databases, the new generation of mail applications follows the client-server architecture. Once considered a single application, mail has since been split into its many component parts: the core engine, the user interfaces, message storage, transport layer, gateways to other e-mail systems, and directory services.

As with databases, this client-server architecture allows each group of developers to concentrate on their strengths. For example, the engine manufacturers can concentrate on better message handling services, while the gateway manufacturers work to write faster and more functional gateways between dissimilar mail systems. Front-end application vendors, in the meantime, can offer e-mail interfaces and then build on top of them.

And like databases, no one mail engine has emerged supreme. Today, four groups are vying for the top spot: Novell, Microsoft, Lotus, and OSI. No clear winner has emerged. Message Handling System (MHS), which has been around since the mid-1980s, is the most mature. Originally developed by Action Technologies, MHS was sold to Novell. At one time, the majority of PC LAN mail applications used the MHS interface. Microsoft will outline its messaging strategy for its applications and network users. [Note: Microsoft ultimately announced its Messaging Applications Programming Interface (MAPI), which has been accepted by Lotus and other important messaging developers.] Lotus has announced the Open Messaging Interface (OMI), plus mail-enabled applications can be built using something as simple as the import/export function in its cc:Mail. [Note: OMI was the forerunner of Lotus's Vendor Independent Messaging (VIM) interface, which has failed to gather industry-wide support.] OSI's X.400 standard offers an internationally recognized method of store-and-forward messaging.

No standard communications language exists for mail-enabled applications in the same way that Structured Query Language has become the accepted method of querying relational databases, even though some differences exist among the implementations.

Instead of supporting each vendor's engine directly, developers could write to a common interface, which talks to the different engines. Developers would not have to write the core mail engine themselves nor would they have to worry about choosing the "right" engine. And developers would not have to spend their resources supporting different engines. Now, if only there were such an accepted, industry-standard interface.

[Note: the next three paragraphs are included for historical reference only—OMI became VIM, which is itself well along the way to the old standards' graveyard.] Lotus has proposed that OMI be that common layer and has placed the specification in the public domain. OMI is an Applications Programming Interface (API) that is published by Lotus, IBM, and Apple, and it offers a common interface for different vendors' mail engines, including directory, transport, and message storage functions. OMI will be available for a variety of platforms, including DOS, Windows, OS/2, Unix, and the Macintosh.

Applications make calls to the OMI interface to send and receive messages and for services such as looking up user names in the directory or storing messages in folders. OMI also provides developers the ability to access e-mail services in a modular fashion, such as directory, message storage, and transport. This way, developers and users can pick and choose services. For example, they may choose to use the network operating system's directory service instead of the mail systems'. This setup prevents developers and end users from being locked into using a particular service or vendor.

So far, Lotus has pledged to use OMI to mail-enable all its applications, including 1-2-3, AmiPro 2.0, and Freelance. IBM says it will include OMI technology in a future OS/2-based offering, and OfficeVision/2 will use OMI. Apple will support OMI in future versions of System 7. Still, OMI is a brand-new specification, and only time will tell if it is adopted. [Time has told—it wasn't.]

Workflow Applications

The personal computer engendered a revolution. Workers gained new freedom when they were empowered by easy-to-use applications running on their desktop computers. Pundits predicted a sharp increase in worker productivity, and corporations spent millions of dollars on personal productivity tools. With word-processing software, typists and administrative assistants no longer had to retype document drafts. Revisions became easy. With database software, vast repositories of data could be created. With spreadsheets, number crunching became a favorite pastime.

Despite the investment, the productivity payoff has not arrived as predicted, in part because these applications deal with only half the work. They deal with the end result—the numbers, words, or products—not the *process* of producing the work. The personal computer is inherently personal, but the work that information workers do is both personal and interpersonal.

Corporations are looking to a new class of applications to improve the productivity of information workers, those people who deal with the process, rather than those who manufacture the end results.

WHY WORKFLOW COMPUTING

Information workers don't enter numbers or type words; they manipulate information, drawing conclusions and making projections. They forward that work or information to coworkers, who then make more projections and draw more conclusions. *Workflow computing* is designed to deal with the process of work, not just the end results.

Workflow computing is inherently a networked application. Although it could take place on a host-centric system, workflow applications take advantage of a network's distributed intelligence. Work can be distributed to the local sites, where workers can continue to use their familiar tools.

A workflow is a description of how work moves among workers and the operations required to process that information as it moves. The work process is decomposed into steps and dependencies. Workflows can be simple or complex. For example, on one end of the spectrum, an intelligent mail application can help prioritize and route a user's mail; on the other end, a workflow application can move a purchase requisition through the approval process.

According to the *Clarke-Burton Report* (The Burton Group, formerly known as Clarke-Burton, Salt Lake City), "The concept behind workflow automation is to extend the reach of computing beyond office automation, [to] bring the process itself—not just the work created by the process—into the realm of the computing system." Market research firm Forrester Research, located in Cambridge, MA, defines workflow computing as "computers and networks adding and extracting value from information as it moves through the organization."

Imagine the work and the process through which a company accomplishes its business as a river. Employees alter, detract, or add to this flow as it begins at the initial customer contact and ends with the product shipment or dispensed service.

Instead of wasting corporate time and money, while paperwork eddies in employees' in-boxes, whirls in their out-boxes, and becomes waylaid in the rapids that fall in between, workflow software routes the work to the proper person. For example, a purchase order must be routed from the requester to one or more managers to the purchasing agent to the supplier and back to the requester. Different purchases require different levels of approval. Workflow software can automate these processes that are now decided manually.

Business cycles can also be shortened. Instead of managers tracking work through engineering, assembly, and marketing, for example, workflow software can monitor its progress, allowing people to concentrate on the specifics of their jobs. Managers and workers can know where a particular item resides in the process. Workflow software can help identify and eliminate bottlenecks.

Workflow software can reduce the difficulties of distance. Companies can more easily distribute their operations as their businesses dictate. Workers in far-flung offices of the same corporation can communicate as easily as if they're local.

Workflow computing can also be externally focused. Companies' desire to communicate with its customers and suppliers will drive workflow computing. Companies will be able to establish tighter links to their suppliers. Customers can more easily communicate with their suppliers. Electronic Document Interchange (EDI) can become more than a primitive reality.

FOUR TYPES OF WORKFLOW

Intelligent routing is perhaps the most important quality of workflow software. Intelligent routing determines who is the next person in the process that must receive the work. This forwarding process can be accomplished in any number of ways, from elaborate process models to complex scripts to ad hoc arrangements.

Workflow computing software must provide facilities to track the flow of work throughout the system and to accommodate existing applications. The flow of work must be tracked and reported, so audit trails can be produced and managers can follow a work's progress. Also, you need to know who is accessing what information. Host-based, client-server, and personal productivity applications must be connected to the workflow system.

Workflow automation comes in four breeds: document flow, process automation, task automation, and workgroup tools. Companies will implement the different types based on their corporate practices and philosophies. For example, a more structured company is more likely to implement a process automation system, while an entrepreneurial company is likely to implement a workgroup or task automation system.

The early workflow systems take a document flow approach. Developed primarily by image-processing companies, these systems automate a paper-based process, such as loan applications or credit card billing. Very often, these systems completely simulate the paper-based process, from file cabinets to paper clips. In automating a purely paper-based process, many of these systems forfeit the benefits of altering the business practice to take advantage of a new technology. Automate an inefficient, manual process, and you will have an inefficient, automated process. These systems are also inflexible in that they create bit-mapped images of documents, which cannot be edited. Few provide automatic routing.

Process automation workflow requires a top-down approach. System designers and business managers analyze the process of work, then build the system based on that model. Once defined, the system is inflexible; it cannot be changed on the fly, forcing workers to adapt to a computerized process. AT&T's Rhapsody and NCR's Cooperation both implement this model.

Rather than automating the entire process, task automation takes the opposite tack and automates the individual tasks that make up the process. This is more of a bottom-up approach. Hewlett-Packard's NewWave Office is one such application, since it enables users to build scripts to accommodate tasks.

However, both process and task automation assume that a process is in place. If the work is accomplished without a formal process in place, neither type is helpful. In this case, workgroup or ad hoc tools are better. Workgroup tools give the power to the user, rather than to the top-level manager. Beyond's BeyondMail, which allows users to build in rules for routing e-mail, is one example. With workgroup tools, workers can define their workflows to their liking. Although they can customize their systems, workflow automation places the burden of system design and administration on the user. This approach is fine for power users, but tentative computer users may balk.

PARTS OR WHOLE?

No clear product strategy or vendor has emerged. Workflow products will come from the traditional office automation vendors, e-mail providers, vertical applications developers, and others.

Some vendors offer a complete system usually built around a shared database. Very often these workflow systems are include bundled or encapsulated applications, such as e-mail, word processing, and print spooling. Essentially, these developers move the model of traditional office automation software into the world of distributed, networked intelligence. AT&T and NCR take this tack.

Other developers are moving toward a component approach. Instead of supplying the whole package from database to workflow, these vendors offer the individual pieces. They may offer one or more front-end pieces that work with other company's workflow database back ends. This pay-as-you-go approach enables corporations and network designers to pick and choose. While this approach is more flexible, it requires the user to act as an integrator, assembling the many pieces of the system.

Much of the current workflow fervor emanates from the electronic mail vendors. Mail-enabled applications are leading the way to workflow computing. The simplest of these provide intelligent mail routing that can be expanded to include routing documents and forms. These applications typically use an e-mail engine or back end of e-mail storage, routing, and directory services. Functionality is added to the e-mail front end until it becomes a full-featured workflow application.

Electronic mail vendors alone can't move the industry forward. Expect to see database vendors team up with e-mail vendors to provide expertise in delivering distributed databases. And to make intelligent routing truly useful, network operating system companies must improve their directory services so applications and users can locate and access networked resources.

SLOWING THE FLOW?

Workflow software is in its earliest evolutionary stages. Office automation software for the mainframe and minicomputer have existed for quite some time; PC groupware products have emerged, but neither offers enough functionality and flexibility. The next generation, exemplified by products such as Reach Software's MailMan or Beyond's BeyondMail will provide the basis for true workflow.

The movement to workflow computing won't happen without pain. Before such systems can become a reality, networks must be built that can mask the differences of incompatible computing systems. Vendors must provide open systems solutions, not proprietary platforms. The kinks of client-server software have to be ironed out.

Many of the challenges are not technical, but rather political or cultural. The impetus for workflow computing must come from a company's uppermost management, since it automates the very heart of the business. Only top management can ensure the steady progress and development of such a system. Also, employees may balk at such systems, which in the wrong hands can be used as a Big Brother monitoring system.

Nevertheless, the benefits of workflow computing can be great. Companies can eliminate steps that were necessary in paper-based systems but that have become wasteful in a world that conducts business online, thereby reaping the profits of just-in-time business.

Messaging-Enabled Applications

E-mail is a form of communication equal in utility to the telephone, fax, and paper mail, but e-mail is much more than sending memos or attaching files. Messaging is a transport for delivering information, and the next generation of messaging software will provide the underpinnings for applications that deliver new productivity gains to information workers.

Not only has this year's workgroup software been designed for a group of users, it is also suitable for the business-line applications, such as accounting, inventory, and materials planning. Scheduling, intelligent mail, forms, and workflow are a few of the applications built on the messaging infrastructure.

SCHEDULING

Scheduling and calendaring are typically the first applications to be added to a messaging backbone. Users can employ electronic calendars within their e-mail to set appointments for themselves and others. A scheduler vendor and an e-mail vendor may bundle their software, or a single vendor can write both applications. The more tightly integrated applications use APIs such as Novell's Message Handling Service (MHS), Microsoft's Mail API (MAPI), or Lotus' Vendor Independent Messaging (VIM).

INTELLIGENT MAIL

In an e-mail-reliant corporation, users can become inundated by the volume of incoming messages, many of which are noncritical or unimportant. Do you really care who has a used Newton for sale? Or if the cafeteria is serving fish sticks on Friday? If e-mail stops enhancing productivity, people will stop using it.

One way for users to handle the e-mail barrage is to ask the software for help. Intelligent e-mail can make message-handling decisions for the user based on a set of rules, such as the message's urgency, the sender's identity, the subject matter, or keywords. Intelligent mail can prioritize, discard, or reroute the messages based on user-defined criteria.

Consider how easily users and administrators can configure and use the rules in any intelligent e-mail package. Users may have difficulty understanding how to configure the rules or how to change the rules for special circumstances, such as when they travel.

FORMS AND WORKFLOW

Electronic forms, or e-forms, also take advantage of a messaging transport. A company typically ventures into workflow with e-forms, because corporations are looking for ways to reduce the volume of paper and because the routing paths and interfaces for forms are straightforward. Many companies start with e-forms and workflow routing for expense reports or purchase order requisitions. Companies such as JetForm (Waltham, MA) have led the way, but WordPerfect has entered the market with its InForms.

If you implement e-forms, you will have to hurdle the security and authorization issue. You can't authorize an e-form by typing your name, because anyone could type your name and it would look the same. Typing your name is the digital equivalent of marking a big "X" in the approval box. You must have a secure form of digital signature. Companies such as RSA Data Security (Redwood City, CA) are tackling this issue.

Electronic forms can also handle the results of database queries. With e-forms for data access, you can turn the query results into an e-mail message. For this setup to work, the e-mail front ends will have to understand SQL and the database APIs, or the database front ends must understand the mail APIs. BeyondMail 2.0 has this capability when used with Lotus Notes.

Workflow's promise lies not in simple tasks, such as routing travel itineraries or filing expense reports; the real utility resides in large-scale corporate applications. Workflow software can automate business processes so the software can routinely decide where to send documents.

For workflow to be effective for business-line applications, the system must be scalable and robust. It must be useable in a wide area network as well

A MESSAGING INFRASTRUCTURE

X.400	SMTP	Mail Gateways	Database Gateways

Message Server

Message Handling System (MHS)	Vendor Independent Messaging (VIM)	Microsoft Mail API (MAPI)

MHS	VIM	MAPI	MHS	VIM	MAPI	MHS	VIM	MAPI	MHS	VIM	MAPI	MHS	VIM	MAPI
Scheduling			E-mail with Rules			Electronic Forms			Workflow			Other Applications		

THE MESSAGE BACKBONE: The next generation of workgroup software, which includes scheduling, intelligent mail, electronic forms, and workflow, will be built on a messaging infrastructure.

as with mobile employees. For these goals to be achieved, messaging and database systems must adopt some of each other's characteristics.

RIVAL ARCHITECTURES

As companies disperse their operations across the globe, they need a way to transport their corporate information. While "transport" implies a messaging infrastructure, business-line applications are primarily database oriented. For an application to be successfully distributed, it needs to adopt parts of a messaging architecture. Distributed applications need to allow access to information from a variety of locations, but users typically don't need quick response times. How updates and changes are distributed, or replicated, is critical to the success of an enterprise workflow system.

Whether you choose a database architecture, a messaging architecture, or a blend depends on your particular needs. For example, for an airline reservation system, a database architecture is better, because a fixed set of people is accessing a fixed set of information. Databases provide fast and robust access to structured data. Don't overlook that databases are a mature, robust, and secure technology with lots of add-on tools and experienced programmers and managers.

But a database architecture isn't always suitable. For example, for an information-publishing service, many different people will be downloading the information, which could be stored in files of any size and type, with graphics and video. Because databases are not flexible in handling unstructured data types and because many paths of communication exist, a messaging structure is better.

When you have a distributed system, you need an efficient way to update each site. A database, because it is built for real-time access, must propagate the changes as they occur or shortly thereafter. But people have a different set of expectations and needs for messaging. Because people don't need the messages instantaneously, the system stores the messages, then forwards them at a slightly later time, whether that interval is every half hour, hour, or day. The slower rate of information exchange makes distribution less costly in a wide area network.

The issue of message storage needs to be resolved. The client's capabilities are tightly coupled with the message storage's functionality. For example, the types of acceptable file formats, such as voice, video, and data, hinge on the message store's capabilities. Some messaging vendors say the message store belongs on the network, while others say it belongs on the client. For example, with Apple's Open Collaborative Environment (AOCE) and Microsoft's Windows 95, the message store and the file store are merged and reside on the client. With MAPI, you can do it either way. Banyan (Westboro, MA) says the message store should be server-based. Having the message store on the client makes users more mobile; having the message store on the server makes the system more robust.

IMPLEMENTATION ISSUES

The highly useful workgroup applications are not shrink-wrapped applications but rather require programming. Whether you rely on systems integrators or develop the experience in-house, customization is expensive. Your business-line applications must justify the development costs. Here's the conundrum: If messaging-enabled applications remain heavily dependent on integrators' expertise, the applications will be available only to the company's most highly leveraged workers. But for workflow to be useful, it has to be deployed across a corporation—it has to be as accessible to the receptionist as it is to the traders.

Lotus Notes is clearly the most successful workgroup software environment, and its base of third-party applications is expanding rapidly. Notes does require customization, but it is an extremely powerful tool.

Shrink-wrapped applications are a must. The first applications to be bundled will be the application suites owned by one manufacturer, such as Microsoft, Lotus, or WordPerfect, since including workflow in the package is considerably easier when one company owns all the applications. Next will come applications that adhere to industry-standard APIs, so users can mix and match.

THE VIRTUAL CORPORATION

The end game of workgroup software is that information sharing will become part of a company's workflow. Information will come from users' personal productivity applications as well as from corporate message servers, database servers, and information servers. If the industry can get information sharing to work, then users can build virtual corporations. Company-to-company communication stands to gain the most productivity from messaging.

Companies create individual departments to increase workers' productivity, but anyone who has worked in a large corporation knows that having departments isn't the most efficient way to work. But what if people in different locations and companies could work together for a project's duration, then form another team for the next project, all the while operating as if they worked in adjacent offices?

Calendars

Corporations accepted LAN-based e-mail as a mainstream application when people could feasibly and practically use different types of e-mail packages to communicate. Before this interoperability occurred, people were restricted to communicating with users of the same e-mail package, which reduces e-mail's productivity gains.

Makers of calendaring and scheduling software are attempting to create the same utility by establishing interoperability among their products. In particular, the MHS Alliance has forged the Calendaring/Group Scheduling Interoperability Specification, which enables different vendors' calendaring software to communicate. As the MHS Alliance, the vendors' first task is to define interoperability for calendars using Novell's Message Handling System (MHS), but they aren't limiting their work to that transport.

"The benefit of interoperability is that it expands the scope of whom you can do group scheduling with, and it expands the value of group scheduling," says Anik Ganguly, co-chair of the MHS Alliance's technical subcommittee on calendaring and scheduling and vice president of product development at Cambell Services (Southfield, MI). "As a result, group scheduling will grow faster and become more valuable."

"People want scheduling to be multiserver and to be a more scaleable solution. People have learned that they need to be connected. They found they can really get work done better with e-mail. Scheduling has that knowledge base to work from," says John Rizzi, president of the MHS Alliance and vice president of strategic marketing at On Technology (Cambridge, MA).

Although achieving interoperability was an important step for the corporate acceptance of e-mail, Ganguly points out an important difference with the scheduling effort. "We are addressing group scheduling more explicitly and earlier in the life cycle of products. There were a lot of point-to-point solutions for e-mail interoperability. There are better ways to solve that problem," says Ganguly.

WHAT A SCHEDULER DOES

Electronic calendars and schedulers replace your paper-based calendar and provide the benefit of performing some of the scheduling footwork for you. For instance, you can use calendaring software to set up a meeting with Melanie, Alan, and Hanna in San Francisco and Dave in Chicago. You enter the proposed meeting time, place, and attendees in your scheduling software, and the software checks the invitees' calendars to see if they are free or busy at that time. The software can also negotiate their busy schedules to find a time when everyone is free. The software then sends a meeting request to the users, which they can accept or politely decline. Each calendaring product has unique architecture and features, of course, but the process works much the same way.

Scheduling meetings is relatively simple if everyone uses the same software, but if people use incompatible schedulers, then they can't exchange schedules unless the vendors wrote point-to-point gateways between their products. Users would be back on the phone, individually asking people when they're free for a meeting.

In theory, scheduling software is a great idea. It's a time saver. But to date, schedulers have met with limited success. Products have been available, but for whatever portable enough, or because of the schedulers' limited interoperability people have not flocked to buy them. Calendar vendors hope interoperability will be the key to widespread usage.

SCHEDULE YOU, SCHEDULE ME

The MHS Alliance Calendaring/Group Scheduling Interoperability Specification, which was published in December 1993, is intended to let different calendaring products exchange information about users and their schedules. Users will be able to schedule and cancel meetings with each other, regardless of their native calendaring application.

Scheduling vendors in the MHS Alliance include Attachmate (Bellevue, WA) and its Zip!Office, Cambell Services with On Time, Microsystems Software

INTEROPERABLE CALENDARING ARCHITECTURE

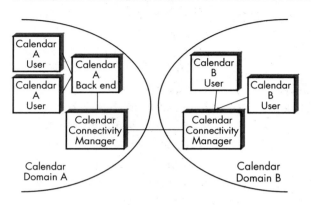

Calendar Domain A — Calendar Domain B

COMMUNICATING SCHED-ULERS: The MHS Alliance Scheduling/Calendaring Interoperability Specification enables users of different calendaring software to communicate. The specification defines calendaring domains of users and products. The Calendar Connectivity Manager knows the internals of the interoperability specification and the product implementations, and it negotiates the differences.

(Framingham, MA) with CaLANdar, On Technology with Meeting Maker, and PowerCore (Manreno, IL) with Network Scheduler 3. (Note: CE Software, of West Des Moines, IA, now markets the software formerly known as Network Scheduler 3 as TimeVision.)

The MHS Alliance's Scheduling/Calendaring technical subcommittee has concentrated its interoperability efforts on the functional blocks of scheduling meetings: inviting people to a meeting, notifying people of a meeting change or cancellation, and choosing a time to meet. The calendaring software must allow a person to select a user in another calendaring system and indicate to the other calendaring software that its user requests a meeting. Selecting a user and requesting a meeting implies that a directory and a facility for directory exchange exists.

The MHS Alliance specification has defined three major message types—events, free/busy time, and directories—and their formats. For example, the specification defines how to request, deny, and reschedule a meeting. It defines how users' free and busy times are published and how users' locations are identified. It provides a way to identify users' time zones. It also handles scheduling for inanimate resources, such as conference rooms and slide projectors. How the message types are implemented is the responsibility of the individual vendor; the MHS Alliance defines only the framework.

To enable interoperability, the MHS Alliance defined a *calendaring* domain, which is determined by the existence of a single vendor's product or a single user directory. The specification does not define the domain; it could be a PC-based system as easily as it could be a PROFS gateway.

Added to the calendaring domain is "translator" software called the Calendar Connectivity Manager (CCM), which enables the interoperability. At one end, the CCM understands the protocols, messages, and data items of the interoperability specification. On the other end, the CCM knows about the internal details of the vendors' calendars.

Each vendor needs to develop a CCM to make its product capable of interoperating. The MHS Alliance's objective is to enable interoperability among scheduling products whole requiring vendors to change little, if any, of their existing code.

The interoperability model works with either the client-server model or the shared-files model used by the scheduling vendors. In a shared-files system, one person can schedule a meeting with another person because the software knows about the files in the calendar and can access them. In a client-server model, the user's software understands how to send requests to the server. The server negotiates setting up the meeting with the other user and returns the answer.

Using the CCM will enable the existing calendaring software to remain largely unchanged. However, most developers will have to modify their calendaring user interface to accept "foreign" names or users who are not in the system. Without interoperability, a calendar is a closed system, in that you can schedule meetings only with people on your user list. With interoperability in place, people can send meeting requests to users who won't necessarily be known to the software. Users must be able to enter names into their address books. The MHS Alliance also has defined the messages required to do directory lookups in other calendaring systems.

Calendar users want to gain interoperability without much performance impact. When users schedule meetings with users of the same type of calendaring system, the calendars work with their native protocols, and the response is speedier.

The CCM translator comes into play only when the user tries to schedule a meeting with a user of a dissimilar but interoperable calendar. Then the calendaring software's architecture plays a role in performance. If it uses a store-and-forward model designed to work with multiple calendaring servers, the performance impact will be less than it would be on a real-time system.

Users' location is the biggest factor affecting performance. If they are remote, they will have to wait for the meeting requests and replies to traverse the wide area network. If they are local, the response time will be quicker. Still, the MHS Alliance predicts that any performance impact will be slight.

A COMMON TRANSPORT

The MHS Alliance calendaring specification assumes that all vendors' CCMs can communicate, which in turn assumes a common transport. However, the interoperability specification is independent of the transport. "The header contains what is essentially an e-mail address. The transport doesn't have a lot of responsibilities," says Rizzi.

The first transport to be used is Novell's MHS. The specification for binding the interoperability code to Novell's Standard Message Format (SMF) is published separately from the interoperability specification. Although the MHS Alliance hasn't settled on the next transport, it has named cc:Mail, Microsoft Mail, Simple Mail Transport Protocol (SMTP), and X.400 as possibilities. Whichever e-mail transport is used, it must reliably deliver and deposit a file. Transports that use a database architecture require more modification than transports that use shared files.

THE XAPIA'S SPECIFICATION

The MHS Alliance isn't the only group working on the timely problem of calendaring interoperability. The X.400 API Association (XAPIA) plans to publish its calendaring interoperability specification in October, 1994. The MHS Alliance and the XAPIA, eager to avoid the API wars that bruised the e-mail vendors, are cooperating. They agree on common interoperability and data models, so after they independently publish their works, one standard with multiple bindings will be published.

A fair amount of cross-membership occurs in the two groups. Most MHS Alliance embers are members of the XAPIA calendaring technical subcommittee. In some cases, no crossover happens. for example, Microsoft is a part of the XAPIA, but is not a member of the MHS Alliance, since it does not have an MHS

NetWare Directory Services

One of the most eagerly awaited aspects of NetWare 4.x is its directory services scheme. It's also one of the most complex to describe. This discussion is necessarily a simplification of NetWare Directory Services (NDS). Since NDS comes from Novell, the NetWare 4.x documentation should be considered the definitive source on the subject. If you're installing NetWare 4.x, follow the 4.x documentation for specifics on NDS. For those wondering whether to make the jump to NetWare 4.x (and hence don't yet have the documentation), here's a brief overview of NDS.

BEYOND THE BINDERY

Versions of NetWare prior to 4.0 built and maintained, on each file server, a special database called the *bindery* to store information on each user, group, or other object the file server had to track. For example, when the supervisor of a NetWare 3.11 file server wants to give a new user access to the server, he or she uses Novell's SYSCON utility to create a new user, entering a new user name (the account name for that user) and telling SYSCON whether or not a password is required.

The fact that each NetWare file server, running NetWare versions prior to 4.0, maintains its own bindery can create a lot of administrative work in organizations with dozens or hundreds of file servers. If a supervisor wants to give a new user access to, say, six servers, he or she must log on to each server and follow the preceding steps. Wouldn't it be nice to be able to say simply: 'Here's the account name for this user. Give her access to these six file servers'? What's needed is some sort of "global" directory, so users and other objects are known to the entire internetwork rather than to a specific file server. NetWare Directory Services has that orientation.

In the *NetWare 4.0 Concepts* manual, Novell defines NetWare Directory Services as a "*global, distributed, replicated* database that maintains informa-

197

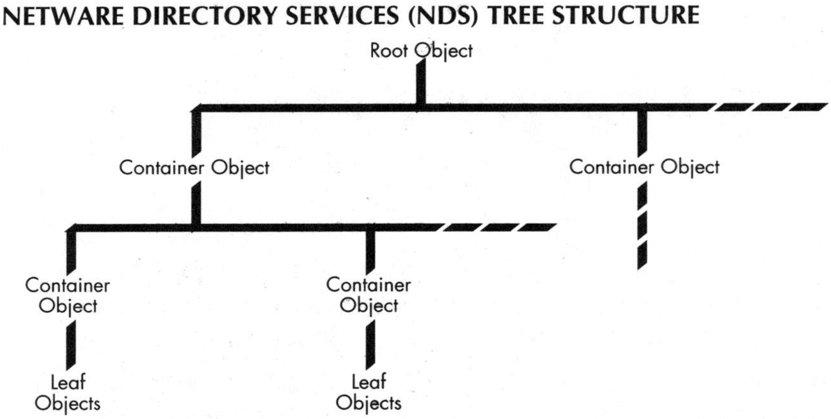

NETWARE DIRECTORY SERVICES (NDS) TREE STRUCTURE

Root Object

Container Object   Container Object

Container
Object

Container
Object

Leaf
Objects

Leaf
Objects

Figure 1. As the dotted lines imply, a directory tree is extensible in breadth and depth.

tion about, and provides access to, every resource on the network." The key words are global, distributed, and replicated. Global refers to the fact that entries in the NetWare Directory database are known to the entire network. Distributed means that portions of the NetWare Directory are replicated (a copy is kept) on various file servers. This setup ensures that, in the event of a file server crash, the NetWare Directory isn't lost. It also means that users won't be locked out of the network because one file server happens to be turned off or is otherwise inaccessible (if a wide-area link is down, for example).

While the bindery is a simple flat-file database, the newer NetWare Directory is hierarchical; it's logically organized in an inverted tree structure, with all key components branching out from the "root" at the top of the tree (see Figure 1). This tree structure also closely mimics the organizational charts of most companies, which permits network administrators to build a structure of account names that closely matches the company's organizational chart.

CATALOGING RESOURCES

Network resources such as users, groups, printers, print queues, and volumes, are cataloged in the Directory as objects. Objects can be either physical or logical. Some examples of physical objects are users and printers. Groups and print queues are logical objects.

NETWARE DIRECTORY SERVICES (NDS) OBJECT HIERARCHY

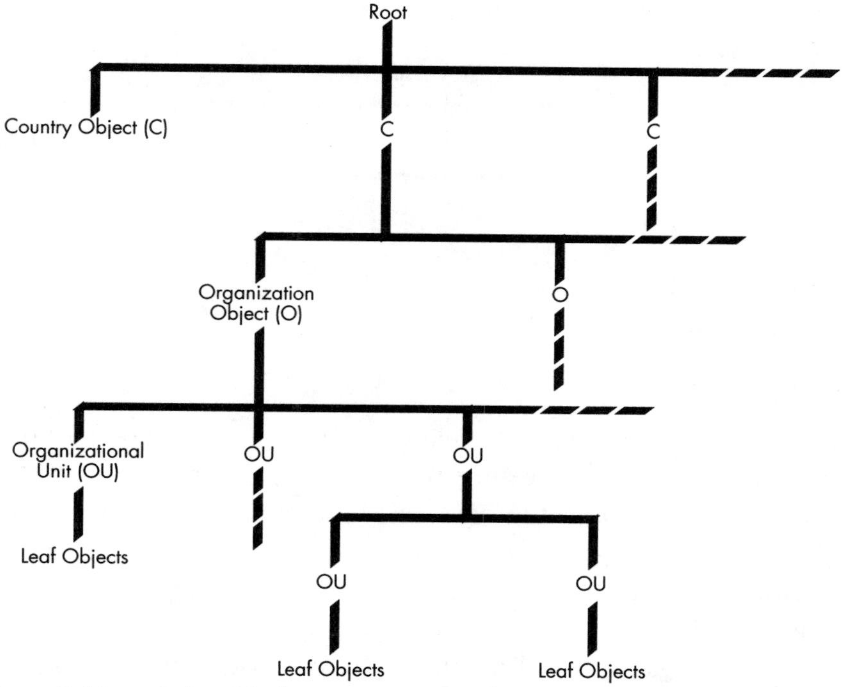

Figure 2. The relationship between various object types.

Objects can also be classified in another way: as *container objects* or *leaf objects*. Container objects are so named because they contain one or more other objects. Leaf objects don't contain any other objects; they're at the ends of branches, hence the "leaf" designation. Some examples of leaf objects include users, NetWare servers, volumes, and print queues.

An object consists of categories of information, called *properties*. Some properties of a user object, for example, include login name, password restrictions, and group membership.

The container objects can be categorized into three types: the country object, the organization object, and the organizational unit. The *country object* is the highest-level container object (next to the root object) in the Directory (see Figure 2). The country object is optional, and it is not automatically created as part of the NetWare 4.x default server installation.

The *organization object* is one level below the country object (if country

A SAMPLE DIRECTORY

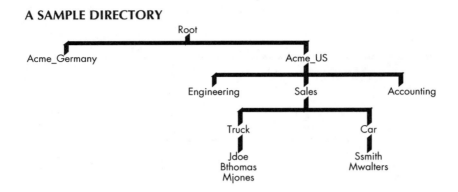

Figure 3. A portion of the NDS directory tree for Acme Auto Co.

objects are used; otherwise it's directly below the root object). There must be at least one organization object in the directory—it's not optional. You would typically use the organization object to designate your company or organization (university or government agency, for example).

A level below the organization object is the *organizational unit.* It can be used to represent a division within your company or organization. There can be several levels of organizational units, so you can use them to designate departments or workgroups.

Note that there can be only one level of country objects (if you use country objects) and one level of organization objects. As mentioned earlier, there can be several levels of organizational unit objects.

Figure 3 shows part of a directory tree for a hypothetical organization, the Acme Auto Company. In this example, the country object is not used, so the organization object occupies the level just below the root object. Acme has operations in Germany and the United States, and the creators of the directory tree chose to use two organization objects: Acme_Germany and Acme_US. Acme_US has three divisions—Engineering, Sales, and Accounting—so organizational unit objects are used to represent them.

Each organizational unit can have subgroups. For example, in the figure, Sales is divided into truck and car departments, so another level of organizational unit objects is used for these. Finally, we get to the users in these departments, who are represented by leaf objects. Each user's login name, which on many NetWare LANs is made up of the user's first initial and last name, is listed.

An object's position within the directory tree is known as its context. In Figure 3, the context for user John Doe is TRUCK.SALES.ACME_US. Most leaf objects have a common name, and for user objects, the common name is the login name.

What Novell refers to as an object's complete name is formed by concatenating the object's common name with its context. In our example, John Doe's complete name is JDOE.TRUCK.SALES.ACME_US.

NetWare Directory Services, Part II

Last chapter, the Tutorial began to explore Novell's NetWare Directory Services (NDS). That tutorial covered much of the basic NDS terminology and examined NDS' hierarchical structure, which resembles an inverted tree. This chapter explores the information in the NDS directory tree, which is distributed and replicated across the network.

The NDS directory is distributed for two major reasons: security and performance. Just as with the NetWare bindery, used in NetWare 3.x and earlier versions, the directory is the repository of all the information NetWare has about users, and it uses that information to control access to NetWare resources. If the directory were lost, no one, including the network Supervisor, would be able to log in to the network. Thus, it's important to have more than one copy of the directory, just in case something happens to the original.

Performance, too, is improved by replicating the directory, particularly in wide area networks. If someone were to log in on a network segment that didn't hold the directory, it could take some time to authenticate the user. Having a copy of the directory reside in each LAN segment eliminates the performance issues.

BREAK IT UP

For large networks, which have a correspondingly large directory, it could be unwieldy to simply have replicas of the entire directory database stored in many different places. Instead, NDS uses a distributed approach, in which the overall database is broken into portions known as *partitions*. (Don't confuse directory partitions with disk drive partitions, however.)

Directory partitioning lets NDS distribute portions of the NDS directory database among the various NetWare 4.x file servers in the internetwork. This arrangement means each file server isn't burdened with storing the entire

NDS DIRECTORY PARTITIONING

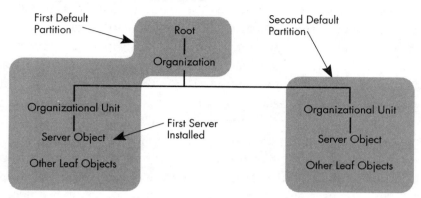

Figure 1. Here is an NDS directory tree with two partitions. The first NetWare 4.x server to be installed is the one on the left, so the installation creates the partition on the left. When a second server is installed later, a new partition is created.

directory database; a given file server might have only a single image of a directory partition, known as a *replica* of the partition.

Figure 1 is an example of how a directory tree might be partitioned, and how partitions are created by default, during the installation of NetWare 4.x file servers. In this figure, the partitions are the areas with a white background. Each partition consists of a container object and all objects contained within it.

IT'S AUTOMATIC

When the first NetWare 4.x file server is installed, the NetWare installation program will automatically create the first partition. The Root object is always included in the first partition.

Whenever an additional NetWare 4.x server is installed in a new container object, the installation program will, by default, create a new partition. This step is also illustrated in Figure 1.

As mentioned earlier, a partition replica is a copy, or image, of a partition. Only one *master replica* can exist for each partition, but you can also have other types of replicas, known as *read/write replicas* and *read-only replicas*. You can have as many of these replicas as you want.

You can view, but not modify, directory information in a read-only replica. Thus, NDS could consult a read-only replica to authenticate a user logging in to the network. Read/write replicas can be updated, so a network manager could add or delete objects within a partition using a read/write replica. Changes to a partition itself, however, can only be made by operating on the partition's master replica. A network supervisor would use the NetWare administrator graphical (Windows-based) utility or the text-based partition manager utility (for DOS-based workstations) to manage partitions and replicas.

The installation program places a master replica of the partition on the first server installed in a container object. If additional servers are installed in the same container object, the installation program places a read/write replica on those servers. By putting two or more servers into a container object, you automatically provide fault tolerance for that directory partition.

When you install a NetWare 4.x server, the installation program checks the network segments to which the server is connected. If it detects existing NDS directory trees, it accumulates the names of these trees. Then you have the option to make the new server part of whichever trees you select.

Once you've told the installation program which directory tree you want the server installed in, you then specify what the server's *context*, or location, in the directory structure, should be. You can specify a context that's within an existing directory partition or choose a new context. In the latter case, the installation program will create a new container object matching the new context, create a new partition, place the container object into the partition, create the new server object (the NetWare 4.x file server you're installing), and place the server object into the newly created container object. It will also create a master replica of the new partition, placing it on the new file server.

IS IT CONSISTENT?

To ensure that read/write replicas and read-only replicas are up to date with respect to their master replicas, servers holding NDS partition replicas frequently compare notes to check for inconsistencies. Any replica that is out of date gets updated from the master replica.

How does does a server know if a replica is out of date, compared to its master? Apparently replicas get time and date stamps, just as conventional files do, and any replica with a time stamp older than its corresponding master replica gets updated.

WHAT TIME IS IT?

It's therefore crucial that all NDS servers be synchronized with each other. In fact, this task is so important that Novell offers several different strategies you can pick from to keep all your servers in sync.

In the *single-reference time server* model, only one server in the entire directory tree is designated as the time server. If you elect to use this model, you designate all other servers as *secondary time servers*. Secondary time servers periodically synchronize themselves with the single-reference time server. When network clients log in, they will have their clocks synchronized to the "nearest" secondary server (or to the single-reference time server, if that happens to be the nearest server).

Servers can use either Novell's Service Advertising Protocol (SAP) to share time information, or servers can be custom-configured to contact specific servers for time updates. The simplest approach (and the default) is to use SAP. For large networks, where frequent SAP broadcasts would be a nuisance, Novell recommends the custom-configured method.

Without going into all the details related to time synchronization, assume that if yours is a small LAN with only a handful of servers, the single-reference time server with SAP communications should probably be your choice—that's the default. For large networks, particularly those with WAN connections, you'll want to carefully study the NetWare documentation to plot your time synchronization strategy.

DEJA VU?

Now for a short digression: Some years ago, a Macintosh networking product named DataClub came to market. DataClub was a "virtual server" that could substitute for an AppleShare server. It represented a clever blending of the peer-to-peer and client-server conceptual models, as data files resided on individual users' Macs throughout the network, yet the DataClub server appeared as an icon on the Macintosh desktop as if it were a single disk volume.

The tough technical problem that DataClub's designers had to tackle was how to build and maintain a distributed directory that could keep track of all those files. The solution: Each Mac that participated in the data "club" had a copy of the directory for the DataClub volume.

This solution presented a problem of its own, however, as any time you distribute a copy of something throughout a network you run the risk that some of the copies aren't in sync with the original. One way to make sure everything is in sync is to immediately update all copies the moment the original changes. But this approach could really slow file access to a crawl. Moreover, Macs that happen to be turned off during a directory update would miss the update and be left with old information.

IT'S A LITTLE FUZZY

The DataClub designers' solution was to design a system where individual Macs on the network would periodically exchange directory information, to get copies of the directory in sync again. The designers referred to this technique as "fuzzy consistency". In other words, at any given moment, one or more copies of the directory might be inconsistent, but over time the system tended toward consistency. It was a clever and technically innovative solution to a messy problem.

It wasn't long before the company that developed DataClub was acquired by Novell. Novell still sells DataClub for the Macintosh.

There are some differences between DataClub's directory of files and the NDS directory of network resource objects. For one thing, each Mac running DataClub has an entire copy of the DataClub volume directory, whereas with NDS the total NDS directory tree is broken up into partitions, so each server need not maintain a copy of the entire directory tree. This approach is probably appropriate, as the DataClub method is best for small networks, while NDS can work with very large networks.

Still, the way that replicas of NDS partitions periodically get updated from master replicas is eerily similar to the way DataClub directory copies get updated. Is DataClub's "fuzzy consistency" one of the enabling technologies behind Novell's NetWare Directory Services? I wonder.

Getting Connected, Part I

"Our company is moving to a new building and I'm not sure if we need Category 3 or Category 5 cable. Does anyone have advice?" "Can anyone recommend a program that will help me monitor my file server?"

These and other questions are asked—and answered—each month in the *LAN Magazine* forum on the CompuServe Information Service. But what is CompuServe? How do you get connected? And how do you find what you need?

In this "Tutorial," I'll describe the whys and wheres of CompuServe.

CompuServe Information Service is the largest on-line commercial service provider in the world. Some people liken it to a really huge BBS (Bulletin Board System) and some liken it to an organized Internet. Both comparisons are somewhat correct.

CompuServe, like any electronic meeting place, has different areas set aside for people to talk about their particular areas of interest. In addition to those areas ("forums" in CompuServe parlance) CompuServe also has a number of magazine, periodical, and newspaper dataases available for searching that focus on such topics as business, computers, and investments. It also has news, sports, and weather reports available. As of this writing, CompuServe has over 2.2 million members worldwide.

GETTING AN ACCOUNT

In order to get connected to CompuServe you need a computer, a modem, and some communications software. Any speed modem will do. At the present time, CompuServe hardware handles speeds from 300bps to 14,400bps, and it is working on 28,800bps connectivity to be available in the near future.

Many software and hardware vendors provide support on the service, and they often include a coupon in their boxes for credit on new CompuServe accounts. You can also call CompuServe directly, at (800) 848-8199, within the United States, or (614) 457-8650. When you sign up you get a startup kit that includes a CompuServe Information Manager (CIM) appropriate for DOS, Windows, or Macintosh. CIM is communications software and navigation software in one program. You can also sign up according to the directions in the *LAN Magazine* forum ad that we often run in the magazine.

IF YOU ARE NOT A COMPUSERVE MEMBER

To join CompuServe and access the *LAN Magazine* forum, set your communications software to 7 data bits, even parity, 1 stop bit. Select your baud rate and find your local CompuServe access number by calling 1-800-635-6225. Respond to the CompuServe prompts as follows:

Host Name: CIS User ID Number: 177000,5605 Password: COMPUSERVE Agreement: LANSIGNUP Serial No: 93010

You will be prompted for billing information and receive a permanent User ID and temporary password online. CompuServe Information Service may be reached at 1-800-848-8199 or 1-614-457-8650.

HOUSE OF COMPUSERVE

When you go to a forum, imagine that you have just stepped into the hallway of a house. There are doors to rooms leading off each side of the hallway. Those doors are marked Announcements, Messages, Libraries, Conference Rooms, and Member Directory.

The Announcements area contains information for new members (you'll be greeted with this automatically when you enter a forum), and information on the rules you'll be expected to follow when you join the forum (if any). In the *LAN Magazine* forum, the rules are in POLICY.TXT in Library 1/General Information. There are also announcements about the other room areas, as well as the Sysops (SYStem OPerators, the people in charge of the forum).

The Messages area will be subdivided into logical areas for that forum. Table 1 and Table 2 contain lists of LANMAG message and library sections.

The message areas are not "realtime." In other words, you don't go on-line

TABLE 1. *LAN MAGAZINE* FORUM MESSAGE SECTIONS
1. General information
2. Client-server
3. Peer-to-peer
4. Interoperability
5. Cabling topologies
6. Operating systems
7. Hardware
8. Software
9. LAN basics
10. Show/meeting reports
11. Management/careers
12. Technology issues
15. Letters to editors
16. Guests
17. The wiring closet

TABLE 2. *LAN MAGAZINE* FORUM LIBRARY SECTIONS
1. General information
2. Reviews
3. Features
4. Guests and interviews
7. Forum member biographies
8. User-to-user
9. LAN basics
10. Thread archives
16. Vendor announcements

and stay on-line to talk with other people. Someone posts a message and other people read that message and respond—or not—at any time convenient to them.

Conference rooms are areas where you talk "real-time" with other members. Many forums have regularly scheduled conferences and members are encouraged to participate.

The Member Directory is a place where you can post some information about yourself and read information about others. The *LAN Magazine* forum encourages people to read about other members—and share information about themselves—via a file called LANBIO.TXT in Library 7/Forum member biographies.

I'M ON-LINE!

Now that you have an account, you need to learn to get around and find all the resources that you're looking for. CompuServe is navigated by GO words (In the CIM programs, GO is a menu option).

Most forums ask you to "Join" the forum. This does not mean you will incur

MESSAGES ARE POSTED IN THREADS

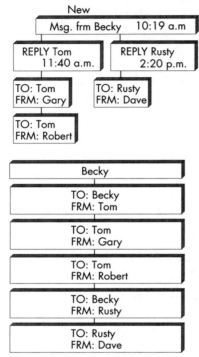

Figure 1. Messages are posted on CompuServe in a "threaded" manner. That is, replies are connected to the messages they reply to, creating numerous threads of postings. When you read postings, then, you will get them in the order in which they were created within each thread.

USERS READ THE MESSAGES LINEARLY

Figure 2. When the group of message threads is translated into a linear listing for you to read, this is the order in which you will read them. First you read Becky's message, then you'll follow the thread of Tom's reply to Becky, and the messages that were then sent to Tom. Then you read the thread started by Rusty's reply.

any additional charges or get on someone's junk mailing list. It's strictly for internal forum accounting purposes. Join away.

The first place you want to GO is PRACTICE. The Practice forum is set up for people to post their first "This is a test" message and get on their electronic feet. When you are in the PRACTICE forum, your connect-time charges are suspended.

Try downloading a file from one of the Practice forum libraries. Library 1/Forum Help & Info has a file called COMPRS.DOC that you might find useful. It has information about the various compression programs that are commonly used on CompuServe. This is an ASCII text file that you can read on-line or download to your hard disk.

If you're not sure how to download a file, or you have another question, leave a message (addressed to All or Sysop) on the forum, and the Sysop or a knowledgeable user will be by shortly to help you. The goal on most forums on CompuServe is to deliver an answer within 24 hours. For many questions it may take considerably less time, but for others, it might be a couple of days. It's important for you to check for a response frequently.

MESSAGE THREADING

Messages on CompuServe are "threaded." That means that you'll not only read messages in the order they are posted, but also in the order they are created in reference to the original message (see Figure 1).

The way you'll actually read these messages is shown in Figure 2. Threading makes it easy to follow conversations on CompuServe.

When replying to a message, it's important to use the Reply function of your software, rather than the Write function, so that the messages can remain threaded.

Each forum can hold a set number of messages; the actual number varies by forum. On the *LAN Magazine* forum, the capacity is about 500 messages, that number will vary by forum.

When someone posts the 501st message on the *LAN Magazine* forum, the oldest message is "bumped" off the forum into the bit bucket. In CompuServe terms, the message "scrolls" off the forum.

The length of time a message stays on a CompuServe forum is measured in days or weeks and depends on the volume of message traffic, which varies for each forum. This is called the "scroll rate." The scroll rate on the *LAN Magazine* forum varies from four days to two weeks. Some forums are so busy they have a 2-day to 3-day scroll rate, which is why it's important to check back for answers within 48 hours.

SYSOPS

The Sysops on CompuServe are not CompuServe employees unless that fact is specifically stated. Each forum tends to have its own atmosphere or "flavor" depending on its Sysop.

In the *LAN Magazine* forum, the current Sysops are Robert Richardson and Tom Henderson. They work to create a friendly and helpful atmosphere. Sysops on CompuServe manage the message base, manage the libraries, and

Getting Connected, Part II

This tutorial is the second in our two-part series about going online with CompuServe Information Service. Last chapter we talked about ways to get CompuServe accounts, navigate around the service, send messages, and join forums. This chapter, we'll let you in on some CompuServe "etiquette," then talk about how you can save time and money when using CompuServe by using autonavigator programs.

MESSAGE MANNERS

Now that you're on-line and ready to commune with your fellow techheads, here are some guidelines and suggestions to help you make the most of CompuServe messaging.

1. *Be polite.* Remember, no one knows you except by what you write. if you get involved in a heated conversation and you feel like the other person has the IQ of a box of rocks, take a break and cool down. Also, swearing is not allowed. If you want to make a point, be creative and use other expressions or words, or substitute letters with punctuation marks (like in the comics). Don't forget that anyone with a CompuServe account can access public forums, including children.

   Also, double-check your messages before you post them. The CompuServe software does not filter messages, nor can a Sysop edit any message. A Sysop, however, can move a message out of public sight if it is deemed grossly offensive or inappropriate.

2. *Stick to the point.* Say enough to get your idea across, and don't ramble. For messages in which you are seeking specific technical advice, be sure to include version or revision numbers.

3. *Limit quotebacks.* When replying to a message, people often like to quote part of the original message as a memory jogger. This is fine, and helpful if you are trying to follow a particularly busy thread. But do not quote back the entire message, or an entire paragraph.

4. *Once is enough.* Never post a message in more than one section of a forum, or more than one forum in a group (such as Microsoft or Novell). Many people read a complete forum or group, and they resent having to waste time and money reading the same message twice.

   If you do not receive a response to your message within two days in a busy forum, then it is OK to post the message in another forum in that same group. The *LAN Magazine* forum is not really intended for urgent technical support, so some messages may not receive a reply until three or four days after posting. Don't worry, though. If no one on the forum has the expertise to help you, the Sysop should be able to suggest another forum where you can get an answer.

5. *No attacks.* Personal attacks are not allowed on CompuServe. If you disagree with what a person says, make sure you disagree with the idea, not the person.

6. *Forget the long signatures.* CompuServe is not the place for Internet-style signature lines. Remember, people are paying for connect time to read or download your messages.

7. *Don't ask for individual advice via e-mail from any Sysop on CompuServe.* That is called "consulting" and it completely misses the purpose of CompuServe. A message posted on a public forum will garner more points of view, spark other discussions, and be a better learning tool for you and other readers.

Vendors who want to sell something on CompuServe must get a store in the service's shopping mall area. CompuServe forum message areas are not an appropriate place to sell your products. *LAN Magazine* realizes that running a network often involves a close relationship with vendors, and a library section has been set aside in the *LAN Magazine* forum where vendors can upload press releases and shareware authors can upload informational files. For *LAN Magazine* vendor guidelines, download POLICY.TXT in Library I/General

Information. Vendors posing as end users and recommending their own products will be shot.

TIME IS MONEY

Many network managers wish for a 36-hour day or an assistant. You might think that adding CompuServe to your routine is the last thing you need. Wrong. Nearly every regular forum participant will tell you that an hour or two of reading messages on the right forums can save you hours of head-banging.

But you need to approach this task in the right way. CompuServe's own software, the CIMs (CompuServe Information Managers), are a great "getting-started" tool. But as you become comfortable with the service and come to depend on it for information, it's time to throw out the CIMs and get some different tools. These tools will help you accomplish the same amount of message-reading in less than half the time.

USING AUTONAV

The tools you need to perform this trick are referred to as autonavigators—autonavs or short—or autopilot programs. They do what their name implies (automatically navigate CompuServe), plus a lot more.

When you use an autonav program, you first specify which forum messages or library files you would like to read or download. Then the program logs onto CompuServe, downloads the appropriate messages or files, and disconnects. Since you can't read at 2,400bps or faster, you might as well download the messages at your modem's top speed for reading later, when you are not paying for connect time.

Once you have finished reading and preparing replies, you use the autonav program to log back on and upload your messages. Not only does this save you money, it gives you a chance to double-check your messages before you post them.

Just as many remote e-mail programs provide filters so you don't have to download every e-mail message when you're on the road, autonavs let you do some filtering before you download messages from a forum. You can decide if

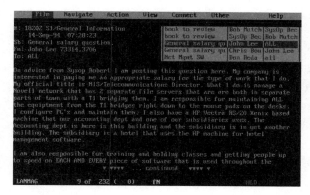

NAVIGATING HELP: With autonavigator programs, you can read and respond to messages off-line, to save both time and money. RECON, available in the TAPCIS forum, gives CompuServe a friendly face.

you want to read all of the messages in a forum, or all the messages from certain sections, or if you simply want to scan the headers in specific sections to see what looks interesting.

The interface used on the CIM products has its advantages, but speed in going from message to message, and especially from one forum to the next, is not one of them. Autonav programs read all or most of the messages from a forum into your computer's memory at one time, making it much faster to go from one message to the next when you read them later.

This difference in speed is dramatic. A forum that might have taken an hour to read on-line with a CIM product can take 20 minutes to a half-hour to read with an autonav program. Instead of spending an hour of connect time, you've spent maybe two or three minutes.

Furthermore, many autonav programs have library management capabilities built-in, so it takes only a couple of keystrokes to download a file that you might otherwise have to spend five or 10 minutes searching for with a CIM product.

Another capability is message management. Since many forums have a three-day to four-day scroll rate (the time a message remains on the forum until it is bumped off by the newer messages), you may see a message you want to read, but not have the time to read it until it's too late. With an autonav program you can download the messages to your hard disk to read at your leisure.

AUTONAV PRODUCTS

Plenty of CompuServe autonav programs are available, and since many of them are shareware, it's easy to evaluate them before you buy. Many are supported on a forum or a section of a forum, and plenty of knowledgeable users are around to answer questions. If your favorite platform isn't listed here, it's easy enough to find a forum where you can make inquiries, using the FIND command.

Autonav programs are available for most platforms. Two popular DOS-based autonav programs are TAPCIS (The Access Program, CompuServe Information Service) and OzCIS. Both can run under Windows or OS/2 if you prefer to run in a GUI environment. And both are shareware programs that can be downloaded from their own CompuServe forums (GO TAPCIS and GO OZCIS).

TAPCIS is arguably the easiest of the DOS-based autonav programs to set up and use, and it requires fewer system resources than OZCIS. On the other hand, OZCIS has more sophisticated built-in features. To get those same features with TAPCIS, you can use an add-on program called RECON (visit the TAPCIS forum for more details; also see figure), which is easy-to-use and is one of the best-supported shareware programs around.

Golden CommPass is the only OS/2-based autonav available at the time of this writing. It is a commercial program available for $99 from Creative Systems Programming (Mount Laurel, NJ). Another product, XC, is the only Unix-based autonav program. It is available for free on the Unix Forum (GO UNIXFO) as a self-extracting ASCII file, or a Gzipped tar archive.

A few Windows-based autonav programs are available, but they have received mixed reviews regarding reliability and speed.

There is only one Macintosh-based autonav available, CompuServe Navigator. You can order it online from CompuServe (GO ORDER); the list price is $70. Complete information about where to download or purchase these programs, along with short reviews, can be found in the AUTOP.INF file in Library I/general Information of the *LAN Magazine* forum.

GET GOING

CompuServe can be a significant resource for network managers, many of whom rely on technical support forums as a first-line resource. For the cost of a few minutes of connect time, they often save their companies hundreds of dollars that would otherwise be spent on technical support calls or contracts. "Lurking," or reading what others are saying without posting any messages, can often accomplish the same thing.

Early last year on the *LAN Magazine* forum, a schoolteacher who was setting up a network lab came to the forum to double-check his contractor's wiring recommendation. Some of the forum's more knowledgeable wiring experts showed him that the contractor was wrong, and he ended up saving a bundle for his school. How sure are you about the advice you're getting?

Threaded Conversation Databases

Groups that work together on a project or process often wish to record, share, track, and refer back to their work. Producing a manual (or a magazine), tracking a complex order or service transaction, and storing histories of problems and their solutions are just a few ways that strung-together chains or threads of conversations have proven their usefulness to organizations.

The basic feature list for a product that collaborators would find useful includes:

- a central storage location to maintain consistency;
- a structuring system that captures messages and responses in order and in the right context;
- remote access to the message store for users;
- control over privacy and access;
- the ability to move, reorder, delete, and duplicate messages;
- the ability to attach non-text documents, such as spreadsheet files, images, and audio clips, to messages and the ability to view or otherwise access them.

Two unrelated technologies—databases and e-mail—are tempting prospects for the job of recording, sharing, and retrieving collaborative work. Unfortunately, both candidates are not quite fight for the job, though it's not immediately obvious why.

WHY E-MAIL CAN'T HANDLE IT

E-mail is a point-to-point technology; an e-mail post office is a transient storage facility, designed to move messages in and out rather than to keep them in one place. If only two people work on a project, an e-mail program with a reply function can serve as an adequate way to track the conversation. Each collaborator has a complete copy of both sides of the ongoing dialogue as the project moves forward. But there is not a single location for the data; responsibility for saving it, much less backing it up, can be clarified only by rules external to the e-mail program.

Now consider what happens with three collaborators, J, K, and L. First of all, there has to be an external rule that each collaborator will cc: the person they are not sending the message to: J messages K and cc:s L. Assume the best case—only one collaborator begins the process. Even if everyone responds to messages in a sort of token passing order, there will be at least one extra message with each "generation" of messages. Of course, in any actual situation, collaboration will not follow a strict synchronous turn-taking model and two people will reply simultaneously to a message. Then the problem of manually incorporating extra messages into the two-way model thread begins to get complicated.

The number of superfluous messages in each generation increases with each additional collaborator. More importantly, the problems of synchronizing responses, manually reordering messages (which are, after all, simply sections of text with a message header), and navigating a long text document without markers and jumping-off points are subject to a sort of combinatorial explosion with additional collaborators. In a very short time, the collaborative message store, which is no more than an undifferentiated text file, will become unmanageable. Using e-mail to track a collaboration involving more than a handful of active participants requires a mass of external rules and a great deal of administrative effort.

CAN DATABASE FUNCTIONS HELP?

Databases have the advantage of storing data in a single place (or in a manageable collection of places). There are two familiar and well-understood database models that can be useful for storing textual data—field-oriented databases and free-form text databases. Field-oriented databases can have their components linked together logically, based on common fields (the relational model), or tied together with pointers (the hierarchical and network models). They are most useful for storing and retrieving sizable chunks of text when each of the chunks or messages is tied to a record with other, relatively short, fields, which can be used for indexing or sorting the database. (Sorting a large collection of messages by their titles or subjects, much less by their contents, would rarely be a useful way to present or browse them.) Typical field-oriented databases have limited functions for searching or otherwise manipulating the content of long text fields.

Free-form text databases usually make no attempt to break up a large body of text; they simply index all the nontrivial words in the text and expedite locating those words. Using Boolean operators to search a massive text can be very fruitful. For example, in a series of messages that track the steps of a LAN enhancement project, searching for "(Category or Type) and (3 or 4 or 5) or coaxial)" should find any messages discussing Ethernet cabling specifications. Such searches work well regardless of how skillfully the subject of the message was named and how well the message focused on a single subject.

Without field-oriented functionality, however, an indexed free-form text file is hard to navigate and only amenable to collaborating people with external rules and a substantial amount of external administration—for example, putting dates on messages and ordering them.

An additional tactic for categorizing pieces of text is assigning keywords— words that characterize the content of the text in some way and can be stored and searched separately. (Keywords can also be useful for keeping track of images and sounds that are not made up of text.) Though very large indexed text databases can be searched fast, the use of keywords can provide even faster performance.

Both database technologies can be useful for tracking threads of messages, but the messages need to be loaded into the database and presented to the collaborators. Establishing threads, notifying collaborators of updates, presenting maps of threads, and many other desirable functions would require custom programming in any of the standard database programs.

The combination of messaging and database functions has converged in several unrelated environments. The first widespread application of threaded conversations was for on-line bulletin board systems. Usenet newsgroups are threaded conversations. Forums or conferences on the commercial on-line services—CompuServe, Prodigy, and GEnie—also take this form. The most

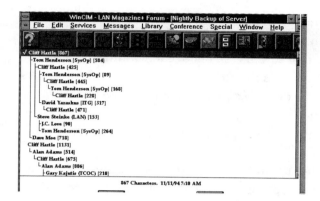

THREAD MAP: CompuServe's forums provide the ability to display a picture of on-line threaded conversations. This excerpt is from the LAN Magazine forum.

ambitious and elaborate commercially available product for tracking threaded conversations is Lotus Notes (Lotus Development, Cambridge, MA). Several other products, including Collabra Software's (Mountain View, CA) Collabra Share, Attachmate's (Bellevue, WA) OpenMind, and Trax Software's (Culver City, CA) TeamTalk have also been introduced to provide this function.

BASIC FUNCTIONS OF A THREADED-MESSAGE DATABASE

Displays. Entering messages must be straightforward, so a user who opens or logs on to the conversation database ought to be able to see a map of the conversation. A hierarchical display, similar to an outline, is a useful way to display sequences of comments and replies. Preset limits to the number of potential levels are probably undesirable. The ability to collapse some or all of the levels helps keep the overall structure clear.

Remote participation. Collaborators must be able to reach the message store over some kind of network. In addition, a gateway to regular e-mail products can let collaborators who don't have full access contribute.

Thread editing. People make mistakes. It ought to be easy to relocate a misplaced message or delete completely irrelevant ones. Actual messages don't always fit precisely in a threaded hierarchy. For instance, a single message may include two or more topics. It should be easy to duplicate a message and insert the copies at the places where they fit.

Scrolling. For large, ongoing threaded conversations, such as those on commercial on-line services, the day will arise when the space that the system has available runs out. For example, there may be a fixed number of message units allocated to a forum; when these slots are filled, each additional message bumps off an older one. This process is referred to as scrolling. A whole series of problems can ensue. It would be desirable to have configurable scrolling settings so that factors such as the message's position in a thread, the relative importance of a thread, or the author of a message could be factored into the scrolling behavior.

Once any message in a thread scrolls off, the meaningfulness of subsequent reply and commentary messages is apt to suffer, even if the title of the thread continues to be carried along.

THREAD DRIFT

A problem that fancy software features are not likely to solve soon has to do with the content of messages and the subject that is assigned to name a thread. Participants in on-line discussions sometimes refer to "thread drift" ironically, when they really mean that someone is drastically changing the subject.

Nevertheless, discussions can imperceptibly veer away from the original topic until the original name of the thread is a completely misleading guide to the content. More generally, there is nothing to stop participants in an unmoderated threaded conversation, or unskilled moderators, from using arbitrary subject names and wrecking the coherence of a conversation. Until the day that computers have the ability to interpret the meaning of sentences and paragraphs, which is nowhere in sight, external rules and human moderators/censors/editors will be necessary to keep threaded conversations coherent to their users.

Section IV

Interoperability

The Challenge of Interoperability

Interoperability is one of the hot buzz words in the network industry. Increasing larger and complex network environments are forcing network administrators to merge heterogeneous computing systems into interoperable wide area networks.

Unfortunately, discussions about interoperability are often clouded in rhetoric or vendor hype, with *multivendor interoperability* meaning different things to different people. For instance, interoperability could mean nothing more than straightforward plug-and-play compatibility, such as connectivity to Ethernet cabling, among different vendors' products. In this case, physical interoperability merely gives users the ability to connect one vendor's computing devices to another's over a network.

This isn't true interoperability, however: Many vendors' equipment, including Digital Equipment Corp. (DEC) VAXs, PCs, and Sun Microsystems' SPARCstations, can be connected to an Ethernet via network adapter cards. But it doesn't mean that VAXs running DECnet over Ethernet cabling can communicate with PCs on a Novell NetWare workgroup attached to the same wire. That's a far more complex task, involving gateways that convert one protocol to another.

Then what is multivendor interoperability? Here's a look at some of the issues involved.

AN INTERNETWORK PROBLEM

Before continuing, one point of clarification: Discussions about multivendor interoperability deal with large, so-called *global* or *enterprisewide* networks. It is in these internetworking environments, where a variety of far-flung (and dissimilar) workgroups communicate with each other, that multivendor interoperability becomes an important factor.

A look at the composition of networks as they "grow up" explains why this is so. Generally, the computers within a departmental workgroup are of a similar kind—all PCs, PS/2s, or compatibles, or all Macintoshes.

There's little diversity of equipment in these environments because people

225

working on similar types of projects and software applications typically use similar kinds of computers. In these situations, all devices operate under the same operating system (OS), network OS and protocol, and media-access method.

Without wide product diversity, multivendor interoperability is therefore not an issue. But the scenario changes radically when organizations begin connecting workgroups into large internetworks. In these environments, which can spread across a building, a campus, or a continent, it's unrealistic and often bad business sense to expect every worker to use the same kind of computer.

For instance, engineers often demand SPARCstations for their design work, while marketing personnel, especially those preparing technical documentation, find the Macintosh ideal for page layout. In addition, both types of users often require access to information stored on a host of some sort. Such an internetwork might also consist of an IBM mainframe communicating with group of PCs through IBM's Systems Network Architecture (SNA), plus a workgroup of PS/2s linked to a NetWare server via Novell's IPX/SPX.

When an organization wants to let users on these diverse networks communicate with each other, it must thus concern itself with interoperability among all these different vendors' products and protocols. For instance, this scenario demands connections between computing products from six separate vendors: DEC, IBM, Apple, Sun, SCO, and a manufacturer of minicomputers.

More importantly, however, this network would require interoperability between six widely differing networking protocols: DECnet, SNA, AppleTalk, Sun's Network File System (NFS), IPX/SPX, and Transmission Control Protocol/Internet Protocol (TCP/IP). All networking protocols, they nevertheless operate differently. The interoperability challenge is compounded by the fact that only one of these protocols—TCP/IP—is an "open" standard designed to support a variety of computing devices. The others were developed primarily to support the vendor's own products, not those of the vendor's competitors.

INTEROPERABILITY'S CAUSES

At the heart of these interoperability issues is the way in which vendors and standards-setting bodies have implemented their respective network protocol stacks. A protocol stack is a predefined, layered set of rules governing the way two networked computing devices exchange information over a transmission medium.

For two computers to communicate over a network, their respective protocol stacks must be able to understand each other's protocol "rules." When two computers communicate over a network, one of them originates data at the top of its associated protocol stack. This data is processed layer by layer down the stack with each layer appending information and/or instructions to the data, creating a frame, as it moves down the stack. The following figure illustrates this stack-to-stack communication process.

Unfortunately, not all protocol stacks are identical. Vendors and standards-setting groups have taken diverging approaches in developing the protocols they use today on networks. As a result, the various available protocol stacks offer services and capabilities that make them incompatible with other protocols.

For instance, compare the Open Systems Interconnect (OSI) reference model, an accepted "open" industry standard for interoperable multivendor networking, and the Xerox Network System (XNS) protocol stack. The two stacks are substantially different, with the most obvious being the number of layers within each protocol stack: The OSI model contains seven layers; the XNS hierarchy five.

Level 0 in the XNS stack corresponds more or less to OSI layers 1 and 2; it handles link-layer access and manipulation of the serial bit streams placed on the network transmission medium.

Level 1 corresponds somewhat to the OSI layer 3, which handles network traffic, while Level 2 protocols perform much the same functions as those in OSI layer 3, which deal with reliably transporting packets to their destinations, and OSI layer 4, which deals with interprocess communications.

Levels 3 and 4 provide capabilities similar to those offered by the uppermost two OSI layers—that is, handling data structuring, process-to-process interaction, and applications. XNS has no protocol that corresponds to OSI layer 5.

INTEROPERABILITY'S SOLUTIONS

Now consider what would happen if an OSI-based computer attempts to com-

THE PROTOCOL PROCESS

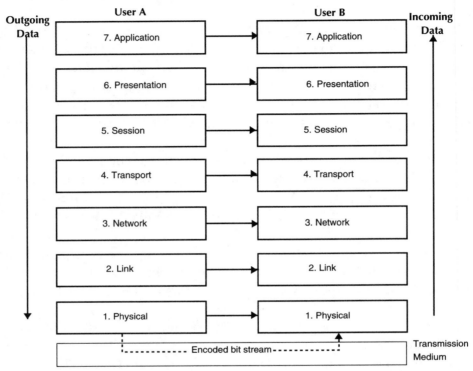

When two computers communicate over a network, one (User A) initiates the process by moving data layer-by-layer down its protocol stack, with each layer appending instructions to the data. After the data is transmitted over a transmission medium the receiving computer's protocol stack reverses this process.

municate directly with one operating under XNS. An XNS-based data packet wouldn't contain OSI layer 5 (session layer) instructions, which establish and terminate process-to-process communications between two computers.

This oversight means that a process running on one computer—for instance, a driver giving the host computer's processor access to a hard disk drive—would not be available to another computer over the network. Without this capability, file servers would not be able to offer remote storage facilities to clients.

How, then, do XNS computers communicate with OSI-based computers? Or OSI-based hosts with VAXs on a DECnet? Communication between computers running different protocols is often handled through devices called *gateways* or via transport services provided by a network operating system.

A gateway is an application-specific device that operates at all seven layers of the OSI protocol stack. In oversimplified terms, gateway hardware includes a processor, memory, and adapter cards. The hardware device maintains separate connections to the networks being combined—for instance, one an unshielded twisted-pair Ethernet cable network linked to a PC workgroup running Novell's IPX; a second workgroup connected to a 3270 coax network with the SNA services running on top.

The gateway runs software that performs protocol conversion on a layer-by-layer basis as necessary.

Network vendors have taken two primary approaches to implementing gateways. Some have developed software-only products that require adding NICs to personal computers or servers. Others market integrated, all-in-one "black boxes" for specific protocols—for example, AppleTalk-to-Ethernet gateways. Either way, the functionality of one system must be mapped to the capabilities of the other system.

In addition, many major network operating system vendors integrate protocol-encapsulation or conversion capabilities into their system software. For instance, Novell's NetWare 3.11 offers native, system-level IPX and TCP/IP transport services.

One protocol may also be *encapsulated* into another. For example, AppleTalk protocols are often wrapped in TCP/IP packets in a process called *tunneling,* which lets Mac users to access TCP/IP services.

These methods provide varying degrees of multivendor interoperability, but none provides a complete answer. Emerging technologies based on the OSI model promise to take interoperability to even higher levels over the next several years.

TCP/IP Protocol Suite

Just about everyone in the networking industry talks about interoperability; the U.S. Department of Defense (DoD), in the guise of the ARPANET (Advanced Research Projects Agency Network) project, actually did something about it when it created the Transmission Control Protocol/Internet Protocol (TCP/IP) family of networking protocols.

TCP/IP is the DoD's answer to connecting its rapidly proliferating—and widely dissimilar—computers and networks into a loosely associated wide area network (now called the Internet). TCP/IP is the DoD's vehicle for providing distributed computing capabilities across a large area.

TCP/IP might also be called the less talented but still much in demand ugly stepsister to the International Standards Organization's (ISO) emerging Open System Interconnection (OSI) protocols. The OSI standards, which vendors are only now, after 10 years of standards-setting work, beginning to incorporate into their networking products promise to eventually overshadow TCP/IP. This eclipse is still several years away, however, and TCP/IP remains the central piece in the complex interoperability puzzle.

A PLENITUDE OF PROTOCOLS

As its two-part name implies, TCP/IP encompasses more than one protocol. It includes a range of protocols that provide distinct services and capabilities necessary for communication between and control of otherwise incompatible computers and networks. In addition to the Transmission Control Protocol (TCP) and Internet Protocol (IP), these include the File Transfer Protocol (FTP), the Simple Mail Transfer Protocol (SMTP), the Internet Control Message Protocol (ICMP), and the Simple Network Management Protocol (SNMP).

Other protocols within the TCP/IP family are the Address Resolution Protocol (ARP), the Reverse Address Resolution Protocol (RARP), the Exterior

230

Gateway Protocol (EGP), and the User Datagram Protocol (UDP). IP, TCP, FTP, SMTP, and Telnet were part of the original DoD military standard, TCP/IP protocols suite promulgated in the late 1970s. Although TCP/IP was the brainchild of and for the military, it has become the de facto protocol for general-purpose intersystem communication.

THE TCP/IP FRAMEWORK

The body of standards making up the TCP/IP suite fit within a four-layer (network access, internet, host-to-host, and process layers) communications framework, shown in the next figure. Before examining these layers individually, however, it's important to first understand several other concepts.

The DoD based its model of data communication on three agents, called processes, hosts, and networks, with processes as the fundamental communications entities. Processes are executed on hosts, which are internetworked computers that can support multiple processes. Hosts in turn communicate with each other via a network. Successful completion of an operation on the internet requires action by all three agents.

The transfer of data from one process to another requires first getting the data to the host in which the process resides, then to the process within the host. In this model, a communications facility must be concerned only with routing data between hosts, with the hosts concerned with directing data to processes.

The network-access layer handles the exchange of data among a host, the network that host is attached to, and a host within the same network. The sending host provides the network with the network address of the receiving host to ensure that the network routes the data properly. The TCP/IP network-access layer services correspond to those provided by the physical, data-link, and parts of the network layers in the OSI reference model.

The specific physical, or media-access, protocol used to put TCP/IP data on the wire is independent of TCP/IP's top three layers. This means that TCP/IP can operate over virtually any media-access protocol, including Ethernet, Token Ring, or FDDI.

The separation of the physical-layer functions from the higher layers also

TCP/IP ARCHITECTURE

Process Layer

FTP

SMTP

TELNET

Host-to-Host Layer

TCP

Internet Layer

IP

Network Access

Layer

The TCP/IP body fits within a four-layer framework.

means that the services provided by the internet, host-to-host, and process layers are not affected by the specifics of the underlying network protocol used. The same high-level software can function properly regardless of the network type a host is connected to.

The internet layer provides services that permit data to traverse hosts residing on multiple networks. The internet routing protocol runs not only on "local" hosts, but also on gateways that connect two networks. A gateway's primary responsibility is to relay data from one network to the other, making sure it gets to the appropriate destination host.

The host-to-host layer ensures the reliability of the data and between two TCP/IP hosts. And the process layer provides protocols needed to support various end-user applications, such as file transfer or electronic mail.

THE TCP/IP PROTOCOLS

Each TCP/IP protocol provides a specific service or set of services to move data from one computer to network to another. The services some of these pro-

OSI AND TCP/IP COMPARED

OSI	TCP/IP
Application	Process
Presentation	
Session	
Transport	Host-to Host
Network	Internet
Data Link	Network Access
Physical	

The TCP/IP network-access layer services correspond to those provided by the physical, data-link, and parts of the network layers in the OSI reference model

vide—the File Transfer Protocol (FTP), for instance—are self-explanatory. Others aren't so obvious.

In the lexicon of the TCP/IP world, an interconnected set of networks is called an internet; the Internet Protocol (IP) is responsible for accepting segmented data (in the form of a Protocol Data Unit, or PDU) from a host computer and sending it across the internet through the required gateways until the data reaches its destination.

The IP delivery process provides what is known as an unreliable connectionless service; proper delivery is not guaranteed by IP. Even PDUs that are delivered may arrive at the destinations out of sequence. TCP must ensure reliable delivery of PDUs. TCP provides the transport mechanism that ensure that data is delivered error-free, in the order it was sent, and without loss or duplication.

TCP's basic role is providing reliable end-to-end data transfer between two processes, called transport users (these include FTP and SMTP). In specific terms, the TCP standard describes five levels of service: multiplexing (the ability to support multiple users), connection management, data transport, error reporting, and a variety of special capabilities.

In the basic data-transfer process, a transport user such as FTP passes data to TCP, which encapsulates the data into a segment that contains user data and control information (e.g., the destination address). TCP ensures reliable data delivery by numbering outgoing segments sequentially and then having the destination TCP module acknowledge arrival by number. If segments arrive out of order, they can be reordered via sequence numbers, and if a segment fails to arrive, the destination TCP module will not acknowledge its receipt, and the sending TCP module resends it.

TCP allows the transport user to specify the quality of transmission service it requires, permits special urgent data transmissions, and provides security classifications that can be used in routing segments to data-encryption devices. In trying to provide high-quality transmission services, TCP attempts to optimize the underlying IP and network resources. Parameters available include timeout delays and message-delivery precedence. Interrupt-driven urgent transmissions include terminal-generated break characters and alarm conditions.

The services provided by TCP and IP are defined by primitives and parameters. A primitive is a mechanism for specifying the function to be performed while parameters are used to pass data and control information.

Only two primitives—SEND and DELIVER—are used to define the IP services. Parameters available with these primitives include source and destination host addresses, the recipient protocol (usually TCP), an identifier that distinguishes one user's data from another's, and user data.

TCP offers two primitives and associated parameters: service request and service response primitives. A TCP client sends service request primitives to TCP; TCP issues the service response primitives to the client. Many of these primitives set off an exchange of TCP segments between host processes or computers, and TCP passes the segments to IP in a SEND primitive and receives them from IP in a DELIVER primitive.

FILES AND TERMINALS

FTP exists to transfer a file or a portion of a file from one system to another under orders from an FTP user. Typically, a user executes FTP interactively through an operating system interface, which provides the input/output facilities that allow exchanging files between systems.

FTP options allow transferring ASCII and EBCDIC character sets and using transparent bit streams that permit exchanging any sort of data or text file. FTP also provides data-compression options and has password/identifier mechanisms for controlling user access.

SMTP provides the underlying capabilities for a network electronic mail facility. It does not, however, provide the user interface. Primarily, it provides mechanisms for transferring messages between separate systems. SMTP accepts e-mail messages prepared by a native mail facility (such as cc:Mail) and—making use of TCP to send and receive messages across the network—delivers them.

With SMTP, users can send mail to users anywhere in the local network as well as to those on the internet.

TELNET outlines a network terminal-emulation standard. It allows terminals to connect to and control applications running in a remote host just as if it were a local user of the host.

In implementation, TELNET takes two forms: user and server modules. The user module interacts with the terminal I/O module, providing translation of terminal characteristics into the network-specific codes and vice versa. The server module interacts with processes and applications, serving as a terminal handler to make remote terminals look as if they are local.

SNMP AND OTHER PROTOCOLS

Among the other TCP/IP protocols, one of the most widely applied is SNMP, the Simple Network Management Protocol. SNMP supports the exchange of network management messages among hosts, including a central host that is often called a network management console.

SNMP was designed to operate over UDP, the User Datagram Protocol. UDP operates at the same level as TCP, providing a connectionless service for the exchange of messages while avoiding the overhead of TCP's reliability facilities. It is useful in transaction-oriented applications.

ARP and RARP provide mechanisms for hosts to learn MAC and Internet addresses. The former allows a host to discover another host's MAC address, and the latter permits a host to find out its own Internet address, an important capability for diskless PCs without permanent ways to store their Internet addresses.

The Exterior Gateway Protocol allows neighboring gateways in different autonomous systems to exchange information about which networks are accessible via a particular gateway. Industry observers once predicted that most TCP/IP users will eventually migrate to OSI. The question is, when? Few commercially available products offer complete OSI functionality. Most OSI protocols remain in the standards-setting phase, and users continue to be satisfied with the level of service provided by TCP/IP.

Novell's MHS

In the early days of mail delivery, letters and packages were transported cross-country by the Pony Express. Although speedy, the Pony Express was not reliable, being subject to the whims of corrupt Pony Express employees and a few Indians.

In the early days of networks, e-mail was a luxury. Receiving quick messages electronically was useful, but not essential. Users paged electronically through long, boring memos from the company management, a minor improvement over reading them on paper. But as networks grew in complexity, and e-mail became more than quick messages or corporate memos, messages had to be delivered to local and remote users in a reliable, speedy, and economical manner.

Message Handling Service (MHS) is to e-mail what the U.S. Post Office is to a letter. As its name implies, MHS handles messages; it accepts the e-mail from the user, concerns itself with the details of addressing, transports the mail, and delivers it. MHS delivers a message whether the recipient is local or remote, and like the Postal Service, will attempt to deliver a message through difficult conditions.

MHS HISTORY

MHS is only one transportation system for e-mail, but it's very important. Others exist, including ISO's X.400, Microsoft's MAPI, and the new Vendor-Independent Messaging (VIM), a spec from Lotus, Apple, Borland, and Novell. Endorsed by Novell, MHS enjoys the largest market share. It facilitates communication among conflicting or incompatible e-mail packages. With vendors and competing standards roiling the e-mail market, MHS's simplicity and compatibility keep it alive when proprietary offerings are pushing their own incompatible transportation systems.

In 1987, Action Technologies released the original MHS to support its e-mail package, The Coordinator. MHS was quite advanced; it proved to be more popular than The Coordinator, and MHS became an open message transportation system for other e-mail vendors.

In 1991, Novell purchased MHS from Action. Novell then integrated MHS *natively* into NetWare, so MHS can run as a NetWare Loadable Module (NLM). But Action is still in the game; it offers MHS versions for Microsoft LAN Manager, Banyan VINES, 3Com 3+Share, and IBM PC LAN Program. So while MHS is bigger than NetWare, Novell is bigger than Action Technologies, and MHS for NetWare is still MHS's big ticket.

INSIDE MHS

MHS was designed as an electronic postal system to warehouse and route e-mail in the background of an e-mail application. Think of MHS as a package delivery service. When you bring a parcel to the delivery company's office, the counters and cashiers are all the same. Once you've properly packaged and addressed the parcel, the delivery company accepts it. It delivers the goods the best way, whether it's a railroad, an interstate highway, or air cargo.

MHS installations are analogous to the delivery service's counters; they are drop-off places where enveloped, addressed messages are processed and routed. MHS connectivity managers, like the delivery company's parcel sorters and handlers, receive, check, log, route, and queue messages for delivery.

MHS Transport Servers reliably transfer messages from one location to another; they are akin to the delivery company's trains, trucks, and airplanes. Finally, the transport servers use data communications links—the LAN or WAN—to deliver the messages.

MHS FROM THE USER END

People don't interact directly with MHS; their applications do. An MHS application packages the text in an MHS envelope, which contains a header plus the text or attached file, which can be ASCII or binary.

Each MHS message is placed in an envelope with a destination and return address. Addresses are two-part: username@workgroup-name. In each workgroup, a user name must be unique. Applications must have names as well (username.application-name@workgroup-name), but application names don't have to be shipped through MHS.

At the user's end, the e-mail software transports the message from the person's PC via the LAN to the MHS *host* and keeps that message safe until the addressee reads it. The MHS host waits to accept a message.

HOSTING MAIL

An *MHS* host is a standalone or networked PC running MHS. The host performs MHS functions and translates between the languages of MHS and the PC network. The host is networked, allowing an e-mail application to send mail to MHS, via the PC network. The host may also contain modems for communication with remote hosts.

Usually an entire LAN is defined as a single MHS host, regardless of the number of workstations on the LAN. Users who work at a host exchange messages among themselves. In a wide area MHS network, messages move from one host to another.

Plan a really big e-mail network, and you'll discover that with enough MHS hosts out there, you'll get tangled in an MHS snarl. Combatting the tendency toward e-mail traffic jams, MHS developers created a host of the hosts, or a *hub*, which performs the same functions as a regular host, except that it routes between other hosts and never talks directly with a front-end e-mail.

MAIL IN THREE PARTS

MHS uses three layers: a *directory manager*, a *connectivity manager*, and a *transport manager*.

The *directory manager* is like a directory assistance operator, containing a routing table with names and addresses of the users, hosts, and workgroups in its domain. However, the directory manager is not a true manager because it doesn't actively manage anything. It is a repository where configuration and routing information is stored. The network administrator manages it manually.

The next layer, the *connectivity manager*, manages the coordination of your local e-mail application with the MHS system. The connectivity manager provides what programmers call *hooks* that an e-mail application uses to communicate with MHS.

The connectivity manager running at each host periodically searches for incoming messages. If the message is for a local user, then the connectivity manager delivers it to a local mailbox. If the message is for a remote user, the connectivity manager consults its routing table and, if all is well, leaves it for the transport manager to deliver it to a remote host or gateway.

What if you had 50 pieces of mail for Denver? MHS's connectivity manager looks at the routing of the messages awaiting shipment and bundles those "envelopes" into a single "packet" for shipment, cutting most of the overhead required for transmission. When the packet arrives at the other end, MHS "bursts" it open to reveal the envelopes for routing to local users or rebundles it for forwarding elsewhere.

In the modem-based, MHS messaging environment, MHS needs two transports to tango. Imagine a shipping department without a receiving department. The transport server delivers messages from one MHS host to another and picks up any messages for its host. The transport layer takes care of pesky modems, cranky phone lines, and fickle transport servers on the other end. It ensures that the messages are delivered error-free. It won't consider the message *sent* until the destination MHS host sends a specific sequence of digits that MHS hosts recognize.

RITUAL MAIL

Remote MHS works either by modem, internetwork, or via gateway.

When MHS was released, a network in San Francisco was probably not physically connected to the Denver office, so MHS designers relied on simple, garden-variety modems to forward messages to distant locations via telephone lines. In MHS lingo, the asynchronous connection transport server transfers messages over standard phone lines using modems.

The Denver host calls San Francisco, checking for Denver-bound mail. Denver is told by San Francisco's MHS that mail awaits for Denver users. Denver's MHS asks San Francisco's MHS host to download (or route) those messages to it. When the process is complete, San Francisco wants to know if Denver holds any mail for the Californians. If so, the transfer process starts again, but Denver's MHS does the sending.

When the MHS hosts finish this ritual, they say goodbye and hang up. The Denver messages now reside in San Francisco's host. It sits until San Francisco's local e-mail application swoops down and interrogates MHS about any mail. The San Francisco local e-mail application sees the Denver messages in the San Francisco MHS warehouse, snatches them up, and informs the end users that a message awaits. This method incurs telephone charges and mail delivery only as frequent as the polling.

On a very large network, the use of direct asynchronous transmission is waning. Internetworks have replaced async connections. The LAN in Denver probably is now directly connected to San Francisco, using a WAN service such as T-1. The internet message server option of MHS takes advantage of the direct connection by letting you set up a directory structure on the Denver file server that the San Francisco MHS host can read on a regular basis.

This "passive" MHS host doesn't run MHS's connectivity and transport managers—just the directory manager and only when a configuration change needs to occur. You are still required by MHS to have a valid licensed copy of MHS resident on your passive host, but the remote MHS host, the active one, moves the mail by itself.

Before a directly interconnected LAN, an MHS host running at both locations was required. In the newer scheme, a single MHS host can cover a wide area network by itself, with no modems.

A gateway server transfers messages into other types of environments, including host-based e-mails such as IBM's PROFS or SNADS or Digital Equipment's All-In-One, and to other message delivery systems such as MCI Mail.

CLIENT-SERVER TO THE CORE

MHS was an early client-server application. The e-mail market is moving toward *client-server*, pulling apart the back-end *engines* and *front-end* user interface.

Therefore, different front-end applications can talk to the same back end. And the same front-end application (with a few modifications) talk to different back-end engines.

Even the manufacturers can be different, provided the interfaces between the back and front ends are well documented. One developer writes the front end, while another writes the back end, each concentrating on their specialty. Front-end e-mail vendors are tightly integrating their products with specific engines. BeyondMail from Beyond (Cambridge, MA) is a front-end mail application that runs on different mail engines. MailMan from Reach Software (Sunnyvale, CA) is another client-server mail application.

There are many ways to skin the e-mail cat these days, but the lack of interoperability among e-mail systems makes MHS—despite its blandness—an extremely important program in the e-mail world. MHS is insensitive to most proprietary aspects of e-mail vendor offerings. Don't dismiss MHS; it still has a mission to perform.

X.400 Messaging

E-mail is an essential application, one that can often justify the installation of a network all by itself. E-mail provides a vehicle for people to communicate regardless of their physical location and time zone. A form of e-mail exists for nearly every type of operating system, from ones running on personal computers to large hosts. Mail-enabled applications can be constructed on the mail system, allowing greater productivity.

A corporation's departments are likely to use a wide variety of systems. IBM'S PROFS and SNADS are commonly used on IBM mainframes; All-In-1 is popular on VAX/VMS systems; WangOffice is used on Wang VS machines; HPOffice is used on Hewlett-Packard minis; SMTP is used on Unix and TCP/IP systems; Lotus' cc:Mail, DaVinci's eMail, and Microsoft Mail are among those used on PC LANs; and CE Software's QuickMail is often used on Mac LANs.

As corporations build enterprise networks, the dissimilar e-mail systems must be connected via a common transport. Very often, that platform is X.400. X.400 is vendor-independent, able to run on a wide variety of computer systems, and internationally accepted and used.

The International Standards Organization (ISO) X.400 Message Handling Systems (MHS) is a suite of protocols that define a standard for store-and-forward messaging. X.400 provides message creation, routing, and delivery services. It runs over an X.25 packet-switched network or asynchronous dial-up lines.

X.400 software is available for a variety of computers, either as native implementations or as gateways.

There are two versions of the X.400 standard: the 1984 and the 1988 specifications. [Note: the specification was further upgraded in 1992.] Most X.400 mail systems implement the older specification. The new spec offers key additions to X.400's flexibility and usefulness. It permits the use of asynchronous lines, a useful tool for PC or laptop users not connected to an X.400 network.

Directory services and security features have been added. As more 1988 X.400 implementations become available, native X.400 usage should rise.

X.400 COMPONENTS

X.400 divides an electronic mail system into a client, called a *User Agent* (UA) in ISO parlance, and a server, called a *Message Transfer Agent* (MTA). Essentially, the User Agent is a mail box; it interfaces directly with the user. It is responsible for message preparation, submission, and reception for the user. It also provides text editing, presentation services, security, message priority, and delivery notification. The User Agent is an interface, not an end-user application, so it does not define the specifics of how it interacts with the user. The product developer decides those issues.

The Message Transfer Agent routes and relays the messages. Its responsibilities include establishing the store-and-forward path, ensuring channel security, and routing the message through the media. An MTA's operation is relatively straightforward. The User Agent sends its message to the local Message Transfer Agent. The MTA checks the message for syntax errors, then delivers the message to a local User Agent, or if the message is not local, it forwards it to the next MTA. That MTA repeats the process until the message is successfully delivered.

A collection of MTAs is known as *Message Transfer System* (MTS). The MTS is usually specialized to a particular vendor's product.

X.400 also uses *Distribution Lists* (DLs), which are like routing lists commonly used in offices.

The *Message Store* (MS) provides a facility for message storage, submission, and retrieval. It complements the User Agent for devices that are not always available, such as PCs or terminals. Essentially, it is a database of messages.

The *Access Units* (AUs) provide connections to other types of communications systems, such as telex and postal services. AUs defined in the 1988 spec are the Telematic Agent for Teletex terminals, Telex Agent for Telex service, and Physical Delivery Agent for connection to the traditional postal service.

A management domain is a collection of at least one Message Transfer Agent and zero or more User Agents that is administered by a single organization. Management domains may be *private* (PDMD) or *administrative*

X.400 MESSAGE HANDLING SYSTEM

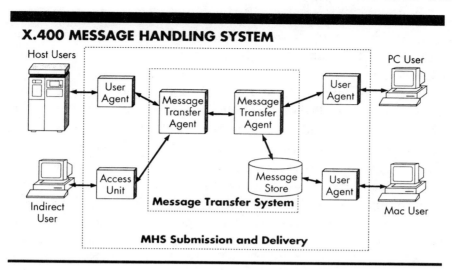

X.400 divides the messaging into client and server portions. The User Agent (UA) interfaces with the user, handling message preparation, submission, and reception. The Message Transfer Agent (MTA) checks the messages for errors and forwards them to other MTAs in a particular X.400 system. A Message Store (MS) facility is provided for PCs and terminals that may not have internal storage space, or that may not be available all the time. Non X.400 users, such as telex and post offices, are accommodated through the Access Units (AUs).

(ADMD). An ADMD is managed by an administration such as a PTT or telephone company, and a Private Management Domain is managed by any other type of organization. A hierarchy of management domains enables the configuration of a worldwide X.400 system with unique addressing.

SENDING X.400 MAIL

An X.400 mail system follows the metaphor of a post office, and X.400 messages follow the metaphor of the letter. Messages are packaged into envelopes, and an envelope describes the control information necessary to deliver the message's content, including the body type, syntax, and semantics. X.400 can deliver messages to other X.400 users via a *message transfer* service or to other communications facilities such as Telex via an *interpersonal messaging* service.

As with the postal services, users and distribution lists must have unique addresses to deliver the message anywhere in the world. X.400 uses two kinds of names, a *primitive name,* which identifies a unique entity such as an employee number, and a *descriptive name,* which identifies one user of the X.400 system.

A name is typically looked up in a directory to find the corresponding address, but X.400 allows a machine name to also be a directory name, which makes it easier for humans to interpret. X.400 addresses consist of attributes that describe a user or distribution list or locate the user distribution list within the mail system. Attributes are personal (such as last name or first name), geographical (street name and number, town, or country), organizational (name or unit within organization), and architectural (X.121 addresses, unique User Agent identifier, or management domain). In practice, X.400 names are lengthy and complex and should be hidden from end users by offering them aliases.

In addition to messages, the message handling system and the message transfer system use probes and reports. A *probe* contains only an envelope—no content—and it is used to determine if messages can be delivered. For instance, a probe may be sent to test out a path, asking the receiving MTS if it can accept a particular message type. By testing the waters with a probe, a lengthy message is less likely to be rejected by the recipient. A report is a status indicator that relates the progress or outcome of a transmission to users.

WAYS OF HANDLING MESSAGES

X.400 defines several protocols for handling messages among the different system components. Two Message Transfer Agents may communicate directly with each other, without the intervention of a User Agent. They do so by using the P1 protocol. If a User Agent wants to communicate with a service outside the X.400 domain, it uses P2, the interpersonal messaging protocol. The 1988 implementation of P2 defined additional body types for messages, so beyond supporting Teletex and Group III fax, P2 supports externally defined body types such as word-processing formats. This specification paves the way for electronic document interchange.

P3 defines the conventions for transferring a message from the User Agent to the Message Transfer Agent. Initially defined in the 1984 spec, P3 assumes that the User Agent is online and ready to accept messages from its Message

Transfer Agent. In 1984, X.400 did not provide for a User Agent that would be online intermittently. In practice, most User Agents are implemented on personal computers, and therefore will not always be online.

To remedy the situation, Message Store was added in the 1988 spec, and P7 was defined for the communication between the User Agent and the Message Store. The Message Store, always connected to the Message Transfer System, stores messages for the User Agents. User Agents submit messages through the Message Store as well as retrieve, list, summarize, and delete messages from the Message Store database. P7 support is crucial for anyone using laptops.

DIRECTORY AND SECURITY ISSUES

The 1988 X.400 recommendations suggest using ISO's X.500 directory service for naming, storing distribution lists, storing profiles of User Agents, and user authentication. By using X.500, users do not have to contend with ungainly machine-oriented names, but can use more intuitive names. However, X.500 is still under development in ISO. Pilot projects are underway, but there are no commercial implementations. No clear-cut solution exists for a directory service that's suitable for a heterogeneous network.

Security is another key issue. The 1988 spec provides facilities to authenticate who originated the message, verify who originated a a delivery or nondelivery notice, check that the message or its contents were not altered and that all recipients received a copy. It also provides return receipt and registered mail services.

Security must be improved beyond these capabilities. Dangers lurk in one user masquerading as another. For example, no facility ensures that a user does not impersonate and misuse a Message Transfer System or falsely claim to originate a message. No facility ensures that message sequence is preserved. If a message were resequenced, messages could be replayed, reordered, or delayed.

X.400 is just one option for building the backbone of the enterprise messaging network; however, it has international acceptance and vendor independence. With the products based on the 1988 specification emerging, X.400 can serve a more useful role.

DOS/Mac Connectivity

It wasn't until after the IBM Personal Computer and its XT/AT successors moved *en mass* into the office computing environment that local area networks became popular. And because MS/PC-DOS-based IBM PCs, XTs, ATs and compatibles were so prevalent, it was only natural that the majority of the office LANs operated in all-DOS environments.

In these homogeneous networks, few users needed connectivity to other operating systems, such as Unix or the Macintosh. A few longtime computer users—generally, those who had used mainframes—may have wished they could access host-based data from their desktop PCs. But the greater majority of PC users had little prior experience with computers, so they didn't even perceive the need for inter-operating system connectivity.

Apple's introduction of the Macintosh in 1984 changed user's perceptions. They found they could use the Mac to produce online charts, graphs, and other illustrations—a capability then lacking with MS-DOS-based PCs.

Inevitably, other applications found their way into the easy-to-learn and use Mac environment. With a Mac, users could combine spreadsheet and/or database files with word processing documents to create attractive, professional-looking reports, and other corporate documents without going to an outside graphics house.

This not only saved their company time and money, it also pointed out the necessity of giving Mac and PC users access to data on the "other" operating system. This was doubly important because most companies using personal computers for bookkeeping, accounting, and customer-profile information do so with DOS-based PCs. It was precisely this data that could make those attractive Mac-generated reports worth reading.

Unfortunately, the MS-DOS and Macintosh file-storage and disk operating systems are incompatible with each other, making it impossible to exchange data directly between them without additional hardware and software. Providing connectivity between PC and Mac systems thus has been a key issue for LAN vendors, especially those selling network operating systems (NOS) and applications software.

INCOMPATIBLE FILE SYSTEMS

The foremost issue they faced was operating system incompatibilities. A glance at the two OSs' user interfaces shows the obvious difference between the Mac and MS-DOS environments. The Mac offers a graphical user interface (GUI), with pictures, or icons, representing files, printers, applications, etc. Mac users "point and click" with a mouse to start an operation or select a file.

PC users interact with DOS through a "command-line interface"—they must type commands. (Recent developments, particularly the release of Microsoft's Windows, have brought a GUI to the DOS world.

The differences between the two operating systems run much deeper than user interface, though. The Mac and PC manipulate and store data in different physical and logical formats—that is, their file systems are totally different. (The Mac's 3½ inch diskettes aren't physically interchangeable with the 5¼ inch diskettes used by the original PCs; this physical incompatibility is rapidly becoming a non-issue, because most MS-DOS-based PCs now support 3½ inch diskettes, and modern Mac diskette drives can read DOS-formatted diskettes.)

Users wanting to share Mac and PC files faced yet another obstacle: Many DOS-based applications store data in proprietary formats that are unreadable by other applications, even other DOS applications. Files from many DOS-based database programs, for example, cannot be "imported" directly into a WordPerfect document file.

A PATH THROUGH THE MAZE

The challenges seem daunting don't they? Fortunately, the path to "transparent" Mac-PC connectivity really isn't as impossible as the above scenario sounds, and many vendors offer several solutions. These range from the fairly straightforward—requiring external floppy disk drives or modem-serial communications packages—to full-scale, server-based LANs that offer a wide variety of network services. Users must simply understand what level of Mac-PC connectivity they need, and plan accordingly.

For simple file transfer between a standalone PC and Mac, one solution is to use a product such as DataViz's (Trumbull, Conn.) MacLinkPlus. MacLinkPlus not only provides the mechanism to transmit data between the two computers, but it also offers "translators" for most applications, ranging from spreadsheets to database programs. These translators convert DOS file formats to the Mac format, while preserving the original file's formatting commands.

MacLinkPlus allows two ways to exchange files: via a connection directly through the two computers' serial ports or via a modem hookup.

Another easy-to-implement solution comes from Dayna Communications (Salt Lake City) DaynaFile external disk drive. DaynaFile allows a Mac to read files from or write files to an MS-DOS diskette; it supports the Mac file system, so DOS files and disks appear on the Mac screen as standard Mac icons. Like MacLinkPlus, DaynaFile also offers a translation function to convert DOS files to the Mac format.

Dayna also offers DOS Mounter, a software package that runs on any Mac with a Hyperdrive. It enables the Mac to mount a 3½-inch DOS diskette to a desktop window and be read just like any Mac diskette. Combined with MacLinkPlus for file translation, DOS Mounter offers Mac users an almost seamless way to read DOS files.

ON TO NETWORKS

These format translation products are inadequate for exchanging files between groups of Macs and MS-DOS computers, however—that's where networking applications begin to make sense (network operating systems such as Apple's AppleShare and AppleShare/PC, 3Com's 3+ and 3+ for Mac, IBM's LAN Server, Microsoft's NT Server, Banyan VINES, and Novell's NetWare).

Naturally, networks require more complicated hardware and software arrangements. Networks need cabling to connect the various computers, net-

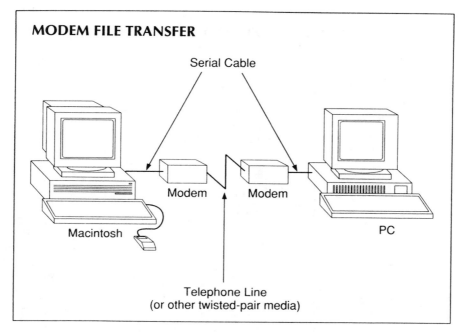

MODEM FILE TRANSFER

Serial Cable

Modem   Modem

Macintosh

PC

Telephone Line
(or other twisted-pair media)

One straightforward way to transfer files between the Macintosh (left) and an MS-DOS-based PC (right) is via modems. Modem connections send a modulated stream of data bits across telephone wire; but they may not transfer formatting commands successfully.

work interface cards inside each networked computer, a network operating system, and a file server. For Mac-PC connectivity, the file server must be capable of communicating with both Macs and PCs.

The figure above illustrates a typical mixed Mac-PC network environment. In this LAN, a LocalTalk network (right) composed of Macs is linked to an Ethernet network via a dedicated file server, which also routes traffic between the networks. Because LocalTalk connections are built into every Macintosh, the Macs on this segment do not require add-in network cards.

That's not the case for the server (a Compaq in this example) and the computers on the Ethernet segment. Because the server requires connection to each type of cabling, it must contain two network cards—one for Ethernet, one for LocalTalk. These adapters provide the physical connection to the two workgroups. In the case of Ethernet, the connection could be via coax cable, twisted-pair wiring, or fiber-optic cable; in LocalTalk, the connection could be via coax cable, twisted-pair wiring scheme or Apple's proprietary shielded twisted-

A MIXED PC-MAC NETWORK

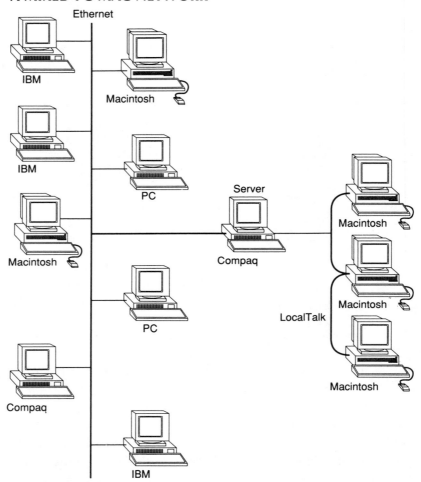

Server-based networks allow fast and easy exchange of data between Macs and PCs, whether the Mac is connected to the LAN via LocalTalk (right) or Ethernet cabling.

pair. The other computers, including the Macs, on the Ethernet workgroup must also contain an Ethernet card.

Each nonserver computer on the network must also be operating with "client" software, which provides the PC or Mac with the commands it needs to "look" to the network and exchange files with the server.

THE FILE SERVER'S ROLE

In addition to providing the physical interface between the two different cabling schemes, the file server in this network also would perform a variety of other tasks. First of all, it must provide all the common file-server services, particularly data-and-application storage and retrieval. These capabilities are controlled and manipulated by a network operating system.

Because this is a mixed PC-Mac environment, this network operating system must be extra "smart": it must "understand" both the Mac and MS-DOS file systems. It must also be able to provide data translation functions that permit users of Macintoshes to access files created and stored by the user of an IBM PC or compatible, and vice versa.

Without these capabilities, Mac-PC connectivity would be severely limited. Networked Macintoshes and PCs could share server disk space and perhaps might even be able to read some data files created by the other.

But the level of functionality available would not be the true transparent Macintosh-PC connectivity required by users of today's increasingly complex heterogenous networks.

IP Addresses and Subnet Masks

As the Internet takes on an ever larger role during our working hours—and perhaps our after-work hours as well—the more people need a better understanding of how IP addressing works and the closely related topic of subnets and how they are defined.

For example, installing IP connectivity software, which the current versions of Windows, OS/2 Warp, and the Macintosh OS all include, on a desktop system generally requires that you know your IP address and your organization's subnet mask. While most organizations administer these setup parameters centrally—typically through the MIS department—it can be useful for people other than the Internet guru to understand how addresses and subnets work. While the topic may seem extraordinarily complex, a little facility with binary arithmetic is sufficient to work out how the system operates.

The Internet address is the first concept you need to grasp. The parsimonious founding fathers of the Internet allowed 32 bits to identify all Internet addresses. (2^{32} =4,294,967,296 addresses, which seems to be a plentiful supply at first glance.) IP addresses are normally written as a sequence of four decimal numbers separated by periods, with each number ranging from 0 to 255. (Each number is an 8-bit byte, or octet in Internet jargon. 2^8 = 256, and 4 x 8 bits = 32 bits.)

So the most common representation of an Internet address looks something like this: 192.228.17.62. Sometimes the four digits of an Internet address are represented in hexadecimal (base 16) notation. As we shall see, it sometimes makes sense to represent them in binary or base 2 notation.

Internet addresses are made up of a network number and a host number. A host can be any device that runs an application. Most hosts are computers—traditionally the term "host" has been reserved for multiuser mainframes and minicomputers, but PCs and workstations are hosts in the Internet sense of the term, as are intelligent hubs, RMON monitors, and other devices.

254

TABLE 1. BINARY REPRESENTATION							
OF THE FIRST OCTET OF AN INTERNET ADDRESS							
Powers of 2	$2^7(128)$	$2^6(64)$	$2^5(32)$	$2^4(16)$	$2^3(8)$	$2^2(4)$	$2^1(2)$	$2^0(1)$
Class A	0	x	x	x	x	x	x	x
Class B	1	0	x	x	x	x	x	x
Class C	1	1	0	x	x	x	x	x
Class D	1	1	1	0	x	x	x	x
Class E	1	1	1	1	x	x	x	x

Hosts whose addresses share a network number can send local broadcasts to one another and communicate without a router. Hosts with differing network numbers can communicate only via an IP router.

The network ID number part of the IP address can be split off from the host ID part in several ways. If the first octet of the Internet address is used for the network number, the last three octets can be used for host addresses. Such networks are called Class A networks, and they can have $2^{24} - 2 = 16,777,214$ host addresses.

If the first two octets are used for the network number, the networks are called Class B networks, and they can have $2^{16} - 2 = 65,534$ host addresses. If the first three octets are used for the network number, the networks are Class C networks, and they can have $2^8 - 2 = 254$ host addresses.

Figure 1 is the binary representation of the first octet of an Internet address. The convention is that if the first (or most significant) binary digit is 0, then the address is a Class A address. Network addresses of 0 (00000000 binary) and 127 (01111111 binary) are reserved, so there are 126 potential Class A networks, recognizable by their having a first dotted decimal digit in the range of 1 to 126. These very large networks have practically all been assigned to large international organizations and government agencies.

Class B addresses are indicated by a 1 in the first bit and a 0 in the second bit of the first octet. Thus they can be identified by their having a first decimal digit in the range of 128 to 191 (10000000 binary to 10111111 binary). The second octet of a Class B address is also part of the network number. Thus there are potentially 16,382 Class B addresses.

Class C addresses have 1s in the first two bits and a 0 in the third bit of the first octet, and use both the second and third octets for the network number. Thus the first decimal digit of Class C addresses ranges from 192 to 223 (11000000 binary to 11011111 binary). There are 2,097,150 Class C addresses.

TABLE 2. DOTTED DECIMAL AND BINARY REPRESENTATIONS OF IP ADDRESS AND SUBNET MASK

	Dotted decimal	Binary representation
IP address	192.228.17.126	11000000.11100100.00010001.01111110
Subnet mask	255.255.255.192	11111111.11111111.11111111.11000000
Bitwise AND of address and mask (resultant network number)	192.228.17.64	11000000.11100100.00010001.01000000
Subnet number	1	00000000.00000000.00000000.01
Host number	0.0.0.62	00000000.00000000.00000000.00111110

Network numbers with the first digit higher than 223 are reserved for special purpose Classes D and E.

WHY DO WE NEED SUBNETS?

A network with 16,777,214 host addresses (Class A) , or even one with 65,534 (Class B), is likely to be unwieldy; even a Class C network with 254 addresses may well be undesirably large for many organizations. As a result of traffic patterns and congestion, upper limits on the number of allowable nodes in a network, distance limitations on LANs, and other reasons, many organizations divide their networks into subnets.

In effect, some number of the leftmost (or most significant) bits of the host addresses are expropriated and used to designate subnets. The subnet is part of the network identified by the network number, but only those hosts that are on the same subnet can communicate without a router. Members of different subnets will not see each other's local broadcasts, and they will need to go through a router to communicate, even though they may be on the same network.

The subnet mask is the method IP software uses to mark off which host bits will be transformed into subnet numbers. A subnet mask is a 32-bit number, often written in dotted decimal form like an IP address—for example, 255.255.255.192. If we write the subnet mask in binary notation (see Table 2), it's easier to see how it works. Think of the subnet mask as a strip of masking tape laid over the host part of the binary IP address wherever there are 0s in the mask.

TABLE 3—DEFAULT SUBNET MASKS

Class A default mask	255.0.0.0	11111111.00000000.00000000.00000000
Example Class A mask	255.192.0.0	11111111.11000000.00000000.00000000
Class B default mask	255.255.0.0	11111111.11111111.00000000.00000000
Example Class B mask	255.255.248.0	11111111.11111111.11111000.00000000
Class C default mask	255.255.255.0	11111111.11111111.11111111.00000000
Example Class C mask	255.255.255.252	11111111.11111111.11111111.11111100

If the subnet mask stops at an octet boundary, it may be the same as the default mask, which is no mask at all (see Table 3). In other words, if you perform a bitwise logical "AND" with a Class B address and the Class B default mask, you get precisely the same network number you would get by simply looking at the first two octets, and there is no subnet number carved out of the Class B host octets.

It is considered good practice to use contiguous bits, starting from the left, for subnet mask values, though it is not always an absolute requirement. Following this rule, decimal representations of subnet mask values follow the sequence 128, 192, 224, 240, 248, 252, 254, 255.

A SAMPLE SUBNET MASK

If you have a Class C network address and you would prefer to configure six networks of 30 hosts each, you would use the subnet mask 255.255.255.224. Subnet 0, with the binary representation 000, is reserved to refer to "this subnet," and subnet 7, with the binary representation 111, is reserved for broadcasts to all subnets on this network. Thus subnets one through six are available. Host number 0 (00000 binary) and host number 31 (11111 binary) are reserved, so there are 30 potential host IDs, numbered 1 to 30, that could be assigned.

With this subnet mask, there are 180 total IP addresses possible on this Class C network (six subnets times 30 host numbers). With no subnetting, a Class C network has 254 total addresses. Subnets clearly can result in wasted IP addresses, although the alternative of not employing subnets at all will likely result in even worse waste—for example, multiple Class C networks being used to segment a small number of users.

In most cases, every host and router on a particular IP network should have the same subnet mask. Exceptions to this rule should be made only by those who understand fully what they want to accomplish in their network design and how using multiple subnet masks on the network achieves that goal.

It's not a good idea to experiment with subnet masks, or for that matter, with IP addresses. Each organization with an IP network connected to the Internet is obligated to request network IDs from the Network Information Center, to which the Internet Activities Board has delegated the responsibility of administering addresses.

Duplicate network numbers, duplicate host addresses, and inconsistent subnet masks can create havoc, and if you are using unregistered numbers, you are presumed to be at fault. If you are installing Internet applications on an organization's network, you must get an appropriate address and the organization's subnet mask from the person in your organization who is in charge of administering them. Aside from the hard-to-find problems that may result from ignorant experimentation with IP addresses and subnet masks, it is a lot of work to go back and reinstall IP software that has been configured improperly.

Section V

Internetworking

Internetworking

As local area networks become more and more prevalent and increasingly vital to the daily operation of an organization, the need to connect multiple LANs together has become as crucial as it once was to link individual PCs into a workgroup. More and more, it's likely that a worker linked into a firm's marketing department workgroup requires access to resources located on another LAN within the company—a database in the engineering network, for example.

This need has spawned one of the fastest growing areas of the LAN industry: The *internetworking* marketplace, composed principally of repeaters, bridges, routers, gateways, and, most recently, hybrid products called brouters and routing bridges. Internetworking products bring interconnectivity to workers linked into large, spread-out groups of LANs. They also play a major role in network management by allowing network administrators to segment, or divide, a single network into an assembly of multiple subnetworks. This subdivision can improve network performance—limiting the number of nodes on a network can reduce traffic over the workgroup wiring. It also facilitates security—internetworking allows restricting individuals to specified resources—and increases system reliability—when one workgroup goes down, it doesn't affect the entire network.

There are four primary types of internetworking products: repeaters, bridges, routers, and gateways. (Beginning in 1994 or so, multiport bridges began to be marketed as switches, but switches usually provide the same fundamental functions as the devices traditionally known as bridges. In some cases, switches actually perform local routing functions as well.) Each internetwork product permits various levels of communication between individual networks; each also functions at a separate level within the OSI model.

REPEATING THE OBVIOUS

Repeaters offer the simplest form of interconnectivity. They merely regenerate, or *repeat* data packets (in reality, electrical signals) between cable segments. In their purest form, repeaters physically extend a network; repeaters operate at the physical layer of the OSI model. Repeaters, for example, allow extending Ethernet network cable segments from 1,000 feet to more than 5,000 feet. In addition, they provide a level of fault tolerance by isolating networks electrically, so a problem on one cable segment does not affect other segments.

Repeaters do not allow a network manager to isolate traffic; they regenerate every data packet or jam signal over all the networks they link. They do nothing to relieve the load on a network's bandwidth.

Bridges, on the other hand, isolate traffic to specific workgroups while still offering the ability to connect multiple LAN cable segments into a large logical network. Bridges operate one layer higher than repeaters in the OSI model; they operate at the MAC sublayer of the data-link layer.

FILTERING TRAFFIC

Most bridges operate only between similar LAN technologies—between two Ethernets or two Token Rings, for example—but some do offer cross-technology capabilities. They regulate traffic by filtering data packets based on the packet's destination address. When a packet's destination address is local, it is not forwarded by the bridge. When the destination address is remote—i.e., to a node on another workgroup—the bridge forwards it. Bridges automatically "learn" the addresses of the devices attached to their subnetwork.

More sophisticated bridges allow filtering traffic on a variety of factors, including packet size, source address, and type of protocol. Because filtering reduces network traffic, it can substantially increase overall network performance. Bridges operate independently of the upper-layer protocols which allows them to handle any transport protocol, such as the TCP/IP, IBM's SNA, and NetBIOS.

Bridges use custom filters to selectively reject or forward packets that match administrator-specified conditions, such as packet size, specific transport protocol (XNS, TCP/IP), or destination address. Custom filters can work on packets whether they're flowing into or out of a network; a filter can also forward only those packets that match user-defined criteria.

System administrators can use custom filters to help set up and manage administrative domains within a network; for example, a network manager could develop custom filters that isolate electronic mail domains. Custom filters can also restrict protocol-specific packets to certain preset domains. Similarly, filters could forward only specified types of packets.

Source-explicit forwarding (SEF) gives administrator-defined workstations exclusive packet-forwarding privileges on the internetwork. Designated stations can forward packets through a particular port on a routing bridge, while the packets of stations without SEF rights will be rejected. SEF thus permits a system administrator to limit access to normally secure or isolated network segments or resources.

These types of controls let network administrators manage their LANs better, permitting them to create secure domains and increase inter-workgroup efficiency.

Traditional bridges have offered transmission capabilities from only a single workgroup to another workgroup, but the move to centralized LAN management centers has prompted LAN manufacturers to market multiport bridges, now commonly called switches. Multiport bridges give network administrators the advantages of modular expansion and/or reconfiguration. By replacing one interface card with another—for example, adding an FDDI link to a modular multiport bridge—the administrator can keep up with an organization's changing network environment without completely rebuilding the network infrastructure.

THE ROUTER ROUTE

Routers operate at still another layer up—at the network layer in the OSI reference model. Routers connect logically separate networks operating under the same transport protocol (i.e., TCP/IP or SNA). Routers are thus protocol-dependent and must support the individual protocols being routed. A router allows multiple paths to exist in an enterprisewide network, and is "intelligent" enough to determine the most efficient path to send a particular data packet through those multiple loops.

In a typical enterprisewide network divided by routers, the separate networks are assigned unique numbers, and each independent network is managed separately. Routers automatically learn changes in a network's configuration, just as bridges do, within the limitation of the network protocol's ability to pass routing information between routing nodes. Routers are more complex

REPEATERS

Application	Application
Presentation	Presentation
Session	Session
Transport	Transport
Network	Network
Data-Link	Data-Link
Physical	Physical

Repeaters operate at the lowest OSI layer: They regenerate electrical signals.

BRIDGES

Application	Application
Presentation	Presentation
Session	Session
Transport	Transport
Network	Network
Data-Link	Data-Link
Physical	Physical

Bridges operate at the MAC sublayer and are capable of modest traffic control and network partitioning.

ROUTERS

Application	Application
Presentation	Presentation
Session	Session
Transport	Transport
Network	Network
Data-Link	Data-Link
Physical	Physical

Routers operate at the network layer and are capable of stringent traffic control and network partitioning.

GATEWAYS

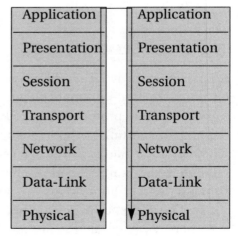

Application	Application
Presentation	Presentation
Session	Session
Transport	Transport
Network	Network
Data-Link	Data-Link
Physical	Physical

Gateways provide translations between two dissimilar computer systems, such as a PC LAN and an SNA network.

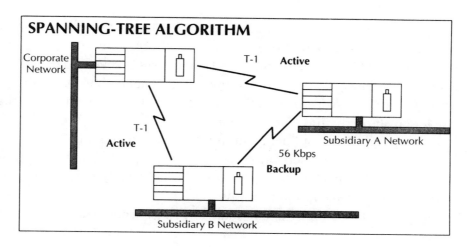

SPANNING-TREE ALGORITHM

Corporate Network

T-1 **Active**

Subsidiary A Network

T-1

Active

56 Kbps

Backup

Subsidiary B Network

The spanning-tree algorithm allows for creation of reliable, fault-tolerant bridged networks. Failure of one of the primary active T-1 lines on a spanning-tree network automatically triggers the use of the 56Kbps backup line, thus ensuring continued network service. When the T-1 line is fixed, the spanning tree algorithm senses its operation and reroutes data over the primary line.

than bridges, however, because routers must know each network's unique number when brought up. This requires users with an in-depth knowledge of data communications, effectively limiting the use of routers to sophisticated environments.

Routers are particularly useful in organizations with multiple large networks connected to a single backbone. Because they must determine which transport protocol is being routed, routers are inherently slower than bridges. Newer routers, capable of routing packets at a LAN protocol's maximum bandwidth (with Ethernet, about 15,000 packets per second), are erasing this limitation, however.

THE SPANNING TREE ALGORITHM

The spanning-tree algorithm allows loops to exist in a bridged Ethernet network. Loops, which are formed when there are multiple data paths between two segments of an Ethernet network, are particularly useful in mission-critical networks because they provide fault-tolerant redundancy and permit internetwork devices to find and use the most efficient routes between the other internetwork devices on that enterprisewide LAN.

In a large multiloop Ethernet, the spanning tree algorithm determines the most desirable path between segments and disables all other paths to eliminate redundant loops. (This path selection process is governed by options that can be selected by the system administrator.) Then, when the active path is unusable for any reason, spanning tree automatically reconfigures the network, activating the most desirable alternative path, until the original active loop is brought back online. Spanning tree permits connecting a corporate network to subsidiary networks via high-speed "active" lines; should either active line fail, a backup loop would be brought online automatically, thus ensuring continued communications.

Spanning Tree's ability to automatically sense trouble areas allows organizations to build large, reliable networks that are still easily managed from a central site; managing similar topologies created with routers alone requires staffing each network segment with network management personnel.

THE GATEWAY

Gateways act as translators between networks using incompatible transport protocols, such as TCP/IP and SNA or SNA and X.25. Depending on the level of incompatibility, gateways operate at the transport through application layers of the OSI model.

One of the more common gateways is a communications gateway between a local area network and a mainframe or minicomputer; such a gateway generally places a special-purpose adapter card with a standard network interface card in a PC that serves as a shared gateway to the host for all the other PCs on the LAN. Such a gateway allows you to use a mainframe or mini as a network server, if desired.

The new internetworking products and features available combined with the old permit creating faster, more secure, and more cost-effective enterprisewide networks—the kind now being demanded by multinational corporations.

Bridges

A data-link bridge is a device that connects two similar networks. It takes packets from one network and puts them on the other, and vice versa. As it does this, it regenerates the signal strength of the packets, allowing data to travel further. In this sense, a data-link bridge incorporates the functionality of a repeater, which also regenerates packets to extend a LAN. But a bridge does more than a repeater. A bridge is more intelligent than a repeater. It can look at each packet and decide on which of the two networks it belongs. Repeaters simply forward every packet from one network to the other, without looking at them.

A bridge looks at each packet as it passes, checking the source and destination addresses. If a packet coming from Station 1 on LAN A is destined for Station 5 on LAN B, the bridge will pass the packet onto LAN B. If a packet coming from Station 1 on LAN A is destined for Station 3 on LAN A, the bridge will not forward it; that is, it will filter it.

Bridges know which packets belong where by looking at the Medium Access Control (MAC) layer information carried in the packet. The MAC layer, which is part of the second layer of OSI Model, defines how packets get on the network without bumping into each other. It also contains information about where the packet came from and where it should go. Because bridges use this level of information, they have several advantages over other forms of interconnecting LANs.

WHY BRIDGE?

The most common reason to bridge is to improve network performance. Dividing one large network into two networks reduces the amount of traffic that flows over the entire LAN and therefore improves performance. Devices on both segments can still talk to each other via the bridge.

267

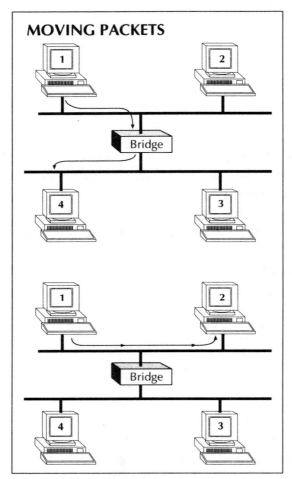

In the first network, the bridge allows a packet from Node 1, which is addressed to Node 4, to pass through based on its source and destination address. In the second network, the packet from Node 1 is addressed to Node 2, so the bridge ignores the packet.

It is possible that a poorly placed bridge can reduce performance by creating a bottleneck. However, it doesn't take too much effort to discover the best place to put a bridge. For example, it doesn't make sense to split up 10 people whose workstations are physically close to each other if they frequently exchange information. A bridge between this workgroup and another workgroup, however, could improve performance dramatically. With the bridge, the two workgroups may still communicate transparently. Only communication between groups, not communication within groups, moves through the bridge.

Another reason to use a bridge is to change from one type of cable to another. For example, you may run twisted-pair cable in the offices and fiber-optic cable between buildings. Segments can be connected with a bridge, so "long distance" traffic can flow freely from one segment to another while local traffic stays local. Broadband and baseband Ethernet networks may be connected this way, too. A 16Mbps Token Ring backbone may use bridges to connect to several local 4Mbps Token Rings.

PROTOCOL IGNORANT

Because bridges operate at the MAC layer, they can interconnect LANs that use many different upper-layer protocols. Bridges are commonly referred to as protocol-independent. For example, the same bridge may connect networks running TCP/IP, DECnet, OSI, IPX, and XNS protocols. All these higher-layer protocols are encapsulated within the MAC layer. That is, the MAC layer is below the network layer where the upper-layer protocol information is kept.

A bridge will not allow a device speaking TCP/IP to talk to a device speaking IPX or OSI. That is a gateway's function. A gateway actually translates between protocols. A bridge simply passes packets back and forth, regardless of the protocols. A bridge will let any two users speaking the same protocol talk to each other.

Many networks have more than one protocol running on them. For example, two groups of Sun workstation users may use TCP/IP most of the time and occasionally use OSI. A bridge between the groups will pass both TCP/IP and OSI packets. In fact, the bridge won't even know which protocol it is passing. But the two machines on either side of the bridge must use the same protocols for the message to make sense.

LEARNING AND FILTERING

A bridge is considered an intelligent device because it can make decisions based on situations it has already seen. To do this, a bridge refers to an address table. When a bridge is plugged in, it sends broadcast messages asking all the stations on the local segment of the network to respond. As the stations return the broadcast message, the bridge builds a table of local addresses. This process is called *learning*.

Once the bridge has built the local address table, it is ready to operate. When it receives a packet, it examines the source address. If the packet's address is local, the bridge ignores it. If the packet is addressed for another LAN, the bridge copies the packet onto the second LAN. Ignoring a packet is called *filtering*. Copying the packet is called *forwarding*.

The basic type of filtering is keeping local packets local, and sending remote packets to the other subnetwork. Another type of filtering is based on specific source and destination addresses. For example, a bridge might stop one station from sending packets outside of its local LAN. Or, a bridge might stop all "outside" packets destined for a particular station, thereby restricting the other stations with which it can communicate. Both types of filtering provide some control over internetwork traffic and can offer improved security.

Most Ethernet bridges can filter broadcast and multicast packets. Occasionally, a device will malfunction and continually send out broadcast packets, which are continuously copied around the network. A broadcast storm, as it is called, can bring network performance to zero. If a bridge can filter broadcast packets, a broadcast storm has less opportunity to brew.

Today, bridges are also able to filter according to the network-layer protocol. This blurs the demarcation between bridges and routers. A router operates on the network layer, and it uses a routing protocol to direct traffic around the network. A bridge that implements advanced filtering techniques is usually called a brouter. It filters by looking into the network layer, but it does not use a routing protocol.

Other bridges are available that do true network-layer routing. These routing/bridges or bridging/routers are often used as the hub of an enterprisewide network.

SOURCE ROUTING

Some Token Ring bridges, notably those from IBM, use a routing scheme called *source routing* to get packets from one network to another. The bridges we've talked about so far use transparent routing, which all Ethernet, and some

Token Ring and FDDI, bridges use. With transparent routing, the packet does not know the route it will travel, nor do the bridges it passes over. Each bridge will forward a packet that is not local, until it finally reaches its destination LAN.

With source routing, the packet itself contains routing information. This information specifies the LANs and the bridges through which the packet will travel to get to its destination. The sending machine is responsible for putting this information into the MAC-layer header, which is the part of the packet that contains the source and destination addresses along with some other information about the packet.

For sending stations to know the route their packets will take, they must learn the layout of the entire network. This is done dynamically through a process called *route discovery*. During route discovery, packets are passed around the network. As they move from LAN to LAN, they are filled with information about the network. Each bridge puts three numbers into the packet: the numbers of the two LANs it connects and its bridge number. This information is then passed back to sending stations. Using this information, sending stations can then create a map of the network and appropriately route their packets.

Source routing is used primarily by IBM on its Token Ring LANs. Source routing does impose some overhead which might diminish network performance slightly. However, this is offset by the advantages of the routing scheme. Because the sending machine knows the route its packets will take, it can always choose the optimal path at the time of transmission, which is not possible with transparent routing. With transparent routing, the optimum path remains so until a bridge or a link fails. Also, source routing provides better management since the path of a packet is immediately accessible from the packet itself. Finally, source routing bridges can be faster than transparent bridges since they do not have to "look up" each packet to see if it must be bridged. The packet tells them immediately.

REMOTE AND LOCAL

So far we have discussed local bridges. Remote bridges connect two geographically separate LANs, mostly over a telecommunications link, such a leased telephone line, a T-1 link, a public data network, or microwave line. In remote bridging, the bridge is split into two devices. A bridge at one end puts packets destined for the other LAN out over the link. A bridge at the other end receives the packets and passes them to its local LAN. The process works in both directions.

Telecommunications links are not the only way to connect long distance LANs via bridge. Broadband networks and fiber-optic links can also bridge geographically distant networks. For example, bridges might be used to pass traffic over a fiber-optic backbone among the buildings of a university or business campus. Technically, this is not a remote connection, but the individual LANs may be several miles apart.

Either way, once bridges connect LANs over a longer distance, reliability and fault tolerance become more important. Bridges at both ends must take precautions against data corruption over the remote link.

SPANNING THE GLOBE

The first step in fault tolerance is redundant bridges. The IEEE 802.1D spanning tree algorithm allows redundant bridges to be configured on an Ethernet LAN. The stumbling block is that introducing parallel bridges creates a loop in the Ethernet topology, which is strictly forbidden by the rules of the Ethernet protocol. However, spanning tree manages those loops, so that packets don't circulate endlessly around the network. Without a backup bridge and spanning tree software, a failed bridge causes the network to be partitioned until the broken bridge is fixed.

According to the spanning tree algorithm, two bridges are set up, side by side. One is designated the primary bridge and it is the only bridge to pass traffic. If the primary bridge fails, the traffic is automatically shunted to the back-up bridge.

Spanning tree overcomes a major obstacle in bridging, but the back-up bridge is idle as it waits for a failure. This is costly. If the back-up link could carry traffic, the cost of the second link could be better justified. Here's where load balancing comes in. Using load balancing, traffic can be divided over the two remote parallel bridges. This provides much better performance since not all traffic is going over one remote link. Since the spanning tree technology is still in place, if one bridge fails, the other can still carry all the traffic.

MANAGING BRIDGES

Since LAN configurations change constantly, it is crucial that bridges be easy to manage. A good bridge management package should allow bridges to be managed from a central location. A LAN manager should not have to be at the bridge but should be able to send instructions from a networked terminal or PC. Critical management functions include enabling and disabling bridges, changing security parameters, and changing the address filters and the protocol priorities dynamically. Many bridges allow the manager to download configuration information, thereby setting up the bridge to work as desired all at once.

Bridges should also provide information about what is happening on an internetwork. For example, a management package should report how much traffic is passing over the bridge, the type of traffic, how many errors occur and so on. With this information, the LAN manager can decide how to configure the network. It might be necessary to move the bridge and segment the network differently. Some bridges allow the LAN manager to set performance or error parameters. If these thresholds are exceeded, an alarm is sent to the manager's workstation.

Many bridges now support the Simple Network Management Protocol (SNMP). SNMP can be used to manage nearly any type of device, from a host computer to a multiport repeater. A bridge must implement the SNMP agent software, which sends information back to the SNMP management station. SNMP is most often used in TCP/IP networks.

Cooperation with an enterprisewide management system is crucial. Such management systems include DEC's Enterprise Management Architecture, AT&T's Universal Network Management Architecture, IBM's NetView, HP OpenView, SunNet Manager, and the OSI Common Management Interface Protocol. These global management systems are essential to fill in the "big picture" of network management.

Total Ring Internetworking

While most of the internetworking frenzy has been directed at internetworking Ethernet LANs, connecting Token Ring LANs encompasses a separate set of issues. Unlike Ethernet, bridging predominates in Token Ring environments. Source routing, which is used in Token Ring, is a more sophisticated form of internetworking than transparent bridging, and this has staved off the onslaught of routing. Yet, as MIS builds increasingly complex networks, routing will become a more critical element in Token Ring internetworks. When internetworking Token Rings, you have three options: source-routing bridging, routing, and source routing transparent.

SOURCE ROUTING

The simplest way to interconnect Token Ring networks is to bridge them using source routing. In transparent bridging, which is used for Ethernet LANs, the internetworking takes place at the Medium Access Control (MAC) sublayer of the OSI Data-Link Layer. In source routing, the internetworking occurs at the Logical Link Control (LLC) sublayer, a half-layer "higher" than the MAC sublayer. This higher level of operation, combined with a richer packet format, gives source routing a higher level of functionality than transparent bridging.

Unlike transparent bridging, in source routing, the sending and receiving devices help determine the route the packet should traverse through the internetwork. The route is discovered through broadcast packets sent between the source and destination packets.

Source-routing bridge hardware is simpler than routers, making them easier to build and less expensive. Source routing also has advantages over transparent bridging. Because the same path is used for the duration of the session, the process is efficient, except for the setup time to determine the route. Source routing optimally uses parallel and redundant paths, so links are not left idle. It also allows IBM controller timing to be properly set for extended LANs.

274

Source routing has its disadvantages. The route discovery process requires more overhead than transparent bridging. If many devices are simultaneously performing route discovery, the network slows down considerably. The bridge selects the best path at the time of the session's commencement; if the link is heavily loaded, the two devices are stuck with a possibly inefficient path for the session's duration. Transparent bridges choose a new path per packet. Source-routing functionality must be engineered into the bridges, making them more expensive and complex than transparent bridges.

Two types of route discovery packets are used: All-Routes Broadcast (ARB) and Single-Route Broadcast (SRB). An ARB packet traverses all possible routes between end stations, while an SRB takes only one route between end stations. To determine the best path between sending and receiving stations, the sending station transmits an SRB.

When the SRB reaches its destination, that station issues an ARB. Multiple copies of the ARB travel over all possible routes back to the originating station. Note that an ARB can never travel the same ring twice nor exceed the hop count limit—source routing uses the spanning tree structure, which can be configured so only one copy of the packet reaches each ring.

As the packet passes through a bridge, the bridge inserts its own bridge number and the numbers of its attached LAN segments into the packet's Routing Information Field. Each Token Ring segment and bridge are assigned identifying numbers, and the combination of LAN and bridge numbers is unique for each bridge. The bridge also indicates the maximum frame size, which will be used to negotiate the frame size for 4Mbps and 16Mbps Token Ring.

The originating station receives an ARB packet back for each possible path from the sender to the destination as well as the maximum frame size. The originating station selects the most efficient path based on the first packet to return, the number of hops between the source and destination, and the packet size. For the transmission session's duration, that route is used.

When a packet already contains a route, the packet's Routing Information bit is set to notify the bridge that routing information is available. The source-routing bridge examines this bit to filter packets. If the bit is not set, the bridge ignores it. If the packet is not a broadcast (and therefore is data) and the bit is set, then the bridge checks to see if its own ring and bridge numbers are contained. If not, the bridge ignores it. If a match occurs, the packet is forwarded over the link to the next LAN. The bridge sets bits to indicate that it has been copied, which prevents packets from circulating endlessly in the network.

The majority of Token Ring networks use source routing, but it is not appropriate in some cases. For example, if you need to connect Token Ring and Ethernet networks, bridging won't be sufficient.

NETWORK-LAYER ROUTING

You can also interconnect multiple Token Ring networks with routers. Whereas bridges operate at the Data-Link Layer, routers operate at the Network Layer, one level higher. Routers deliver a higher level of functionality than bridges, but they incur greater overhead. Routers must be built specifically to handle Network-Layer protocols, such as TCP/IP or IPX/SPX. Many also include bridging functionality for protocols that can't be routed.

As MIS departments consider consolidating SNA and PC LAN networks into one "super-network," many are looking to routing. Companies with Token Ring LANs also look to routing to provide the same level of security, flow control, and path control that Ethernet LANs and routers provide.

In a routed network, routers communicate with each other, learn where the end-station devices reside, and manage the traffic flow. They require a specific protocol to do so. For example, most TCP/IP routers use the Routing Information Protocol (RIP), but some use Open Shortest Path First (OSPF). Routers can detect congestion on a particular link and send network traffic over a less congested link.

If a particular link fails, the router reconfigures the network around the failure. This convergence presents a strong advantage over bridging. Source routing determines its paths statically; if a link fails, the session must be restarted. With routing, if this convergence happens quickly enough, the user won't notice the difference. If the network does not converge quickly enough, the session is dropped and the user loses the connection.

One problem with routers in Token Ring LANs is most IBM networks don't include routable protocols. SNA/SDLC and NetBIOS are not routable protocols. They both lack Network Layers and thus can't be handled by routers.

One solution is to use a router that encapsulates Token Ring traffic into

TCP/IP packets. This method adds the overhead of encapsulating your traffic into TCP/IP at the transmission side and de-encapsulating it at the receiving end.

If you encapsulate SNA traffic, you may run into timing issues. In an SNA network, the session will be dropped if the controller does not respond within the preset time. Some MIS shops reconfigure their VTAM tables to allow for a slower response time. Some manufacturers add controller-like functionality into their routers to fool the front-end processor into thinking that the router is a cluster controller. "Poll-spoofing" is a tricky feat to accomplish. Test this solution carefully before you implement it in a production network.

Another solution is to add TCP/IP to your network. If TCP/IP runs on all hosts and LAN servers, TCP/IP routers will manage the traffic. This solution makes the most sense if you are largely a TCP/IP shop or if your MIS department is willing to invest in learning TCP/IP technology.

A third solution is to implement a nonstandard routing method (available from different manufacturers) that gives good response time and can quickly reconfigure a network after a failure.

SOURCE ROUTING TRANSPARENT

Source routing transparent is a truce between the Token Ring source-routing camp and the Ethernet transparent-bridging camp. It provides a way for Token Ring and Ethernet LANs to interoperate.

Source routing cannot operate in a transparently bridged LAN, since the packets lack routing information and the bridge has no way of knowing that the packet should be forwarded. You can use transparent bridges in a source-routing environment; however, the routing information is ignored and the advantages and overhead of source routing are wasted.

Packet size is a problem when you have both 4Mbps and 16Mbps rings, since transparent bridges can't indicate the correct packet sizes, while source-routing bridges can. In many instances, duplicate transparent and source-routing bridges must be used to carry the two types of traffic, which clearly is inefficient.

The upcoming IEEE Source Routing Transparent (SRT) specification addresses the coexistence and interoperability of Ethernet, Token Ring, and

FDDI. A source routing transparent bridge allows both source-routing and transparent data to be passed. An SRT bridge will source-route packets with embedded routing information and transparently bridge those that lack this information.

Source routing transparent implements two logical paths for the two packet types. All packets are filtered to determine if the routing information bit is set. If it isn't, the packet takes the transparent path. If it's set, then it takes the source-routing path.

Source routing transparent defines three packets that can be used for route discovery: All-Route Explorer (ARE), Specifically Routed Frame (SRF), and Transparent Spanning Frame (TSF). The ARE frame is equivalent to source routing's ARB packet; it traverses all routes between end stations. The SRF is issued in response to the ARE. The TSF lacks routing information but performs the SRB's function.

These new route discovery methods are not supported by all IBM source routing software, so changes in some end-station source-routing software will have to occur.

The SRT standard allows the end station to discover the route, which source routing does not permit. The destination station performs this function in three instances: when it becomes the source, when it gets routes from the ARE sent by the source, or when the destination picks up the route from the data packets that were sent from the source. The latter allows the destination to discover the route without creating overhead.

In SRT, end stations have more robust options for choosing the best route for a particular session. For example, they can reserve more than one route to be used as backup if the primary route fails during transmission. Route selection criteria include the first frame returned, the lowest number of hops, the first route returned with the largest frame size, or any combination of the above. Once the route is determined, the path is inserted in the data packet, and the bridge decides whether or not to forward it based on the routing information.

SRT does not enable a transparently bridged LAN to talk to a source-routed LAN; it cannot translate among different packet formats. SRT allows the mixing of source-routed and transparently bridged networks on the same internetwork, alleviating the need to purchase duplicate hardware.

Routing Protocols

Large internetworks spanning multiple workgroups, subnetworks, and host computers create special problems for system administrators. Like managers of local networks, they must deal with products from multiple vendors, get different network operating systems to communicate, and justify the costs of new services and applications.

But they also face the task of selecting, managing, and maintaining bridges, routers, and gateways—the internetworking devices that permit widely separated clusters of networks to communicate. These products offer important capabilities to help network managers solve particular problems, but each poses special implementation challenges, too.

This is especially true of *routers* and their associated routing protocols. Routers, connect logically separate networks operating under the same transport protocol, such as the Transmission Control Protocol/Internet Protocol (TCP/IP).

Routers, which operate at the network (or third) layer of the Open Systems Interconnection (OSI) reference model, are *protocol-dependent* devices. That is, they must support each routing protocol on that LAN.

A WEALTH OF PROTOCOLS

A wide variety of routing protocols can be found on enterprisewide networks today. Some are proprietary, or single-vendor, solutions developed specifically for use with a vendor's own products. Others are "open" in that they have been standardized by official sanctioning agencies.

Among the proprietary ones are the Internetwork Packet eXchange (IPX) protocol used by Novell's NetWare and the Interior Gateway Routing Protocol (IGRP) used by Cisco Systems. Open protocols include the Routing

279

Information Protocol (RIP) for use with the TCP/IP suite and the OSI Intermediate System-to-Intermediate System (IS-IS) protocol. These were formulated or standardized by the Internet Activities Board (IAB) and the International Standards Organization (ISO), respectively. Since they are open, they can be used with multiple vendors' products in heterogeneous networks.

Other widely used routing protocols include the IAB's Open Shortest Path First (OSPF), DECnet Phase IV, the OSI's Connectionless Network Services (CLNS) protocol, and Apple Computer's Datagram Delivery Protocol (DDP).

ROUTING ALGORITHMS

The primary role of a router is to transmit similar types of data packets from one machine to another across wide area communications links such as T-1 lines or Fiber Distributed Data Interface (FDDI) rings. Ideally, the router exchanges data by selecting the best path between the source and destination machines. It determines what is best via *routing algorithms,* which are complex sets of rules that take into account a variety of factors.

In operation, these algorithms' first task is to determine which of the paths on the internetwork will take a data packet to its destination. Because multiple paths often exist between any two routers, the algorithms are used to select the best paths. These decisions are based on a prescribed set of conditions, which might include the fastest set of transmission media or which network segment carries the least amount of traffic.

FLOODING THE NETWORK

Without microprocessors to perform the complex mathematical calculations required by routing algorithms, early routers were slow. The networks they ran on were equally low-powered, with little bandwidth and not complex. This meant that routers could be simple and operate without knowing where the other routers on the network were located.

These types of routers were isolated in that they did not exchange network routing information with other routers on the network. As a result, they forwarded data merely by flooding every path with packets. Data packets eventually reach their destination in this scheme, but flooding also risks creating routing loops, in which certain packets can travel around the network indefinitely.

Several measures can be taken to help flooding-type routers choose reasonable paths. One is called *backward-learning*. In this scheme, a router remembers the source addresses of all incoming packets and notes the physical interface it came in on. When it's time to forward a packet to that address, the router bases its decisions on this stored information.

Some routers avoid the entire issue of path-finding by relying either on a human or host computer to make these decisions. In the former case, the network manager provides each router with a block of *static* routing configuration information at start-up, including the information needed to make routing decisions.

In the host-router implementation, end hosts place information in every packet they place on the network. This information indicates every path and the immediate router the data must pass through to get to its destination. This is *source-routing*.

ADDING COMPLEXITY

More complex networks require dynamic routing solutions. In large wide area networks with multiple links between networks, routers perform more efficiently when they understand how the network is linked together. An *integrated router* does this by exchanging information about the network's topology with other integrated routers. As a result of this exchange, integrated routers create *routing tables* that show the best paths between the various links on the internet.

Algorithms for integrated routers must be able to quickly determine the network topology. This process, called *convergence*, must take place rapidly, otherwise routers with obsolete or incorrect data about the network can send data into dead-end networks or across unnecessary links.

DISTRIBUTED ROUTING

Routers can be arrayed in centralized or distributed configurations. Central routers with intensive CPU resources and lots of memory control how data packets are moved around. These relatively expensive central routers receive topology information from remote, less-powerful "slaves," then build routing tables and pass them along to the remote routers as needed.

The newer, increasingly sophisticated routers with their own CPU and memory resources available make centralized routing obsolete. In the *distributed routing* environments now prevalent, all routers on the internetwork can calculate routing algorithms quickly and efficiently.

The two main distributed-routing algorithms are a *distance-vector* algorithm, or the *Bellman-Ford* algorithm, and a *shortest path first,* or *Dijkstra* algorithm. Both are in wide use, in proprietary and standard protocols. For instance, RIP (used with TCP/IP, Xerox Network Systems [XNS], and IPX), DECnet Phase IV, and Cisco's IGRP implement distance-vector algorithms. OSPF, used in TCP/IP, is a shortest path routing algorithm.

Distance-vector routers create a network map by communicating in a periodic and progressive sequence with each other. This information exchange helps them determine the scope of their network in a series of router hops that reveals more information about the network.

Here's how the algorithm works: When the network is started, each router knows about only the networks it is connected to directly. Each router then advertises information about its immediate connections to the routers it is directly connected to. By incorporating the updates it receives from routers nearest to it, each router learns about networks connected to its neighbors, two router hops away. Additional updates expand each router's knowledge hop-by-hop.

Shortest Path First (SPF) routers update each other and learn the topology of an internetwork by periodically flooding the network with *link-state* information. Link-state data includes the cost and identification of only those networks directly connected to each router.

SPF routers send link-state data to all routers on a LAN. This allows OSPF routers to perform two important subsequent steps. First, they use the link-state data to build a complete table of router and network connections. Then each router calculates the optimal path from itself to each link. In this repetitive process, each router checks the potential pathways between the links on the network, eliminating the most indirect path in favor of the shortest. That

INTERNET ROUTING ARCHITECTURE

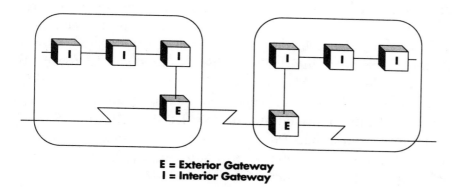

E = Exterior Gateway
I = Interior Gateway

The TCP/IP routing scheme used in the Internet relies on interior gateways, or routers, (noted with "I" in the illustration), to move data packets within an autonomous system, such as the network at a university campus. Exterior gateways, or routers, (noted with "E"), pass data packets between these autonomous systems.

path, with any routers connected to it, is put on an active list. This process goes on until all possible shortest links are active.

TCP/IP ROUTING

The TCP/IP protocol suite offers a slightly confusing routing picture, partly due to its nomenclature, and partly due to the structure of the internetwork that spawned TCP/IP.

The Internet community uses the word "gateway" to describe a device that the rest of the internetwork marketplace calls a router. In the Internet, the devices serving as gateways do so within two interconnected environments: One, they link the subnetworks within individual universities and research institutions into a large network, and, two, they act as the physical links between individual universities and research institutions.

Also confusing is the Internet's use of the terms *interior gateways* and *exterior gateways* to describe certain gateways, or what are normally called routers. These gateways (hereafter called routers) perform specific duties within the hierarchical Internet architecture, with the duties matching the services required by this structure.

The TCP/IP routing scheme used in the Internet relies on interior gateways, or routers, (noted with "I" in the illustration), to move data packets within an autonomous system, such as the network at a university campus. Exterior gateways, or routers, (noted with "E"), pass data packets between these autonomous systems.

An interior router moves information *within* an *autonomous system*. An autonomous system is a group of networks under the control and authority of a single entity. An example is the networked computing resources at a single university. Among the Interior Gateway Protocols (IGPs) are RIP and OSPF.

An exterior router moves data from one autonomous system to another—that is, from one university's internet to another's. The TCP/IP Exterior Gateway Protocol (EGP) is an example of this type of protocol.

Mainframe Gateways

MIS is experiencing a revolution. Data is no longer locked up in the glass-walled, air conditioned, computer room. Information is a key part of a company's strategy, and as such, must be easily accessible. The local area network can be used to bring that corporate data to the desktops of the users. Once the data appears on the user's PC, he or she can manipulate it by changing variables, trying different views, and plotting graphs. Or the LAN-to-mainframe link may be part of a mission-critical application such as an airline reservation system. Or perhaps users simply need to share electronic mail with mainframe users.

Getting this information requires a physical link between the PC and the host. A mainframe gateway is a combination of hardware and software that allows PCs, PS/2s or Macintoshes on a LAN to communicate with a mainframe. We will limit our discussion to gateways to IBM SNA mainframes, such as the 30xx, 43xx, and 9370.

GATEWAY TYPES

The hierarchy in the mainframe world is straightforward. The mainframe is the central repository of data and applications. Access to this information is granted through a system that runs on the mainframe. This system is usually Virtual Telecommunications Access Method (VTAM). VTAM contains information about every device on the SNA network. Terminals are wired to cluster controllers. The terminal family is referred to as 3270.

Introducing PCs into the equation allows more sophisticated applications to be put into place. It also disrupts the hierarchy, since a PC can act as both a terminal and a cluster controller. Most importantly, the PC brings about drastic changes in the politics in MIS.

The most basic micro-to-mainframe link is the *coax adapter*. The two de facto standard coax adapters are from IBM and DCA (now Attachmate). The PC also runs terminal emulation software so it can act as a 3270 terminal. But the coax adapter is not a LAN-to-mainframe connection. Each PC must have an adapter and coax cable. If it is remote, it needs its own synchronous modem. With a network, however, fewer of these components are needed and their cost can be distributed among a number of users.

A *DFT coax gateway* is basically a LAN version of the coax card. Unlike the other types of gateways, a DFT gateway allows a PC to emulate a terminal. Distributed Function Terminal (DFT) is a terminal mode that has largely replaced the older Control Unit Terminal (CUT) mode. DFT assumes the device talking to the mainframe is intelligent (as opposed to a terminal). In CUT mode, the cluster controller is responsible for displaying the data, whereas in DFT mode, many of the controller's functions are distributed to the intelligent device.

Like a DFT terminal itself, a DFT coax gateway may have up to five concurrent sessions. This means that at most five people can communicate with the mainframe at the same time. One way to increase the number of concurrent sessions is to install multiple coax cards in the gateway PC. Another method is to buy a coax gateway that uses multiplexing to support up to 40 sessions on a single card.

A DFT gateway is cost efficient if you already have a cluster controller in place. They are also relatively easy to install. However, they have few sessions to offer users.

Because most users are located at a different location than the mainframe, the *SDLC gateway* is widely used. A Synchronous Data Link Control (SDLC) gateway connects geographically remote users to a mainframe using modems and telephone lines. One PC on the LAN is designated the gateway and it emulates the 3174/3274 controller. This PC contains the SDLC board, gateway software, and a synchronous modem.

Typically each SDLC gateway supports up to 32 workstations with a total of 128 simultaneous sessions. (The 128 limit was traditionally a limitation of NetBIOS.) As for modems, 9600 bps and below is fine for interactive work, but file transfers and remote applications will require 19.2 Kbps and above. An AT with a standard gateway adapter will support speeds up to 19.2 Kbps. For speeds of 56 Kbps, an intelligent gateway adapter will be required.

Keep in mind that the modem bandwidth and the adapter card's CPU must be divided among the users. Although 128 simultaneous sessions is the theoretical limit, the practical limits are set by the type of applications the users run.

The *Token Ring Interface Coupler* or TIC is the newest method of connection. Made by IBM, the TIC makes is basically a Token Ring interface adapter for cluster controllers, midranges, front-end processors, and mainframes. It can be a local or a remote connection.

Depending on the TIC card and Token Ring, transmission is at 4Mbps or 16Mbps; at either speed, it is significantly faster than coax or SDLC methods. The TIC is the most logical method if users on an existing Token Ring need access to a local mainframe. A TIC is also essential for cooperative processing applications built on APPC.

Each workstation on the Token Ring can be addressed directly, or one PC may be set up as the gateway. Although direct addressing provides performance benefits, it increases management efforts. Each workstation must be defined in VTAM as a Type 2 Physical Unit, thereby adding overhead at the mainframe level and increasing the amount of work for the people who maintain the system. From the CPU's and systems programmer's point of view, it is more efficient to designate one PC as the gateway. The mainframe polls the gateway PC, and the gateway is responsible for polling each workstation.

A fourth gateway type is a *channel-attached gateway.* This is the highest performance method, and is most often used when other mainframes, minicomputers, and engineering workstations need to communicate with the mainframe. Because a coax gateway and an SDLC gateway communicate through a cluster controller or front end processor, they are limited by the controller to a raw throughput of 56 Kbps. A channel-attached gateway is connected directly to a mainframe's I/O channel, and while speed varies according to manufacturer, you can get bandwidth of about 20Mbps.

SESSION ISSUES

Most gateways are PC-based. The gateway PC can run either DOS, Windows, or OS/2. The workstations communicate with the gateway via a communications protocol, most often NetBIOS. Some gateways tailored for the NetWare environment use IPX. The OS/2 gateways generally use Named Pipes.

The most basic function of a mainframe gateway is distributing the mainframe's sessions to the PC users. Gateways allocate these sessions or Logical Units (LUs) statically or dynamically. A PC or terminal explicitly defined in VTAM is said to have static or dedicated LUs. So a particular user, say John in Accounting, always gets a particular session, say LU #2. In dynamic pooling, sessions are grouped together. So one pool could be printer sessions, another, terminal sessions. Pooled sessions are distributed on a first-come, first-served basis.

Users with high priority or who deal with sensitive information should have dedicated sessions. Dedicated LUs simplify management, since the mainframe personnel always know who has access to which session. The disadvantage is that VTAM tables become very large. And every time a user is added, the tables must be updated. Dynamic allocation insures flexibility and eliminates waste. A mainframe gateway should support both methods.

On the whole, mainframe gateways offer very little in the way of management capabilities. Functionality can range from the very simple—reporting which user has which LU—to the very complex—reporting information back to IBM's NetView. This is one area where improvement is needed.

WORKSTATION SOFTWARE

The gateway PC takes care of the basic communication and session handling with the mainframe. But each workstation must run software as well. The first key item is terminal emulation. The PC running DOS, OS/2, Windows or the Macintosh must be able to act as a 3270 terminal. Of the 3270 family, the 3278 and 3279 color displays are the most widely emulated. The 3178 and 3278 monochrome displays are also popular. If you need to display the full screen formats of the larger displays, each PC may need to be equipped with a VGA or better graphics adapter.

In addition to terminal emulation, a gateway may also need to provide printer emulation. This will permit PC users to print mainframe data to their local and LAN printers. Most gateways emulate the 3287 printer; some emulate the 3286.

File transfer is as essential as terminal emulation. Most support IBM's host-based file transfer program called Send/Receive or IND$FILE. Most have a proprietary file transfer that is generally a great deal speedier than IBM's. Some increase the speed of Send/Receive by using larger buffers. On the other hand, that requires more memory on the PC side. The gateway should also allow users to transfer files in background mode. With background file transfer, a user can set up a file transfer and switch to an interactive terminal session while the transfer takes place.

Most gateways allow users to have multiple, simultaneous sessions on the mainframe. Some gateways limit this to a specific number, say two terminal sessions and one printer session per user. Others allow one user to hog every session the gateway has available. Most people would find it difficult to keep track of more than three simultaneous sessions (one for calculation, one for interactive work, and one for printing). It is very useful if the software supports windowing, so the various sessions can be overlaid on a single screen.

The PC keyboard must be remapped to emulate the 3270 terminal keyboard. The difference between the <ENTER> and <RETURN> keys on the 3270 keyboard must be reconciled. The PF keys must be added to the PC keyboard. These problems are compounded by the differences in the XT and AT keyboards. Often, the workstation software allows the user to pop up a map of the keyboard. Some allow the user to remap the keys on the fly. Another handy feature is to allow users to build macros to automate common functions, such as logging in or retrieving mail.

If the users need to access a mainframe application that makes use of SG2 or APA graphics, special software is required. SG3, the older graphics method, has been replaced by vector graphics (which is also called All Points Addressable). In APA graphics, the mainframe sends only the vector points, and the terminal draws the image on the screen. The 3179-G and 3279-SG3 displays support graphics.

By the time an operating system, a network operating system, and gateway software is loaded into a PC's memory, there's precious little RAM left. Generally, the amount of available RAM and the functionality is a tradeoff. The high end functions, such as graphics or APPC, tend to require a great deal of RAM. If you need these high-end features, consider a gateway that supports expanded or extended memory or one that is able to page to disk. Or consider one that supports OS/2 workstations.

This brings us to a hotkey to DOS. While many gateways offer the user the ability to hotkey to DOS, in reality, there is often little RAM left to do more than a directory listing. Also, when you switch to DOS, often times the file transfer or other process will stop because DOS is not a multitasking operating system. Some vendors have developed a workaround. But if you want true multitasking, you will need OS/2, 32-bit Windows, or UNIX.

PROGRAMMING INTERFACES

Terminal emulation, file transfer, and print services are basic, but essential functions. As the PC becomes a partner with the mainframe, rather than a souped-up terminal, more sophisticated applications are possible. Application programming interfaces (APIs) are the enabling mechanism. APIs allow programmers to move part of an application down from the mainframe and onto the PC. So for example, a loan application can be entered and verified on the PC, then sent to the mainframe. Mostly, APIs are used for far simpler tasks. Users can automate simple tasks, such as downloading files.

Nearly all gateways have some type of programming interface, whether proprietary to that manufacturer or compatible with IBM's. HLLAPI (High Level Language Applications Programming Interface) and 3270-PC API are two of the best-known IBM APIs. They allow you to present information in a way different from the traditional mainframe. For example, mouse support is enabled through HLLAPI. EEHLLAPI or Entry Emulator HLLAPI is a subset of HLLAPI. These APIs are popular because they do not require any changes to be made on the host side.

Enhanced Connectivity Facilities/Server Requester Programming Interface (ECF/SRPI) is a newer API for cooperative applications. It is easier to implement than Advanced Program-to-Program Communications (or APPC). APPC is used in applications where the PC or midrange is considered the peer of the mainframe. This is a radical departure from the traditional terminal-midrange-mainframe hierarchy. APPC is primarily used in high-end transaction processing applications, such as done in airline reservations or banks.

SNA and LU6.2 Connectivity

When IBM introduced Systems Network Architecture (SNA), its strategic wide area networking product family, in 1974, mainframes dominated computer environments. Because they were ruled by mainframes, the computer networks in use were hierarchical, or tree-structured, with the mainframe at the top of the inverted tree. This arrangement required lower-level systems on the network to communicate with each other through the mainframe rather than directly with each other, which was a tremendous waste of host-based resources.

The popularity of personal computers in the 1980s changed the structure of corporate computing, however, No longer were computing resources located in or controlled from a centralized location: They were now distributed throughout an organization, in dozens (even hundreds) of PCs as well as the mainframe.

The growth of PC-based networks further strengthened this distributed environment. With hundreds of PCs connected to networks—all needing to communicate with each other—it became intolerable for most organizations to rely solely on the traditional SNA-type network. No longer could they allocate host resources to managing communication among the dozens of computers on the network.

In 1982, IBM responded by adding a protocol called Logical Unit (LU) 6.2 to SNA. LU6.2 makes all computers peers on an SNA network, including hosts. With LU6.2, the mainframe no longer plays dictator to its "slave" counterparts on the network.

LU6.2 brought other changes to SNA as well. Rather than forcing devices connected to SNA to act as dumb terminals incapable of handling processing, LU6.2 permits cooperative processing. Each processor on the network can do what it does best rather than rely on the mainframe. It also allows the dynamic allocation and tuning of SNA networks, substantially reducing the need for operator intervention.

SNA'S STRUCTURE

SNA, with IBM's market presence behind it, has been a *de facto* data processing and networking standard for many years. IBM has developed and installed sufficient hardware and software to make SNA the world's most widely installed network topology, with more than 22,000 sites.

As a protocol suite, SNA offers functionality similar (and is an alternative) to the Transmission Control Protocol/Internet Protocol (TCP/IP) and Open Systems Interconnection (OSI) protocols. Like these protocols, SNA offers a layered approach to communications. From the top down, SNA's seven layers are: end-user, network-addressable unit services, data flow control, transmission flow control, path control, data link control, and physical layers. Together, they provide services that are more or less synonymous with those of OSI and TCP/IP. However, the layers' functions do not completely correspond from one protocol to another.

These layers handle the following tasks. The physical layer (layer 1) moves data between computers on a network. The data-link layer (layer 2) uses the Synchronous Data Link Control (SDLC) protocol to pass data across the physical interface. The path control layer (layer 3) manages routing and traffic control, packing data together to increase throughput. The transmission control layer (layer 4) initiates, manages, and concludes transport connections or sessions, controlling the data-flow rate between layers 3 and 5. The data-flow control layer (layer 5) determines which LU can transmit next and helps manage error recovery. The NAU services layer (layer 6) handles presentation services to layer 7. The end-user layer (layer 7) provides the user interface.

In practice, SNA and LU6.2 use only layers 4 through 6. In this tutorial, we'll describe the functions and features these layers provide.

LU, PU FUNCTIONS

Before continuing, let's define *logical unit,* and its hardware-specific counterpart, the *physical unit.* Logical units (or LUs) and physical units (PUs) are the two primary functional entities in an SNA network. Both LUs and PUs are also referred to as network-addressable units (NAUs).

In SNA parlance, PUs are physical systems or nodes connected to each

		SNA		OSI
User Interface	7	End User		Application
	6	NAU Services		Presentation
Logical Services	5	Data Flow Control		Session
	4	Transmission Control		Transport
	3	Path Control		Network
Physical Services	2	Data Link Control		Data Link
	1	Physical		Physical

Although SNA is a seven-layer protocol, in practice it provides functionality in only layers 4 through 6. These four layers offer functions roughly equivalent to those provided by layers 4 through 6 in the OSI reference model shown on the right.

other via cabling. PUs are also known as Node Types, or NTs. IBM has defined five node types, including hosts (PU5) and terminals (PU2), and left a sixth available for future definition. For the sake of simplicity, we'll refer to node types/physical units only with the PU designation—such as PU2.0—although it's just as accurate to label PU2.0 as NT2.0.

Logical units are electronic entities connected by sessions. Just as there are five PUs, there are five LUs, including LU6.2, that make SNA network resources, including disk files and processing cycles, available for application software. A node on an SNA network can be a physical unit (such as hardware) as well as a logical unit (such as a logical session connection).

In essence, LU6.2 acts as an interface, or protocol boundary, between SNA and an end user's application. Closely associated with LU6.2 is PU (or node type) 2.1, which is an enhancement to PU2.0 for cluster controllers. PU2.0, also known as 3270 terminal emulation, is the protocol most often used to connect personal computers into an SNA network. PU2.0 also lets other devices on an SNA network access a mainframe by emulating a cluster controller.

PU2.0 has some limitations, however. Most importantly, it allows devices to access only a host, not other peer nodes. And it requires one or more System Service Control Points (SSCP), which start and stop sessions. PU2.1 remedies these shortcomings.

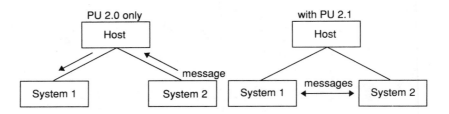

Physical Unit (PU) 2.1 brings peer-to-peer communications to SNA. With PU2.1, the two nodes at right can communicate directly between themselves, without intervention from the mainframe computer. Contrast this to SNA with PU2.0 (left), in which all communications between network nodes must go through the host, wasting host resources.

PU2.1 includes all the features of PU2.0, with major upgrades. It allows SNA devices to connect to peer nodes without mainframe assistance, and it permits running multiple sessions simultaneously. And while PU2.0 permits only peripheral node connections, PU2.1 provides peer-to-peer connectivity. PU2.1 also requires no central control point to manage session services. The next figure highlights the differences between PU2.0 and PU2.1 communications.

LU AND PU TYPES

There are five LUs and an identical number of PUs. We've described one of each already. The table provides a brief description of the full set of physical and logical units.

Of the logical and physical units listed in the table, LU3 is outdated. LU6.2, which can be considered a subset of SNA, consists of a base set of features plus 41 options. IBM implements LU6.2 across its entire product line, although the specifics vary from product to product. In its most popular form, users know LU6.2 as Advanced Program-to-Program Communication (APPC).

Users purchase APPC in the form of a developer's toolkit, which allows them to create transaction programs capable of using entities called APPC *verbs*. These APPC verbs are used within the transaction program to get LU6.2/APPC to perform functions the program needs carried out. Although APPC and LU6.2 are synonymous, their verb names differ slightly. With a few

DEFINITIONS OF PHYSICAL AND LOGICAL UNITS

Physical Units		Logical Units	
No.	What It Defines	No.	What It Defines
PU1	Terminals	LU0	Application presentation services
PU2	Controllers	LU1	3287 emulation, network & remote job
PU2.1	Enhances	LU2.0	Entry
PU3	Not defined	LU2	3278/9 Terminal emulation
PU4	Front-end processors	LU3	3270 Printer connections
PU5	Mainframe hosts	LU6.2	Peer-to-peer communication

exceptions—for example, APPC/PC does not support some of the more obscure features of LU6.2—APPC functionality is virtually identical to that of LU6.2.

LU6.2/APPC functions primarily as a resource allocator and controller. This means that LU6.2/APPC ensures that programs have access to network resources when they need them, and that network resources are not corrupted, such as when two users attempt to make simultaneous updates to the same file.

IBM has made APPC its preferred LU6.2 implementation in a variety of its systems, including its PCs, System/38/36, AS/400, and 9370 mainframe. IBM has said that APPC is its strategic product for distributed processing in the minicomputer and PC environments. IBM sees APPC as one way of taking PC-to-mainframe market share away from terminal emulation applications.

ON THE PC SIDE

APPC/PC is IBM's offering at the low end of the LU6.2 market. Two versions are available. Version 1.1 is designed for IBM's Token Ring and PC LAN Program networks and stand-alone micros. The OS/2 Extended Edition APPC is part of the Communications Manager for OS/2.

While backed by IBM, the memory-resident APPC/PC program has met resistance from end users. It consumes 164 KB of RAM, which is too much for most PC users to spare. With only 640 KB of DOS-addressable memory, many users don't have enough RAM to run DOS, APPC/PC, and applications software on a network. This is not an issue for end users running OS/2, which can access up to 16MB of memory; however, only a small percentage of users in the PC environment are using OS/2.

Because of the memory limitation, third-party applications developers have been slow to release software that takes advantage of APPC/PC. If more users migrate to OS/2, developers are likely to release more applications written to APPC/PC.

Another of IBM's LU6.2 implementations is Advanced Peer-to-Peer Networking (APPN). APPN adds network management capabilities to LU6.2 peer-to-peer communications services. APPN also includes a routing capability that can create new routes between nodes on a network dynamically.

Wireless WANs

How many times have you rushed through the airport, notebook smacking against your leg, trying to find a pay phone with a phone jack so you can dial in for messages between flights? For the most part, airport pay phones don't have jacks, and you can't use your wired modem.

And how many times have you checked into a hotel room, only to discover that you can't plug your notebook's modem into a jack in the room? The jack and wires are fused, or the jacks are nonstandard. "DataPorts" on hotel phones are few and far between, though they are very welcome.

You're trying to mate a mobile technology—notebooks—with a stationary concept—dial-up. With your notebook, you can compute anywhere, but the need to communicate with your office or with your customers ties you back down to land.

Then you eyeball your portable cellular phone, sitting there in your brief-case, right next to your landlocked notebook. You're not the only one. Wireless technologies will be able to provide communication for laptops, notebooks, Personal Digital Assistants (PDAs), and even less intelligent devices, such as soda machines.

Talk of wireless networking has accompanied the arrival of notebooks and the talk of PDAs. To be successful, PDAs will have to be wireless. Notebooks are likely to exist in a quasi-wired world; they could go either way. Most of the loudly discussed wireless technologies are for in-building, or local, usage.

Companies such as Motorola, NCR, and Windata are building wireless network products that are designed to be used locally. Even the companies coming out with wireless PCMCIA cards, such as Xircom and Proxim, are using spread-spectrum technology, which is designed for local transmission.

But as the universe of roaming computer users grows, they'll roam farther. And they'll need universal connectivity—wireless connectivity.

UNWIRING THE WAN

Five types of wireless technologies may serve: packet radio, packet cellular, circuit cellular, satellite, and paging. Packet radio, packet cellular, and circuit cellular are the most important.

- **Packet radio.** Mobile users can use the existing packet radio networks, such as RAM Mobile Data and ARDIS, to connect their computing devices to their networks.
- **Packet cellular.** Data communication can also take place over the US cellular network.
- **Circuit cellular.** Data can be carried over cellular voice channels today, in a manner similar to the way data is carried over analog lines by conventional modems. Modem vendors, including AT&T, PowerTek, and Vital, will play a big role in this market.
- **Satellite.** Low earth orbit satellites will carry voice and packet data. Motorola is building its Iridium network to provide worldwide voice coverage by 1996. Satellite bandwidth will be too small to serve the needs of most LAN users.
- **Paging.** The same networks that serve beepers may apply, despite low bandwidth.

FOUR FACTORS

Which technology or technologies take hold depends on their coverage, cost, performance, and adapter.
Service coverage must be nationwide and penetrate buildings. Many current wireless LANs fail in that they are local—and often can't cross buildings or even floors.

For nomadic computing to take off, communication coverage must be ubiquitous. Both packet cellular and circuit cellular will offer greater geographical coverage than the packet radio networks, because a huge cellular infrastructure already exists to handle voice calls. Advantage in for packet and circuit cellular.

What is the market price of convenience? Dialing out from hotel rooms and racing from pay phone to pay phone in airports will be cheaper than using wireless communication. According to Forrester Research (Cambridge, MA), circuit cellular costs $.50 per minute, while packet radio and packet cellular charge $.04 per packet and up. Advantage in for packet radio and packet cellular. Cost and performance are a delicate balance. Although packet technologies are lower cost, they cannot elegantly handle fax. Packet cellular has been demonstrated at 19.2Kbps, which is a far cry from the speed LAN users are accustomed to. Fax service, because of the nature of the transmission, requires a circuit connection. For those on the road, faxing is as important as dialing back into the company network. Ad in for circuit cellular.

The adapter is critical. The different technologies' adapters vary in size, weight, cost, and power consumption. The new PCMCIA cards will help reduce the footprint of these adapters from the size of a brick to the size of a credit card.

Initial PCMCIA cards will use spread-spectrum technology (for LAN usage), as well as circuit cellular (for WAN usage). The adapter should be a fraction of the notebook or PDA's cost—anywhere from 10 percent to 25 percent.

The adapter must also be simple to insert and remove. Make the adapter too big or difficult to install, and no one will want to transport it or figure out how to connect it.

Power consumption is key. The adapters draw power from the notebooks, placing yet another demand on the notebook's already short-lived battery.

Wireless vendors are acutely aware of the power crunch and are working to manage the power consumption. A packet cellular adapter can be combined with a cellular phone and use the same radio and antenna. The circuit cellular modem cards. as mentioned, will be implemented as PCMCIA cards,

A LOOK AT PACKET CELLULAR

Forrester predicts that by 1997, packet cellular will have an installed base of 1.4 million users in the US, which will be more than half the wireless installed base.

CelluPlaN. in particular, is projected to be the leader. It is a consortium composed of IBM and these nine cellular carriers: Ameritech Mobile

Communications, Bell Atlantic Mobile Systems, Contel Cellular. GTE Mobile Communications, McCaw Cellular Communications. Nynex Mobile Communications, PacTel Cellular. Southwestern Bell Mobile Systems, and US West NewVector Group. Together, they propose a cellular packet technology called Cellular Digital Packet Technology (CDPD).

Packet cellular has a number of advantages. Because the technology relies on the existing cellular voice network (with some modifications), current cellular users will be familiar with it: they'll see cellular packet as an extension of their existing voice service. They'll feel comfortable buying and using it.

Packet cellular used the existing cellular infrastructure, with some modifications. The initial investment in CelluPlaN was $400 million added to the $9 billion cellular partners can use to subsidize their data service investment off their substantial voice revenues.

Also key to packet cellular's future success is its use of existing cellular radios and antennae. The cellular companies have the infrastructure in place-they can simply add a few more components. Most of the carrier and end user components will cost less because they're already manufactured in such high volume.

ARDIS and RAM, the packet radio networks currently in use, cannot match packet cellular on a number of points. ARDIS and RAM have fewer users, smaller geographic coverage, lower bandwidth (from a LAN point of view), and require specialized equipment.

THE TECH BEHIND THE CURTAIN

The technology behind CelluPlaN is CDPD, which allows data transmissions to be overlaid onto the existing analog voice networks. With CDPD, data is transmitted in short bursts and only when the system detects an idle time between voice calls. Data can be sent without needing a dedicated channel, so data transmission will not impact the system's ability to carry its bread-and-butter—voice.

CDPD sends packets (just like on LANs) across one or more channels as the idle time occurs. Even during peak times, channels are idle between the time when a call is terminated or handed off and the time when the channel is reassigned to a new call.

A technique called channel hopping is used to select the channel that is least likely to be used for a voice call. This technology exists in today's cellular systems to hand calls off to new cells.

Cellular poses a few unique problems for data. When talking over a cellular phone, you can (impatiently) wait out the clicks, blackouts, and detect the control and user-identity information, and user-authentication procedures are also in place. When a user connects, the system assigns a temporary ID for addressing. With nationwide cellular handing calls from cell to cell, it will be harder to physically eavesdrop—you would have to be sure you hit the right cell control site. The advent of digital cellular will make it harder still. But data encryption seems like the sensible thing to do.

CDPD proponents are publishing their specifications, which will allow multiple vendors to implement the technology'. The proponents, except for IBM, are service providers and therefore benefit from other companies manufacturing adapters, modems, and other equipment. The CDPD organizers are also working with the Cellular Telecommunications Industry Association and the Telecommunications Industry Association to make it a standard.

BEYOND THE USUAL APPLICATIONS

The target users of wireless WANs are no surprise: people in sales, service, or those who travel frequently. By giving salespeople a "nomadic office", they're forced to spend more time with customers and less time at their desk. With networks, they can get more immediate access to information, such as inventory and pricing. Service providers can also use wireless WANs. Typical users may be rental car agencies, waitresses, baggage handlers, and loading dock workers. Traveling managers can stay in touch with their offices via e-mail and wireless connectivity.

But some applications may be unique. Consider for example, the soda vending machine that calls a central computer when it runs low on change or out of Mr. Pibb. Gas and electric meters could be imbued with intelligence so they notify the utility company how much gas or electricity the customer has used, and meter readers no longer knock on doors. Parking meters could do the same thing, I suppose.

Dial-up Internetworking

Enterprise network occupies a large slot in the industry's lexicon. The term conjures visions of an intercontinental network connecting hundreds of sites and tens of thousands of computers. But enterprise networks of this scale exist in only a small number of companies.

The vast majority of networked companies doesn't have a multitude of offices flung across the globe, populated by workers who need constant, heavy-duty access to each other's information. Most companies only need remote access on an occasional basis and make relatively minimal demands of many applications.

Look at companies' telephone line purchase patterns. Most phone lines used for data purposes are digital leased lines; to a lesser extent, companies buy fractional T-1 and full T-1. 56/64Kbps leased lines fill most of the need.

Cost is one reason for the plenitude of 56Kbps lines. Most companies outside the Fortune 1000 can't justify the high price of a T-1, unless they piggyback data on their existing private T-1 network used for voice traffic. Per month, a 56Kbps line costs in the hundreds of dollars; monthly costs for a T-1 fall in the thousands.

ON A SMALLER SCALE

The term *enterprise* can and should be applied on a smaller scale. An enterprise network connects every location in your company—even if there are only a few zone office locations. For these smaller, but no less important, networks, internetworking solutions—outside of the usual recommendations of high-speed multiprotocol routers pumping data down multiple T-1 pipes—apply. Smaller sites need the same level of connectivity but not the same level of horsepower. If your site is one of these smaller networks, dial-up internetworking is likely to play into your plans.

Most companies don't build private networks for voice, but many build private data networks. Still, for most companies, dial-up lines are the most con-

DIAL-UP VS. LEASED LINE COSTS

Distance	Dial-Up Service	Leased 56KBps Line	No. of Hours to Break Even Price
10 miles	$12 per month + $.60 per hour	$137	208
10 miles	$12 per month + $9.60 per hour	$732	75
10 miles	$12 per month + $14.40 per hour	$1,224	84
10 miles	$12 per month + $15.00 per hour	$1,759	116
10 miles	$12 per month + $15.00 per hou	$1,931	128

Source: Infonetics, San Jose, CA

Figure 1. Dial-up internetworking can be more cost effective than leased 56Kpbs lines for users who require a part-time connection between two sites.

venient way to communicate. The public switched telephone network is never more than a phone jack away. It's convenient, it's cheap, and it's reliable.

For data, the drawback has historically been speed. For dial-up, 2,400bps and 9,600bps modems may be the norm, but they provide insufficient speed for more than a single user running an application that requires minimal bandwidth.

Advances in technology have made dial-up a more viable alternative. The majority of the telephone infrastructure is fiber optic, not copper, which reduces the number of transmission errors and translates into higher throughput. With VLSI integration of chips and the use of digital signal processors, modems can operate at higher speeds, at a lower cost. Add some compression software, and a 14.4Kbps modem can achieve data throughput of 20Kbps to 57Kbps. These aren't exactly Ethernet speeds, but neither are they at the 2,400bps modem level.

The bottom line is always the biggest motivator; cost is a reason for using dial-up lines over leased lines. With dial-up lines, you pay for what you use, and only what you use.

With leased lines, you pay a flat rate, no matter how much or how little you use them. For occasional usage, dial-up lines make firm financial sense. According to the calculations of market research firm Infonetics (San Jose, CA), shown in Figure 1, if a company needed one hour per day of connectivity between San Francisco and Pittsburgh, the cost of a leased 56Kbps line would be $1,759 per month, but with dial-up networking, the same connect time would cost $327. That's a savings of $17,000 per year. Think about how many hours of usage you would actually need. An hour a day is enough time to exchange 60MB of information, assuming the connection operates at 25Kbps, according to Infonetics.

The flip side of the raw cost consideration is the throughput cost. Although the cost of using POTS (Plain Old Telephone Service) is cheaper, the time costs are less apparent but are of increased importance if the throughput becomes a problem. After all, there is also a cost factor in the time it takes to transfer files or to run an application.

SPONTANEOUS INTERNETWORKS

You could benefit from dial-up networking if your company has any one of the following scenarios:

• **You want to connect multiple remote offices that have relatively low traffic demands.** Most offices don't need constant, heavy access either back to headquarters or to their branches. Users transfer some files and log into e-mail. The high cost of leased lines has typically prohibited offices with low bandwidth requirements from internetworking, but with the lower costs of dial-up internetworking (and advances in speed), such connectivity can be cost-effective. Small offices can benefit from the increased communication that, until recently, companies with big budgets have been enjoying.

For example, a headquarters may allow access to its networks from various branch offices. Another scenario is to let one company access a particular portion of another company's network, say an inventory database or online information service. Many companies have already done so on an informal basis, quite successfully, using standard telephone lines.

• **You want to telecommute.** As notebooks proliferate and as workers become increasingly mobile, the need to access the home network becomes paramount. Dial-up internetworking provides one solution. Asynchronous communication servers and cellular communication are others. Anyone who has used remote communications software to dial in to a network knows the pitfalls. Remote communications software over a modem can be slow and doesn't always work well. And you can't run any significant applications; at best, you can download or upload a small file (hopefully a compressed one).

Cellular holds holds some promise, but until digital cellular is implemented, the bandwidth offered on the voice network is pitifully low.

With dial-up internetworking, the remote user participates as a full-fledged node on the network, entitled to all of his or her access rights and applications. With communications software, you are merely an emulation of your former self.

Although with dial-up, the speeds can be slow and you wouldn't be eager to restructure a database while remote, you can easily check your e-mail and run similar applications. (Hint: Keep your applications software local. You might also want someone at headquarters to administrate your electronic mailbox for you; it can be dreadfully slow if done remotely.)

With higher speed lines such as Switched 56 or ISDN, you could run a CPU-intensive application, such as a database or CAD program.

• **You want to manage networks.** Remote communications packages are the tried-and-true answer to remote network management, yet these applications provide relatively limited control and functionality. With dial-up internetworking and the capability to run as a full network node, you can do anything remotely that you can do locally. Systems integrators and in-house administrators can take advantage of such products to provide support remotely for their customers.

• **You want to back up leased lines.** Leased lines are typically quite reliable but nevertheless subject to outages. Dial-up routers can be in place waiting to provide a backup to a leased-line service. When you need the bandwidth, it's there. In this way, you can build a hybrid of a public and private network.

HOW TO DO IT

To engage in dial-up internetworking, you don't need much equipment: a dial-up router on both ends of the link and a telephone line. Dial-up routers are new, with products currently or shortly available from Centrum Communications (San Jose), CMC (Santa Barbara, CA), DCA/ICC (Alpharetta, GA), NEC (Sunnyvale, CA), and Telebit (Sunnyvale).

In essence, a dial-up router isn't much different from a "regular" router, except that it handles dialing up the remote site for the user. When the router detects traffic coming in, it checks whether the data is destined for a remote site. If so, the dial-up router uses its built-in modem to dial that site's telephone number, establishes the connection, and transfers the data.

After a certain period of inactivity, the router breaks down the connection. Dial-up routers will most likely end up in locations where the users lack computer expertise, so find a product that requires minimal human intervention (and, of course, supports remote management).

As with ordinary routers, support for multiple protocols, such as NetWare IPX/SPX, TCP/IP, and Apple AFP, is critical. The router must be able to accommodate the different network users who dial in. Also look for standards-compliance. A TCP/IP router that uses Point-to-Point Protocol (PPP) will be able to communicate with other TCP/IP routers using that protocol; a router implementing a vendor's proprietary WAN protocol will be able to communicate only with its own kind.

Look for routers that are designed to survive in a WAN environment. With a dial-up, you pay for every packet sent over the wire; operating in that environment requires you to be packet-wise. NetWare routers should implement Burst Mode and filter Service Advertising Protocols to reduce the sheer numbers of unnecessary packets.

Some dial-up routers locally acknowledge a NetWare server's keepalive packets, a process that also reduces overhead. "Spoofing" the server with local acknowledgements can be tricky business, and it has to be carefully implemented. Whatever the network protocol, compression is key, both for the packet header and for the actual data portion.

Security is of paramount importance. Dial-up lines are inherently less secure than leased lines; you don't know where the line physically goes and who can access it the process. Passwords are the bare minimum. Call-back, where the user calls in and the router calls back to a predetermined number, is useful. Tighter security, including better authentication schemes, is needed.

This tutorial has focused on low-speed dial-up lines, but other options exist. Switched 56 is a dial-up. circuit-switched service that provides 56Kbps of bandwidth. Available only in the United States, the phone companies have prices Switched 56 rather aggressively, With the impending deployment of National IDSN, IDSN may indeed become a real service. A basic rate ISDN interface can deliver 64Kbps or 128Kbps of bandwidth for the cost of one or two Switched 56 lines

Frame Relay

For LAN/WAN interconnections, frame relay was proffered as the solution to expensive leased lines and to slow packet-switched networks. To date, end users have not necessarily embraced frame relay with unbounded enthusiasm, although it is experiencing a surge in interest. Will frame relay win the race, or will it go the way of ISDN?

Oddly enough, frame relay is a byproduct of the ISDN standards work. Frame relay will eventually be offered on Broadband ISDN networks, but it is currently marketed as an upgrade to X.25 packet-switched networks.

Frame relay makes sense if your enterprise network interconnects more than four sites and network traffic is fairly heavy. If your network traffic is primarily from terminals, then X.25 is a better service option; however, if your network traffic is from workstations and PCs, then frame relay is probably your best bet. Nevertheless, frame relay suffers from growing pains.

BACKTRACK TO X.25

Packet-switched networks are suitable for connecting geographically dispersed locations, because instead of directly connecting each remote site to the headquarters or connecting each site to every other one, packet switching provides a "cloud" network into which sites can connect. Once attached to the cloud, any site can communicate with any other. Each site has a local connection, which is then connected into a larger packet-switched network.

Packet-switched technologies maintain virtual connections between two users. It appears to the end users that they are directly connected, when, in reality, the connection may go through intermediate points. Virtual connections can either be permanent or temporary. A permanent virtual circuit is guaranteed to be available at all times. With a temporary, or switched virtual circuit, the connection is set up for the duration of the transmission, then broken down.

307

X.25 is a packet-switched technology that has been used for more than 10 years. It was designed to transport character data from host terminals, and for such low-bandwidth applications, X.25 delivers adequate performance. But stuffing Ethernet or Token Ring traffic through a 56/64Kbps X.25 virtual circuit is much more difficult.

X.25 was developed when the telephone system was built from copper lines, and it necessarily included a large number of error-detecting and -correcting routines to handle the effects of noise, dropped calls, and other problems. However, since the vast majority of the U.S. phone network is fiber-optic, the error-detecting and -correcting code in X.25 can be unnecessary overhead.

And so frame relay was developed—originally to run in the ISDN "D" channel. Frame relay retains many of X.25's good traits, including packet switching, while dropping other traits, such as the overhead. Frame relay was developed under the aegis of the CCITT I.122 and the corresponding American National Standards Institute committee 1.606.

JUMP TO FRAME RELAY

Frame relay's benefits include low overhead, high capacity with low delay, and reliable data transfer over existing public networks. It is largely designed to be a public service for interconnecting private local area networks, although private networks can be built.

Frame relay is generally considered to be able to provide service at speeds up to 2.048Mbps, although some service providers claim that they will be able to squeeze out 45Mbps. Public frame relay carriers have rolled out frame relay services in the increments of 56Kbps, fractional T-1, and full T-1. Frame relay services will come from the RBOCs, interexchange carriers, and value-added networks (VANs), including British Telecom, Pacific Bell, CompuServe, and Wiltel. More than 10 companies offer frame relay service.

Frame relay operates on OSI Layers 1 and 2, whereas X.25 operates on Layers 1, 2, and 3. Because frame relay operates under the network layer, it is independent of the upper-layer protocols, such as TCP/IP or IPX. This arrangement delivers greater flexibility.

Frame relay achieves high throughput with low delay by eliminating the overhead of error detection and correction. Data integrity is insured only through a cyclic redundancy check, and any corrupted packet is discarded. When necessary, the network-layer device—usually a router—handles retransmissions. That device must detect the transmission failure and request a retransmission. Although errors will occur less frequently because of the more reliable phone lines, the responsibility of handling them has simply moved to another device that must be capable of handling the added work. Frame relay will also drop packets when the network is too congested.

Frame relay offers some pricing advantages over other WAN technologies. It is priced on a distance- and usage-intensive basis. T-1, for example, is priced according to the distance between the two sites; the greater the distance, the more expensive the T-1 line. X.25 is priced based on usage; the higher the volume of traffic, the more you pay.

X.25 is used rather infrequently in the United States because leased lines are plentiful and relatively inexpensive; however, X.25 is widely used internationally. X.25 is often the only reliable WAN method, as many countries' phone systems are outdated and leased lines are not readily available. As a follow-on to X.25, frame relay will be popular in Europe as well as for connecting U.S. sites to those abroad. With 11 sites, British Telecom is the only carrier to offer international frame relay service.

FRAME RELAY AND YOU

Like LANs, frame relay uses a variable length packet, with sizes ranging from a few bytes to more than 4,000 bytes. A variable packet length enables it to accommodate the LAN's bursts in traffic; however, because the delay is unpredictable, frame relay is not suitable for voice or video traffic—only data.

Each frame includes an 11-bit address field, the Data Link Connection Identifier (DLCI), which supplies the virtual circuit number that corresponds to a particular port on a router. Frame relay offers independent packet addressing, which also reduces overhead. Private virtual circuits may be set up between addresses.

A variety of devices can be used to bring frame relay to your LAN. If you choose a public frame relay service, you'll need frame relay equipment on your premises, as well as a connection to the frame relay network via the local loop.

Most corporations use a router with a frame relay interface card. These routers may use specialized hardware or run on a PC.

You can also use a multiplexer, commonly referred to as a mux, that accepts data from the LAN and forwards it to the frame relay network. A mux is handy in a point-to-point configuration, but if your network uses multiple protocols or has a complex configuration, then you should use routers.

If you implement a private frame relay network because of security, reliability, or control issues, you will need to purchase frame relay switches. The added benefits may offset the costs of investing in your own switching equipment.

Frame relay equipment has the advantage of being relatively similar to X.25 equipment. In many cases, the manufacturer does little more than change the software to give an X.25 device frame relay functionality. This similarity can make upgrading from X.25 to frame relay more cost-effective than switching to another WAN technology.

FRAME RELAY FOIBLES

Frame relay seemed to have been met with astounding acceptance—until you began to measure actual usage. Like any new technology, frame relay was hyped by the manufacturers and the media, and when customers went to purchase it, many were disappointed to discover that frame relay coverage was spotty, the standard is not complete, and the technology did not work as promised.

Frame relay comes in two versions: *Frame relay 1* sets up a permanent virtual circuit, in which the connection must be maintained at all times. One of the touted benefits is that frame relay offers "bandwidth on demand." This benefit should not only mean that you can dial up extra bits per second when the LAN traffic surges, but also that you can dial up the service itself as needed.

The next version of the standard, *frame relay 2*, will offer this switched virtual circuit service. When switched virtual circuits do become available, frame relay will become more flexible, since users can dial up the service.

Frame relay does not handle congestion with grace. When there's too much traffic on the frame relay network, the frame relay equipment drops frames. Because network traffic travels in bursts, the receiving device's buffer can easily become overloaded. The device discards the packets and waits for the end nodes to notice and retransmit. This strategy is not reliable for mission-critical networks.

The two methods for handling congestion within frame relay are Explicit Congestion Notification (ECN) and Consolidated Link-Layer Management

(CLLM). Neither method is standard, and it remains the prerogative of each vendor and service provider to implement it differently or not at all. This lack of conformity makes communication among different vendors' frame relay products difficult at best. ECN offers the ability to communicate traffic overload problems downstream and upstream. ECN can be done from the source node in the direction of the data flow, which is called *Forward ECN*. Or it may be done from the data flow back toward the sending node. This process defines *Backward ECN*. The congestion flag is set in the DLCI address, so that all sending and receiving nodes know that the network is congested. With CLLM, one of the DLCIs is used to send link-layer control messages. These messages can be coded to include the type of congestion and the addresses of the DLCIs involved.

In addition to ECN and CLLM, the router can handle the congestion, although errors can be handled more quickly at the lower layers of the OSI stack.

Each frame relay carrier offers a different set of access rates, pricing, and price discounts. When selecting a frame relay carrier, check the link speed and the committed information rate, or the data rate between two sites, that the carrier guarantees. You should specify a committed information rate that's below the link speed you think you'll need; this way the frame relay network can accommodate bursts of LAN traffic. In some instances, you'll have to lease a line between your site and the frame relay point of presence. Also, because few service providers actually offer the service, the area of coverage is currently limited.

WHAT TO DO, WHAT TO DO

Frame relay is a good interim media. Technically, it's better for LAN traffic than is X.25, and it has particular applicability for international networks. Yet its ultimate success will be determined by factors beyond technology. If the service providers price frame relay aggressively, then users will be encouraged to try a new service. Frame relay's success may be dampened by technologies such as ATM and SMDS that not only offer high speeds but, more importantly, are able to carry voice and video as well as data. For it is in the high-speed integration of data and voice that a true enterprise LAN/WAN can be constructed.

An ISDN Issue

ISDN has been a much-maligned telecommunications service. Saddled with secondary meanings of "I Still Don't Need it", and "I Still Don't Know", ISDN may be regaining some respect.

ISDN—Integrated Digital Services Network—has had limited success as a telecommunications service offering in the United States, primarily because of incompatibility and tariffing problems. Various ISDN switch manufacturers implemented different versions of the Consultative Committee for International Telephony and Telegraphy's 1988 ISDN specification, making one vendor's equipment unable to communicate with another's. The best you could hope for was pockets of ISDN. Service coverage had been limited to large metropolitan areas, and when available, ISDN equipment and installation costs, as well as tariffs, are higher than those for the public switched telephone network and packet-switched networks.

So while the Regional Bell Operating Companies (RBOCs) have proposed ISDN for more than a decade, it has not been widely deployed. In its stead have come less-expensive and more-available services from the RBOCs, local exchange carriers, and public-switch network providers, including Switched 56, fractional T-1, and frame relay. And X.25, while geriatric, provides world-wide coverage for data communications.

But with the November 1992 ratification of National ISDN-I, a single specification finally exists for ISDN service across most parts of the United States. But national coverage still has limitations. In the first phase, only Basic Rate service is offered, meaning users have a maximum of 144Kbps of bandwidth. AT&T and MCI were initially the only long-distance carriers. Some RBOCs, notably US West and Southwestern Bell, initially opted not to upgrade to ISDN-I. Compatible ISDN will be available in isolated islands across most of the country.

OVER HERE, OVER THERE

The Corporation for Open Systems proposed National ISDN-I in February 1991 to stop the squabbling among the ISDN switch vendors. The November, 1992 issue represents its first fruits. Meanwhile, in Europe and Japan, vendors haven't been bickering; they've been installing ISDN to upgrade their aging X.25 packet-switched networks.

According to Frost & Sullivan (New York), the total European ISDN market was $4.62 billion in 1992, and the market research firm expected the figure to be $5.91 billion by 1994. By 1997, the ISDN market should be $10.23 billion. Germany leads the world market with the largest installed base of ISDN, holding a 30-percent share. The United Kingdom maintains a 25-percent share and France holds 20 percent. Frost & Sullivan expects to see the most growth in Spain and Italy. A standard ISDN service that will become available in several European countries starting this year will encourage market growth.

Declining prices remain key to the growth of the market. By 1997, the cost of ISDN Customer-Premises Equipment (CPE) will fall to one-twentieth of its 1992 cost. An ISDN PC terminal adapter that costs $1,000 today will cost $50 by 1997. While the greatest market growth will come in ISDN-capable PBXs, Frost & Sullivan expects to see significant growth in the PC workstation market as well as the PC board market because of the use of LANs and fax cards.

AN APPLICATION PUSH

Manufacturers often avoid the term *ISDN*, because of the negative connotation that ISDN has in the United States, instead referring to the service as "bandwidth on demand". But the manufacturers' interests are piqued. Sun Microsystems (Mountain View, CA) shipped SunLink ISDN, an adapter card that provides Basic Rate Interface service to Sun Sparcstation 10 workstations running TCP/IP. The card is certified in France, Germany, the United Kingdom, Japan, and the United States. Sun also plans to OEM the card. Although Sun also offers a frame-relay card, it contends that the real global connectivity will be performed using ISDN.

Vendors such as Ascend Communications (Alameda, CA) offer LAN bridges that will connect LANs using ISDN. Ascend's Multiband LAN Service Unit can use ISDN in addition to leased 56Kbps lines, full and fractional T-1, and Switched 56 to interconnect LANs.

Despite the product-development and marketing efforts of the vendors, ISDN's utility will determine its success. ISDN was once positioned as the way to provide simultaneous digital-voice and data connectivity to the desktop. Stock brokers, engineers, and the like were supposed to benefit from the full integration of voice and data on the same terminal. ISDN was also positioned to deliver videotext, facsimile, and advanced call management services. But ISDN did not combine the telephone and computer into one device. And LANs exploded. ISDN has been repositioned to provide services to residential users, people who work at home, and small businesses. For example, Microsoft is testing ISDN as a way to connect its employees who work at home back to the corporate LAN.

ISDN's technical details have not supported image, video, and telemetry. But its applicability has mutated. ISDN will also prove useful for users at remote sites who need real-time access to corporate databases and services. Document conferencing is also possible if a shared workspace is provided.

In addition to providing connectivity for people working at home and for small businesses, ISDN should prove useful for providing desktop videoconferencing, dial-up data services, and LAN or host interconnection. ISDN can be used to provide connections between LANs as they are needed—a feat leased lines cannot perform. Because of this flexibility, ISDN can be used to accommodate periods of heavy traffic flow, for network backup, and for disaster recovery, where ISDN connections can be set up for short periods of time or according to traffic patterns. For example, a large credit-card company uses ISDN to provide for overflow bandwidth. Instead of leasing a dedicated line to accommodate its two days of peak demand—the day after Christmas and the day after Thanksgiving—the company can use ISDN to provide bandwidth as needed.

A TOUGH MARKET

In this "bandwidth-on-demand" market, ISDN faces some stiff competition. Switched 56 and frame relay also provide similar services. Switched 56 is inexpensive and widely deployed. Because it is a switched service, it is not suitable for voice traffic, but it can carry data and digitized video.

Frame relay, ironically, is a byproduct of work on ISDN. Frame relay is still quite new—equipment is expensive and service coverage is limited—but it has gained momentum. Still, frame relay only operates at speeds up to T-1 (1.544Mbps), whereas ISDN can provide for greater bandwidth.

Switched Multimegabit Data Service (SMDS) is another potential competitor. Currently, it suffers from limited service coverage and overall newness of service and equipment, but SMDS is capable of carrying voice, video, and data at 45Mbps.

Which technology succeeds will be determined by service coverage, service cost, product availability, and ease of use.

In general, a switched service such as Switched 56 or ISDN will make sense over a leased-line service such as fractional or full T-1 when you use the link between five hours and eight hours per day.

According to Ascend Communications, a manufacturer of customer premises switched-digital access equipment, a full T-1 between New York and San Francisco will cost $22,400 per month and a 384Kbps fractional T-1 will cost about $7,500 per month. A six-channel 56/64Kbps switched service will cost about $5,000 per month for five hours of usage per day and about $7,500 to $11,000 for eight hours of usage per day, making switched services fiscally wise. For an international link, the break-even point with a 384Kbps fractional T-1 line is between five hours and seven hours of usage per day.

WALK ON THE TECHNICAL SIDE

ISDN consists of a Basic Rate ISDN (BRI) and a Primary Rate ISDN (PRI) service. BRI is two "Bearer" (B) channels for user-data transfer plus a "Data-link" (D) channel for control and signaling information. BRI provides a total of 144Kbps of bandwidth. In the United States, the Primary Rate access is equivalent to a 1,544Mbps T-1 circuit, and it supports 23 B channels plus one 64Kbps D channel—usually written as 23B+ D. In Europe, the PRI is 30 B channels plus one D channel, since the European equivalent to T-1 is a 2.048Mbps E-1 circuit. The European PRI is typically written as 30B+D. ISDN service can be carried out over a circuit-switched or packet-switched network, although most will be circuit-switched.

Three types of ISDN channels are defined: B, D, and H. The B channel is a 64Kbps clear channel that can carry any digitized data, voice, text, image, or video. A clear channel means no signaling information is sent; it is an open communications line.

The D channel, used for signaling information, can operate at either 16Kbps or 64Kbps. The D channel can be used for common-channel signaling, telemetry, monitoring, alarm signals, videotext, and telephone-to-telephone text messages.

There are three H channels, all providing higher-speed transmissions than the D channel. The HO channel operates at 384Kbps and can be used for switched-video conferencing, high-speed fax, or packet-switched data. Up to four HO channels can be multiplexed into a single H1 channel, which operates at 1.544Mbps. The H1 channel can be used for high-speed data communications or LAN interconnection. The H2 channel, which operates at 1.9Mbps, is available only in Europe.

Two types of services are defined: bearer services and teleservices. Bearer services correspond to a basic service that operates over one or both of the B channels and provides lower-layer functions that are equivalent to those of OSI Layers 1 to 3, such as establishing, holding, and releasing a telecommunications path. Teleservices are the higher-layer services, such as X.400 message handling, videotext, and fax. ISDN services are separated into different layers, as is the OSI model, which provides for greater flexibility for product designers and users.

ISDN, once positioned as the way to provide simultaneous voice and data service to the desktop, is now positioned at the low end, where it will provide services to residential users, home offices, and small businesses. ISDN can provide videotext, dial-up data services, desktop teleconferencing, and advanced call management to the many users who work at home or out of small business offices. It can also deliver bandwidth to LAN users who do not need the constant connection provided by a leased-line service. Although ISDN-1 has resolved the problems of incompatibility and ISDN-2 will resolve the limited geographical availability, ISDN has to fight for its share in a market crowded with WAN service offerings.

Inverse Multiplexing

Where are you most likely to find an inverse multiplexer?

1. In the aisle with the Sears Craftsman tools, next to the extruders.
2. In the classified ads of the sort of magazine that comes wrapped in brown paper.
3. On a rack in the wiring closet.

Inverse multiplexers may not yet be de rigueur for wiring closets, but they're a tool for merging the LAN and the WAN within a budget.

GO WIDE, YOUNG MAN

MIS shops are scrambling to accommodate the convergence of data and the WAN. LANs pump more and more bandwidth to the WAN's edge, but few network engineers have optimized their systems to a WAN environment, where bandwidth is limited and you pay for every transmission.

The traditional WAN solution was leased from one of the phone companies. Leased services, although they provide the greatest amounts of bandwidth, are expensive. Depending on the distance between the two points, T-1 lines can run you a five-figure bill per month.

In response to the constricted economy and the advent of LANs, WAN-service providers developed options more attractive to data users both in price and technology. The Regional Bell Operating Companies, interexchange carriers, and value-added network providers are heavily promoting these services, including frame relay, ISDN, and SMDS.

But you don't have to venture into a new and unproven technology to get better service; you can recycle what you already have. The public-switched network offers time-proven service, and the prices are low. A 56Kbps data call now costs about the same as a voice call.

INVERSE MULTIPLEXING

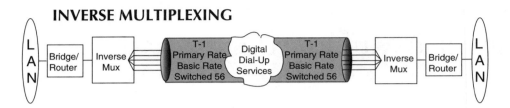

Figure 1. An inverse multiplexer makes multiple lower-speed (and lower-cost) lines look like a single higher-speed (but still lower-cost) line to the applications at either end.

Bandwidth on demand dictates that users can access dial-up lines to call up additional WAN bandwidth. So when a LAN application bursts and more data needs to be sent than there is pipe to send it through, another switched-service line can automatically be called into action.

From bandwidth on demand comes inverse multiplexing.

MORE ELEGANT THAN ITS NAME

What inverse multiplexing accomplishes is more elegant than its moniker suggests. Ordinary multiplexing takes multiple low-speed lines and puts them onto one high-speed line. Inverse multiplexing spreads a high-speed output over multiple low-speed (and presumably lower-cost) lines, while maintaining the appearance of a high-speed transmission. Hence the name "inverse."

Inverse multiplexing works as follows. A T-1 line is made up of 24 channels, each running at 64Kbps, for a total bandwidth of 1.544Mbps. Each channel only has 56Kbps of throughput, because 8Kbps is necessary for in-band signaling. The key is that a T-1 line consists of 24 separate channels.

For example, you can inverse multiplex two 56Kbps lines into what appears to the application to be one 112Kbps pipe. (The number and speed of lines is indicated using Nx, where the "N" denotes the number of lines and the speed follows the "x." So two 56Kbps lines are referred to as 2x56.) Inverse multiplexing typically uses multiple 56Kbps leased or switched lines, although 64Kbps lines can be used internationally. You can also use ISDN Basic Rate Interface, ISDN Primary Rate Interface, ISDN HO Switched 384, or full T-1 (see Figure 1).

The benefit is that you are buying low-cost, low-speed lines and ratcheting up the speed yourself. With inverse multiplexing, you can get the bandwidth

INSIDE INVERSE MULTIPLEXING

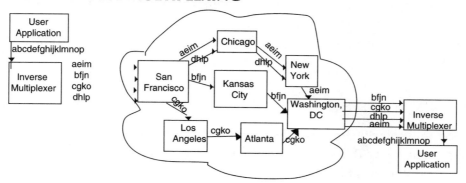

Figure 2. An inverse multiplexer aggregates different data streams over higher-speed lines. The separate channels take diverse paths through the network and arrive at their destination but not necessarily at the same time or in the right order. The inverse mux puts the packets back in the proper order and adjusts for any delay.

equivalent of a T-1 but at a much lower price. You can buy fractional T-1 today, but the applications view the channels as separate.

Inverse multiplexing will be most beneficial if you are trying to internetwork several LANs, but it is also applicable for videoconferences, traffic overflow, and disaster recovery.

INSERT THE INVERSE MUX

Figure 2 shows how an inverse multiplexer works. Multiple high speed data streams are input into the inverse mux. These data streams can come from the different ports on the same device, perhaps a router, or they may come from different sources, perhaps a router, a terminal server, and a video codec. The inverse mux uses time-division multiplexing to split the data stream into multiple 56Kbps channels.

The separate 56Kbps channels take diverse paths through the public switched network-unbeknown to the application. For example, Figure 2 shows that the "abcdefghiijklmnop" message is broken into four streams: "aeim," "bfjn," "cgko," and "dhlp." the "aeim" stream goes from the switch in San Francisco to Chicago and New York before it reaches Washington, DC. The "cgko" packet goes to Los Angeles and Atlanta on its way to the District. The four data streams arrive at the same destination but not necessarily at the same time or in the right order. then, like a router, which segments and reassembles packets, the inverse mux buffers the arriving packets, and puts them in the proper order. It then passes the intact information to the router, then the user's application.

A STANDARD METHOD

Inverse multiplexing improves on a feature some routers offer—load balancing or load sharing. With load sharing, the router tries to balance the traffic across multiple outgoing ports; however, load sharing adds about 30 percent overhead to the transmission. Also, each vendor's implementation is unique, so one vendor's implementation will not work with another's. You're locked into a proprietary solution.

Inverse multiplexing accomplishes the same function but uses a standard called Bonding. This specification was written by the Bandwidth on Demand Interoperability Group, a consortium of 40 manufacturers, and has been passed to the American National Standards Institute TR41.4 group.

Bonding supports four modes. Mode 0 is a special mode for dual 56Kbps calls, which offers special economies when both sides are using 56Kbps lines. Mode 1 works with any number of lines (called Nx) and has no subchannel. The subchannel can be used for control signaling and other types of information. Mode 2 is also Nx but has an in-band subchannel overhead of 1.6 percent. Finally, Mode 3 is also Nx with an out-of- band subchannel.

Ascend, a leading manufacturer of inverse muxes, has its own protocol—Ascend Inverse Multiplexing (AIM)- which it recommends for higher performance. AIM supports four modes: Static, which has no subchannel; Manual, which has an in-band subchannel overhead of 0.2 percent; Delta, which is an out-of-band subchannel; and Dynamic, for dial-up bandwidth.

The ISDN H.221 specification can also be used for inverse multiplexing, but it is primarily used for video, not LAN, data.

IMMEDIATE GRATIFICATION

Inverse multiplexing offers a way to "roll your own" dial-up bandwidth service immediately. You don't have to wait for the phone companies to tariff new service offerings.

Later this year, the WAN-service providers will step up their offerings of commercial services that will deliver the equivalent of inverse multiplexing. For example, AT&T currently offers Switched 384, which provides the same bandwidth as six 64Kbps lines and an inverse mux. Yet 384Kbps is a rather unwieldy chunk of bandwidth and so less attractive to LAN users.

But later this year, the long-distance carriers will offer dial-up service in more manageable increments. ISDN HO Switched 384, ISDN HI Switched 1536, and ISDN Multirate (Nx64) services are becoming available.

The carriers may make inverse multiplexing less attractive in another way. When you dial up additional lines using an inverse multiplexer, you are charged for each call setup. So if you dial up six 64Kbps lines, you are charged for six separate calls. If you buy Switched 384 or similar service, you are charged for only one call.

Ethernet Switching

If an Ethernet network begins to display symptoms of congestion low through-put, slow response times. and high rates of collision the reflexive response is to plan installation of pervasive higher-speed connections. However, it may not be necessary to make huge investments in Fiber Distributed Data Interface (FDDI) or Asynchronous Transfer Mode (ATM) technology.

Several approaches exist that can preserve much or all of the existing network's cabling and workstation interface card infrastructure while still greatly enhancing the throughput for users, even if demanding applications, such as multimedia production and video conferencing, are on a company's horizon. The most promising techniques, as well as the best return on investment, could well consist of installing the right mixture of Ethernet switches.

An Ethernet switch is, in principle, a multiport bridge. It concerns itself with the OSI layer two media access control (MAC) information in the frames it processes. It learns the MAC source addresses associated with each port as traffic appears, so little or no manual administration is required.

When a frame arrives at a port, the switch examines its MAC destination address. If the destination is local to the segment the frame is on, the switch filters the frame—that is, it ignores the frame and does not retransmit it. If the switch's address database associates the destination with another port. the frame is forwarded (or transmitted) on that port. If the frame's destination is unknown, the switch transmits it to every port except the incoming one.

Like bridges, switches segment traffic on one port from traffic on the others. Therefore, groups of heavy traffic producers, such as programmers, CAD jockeys. or multimedia producers, with their servers, can be isolated from more mundane users. The light-duty users will no longer be slowed by the traffic of heavy users, and the heavy users can be provided with as much as 10Mbps or more of dedicated throughput if needed.

Aside from having the marketing advantages of a hot new name, switch, rather than a tired old one, bridge, the current generation of switches also has some technical advantages over the bridges of yesteryear.

Switches often have a high-performance backplane that can support very high throughput—as high as the number of paths through the switch, multiplied by the throughput of each paths—from 60Mbps for a 12-port 10BaseT switch, to multiple Gbps for large switches with 100Mbps ports. Unlike traditional bridges, the optimal deployment of switches can result in aggregated total throughput; when everything works right, each additional switch can add to the total performance of the system.

Switches can also employ new tricks to overcome the historical drawbacks of bridges. Some switches read beyond the data link header in each frame and identify the network layer protocol. With information, the switch can selectively filter specific protocols for security or performance purposes.

Other switches creatively deploy queuing buffers to combat the phenomenon known as blocking, in which particular paths experience a backlog or latency despite the ready availability of alternate paths. The advances in Application Specific Integrated Circuit (ASIC) technology that we have come to take for granted elsewhere have also bolstered the performance of switching devices.

SHARED 10MBPS PORTS

The earliest Ethernet switches, introduced by Kalpana (Sunnyvale, CA, now a subsidiary of Cisco Systems) in 1990, had sharable 10Mbps ports. The Kalpana switches use "cut-through" methods; unlike traditional bridges, which are classified as "store-and-forward" devices, the Kalpana switches begin forwarding a frame as soon as they read the destination address and look it up.

The cut-through technique reduces the latency, or delay, for a forwarding operation to about 40 microseconds compared to as much as 1,200 microseconds for a store-and-forward bridge (see figure). Latency is a major factor for protocols such as NetWare's IPX (before burst mode became available), which have a lot of frame-by-frame acknowledgment, but is less of a factor for protocols such as IP, which can handle acknowledgment activity more efficiently. Cut-through switches look their best on traditional NetWare networks.

SWITCHING AN ETHERNET FRAME

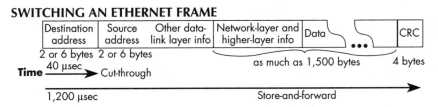

CUT-THROUGH VS. STORE-AND-FORWARD: A cut-through switch begins forwarding frames as soon as it reads the destination address. To perform the CRC data integrity function, a store-and-forward switch must read the entire frame before forwarding it.

However, the cut-through method of forwarding can perpetuate and aggravate problems. Store-and-forward devices use the cyclic redundancy check (CRC) field to verify that frames are well-formed; they discard runts (short frames typically disrupted by a collision) and jabbers (overly long frames sometimes caused by a defective NIC). Cut-through switches pass these bad frames along. Jabbers often look like broadcast frames to a cut-through switch, and can be cascaded all over the network if nothing is done to eliminate them. Some switch producers let network managers choose between cut through and store-and-forward operation.

Shared 10Mbps switches require no other changes to the network. Existing hubs. NICs, and cable can be used transparently.

Interesting variants of this class of switch are produced by Matrox (Dorval, Quebec) and XNet Technology (Milpitas, CA). These switches are cards that plug into the ISA or EISA bus of a PC and provide as many as 16 ports at a very low per-port cost in comparison with standalone switches.

DEDICATED 10MBPS PORTS

Workgroups with many high-bandwidth users may be interested in a class of Ethernet switches, pioneered by Grand Junction Networks (Fremont, CA), that segments a network giving each node its own port. Each user or device on one of these switches has a dedicated, collision-free 10Mbps connection to any other node. Because of the simplifications that result from unshared segments, these dedicated workgroup switches cost much less than switches that support multiple MAC addresses per port.

Like switches with shared 10Mbps ports, dedicated port switches use existing NICs, cable, and hubs. However, none of the ports can be shared by multiple users.

FULL-DUPLEX PORTS AND 10MBPS PORTS

A dedicated Ethernet connection doesn't need to listen for collisions, because no other traffic source is there to collide with. For this reason, such a connection can freely receive and transmit at the same time; in other words, it can operate in full duplex mode rather than the usual half-duplex. If incoming and outgoing traffic is perfectly balanced. the throughput on existing cables could be as high as 20Mbps.

At first glance, the advantage of full-duplex operation seems marginal because most workstation applications seem to receive much more traffic than they transmit; the "additional" channel will be idle much of the time. However. a lot of invisible acknowledgment and housekeeping traffic takes place on most networks, so, if the added cost of full-duplex cards and switches is not high, the purchase may be worthwhile for workstations.

In any case, server-to-switch traffic is likely to be better balanced between transmitting and receiving, and the added cost of a server NIC and one or two full-duplex ports on a switch can be more readily justified than the cost for upgrading a workstation to full duplex. Full-duplex workstation attachments could also be cost-effective for video conferencing, which normally produces symmetrical data traffic in both directions.

An additional option for server connections on NetWare networks is to connect more than one server NIC, either full- or half-duplex, to a switch. This solution requires a special NLM on the server that balances traffic between the NICs and overcomes NetWare's reluctance to permit the same network segment to have multiple server connections. Network Specialists (Lyndhurst NJ) and Kalpana were the first companies to introduce these NetWare add-ons.

SWITCHES WITH HIGH-SPEED PORTS

If full-duplex or combined 10Mbps connections to a server (or a backbone) are

AGGREGATING BANDWIDTH WITH SWITCHES

FastSwitch
10/100 AG

- - - Dedicated 10Mbps
bandwidth to each node
— Dedicated 100Mbps
bandwidth to server
▬ Shared 100Mbps
bandwidth hub
interconnection

1-25

FastSwitch
10/100

FastSwitch
10/100

26-50

51-75

SCALING FOR POWER USERS: Each of the 125 nodes has a private Ethernet connection. Each server receives 100Mbps of bandwidth. The connection between switches is a shared 100Mbps link. Aggregate forwarding bandwidth is 850 Mbps.

FastSwitch
10/100

FastSwitch
10/100

76-100

101-125

Source: Grand Junction Networks

still a bottleneck, the next approach is obtaining a switch with at least one 100Mbps port. FDDI is a mature, standardized, widely implemented technology. NetWorth (Irving, TX) and 3Com (Santa Clara, CA) are some of the leaders in providing combination FDDI/Ethernet switches.

For a high-speed server or backbone attachment, an alternative to FDDI is 100BaseT Fast Ethernet. Grand Junction has introduced a product with 24 dedicated 10Mbps ports and two 100BaseT ports. In theory, a 100BaseT switch could outperform a switch based on FDDI, because it would not have to perform translational bridging between FDDI and Ethernet.

With switches that include high speed ports, the NICs and cable that connect workstations and printers are unchanged. Only the connections to servers, routers, other switches, or workstations that require 100Mbps throughput need to be upgraded.

ATM Basics

Asynchronous Transfer Mode—what a mouthful of vague abstractions. If there weren't so much money and job security riding on ATM, it would be awfully tempting for many of us to ignore it. A transfer mode is a method of transmitting, multiplexing, and switching data in a communications network. (Multiplexing is combining multiple streams of data on a single circuit; if it weren't for multiplexing, the view of the sky in our cities would be blocked by telephone wires.)

It's only possible to understand "asynchronous" by getting a grasp on "synchronous," The terms refer to digital signals; more specifically, they identify two ways that units of data are framed or blocked within a stream of bits. Synchronous signals are closely tied to some sort of clock, so each unit of data begins, for example, precisely at 0.0ms, then 7.5ms, then 15.0ms, then 22.5ms, and so forth. Asynchronous signals are not bound tightly to a clock—perhaps their data units have a start and a stop bit, or some kind of unique bit pattern to identify the beginning and end of a character or a packet.

Most serial communications and practically all LAN communications are asynchronous, but most data transfers in and out of your microprocessor, the traffic on your parallel port, and the traffic on your computer's bus, are synchronous. Given a steady stream of data, synchronous transmission tends to be more efficient than asynchronous, while asynchronous transmission tends to be more flexible and resilient.

The telephone companies, who incidentally built the infrastructure for wide-area computer data communications when they built their voice networks, can be forgiven for concentrating on a data type—human speech—that is highly intolerant of timing variations. As they built equipment to handle thousands and millions of simultaneous conversations, they developed techniques for multiplexing numerous digital voice circuits on single lines first copper wires, then fiber optic cable.

Time division multiplexing turned out to be the best way to combine many

CARRYING A BIT STREAM

VOICE DATA: With its ability to carry data a high speeds and its small cells, ATM need not maintain strict synchronization for boice bit streams. Source: ATM Forum

telephone circuits on a single physical cable. At each level of concentration, a 64Kbps telephone circuit is tied to a specific time slot. If the timing of a telephone call is disrupted, perhaps through being routed via a satellite or as a result of some malfunction, we might hear a slightly delayed echo that makes it nearly impossible to keep talking, or the whole conversation may be unintelligible. Synchronous communication is well matched to the voice data type.

Video and much multimedia material also matched well with the characteristics of synchronous communication. Not only is there often human speech or other sound involved, the sound can't be allowed to wander away from the image; if it does, the video or multimedia session starts to feel like a badly dubbed Japanese sci-fi movie.

Unfortunately, most computer data communications do not fit well with synchronous methods. For one thing, they tend to be bursty, meaning the ratio of the peak data rate to the average data rate is high. (Synchronous data links have no time gaps—the peak data rate is the same as the average data rate.) Thus, data communicators face the quandary of either paying huge amounts for data pipes that are mostly idle except at peak usage times or suffering through long delays at peak times with a less-expensive small data pipe. The telephone network is not well suited to supply bandwidth-on-demand.

ATM is the result of a compromise among all of the data-type constituencies to find a single common denominator for all types of data. One alternative to time division multiplexing is to use packet or cell multiplexing. A stream of bits is broken up into discrete packets or cells, each of which has a header indicating its path and other worthwhile information. If the cell size is made small, and the overall throughput of the circuit is high, delay-sensitive traffic can be carried along with bursty types of data successfully, and everyone gets what they need from the data link. Voice and video work without glitches, and data customers (potentially) get bandwidth-on-demand. As a universal transport, ATM can plausibly be installed on the desktop, on departmental and campus backbones, on high-capacity wide area services, and even on a global information superhighway system.

During the development of the fundamental ATM definition, the voice interests—particularly the European telephone providers—wanted a 32-byte cell with a 4-byte header, while many North American interests preferred a more efficient 64-byte cell with a 5-byte header. The compromise of a 48-byte cell with a 5-byte header was reached, so, an ATM cell is a 53-byte entity.

ATM AND NETWORKS

Like frame relay and X.25, ATM protocols are connection oriented. ATM sessions take place over virtual circuits (virtual because they need not use particular physical paths, although once the virtual circuit is established, it stays in place for the duration of a session). Most, if not all, of today's ATM services offer only permanent virtual circuits (PVC); setting up and tearing down PVCs is a job for the telephone company unless the ATM network is completely private. The real promise of bandwidth-on-demand will be fulfilled when switched virtual circuits (SVC) become available. PVCs are comparable to leased lines, while SVCs are comparable to dial-up voice service. An ATM SVC will typically take only a fraction of a second to be established, however.

With its connection orientation, ATM does not readily compare with shared medium protocols, such as Ethernet and Token Ring, or with connectionless protocols that perform routing, such as IP and IPX. With the development of LAN emulation standards, ATM services can be made available to Ethernet and Token Ring networks. Products for translating frame relay data to ATM have been announced. IP and Address Resolution Protocol over ATM are

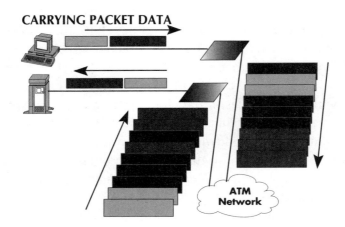

CARRYING PACKET DATA

ATM
Network

COMPUTER DATA: Packets of computer data are chopped up into ATM cells for transit over the ATM virtual circuit, then reassembled at the receiving end. Source: ATM Forum

described in the Internet RFC1577. In general, ATM fits into the data link and physical layers, but because connection-oriented protocols don't require routing, it is possible for ATM to provide services to the upper layer protocols directly. This is the sense in which ATM is supposed to sound the death knell for all routers.

AIM PROTOCOLS

The top layer of the ATM protocol stack is the ATM Adaptation Layer (AAL). Different AALs correspond to the different data types ATM supports. Thus AAL1 permits the ATM device to closely resemble a constant bit-rate voice circuit; AAL3/4 and AAL5 are used for variable bit-rate data types, which are those typically found on computer networks. The AAL is also responsible for integrating the inherently connection-oriented ATM with connectionless data sources, enabling ATM clients to emulate broadcasting and multicasting.

The ATM layer is the common core of all ATM technology. There are multiple AALs and multiple physical layer options, but the protocol that describes the cell header layout and governs the actions of switches on the cells is a constant. The ATM layer is responsible for cell routing, multiplexing, and demultiplexing.

Before any user data can flow over an ATM virtual circuit, each intermediate switch must create a local routing table entry that maps the inbound virtual channel identifier to an outbound port. In order to simplify the routing overhead for intermediate links, ATM defines virtual paths (VP), which are basically virtual channels defined over two or more physical links that are treated as a unit. VPs are semipermanent connections, and their routing tables may be set up in advance. A packet that travels along a VP will not have to be rerouted at each of the component VCs.

Based on the type of data carried in cells, the ATM layer interleaves multiple streams together based on the priority of each type. It is also responsible for identifying congestion, managing faults, and managing traffic.

At the physical layer, now customarily referred to as PHY, ATM supports (or will support) multimode optical fiber, single mode fiber, STP, coaxial cable, and UTP, at throughputs as high as 155Mbps, although the speed of ATM can be extended as far as the market's ability to pay for it. ATM traffic can readily fit into SONET or SDH (Synchronous Digital Hierarchy, the international superset of SONET standards) data streams—the 155Mbps single- and multimode fiber physical layer standards are based on SONET frames. A 44Mbps standard for the DS3 interface, which uses coaxial cable, has also been defined. DS3 facilities are much more widely installed in North America than SONET facilities. At 100Mbps, ATM can use the physical standards defined for FDDI.

The ATM Forum has chosen to adopt existing physical layer standards wherever it can. Potential future standards may include: 52Mbps over Category 3 (or higher) UTP; 155Mbps over Category 5 UTP; and 1.544Mbps for T-1 (or DS1) lines. IBM and several allied companies have also proposed a 25Mbps standard for desktop connections using Category 5 UTP cabling.

The ISDN Connection

To really understand the Integrated Services Digital Network (ISDN), you need to put it into context. You need to see what's come before it to more fully comprehend what the new technology brings. This Tutorial, briefly reviews the existing conventional telephone system before discussing how ISDN departs from the norm.

The conventional telephone system—often referred to by the acronym POTS (meaning plain old telephone system)—is an analog system. The pattern of voltage variations on the telephone line is a direct analog of the acoustical pressure variations that produced them.

The telephone line in your home is typically a single unshielded twisted pair (UTP) of copper wires that runs to the telephone company's central office (CO). This line is usually referred to as the subscriber loop or local loop.

The central office is a key concentration point for telecommunications. Inside the central office is a telephone switch that connects your line with that of the person you want to call, establishing the circuit.

ISDN SPELLED OUT

What's different about ISDN compared to POTS? First, it's digital instead of analog. Second, the "integrated services" portion of the name is a reference to one of the basic goals of ISDN—to provide integrated, multipurpose voice, data, and video communications, all over a single system. Contrast that with today's norm, where you typically need three services to provide the same communications ability: dial-up analog phone lines to carry voice, digital leased lines for data, and coaxial-cable networks (cable TV) for video. The idea that one network can handle all communications types is obviously appealing.

There are two levels of ISDN service. The Basic Rate Interface (BRI) is lower in cost than the other option, and it can run over typical residential subscriber loops without rewiring. BRI consists of three separate channels—two bearer channels (B channels) and one data (or D) channel. Each B channel has a data rate of 64Kbps, while the D channel is 16Kbps. The D channel is used for signaling, such as call setup and tear-down. The B channels carry user data, which might be digitized voice, binary data, or digitized video.

The Primary Rate Interface (PRI) might be used at a business headquarters site. It consists of 23 64Kbps B channels, plus one 64Kbps D channel. Again, the B channels carry the payload (voice, data, or other user information), while the D channel carries telco signaling. To get PRI service, you'll need a T-1 line from your site to your local exchange carrier's CO.

In Europe, the commonly used digital data line that's roughly equivalent to the T-1 line used in North America is known as E-1, and it has a higher capacity than the T-1—2.048Mbps vs. 1.544Mbps. European ISDN PRIs take advantage of the increased capacity and carry 30 64Kbps B channels, plus one 64Kbps D channel.

With POTS, it's a given that one phone line lets you make only one call at a time. If you're on the line when other people try to call you, they'll get a busy signal and will have to wait until you've finished your call before they can get through. With ISDN, it's a little different. With an ISDN BRI, you get two phone numbers—one for each B channel. Consequently, you could make two separate phone calls to different destinations, even though you've got only a single phone line.

PRI B channels are the same as BRI B channels; you can place a call from a BRI to a PRI, or vice versa, linking one of the BRI's B channels to one of the PRI's B channels. With 23 B channels, you could simultaneously have 23 separate ISDN calls going out over a single Primary Rate Interface to the telco, even though each of these calls has a separate destination.

ISDN is a digital, synchronous, full-duplex link. When voice is carried over ISDN, it's digitized at the telco standard of 8,000 eight-bit samples per second. This analog-to-digital conversion is performed by a compression/decompression (codec) device in the ISDN phone. If a conventional analog phone is used, it must be adapted to the network by an ISDN terminal adapter (TA). In this case, the codec is part of the TA.

The sampling rate and sampling precision is the reason 64Kbps was chosen for bearer channel data rates. Eight bits sent 8,000 times per second equals 64,000 bits per second.

ISDN'S BIG PICTURE

The block diagram in the figure shows how user equipment interfaces with the telco-provided ISDN BRI connection. A key feature of the BRI is that it can run over most existing subscriber loops, which are two-wire (single-pair) UTP. On the left side of the diagram (everything left of the letter *U*) is the customer premises, while the right side is the telco side, including the central office ISDN switch.

The telcos don't want customer equipment to connect directly to their networks, for fear of faulty or poorly designed equipment disrupting operation of the network. So the telcos interpose a device known as a network terminator (NT1) between the subscriber loop and customer equipment.

The customer's equipment is referred to as terminal equipment (TE), and there are two classifications of these: TE1 and TE2. TE1 equipment is digital equipment that's ISDN-capable. An ISDN phone is one example of a TE1 device. A TE1 can plug directly into the NT1.

A conventional analog phone or an ASCII data terminal (or the RS-232 serial port on a computer) represents equipment that's not ISDN-ready. Such terminal equipment is classified as TE2. These devices must have an ISDN terminal adapter interposed between them and the NT1. The terminal adapter makes the TE2 equipment ISDN-capable.

If a customer premises switch, also called a PBX, is used to connect an ISDN line to the terminal equipment or terminal adapter, it will reside between that equipment and the NT1. PBXs are classified as NT2 devices.

The figure shows an example of a TE1 and TE2 connected, through a PBX, or NT2, to the NT1 and the subscriber loop. For the TE2 connection, the setup calls for a terminal adapter. At the other end of the subscriber loop is the telco's central office switch. Various reference points have been defined by the standards, and these are shown in the figure as the letters R, S, T, and U.

In the United States, the demarcation point between the telco's network and the customer premises is located at the customer end of the subscriber loop—the point marked *U* in the figure. Martha Haywood, director of engi-

CONNECTING TERMINAL EQUIPMENT TO ISDN

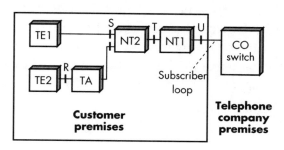

MAKING THE CONNECTION: An ISDN network terminator (NT1) must be placed between the telco's network and customer equipment. Customer equipment (also called terminal equipment or TE) is shown on the left side of the figure. TE1 represents ISDN-capable terminal equipment, while TE2 is non-ISDN equipment, for which an ISDN terminal adapter (TA) is required. Some sites will have a PBX switch on the premises, as shown in NT2.

neering at Telebit (Sunnyvale, CA), a manufacturer of both ISDN- and analog-based remote LAN access equipment, reports that in Europe, the NT1 is traditionally owned by the telecommunications provider, even though it's installed on the customer's premises. Therefore, it is part of the telecommunications network. Because of this, the International Telecommunications Union (ITU) standards body recognizes the T reference point as being the demarcation between the customer's and the telecommunication provider's respective portions of the network.

A customer premises switch (NT2) will most likely be used with PRIs, rather than BRIs, but it's shown in the figure to indicate its place in the overall scheme of things. On most BRIs, TE1s and TAs will be plugged directly into the NT1. The S and T reference points are thus essentially interchangeable; the switch merely serves as a line selector.

Some manufacturers of ISDN terminal equipment and terminal adapters incorporate an NT1 right into the product. In this case, the device is said to have a U interface, since it can plug directly into the subscriber loop. Having a built-in NT1 means there's one less thing to buy, but Telebit's Haywood points out that there can be drawbacks, too. For example, the ISDN standards permit up to eight TEs to be connected to a single NT1. (This doesn't mean that all eight can be active at the same time; only one TE at a time can use a B channel. Thus, a BRI can support only two calls at a time.)

In the case of the BRI, which has two B channels, a terminal adapter and an ISDN phone could both be on-line at the same time, with each device using one of the B channels. But if the terminal adapter had a built-in NT1, you couldn't plug in another device—unless the designers of the terminal adapter had the foresight to put in a port for a phone—because the subscriber loop itself cannot be shared. In other words, there can be only one NT1 per BRI.

Haywood says that initially, there may be strong interest for products with built-in NT1s, but as customers gain experience with ISDN, they'll begin to see the advantage of keeping the NT1 as a separate device.

ACKNOWLEDGMENTS

Thanks to Martha Haywood and Mike McLaughlin, product manager at Telebit, for information they provided.

There's a wealth of information available on ISDN. If you're interested in delving further into the subject, refer to the following sources:

Bell Communications Research (Bellcore), the research arm of the Regional Bell Operating Companies (RBOCs), maintains a World Wide Web site that contains a great deal of information compiled by the National ISDN Users Forum (NIUF). This information is in encapsulated PostScript (EPS) format. To access it, set your Web browser to:

http://info.bellcore.com.

Pacific Bell's Market Applications Lab (510-823-1663) can answer questions about the suitability of ISDN for your application, and what types of equipment you should consider.

Pacific Bell Applications BBS (510-277-1037) has an ISDN tutorial that can be downloaded.

For more information, try the following books on ISDN:

Digital Telephony and Network Integration, Second Edition, by Bernhard E. Keiser and Eugene Strange, Van Nostrand Reinhold, New York, ISBN 0-442-00901-1.

ISDN, Second Edition, by Gary C. Kessler, McGraw-Hill, New York, ISBN 0-07-034247-4.

ISDN and Broadband ISDN, Second Edition, by William Stallings, Macmillan, Englewood Cliffs, NJ, ISBN 0-02-415475-X.

Telecommunications, Second Edition, by Warren Hioki, Prentice Hall, Englewood Cliffs, NJ, ISBN 0-13-123878-7.

Remote Access

Two distinct technologies for out-of-the-office LAN users.

There are two basic ways to access your network from a hotel or from your office at home: a remote control connection or a remote node connection. The first option is conceptually simple. In effect, the dial-up telephone line becomes an extension cord for the monitor, the keyboard, and the mouse, connecting them to a computer at the host site that can log on to the network. (Remote control is possible with non-networked PCs, too.)

In this approach, the remote PC performs no processing operations beyond executing the remote control software itself—it simply updates the display and sends keyboard and mouse input to the host. Exchanges between remote control computers and their hosts take place at the Application level, although some remote control applications can run over networks and therefore use the network protocol stack.

Over telephone lines, direct serial links, and wireless connections, remote control programs are indifferent to whether the host is on a network. Except for the ability of remote control software to perform file transfers to and from a host, remote control is a kind of terminal emulation.

Some of the most popular remote control programs are Symantec's (Cupertino, CA) pcAnywhere, Microcom's (Norwood, MA) Carbon Copy, Traveling Software's (Bothell, WA) LapLink for Windows, Stac Electronics' (San Diego) ReachOut, and Farallon's (Alameda, CA) Timbuktu.

The principal problem with remote control solutions is their expense. A host computer with a network interface, modem, and telephone line, and a remote PC and modem, must be dedicated to every remote session. If the host machines are distributed among different offices, there are potentially serious management problems—primarily the difficulty of providing adequate security and technical support. Finding someone to physically reboot a host machine after it crashes is a potentially difficult problem. Logged-in machines spread throughout the building—with no local users—are a big security risk.

A chassis- or rack-based system of host computers on plug-in boards, such as those provided by Cubix (Carson City, NV) and J&L Information Systems (Chatsworth, CA), can enable network managers to install a high density of remote-session hosts in a central, controlled location and provide some extras such as remote rebooting capabilities and remote management. Unfortunately, the initial cost per host of these systems can be higher than the cost of most standalone PCs with comparable horsepower. (Of course, reduced support, management, and administration costs will offset the initial price difference and save money in the long run.)

In light of the obstacles to providing broad-based remote control capabilities to users, remote node software offers some significant advantages. Unlike remote control, which requires a remote user to have a dedicated modem, a PC, and a network interface, remote node sessions need only a dedicated modem and a serial port. Multiple sessions can readily share a single processor and network interface.

A remote node server is essentially a router (or sometimes a bridge) that translates frames on the serial port to a frame layout that the LAN can accommodate and then passes them along. The processor is required only to route or bridge incoming and outgoing traffic, and it would take more than 150 64Kbps ISDN sessions and more than 1,000 9,600bps asynchronous connections to match the throughput of a 10Mbps Ethernet link—supporting a few remote nodes doesn't take a state-of-the-art microprocessor.

An approach that some software vendors have taken is to combine remote control and remote node software in a single package. Users of these products gain flexibility in matching their access method to various applications and systems.

Remote node servers can be purchased with built-in modems or with serial ports that can be connected to external modems (or to other wide-area links, such as ISDN lines).

REMOTE NODE SERVERS

REMOTE NODE HARDWARE: Self-contained remote node servers are a complete solution, with telephone and LAN interfaces built in. Remote routers and bridges often are supplied with a generic WAN port, which requires an external modem or, if ISDN lines are used, an external terminal adapter. Server-based remote nodes provide the ultimate in flexibilty—even the software must be configured.

ACCESS SERVER HARDWARE

Remote node services can be provided through numerous hardware configurations (see figure). Router or bridge processing can be accomplished on a processor in a dedicated box, on a communications server (including those that provide remote control services), or on a file server doing communication duty, as well as on a product sold as a router or bridge. (The file server must be able to accept add-on software that performs the routing or bridging jobs.) Multiple serial ports may be built in to a dedicated access box or mounted on boards that plug in to the communications server or file server. Standalone modems may be mounted in an external rack and plugged into serial ports. Internal or modular modems may be installed on plug-in boards, or mounted in PC Card (PCMCIA) slots.

Remote connection ports may also support high-speed ISDN connections. ISDN ports may be supplied on plug-in boards for PC-type servers, on modular boards for dedicated servers, or on standalone terminal adapter units (sometimes called "digital modems") that connect to a serial port. Some terminal adapter boxes (and terminal adapter boards that plug into a PC's bus) have integral NT1 functions, so they can connect directly to the ISDN telephone jack. Others require an external NT1 unit to provide an interface between the terminal adapter and the telephone line. To achieve the maximum possible throughput on low-cost dial-up lines, some ISDN access devices support inverse multiplexing of the two 64Kbps B channels to provide as much as 128Kbps throughput.

In many cases, dedicated remote access boxes are the easiest way to provide network access to remote users. Configuration problems are minimal; in fact, some of these products approach the plug-and-play level of installation ease. They may not be the least expensive solution, however, and they are not likely to offer the most flexibility for upgrading and expanding. Routers and remote bridges may be effective remote node solutions when an organization has standardized on a family of devices and wants to maintain consistency. Some devices that have been designed specifically for remote access are just about as easy to set up as a dedicated box—the primary difference is that modems or ISDN attachment equipment must be configured. PC servers that function as remote node servers will offer the biggest configuration challenges—software will have to be configured, as well as the ports that attach to the dial-up lines.

SOFTWARE OPTIONS

Remote access software also comes in many flavors. Dedicated access boxes, such as those made by Shiva (Burlington, MA), Telebit (Sunnyvale, CA), and 3Com (Santa Clara, CA), run their own routing software. The U.S. Robotics (Skokie, IL) remote node server runs Cisco's (San Jose, CA) Internetwork Operating System. IBM's LAN Distance server software runs on OS/2, and AppleTalk Remote Access (ARA) can provide remote node services to Macintosh clients.

Supporting DOS and Windows remote node connections and ARA clients, Novell's NetWare Connect also provides dial-out capabilities (for DOS, Windows, and OS/2 machines) so local network clients can share modems. Windows NT includes Remote Access Server. Attachmate's (Bellevue, WA)

Remote LAN Node (RLN) software supports ARA clients as well as DOS and Windows. (There is also an RLN Turnkey Server, replete with a dedicated box.)

While most traditional remote node applications use some form of proprietary interface for remote client-to-node server sessions, PPP is beginning to dominate the field. Unlike its predecessor, SLIP, PPP supports most ordinary LAN protocols—not just TCP/IP. Defined by the Internet Engineering Task Force (IETF) request for comments (RFC) process, PPP is a variant of the High-level Data Link Control (HDLC) protocol and can be thought of as a (usually slower) alternate to Ethernet or Token Ring at the Data Link layer. PPP can work with Physical layers that consist of modems and analog telephone links as well as with ISDN telephone lines. In remote node clients and servers, PPP support holds out the promise of interoperability among products from multiple hardware and software vendors.

WHICH ONE WHEN?

Remote node access is ideal when the remote client machine has applications installed on it and the purpose of the connection is to transfer or manipulate data in relatively small doses. SQL-based database operations and desktop applications that use shared directories on a LAN for data storage lend themselves to remote node services. Because the remote pipe is a thin one—especially if modems sit between the remote client and the server—it is best to avoid 1MB- or even 100KB-sized data transfers. For example, login.exe has some 111KB. Executing this program to log in remotely can be slow if it must first be loaded over a 9,600bps connection. Remote node users should keep local copies of both essential network utilities and their applications.

Traditional desktop databases, such as dBase, want to load data files into local RAM—the client itself is the database "server" and the network drive is simply a file server. Over a remote node link, access to a 1MB database will be painfully slow even if the application is installed on the remote client machine. Graphics applications also involve notoriously large files.

With large data files, and when applications are installed only on the host system, remote control provides a huge performance advantage. Because the files move across only high-speed local links and program execution is local, the thin pipe—which updates only the screen and keyboard/mouse actions—doesn't become a bottleneck. In fact, a remote control client with a pitiful 386 can take over a state-of-the-art processor at the host.

Remote e-mail is a special case. The remote clients provided by e-mail vendors such as Lotus cc:Mail (Mountain View, CA) connect via a sort of application-specific remote node connection. These connections can be assigned to a specific telephone number and the security of the connection can be managed. The remote e-mail software posts mail to the mother ship post office and downloads new messages, but will not necessarily display old messages, BBSs, and other material that would appear locally. For full-featured e-mail access to a single, complete in-box, remote control is the best choice.

With the increasing availability of ISDN connections and advances in compression technology, the demand for remote control may not grow as fast as the demand for less-costly remote node connections. Nevertheless, programs keep getting bigger and multimedia files are generally many times the size of traditional text files, so the need for remote control won't disappear soon.

Section VI

Network Management

Network Management

Although the physical location of the personal computers on a local area network seldom changes, networks are still dynamic entities. That is, the logical makeup of any network fluctuates from moment to moment.

For example, the number of data and application files in use or stored away, the amount of available disk storage space, the number of users logged in to the LAN, and the volume of traffic passing through the network cabling all change continually. Moreover, a network offers users a distributed-processing environment, with some processing performed by a centrally located server, some done at users' workstations, adding even more activity to the LAN.

Keeping this conglomeration of network hardware, software, cables, and the people using them working efficiently comes under the ambiguous term of *network management*. it's ambiguous in that managing a network can range from the simple to the complex, from a moment's quick fix of plugging in a misplaced network cable to a day-long search for an obscure disk problem.

Network management can be as simple as creating a boot diskette for a new user and making sure that user has proper access to network resources. (Although in truth these jobs may not be all that simple in some widely distributed networks.)

Or managing a network can include daily disk-maintenance duties—backing up network files or defragmenting disk directories. Or it may mean troubleshooting the LAN, trying to discover why some users are experiencing slow network response. Or it may include reconfiguring a remote internetwork device to improve overall system performance.

In short, network management incorporates an almost unlimited list of duties—basically, doing whatever it takes to keep the LAN running smoothing and efficiently, with minimal or no downtime.

This job has grown even more difficult as networks have become larger and more complex. The evolution from small workgroups of often identical PCs to large internetworks made up of dissimilar machines—IBM PS/2s, Macintoshes, PC clones, printers, communications gateways, and bridges and routers—has brought more power to the desktop while adding immense complexity to the network manager's job.

Fortunately, vendors are developing more and better tools—some software-based, others complete systems that provide onscreen maps of network resources—to help in the endless task of managing a network.

FROM SIMPLE TO COMPLEX

Network management tools, whether they are as application-specific as a performance monitor or as comprehensive as IBM's mainframe-based NetView, help bring some order to the potentially chaotic network management environment. They give network managers information and capabilities they can use in the battle to keep their LANs running trouble-free.

Whether they are intended to merely find cable breaks or to pinpoint the cause of a network slowdown, network management tools are vital to the network manager's day-to-day life. They can help ensure uptime and network reliability, maintain predetermined performance levels, manage LAN resources optimally, plan for expansion, maintain company security, track network use, and provide a basis for charging customers for network time.

For example, knowing how many network users regularly access a laser printer—and how long they have to wait for their printed material to appear—can help a company decide when it's time to add a second printer. Knowing which workstations generate the heaviest traffic lets a network administrator predict possible bottlenecks—bottlenecks that can be avoided by adding inter-network devices such as bridges or routers.

FIVE FUNCTIONAL AREAS

At the very basic level, network management requirements generally fall into five functional areas: configuration management, fault management, security management, performance management, and accounting management.

Configuration management applications deal with installing, initializing, booting, modifying, and tracking the configuration parameters or options of network hardware and software.

Fault management tools provide an audit trail, or historical overview, of a network's error and alarm characteristics. These types of tools show a LAN manager the number, types, times, and locations of network errors. These errors might be dropped packets and retransmissions (on an Ethernet) or lost tokens (on a Token Ring).

Security management tools allow the network manager to restrict access to various resources, from the applications and files to the entire network itself; these generally offer password-protection schemes that give users different levels of access to different resources. For instance, a user in marketing could be allowed to view, or read a data file in accounting but not be permitted to change or write to it.

Security management is also important in managing the network itself— for instance, only certain individuals (such as network administrators) should be permitted to change configuration settings on a server or other key network devices.

Performance management tools produce real-time and historical statistical information about the network's operation: how many packets are being transmitted at any given moment, the number of users logged into a specific server, and utilization of internetwork lines. As already noted, this type of information can help network administrators pinpoint areas or network segments that pose potential problems.

Performance management tools generally allow polling individual network devices for component-specific information. A communications server might provide information on throughput for each serial port, while a file server might report the number of users logged in, what applications they are using, and the number of active files. This information can then be studied to determine which gateways, servers, or routers are being used heavily and may need added capabilities in the future.

Accounting management applications help their users allocate the costs of various network resources—a public data network gateway, access to a mainframe session, or printer time—to those using them. These applications provide information about session start up/stop, user logins and resource use, and audit trail data. Companies can then use this information to bill departments internally or customers for computer and/or network time.

BUILT-IN NOS MANAGEMENT

Most network operating systems (NOSs) provide some level of network management capabilities; in particular, almost all the leading NOSs offer password-protection schemes that limit users' access to network resources. Novell, for instance, implements its NetWare management scheme through user profiles, which define not only the user's access rights, but the users' classifications (supervisor, workgroup manager, console operator, or user), which also determine the resources they can access.

In this scheme, a supervisor has access rights that allow reconfiguring and upgrading the entire system. The workgroup manager, available with NetWare 3.X, controls only the resources of a single user or user group. This concept allows a supervisor to distribute some of the responsibility for maintaining the network to others around a large network.

A user with console operator access rights can run NetWare's FCONSOLE utility, which allows monitoring and controlling a variety of network performance criteria, such as print queues. The user can access only those resources allowed by the supervisor (or workgroup manager with NetWare 3.X). Although users can access the NetWare management utilities, their rights to actually perform management functions are severely limited.

Although other NOSs' access schemes may differ in specific features from NetWare's, they all offer similar resource-restriction capabilities that give the network managers control over their LANs.

PROGRAMMABLE MANAGERS

Many other network product vendors also offer specific network management products that address more-detailed needs. These include Sun Microsystem's SunNet Manager [now known as Solstice], Hewlett-Packard's OpenView, and IBM's NetView for AIX, and Cabletron's Spectrum.

Both Sun and Hewlett-Packard designed their network management applications to work with other vendors' "agent" applications that add specific functionality to a system. For example, various agents can perform monitoring and controlling capabilities on gateways and routers.

Other products, however, deliver only partial solutions. These devices include protocol analyzers, which provide configuration and performance data but no accounting management capabilities. Often these applications are integrated into a device management application.

MANAGEMENT STANDARDS

As networks have grown larger and become increasingly heterogeneous in nature, so has the need for industry-standard network management protocols (and products) that operate across a wide range of vendor offerings. The first of these protocols, the Simple Network Management Protocol (SNMP), was developed by the Internet Activities Board in 1988. SNMP generally relies on the User Datagram Protocol/Internet Protocol (UDP/IP) as the underlying mechanism for transferring data between different types of systems and networks, though IPX and AppleTalk have been employed successfully by some products.

Briefly, SNMP is a protocol that defines the communication between a network management station and an device or process to be managed. SNMP's three-layer architecture (network management stations, agents, and a common set of protocols that binds them together) operates with a management information base (MIB) and a structure of management information (SMI). The MIB and SMI are network management concepts that allow defining each network element so these elements can be monitored and controlled by the management stations.

Though widely accepted, SNMP has several limitations. For one, it is considered by some to be too simplistic for managing the large, global-style networks evolving today, and its manager-to-agent architecture leaves it incapable of managing true enterprisewide LANs, which can require manager-to-manager systems as well.

Eventually, the evolving Common Management Information Protocol (CMIP), the network management standard for Open Systems Interconnection (OSI) networks, may overshadow TCP/IP. However, CMIP will have difficulty dislodging the huge installed base of SNMP applications and overwhelming industry support. Because products based on it are widely available—hundreds of vendors make compatible products—SNMP remains the network management protocol of choice for most PC-based network managers.

HOST-BASED SYSTEMS

Two mainframe-based network management systems with wide industry support are IBM's NetView and AT&T's Unified Network Management Architecture (UNMA.

Although proprietary in nature, these products enjoy broad end-user support because of their associated vendors' large installed bases of computers. With the protocols already available, many users incorporate their primary vendor's network management products into their LANs as a matter or course.

IBM's NetView permits non-IBM networks to access the NetView host via its NetView/PC and LAN Network Manager gateway products. IBM also supports SNMP in many of its products.

Backup

Making copies of the program and data files on the network is called *backup*. Backup is the most important thing you can do for your LAN. You can buy the fastest file server, the slickest workstations, the newest operating system, and the fanciest application software, but without backup, the network could become nothing very easily.

Catastrophic failures aside, people make mistakes. Users regularly delete files by accident. Even network administrators are not immune to slips of the fingers. Sometimes they inadvertently delete entire directories or even volumes. It's one thing if the deleted file held a short memo. It's another thing if those were the figures for the shareholders' meeting tomorrow or an entire day's worth of data entry. Sure, people can print files so they always have a hard copy, but then someone has to rekey all that data. And a hard copy does nothing when a program's executable files are deleted or corrupted.

Humans make mistakes. So does hardware. Even though hard disks often have a mean time between failure greater than 100,000 hours, the server disk could experience a head crash, rendering your company's vital information nonsensical. There are plenty of shocks great enough to crash the heads, even though disks can withstand several Gs of force. The power does surge and sag, blowing unprotected disks left and right.

Network operating systems have glitches. Mysterious system errors can cause files to disappear. Viruses don't just make good headline news stories. They are rare, but when they appear they can be responsible for vast amounts of damage.

Natural disasters do strike. Earthquakes, floods, and tornadoes really happen.

MIS departments wouldn't dream of running minicomputers or mainframes without backup systems and procedures. A PC LAN is no different.

351

BACKUP OPTIONS

Two backup options exist: tape or disk. The simplest method, to back up to floppy disk, is really only suitable for standalone PCs with small hard drives. If a server has a mere 40MB drive, and 20MB are used, it would take 14 floppies to back up that information, and that's if you use 1.44MB diskettes, the highest capacity available. And most servers have at least several hundred megabytes, if not gigabytes, of storage.

Backing up to floppies is even marginal for users. Users have less disk storage than servers do, but its hard for the network administrator to ensure that the users will really back up their data. Most users will back up only after they have lost important data, and then only until they feel invincible again.

In practice, it is ridiculous to back up the server to floppies. You can, however, back up the server to another hard disk, either removable or fixed. Removable disks are handy because if the server or disk fails, you can pop out the damaged equipment and pop in the backup disk.

However, the vast majority of network administrators backs up to tape. Tape is inexpensive, convenient, and widely available. Network managers may complain bitterly about tape and its ills, but basically, it is the backup medium of choice.

A new option in the backup bag of tricks is optical disks. The Write-Once-Read-Many (WORM) drives are more useful for archiving than daily backups, since you cannot change the data once it is on the disk. The newer rewritable optical disks are handier for backup, since they boast a huge amount of storage and are reusable. Optical disks don't wear out as quickly as tape, but they are much more expensive.

TAPE FORMATS

The most common tape format is standardized by the *Quarter Inch Committee*. The tape is a quarter-inch wide with nine parallel tracks, enclosed in a plastic housing about the size of a VCR tape. 3M's DC600 is the most popular of the formats. A DC600 fits into a standard 5¼-inch form factor, so it can be internally mounted in a PC, although the vast majority of drives are attached externally. The standard tape length is 600 feet. The extended length cartridge has 600 feet

STREAMING TAPE

Beginning
of Tape

End
of Tape

HELICAL SCAN

Directory

Beginning
of Tape

End
of Tape

In streaming tape, the ¼-inch tape is moved across the stationary read/write head. The data is laid down in a serial track until it reaches the end of the tape. It then reverses itself and lays down another track parallel to the first.

In the newer helical scan method, both the tape and the read/write head move. The tape is wrapped around a cylindrical drum on which there are several read/write heads. The data is laid down in diagonal strips on the tape. Helical scan not only increases the tape capacity, but also increases the throughput. Both the 8 mm and the 4 mm DAT can use helical scan.

of tape. The newer DC2000 format uses the same ¼-inch nine-track media but the cartridge fits into the 3½-inch form factor, which is perfect for a PS/2.

Digital Audio Tape (DAT) is the newest backup medium. DAT for data is the same DAT tape that excites audiophiles. DAT can store several gigabytes of information on a cassette the size of a cigarette pack. DAT will offer terabytes of storage in the future. The difference is DAT uses digital recording.

DAT drives use *helical scan*. In this method, both the tape and the read-write head move. With streaming tape, only the tape moves. In helical scan, the tape is wrapped around a cylindrical drum on which there are several read-write heads. The data is laid down in diagonal strips on the tape. Helical scan not only increases the capacity of the tape, it also increases the throughput rate. Both the newer 8 mm tapes and the 4 mm DAT can use helical scan. With its multiple gigabyte capacity, 8 mm tape is attractive for high end applications.

TAPE METHODS

There is very little difference among the various tape drives. Basically they are made by a small number of manufacturers and resold by companies that make backup software. This venue is currently changing, since the tape drive manufacturers are beginning to sell directly to the end users and dealers.

There are two methods of operation: *image* and *file-by-file*. Image backup is more primitive and less desirable. A drive performing an image backup takes a complete image or snapshot of the disk, not concerning itself with the disk's file structure. It just copies all the bits onto tape. Due to this lack of overhead, image backup is fast. But it is not the most efficient. An administrator who wants to restore a single file will have to restore the entire disk, which can take hours.

File-by-file backup is far more efficient. In this method, data from each file is copied to tape before moving onto the next file. It takes longer to reconstruct the fragmented files into whole units, because the disk head has to jump around, but you can restore individual files much more quickly. Also, with file-by-file, you can back up selected files, since only a small percentage of the files are changed each day.

WHAT AND WHEN

Backup is not effective if you only do it occasionally. It's like exercise. It doesn't matter what you do as long as you do it regularly. You aren't going to have the body of Mel Gibson if you have the workout routine of Peewee Herman.

A rule of thumb is to back up the files that change every day, and back up the program executables once a week. Then the worst that could happen would be that the users would lose one day's work. But even if you don't take the time to back up every day, at least do a complete backup every week.

Don't use the same tape cartridge every day. A generational backup system is the best. Have tapes marked Monday, Tuesday, etc. and use them accordingly. Then save those tapes for three or four weeks before you reuse them. (Some viruses are time-release.) If you don't want such an elaborate system, at least alternate the tapes every other day. That way if you discover that the drive can't read yesterday's backup, at least there is a tape from the day before. Tape is cheap. Use it. Use a lot of it.

Nights and weekends are the best time to do backup. Sending all the files that were changed that day will bog down the network. A more important reason is that open files can't be backed up. Some software packages will simply skip the open files, inviting a catastrophe. Others will wait until those files close, which could leave the tape system waiting forever. Either make sure all users are logged off the system by a certain time or buy a package that lists the open files, so you can back them up later.

The software should allow you to write a script to tell it what files to backup and when. In addition to allowing you to run backup unattended, the software should let you back up the server from any workstation. This way, the network administrator can perform backups from his or her desk, and the server can be safely locked away in the closet or computer room.

The software should allow local workstations to be backed up. Users won't remember to back up their local hard disks regularly.

Security is a major issue. You don't want someone with a tape drive to walk off with the contents of the server disk. The software should require a password. Some products require that the software log in as the supervisor, which is bad, because the person performing the backup should not necessarily have access to every bit of information on the network.

BEYOND BACKUP

If you do it right, backup will ensure that you will lose only a day's work. But even a day's lost work can be too much. In that case, you should move into the fault tolerance world, and use disk mirroring and duplexing. Disk mirroring uses two disks and one controller and all writes are made to both disks. Disk duplexing takes fault tolerance one step further and duplicates both the disk and the controller. It affords twice the protection at twice the cost. In either case, a copy of the server disk is ready to go online at any time. Depending on the software package and hardware configuration, the switch to the backup disk could be instantaneous.

However, backup is sufficient for most LAN installations. And tape is the most cost effective method. Use it.

Security

Prevention is key when it comes to LAN security. Identifying and stopping intrusion—in all its forms—is what security is all about. But identifying a potential intrusion is not always obvious, or likely. The usual security suspects—Soviet spies, CIA agents, and industrial espionage—make great headlines, but they don't pose real risks to the average company. However, just because you're not building the next secret weapon doesn't mean that you're not at risk from security breaches. Far more often, security risks come from acts committed out of human error, greed, malcontent, or machine error.

Physical theft, electronic tampering, and unauthorized access are just three of the more obvious threats to LAN equipment and data. Physical theft includes people stealing computers, taking floppies with data, and tapping into the cable to siphon off information. Electronic tampering covers computer viruses and other malicious reprogramming. Unauthorized access, the most common threat to security, usually occurs when people see information they shouldn't.

There are literally hundreds of approaches that can be taken to deal with these threats. Just as there are many forms of home security—from a lock on the door to a 24-hour guard—there are many forms of LAN security. And as the type of home security you use depends on your neighborhood, valuables, insurance, and the amount of money you have, the type and amount of prevention your LAN needs depends upon the importance of the company's data, the expense of computer equipment, the likelihood of intrusion, and the amount of money you can afford to spend.

NETWORKING IS A RISKY BUSINESS

Networks seriously increase access to your information, and with access comes the responsibility of restriction and control. In addition to the usual sources of

356

security breaches—people taping passwords to their monitors and using scanners to electronically eavesdrop—networks invite a whole host of other vulnerabilities. It's easy enough to drop another workstation or server on the network or add another application. Add the ability to dial into the network system, and you pose an even greater risk.

There is no simple formula for calculating your security needs. The amount of security depends upon the threat you perceive. In some cases, the need for security is clear: banks, airlines, credit card companies, the Department of Defense, and insurance companies. In other cases, the risks may be less obvious. Allowing any worker to examine the payroll file makes for disgruntled employees. Your personal calendar indicates when you are out of town. The following are some of the more common risks to network security.

- Your network can be a danger to itself. Being made of mechanical components, a network can do itself damage when disk heads crash, servers fail, and power supplies blow. Tape and disk platters get old and go bad. Bugs, such as in an out-of-control operating system process or one with a faulty memory mapping, destroy data. Monitor mechanical equipment for wear. For critical components, keep spares onsite or, if warranted, online.
- Your network is physically vulnerable. Thieves and other intruders can physically break into your building, wiring closet, or server room and steal or vandalize equipment and data. When a file is erased, very often it physically remains on disk or tape—only the entry to the directory structure is removed. Sensitive documents may be printed out and left lying around the office, waiting for prying eyes or thieving hands.

Your first line of defense is the simplest: Use locks, guards, and alarms to protect against these physical vulnerabilities. Lock servers in a room and lock wiring closets, permitting access to only those with a key. Sensitive data must be completely wiped off the media when deleted. Shred all sensitive printouts. Bolt expensive equipment to the floor or to a desk. A slew of products exist to prevent intruders from physically taking equipment. Most involve locking equipment with metal bars, in steel cabinets, or with large chains. Others sound loud alarms to deter the thief. These products can help to keep your equipment from being physically stolen (it also makes them difficult to move from one station to another). If your security needs are extreme, you might employ biometric devices. Biometric devices use a physical aspect of people, such as their fingerprints, to verify their identity.

The next step is to secure the cable. Copper cable gives off electromagnetic radiation, which can be picked up with listening devices, with or without tapping into the cable. One solution is to switch to fiber-optic cable, which does not emit electromagnetic signals and is more difficult to tap without detection.

Diskless PCs are a popular security measure. A diskless PC lacks floppy and fixed drives. Users must boot the computers off the file server. With no drives, no way to remove data physically exists. However, be aware that diskless PCs with serial and parallel ports and expansion slots are insecure. A user can insert a removable disk into an expansion slot and remove data. Or the user can attach a printer.

Another step is to physically limit access to data sources. Use the keyboard lock on PCs and file servers. Lock file servers in closets or computer rooms, thus preventing direct access and forcing intruders to circumvent network security. Rooms with doors and locks are good places for printers and other output devices since printed data may be as sensitive as electronic data.

- Viruses are potentially the most dangerous and costly type of intrusion. Although they are relatively rare to a well-kept network, the penalties inflicted by a virus can be severe. Your network is vulnerable at any point it contacts the outside world, from floppy drives to bridges to modem servers. At these external contacts, your network's messages can be intercepted or misrouted. Workers take notebooks on the road and may come into contact with a virus-infected computer. Users may take work home, where their home computers are infected. Demonstration programs, bulletin boards, and even shrink-wrapped software may have viruses.

  Protecting your LAN against a computer virus is much the same as protecting it from unauthorized access. If an intruders can't access the LAN, they can't unleash a virus. However, many viruses are introduced by unwitting, authorized users. Any new software should be suspected of having viruses. Although programs from bulletin boards may sometimes be infected, several software companies have shipped shrink-wrapped software that was infected with a virus. While specialized programs can look out for viruses and limit the havoc they wreak, no program can prevent a virus. It can only deal with the symptoms.

- Intentional threats are also potentially damaging. Employees and outsiders pose intentional threats. Outsiders—terrorists, criminals, industrial spies, and crackers—pose the more newsworthy threats, but insiders have the decided advantage of being familiar with the network. Disgruntled employees may try to steal information, but they may also seek revenge by discrediting an employee or sabotaging a project. Employees may sell proprietary information or illegally transfer funds. Employees and outsiders may team up to penetrate the system's security and gain access to sensitive information.

- Workstation file systems present a threat to the network. DOS is easy to circumvent. Intruders can use the many available programs to get at a hard disk and remove data, even if security programs are at work. For this reason, high security installations may want to use a different operating system, one with a different file system. Unix has sophisticated file security and additional programs are available for even more protection.

- Your network radiates electromagnetic signals. With an inexpensive scanner, experienced electronic eavesdroppers can listen in on your network traffic and decode it. Shielded cable, such as coax and shielded twisted pair, radiates less energy than unshielded cable, such as telephone wire. Fiber-optic cable radiates no electromagnetic energy at all—since it uses light instead of electrical signals to transmit—and it's relatively easy to detect taps into a fiber cable, since these decrease the light level of the cable. If your installation demands maximum security, Tempest-certified equipment shields electromagnetic emissions.

- By far the most common network intrusion is unauthorized access to data, which can take many forms. The first line of defense against unauthorized access should be the workstation interface. Login passwords are a must. Nearly all network operating systems will not give workstation users access to network resources without the correct password. To make passwords more effective, the administrator should assign them and change them at random intervals. Don't let users post their passwords on their monitors or desk blotters. Use mnemonic passwords to help users remember.

Software is available to blank a user's screen or lock the keyboard after a certain definable period of inactivity. Other software will automatically log a user out of the network. In either case, a password is required to renew activity. This prevents the casual snooper, but not a determined one.

A more secure method to stop unauthorized access is an add-in card for each workstation. This card forces the workstation to boot up from a particular drive every time. It can also enforce some kind of user validation, like a password. If the card is removed, the workstation is automatically disabled.

- Your network administrators present yet another risk. If you give them free reign over the applications and data, you're exposing your network to unnecessary risks. Your network administrators manage the network, not the data on it. Administrators should not have access to payroll information, for example. Similarly, don't fall victim to the fallacy that the department heads should have complete access to the network and its information just because they are in charge.
- Finally, your network is subject to the whims of nature. Earthquakes, fires, floods, lightning, and power outages can wreak havoc on your servers and other network devices. While the effects of lightning and power outages can be minimized by using uninterruptible power supplies, you'll need to store backups of important data (and perhaps even equipment) offsite to deal with large-scale disasters.

THREE FORMS OF DATA SECURITY

Information security entails making sure the right people have access to the right information, that the information is correct, and that the system is available. These aspects are referred to as *confidentiality, integrity,* and *availability.*

Information stored on a network often needs to be confidential, and a secure network does not allow anyone access to confidential information unless they are authorized. The network should require users to prove their identities by providing something they know, such as a password, or by providing something they possess, such as a card key. Most network operating systems and many applications packages use passwords.

In government circles, this aspect of security hinges on secrecy; access to information is granted according to security clearance. In commercial circles, this aspect of security comes more from confidentiality, where only users who need to know the private information have access.

Guarding access to information is one aspect of security; the security system must also guarantee the information itself is accurate, referred to as data integrity. In providing data integrity, for example, a network ensures that a $14,000 bank account balance isn't really supposed to be $14 million. The system must verify the origin of data and when it was sent and received. Network operating systems grant users access to files and directories on a read, write, create, open, and delete basis. Word processors lock files so more than one user cannot modify the same file at the same time. Databases use record locking to provide a finer granularity of access control.

The third aspect of security is network availability. Although not commonly thought of as part of security, a secure network must also ensure that users can access its information. The network must continue to work, and when a failure occurs, the network devices must recover quickly.

SOLVING SECURITY PROBLEMS

Whatever type of security you implement, diligent watchfulness is important to its success. To help, several LAN operating systems include audit trails that track all network activity, including which workstation has tried to login to a file server three times unsuccessfully or which files have been changed when they should not have been altered.

Some audit trails can sound alarms when certain events take place. For example, the system manager may want to know when certain files are open, or when unusual traffic takes place. Audit trails will also keep a running log of all that takes place, so the LAN manager may be able to detect a pattern of intrusion.

Protecting against internal threats requires you to control access to files and applications on a need-to-know basis. Only grant access if users present valid reasons to access the application or data. Use the network operating system's security features to restrict access. Keep audit trails of who accesses what files and when. Enforce the use of passwords.

Such access privileges may be assigned by file, by user or a combination of both. For example, users with a certain security level may read and write to certain files. Those with lower security levels might be restricted to reading these files.

The LAN manager should create a profile of access privileges for each user. This profile, which is executed when the user logs on, restricts the user to authorized data and devices. Profiles may also be set up for data and devices, limiting their access to only authorized users. Profiles make managing security easier since they provide a consistent method of assigning and maintaining network privileges.

Once a user has workstation and network access, other security barriers can be put in place. Most network operating systems have many levels of access control that limit what resources are available, which data can be accessed, and what operations can be performed. These include restricting who can read and write to certain files, directories, applications, servers, and printers.

To reduce the risk, limit connections to the outside world. When you must make connections, use call-back modems, encryption, and virus-detection software. With call-back modems, users must dial into the system, verify their identity, then the modem calls the user back at a predetermined telephone number to establish the connection. Encryption scrambles data into an unreadable format so even if the packets are intercepted, the message remains nonsensical. Upon receipt of the message, only the people who know the private code, or key, can unscramble the data. Virus-detection software will identify many viruses and disable them if possible.

Biometric devices are a rather drastic security measure. Biometric devices use a person's physical characteristics to verify an identity. The verifying physical characteristic varies. Some use fingerprints, others use voice recognition, others scan a person's retina. Biometric devices are quite costly and are for highly secure environments.

ENCRYPTION

Passwords, locks, access privileges, and even biometric devices do not always deter the determined intruder. A common tool like a protocol analyzer can be hooked up to the network and the intruder can watch all data, including passwords, pass by. Data encryption is the answer.

With encryption, data is scrambled before transmission, making it unreadable as it passes over the wire, even if it is intercepted. To scramble or encrypt this data, its bits must be transformed according to an algorithm. The data is transmitted, and at the receiving end, a system of keys is used to decode the bits into intelligible information. Keys are necessary for encoding and decoding.

Encryption usually requires extra hardware because of the processing power required. Hardware-based encription schemes are more difficult to crack than software-based methods.

A common data encryption standard specified by the U.S. government is Data Encryption Standard (DES). Another standard used by the government, called CCEP, is more recently developed than DES, and will someday supplant the older standard.

DES defines how the data should be encrypted and the specifications for an electronic key. It uses one 64-bit key for encryption and decryption. This can cause problems because the key must be in the hands of the sender and receiver. The only way to get it from place to place is to transmit it. Transmitting the key introduces a security threat.

The Public Key System is a solution. Under this setup, each user has two keys, one public and one private. The public key is made available to all senders and is used only for encryption. The private key is used only for decryption and remains exclusive to the receiver. So everyone can encrypt files, but only the intended receiver can decrypt files and there is no need to transmit private keys.

Encryption may be done before data is stored or transmitted. Some networks only encrypt data when it is sent, which makes wire tapping more difficult but does not keep intruders from taking data from a disk. Other networks also encrypt data on the hard disk. Data is encrypted as it is written and decrypted as it is read from the disk. Having encryption working in both places keeps network data much more secure. Encrypting passwords, as NetWare 386 does, is sometimes sufficient to deter the casual data thief.

To further enhance encryption's effectiveness, keys should be changed at random intervals. This prevents intruders from discovering either the key or the time the key is changed. Alternative keys should be available, too, in case the original set is compromised.

The best network encryption schemes hide much of the encryption hassle from end users by taking care of key management and encryption automatically.

DEVELOP A SECURITY PLAN

Make a planned attack to secure your network. Once your network has been hit by a virus or a data thief, it's too late to start thinking—you should already be acting. Start the planning process by naming a security administrator, who may or may not be the same person as the network administrator. The security administrator works with the network administrators and department heads to develop a security plan.

You must evaluate the dangers to your network. You need to examine its vulnerabilities, the points at which it is susceptible to attack. Then you must identify the threats, or possible dangers to the system, such as a person, an object, or a natural disaster. Vulnerabilities take several forms, including physical, natural, mechanical, communications, and human.

Unintentional, intentional, and natural threats exist in your network, but the majority are unintentional. Users and system administrators commit errors—they delete the wrong file, they disable access to a directory, they corrupt a data file, they never change their passwords, or they write them on their desk blotters. To counter unintentional errors, train your users and administrators about the network and its applications. Keep regular backups of the applications and data, for after a virus infection or data loss, restoring the damaged or lost files may be your only choice.

Reinforce the need to not write their passwords next to their computer or give them to anyone else. They should use passwords that are fairly difficult to guess. For example, users' passwords should not be their first names or spouses' names. Passwords that include numbers are much more difficult to guess. Users shouldn't type their passwords while someone is watching. Users and administrators should change their passwords frequently. Administrators shouldn't use supervisor logons as their "usual" logons.

Don't over-secure the network. Security procedures generally limit freedom to access the network, so implement them carefully. If you restrict access to certain directories, users may not be able to cut and paste freely from one document to another. Users will balk at elaborate security procedures that interfere with their jobs. They will find ways to circumvent the network security procedures, such as storing data on their local hard drives, not on the server, where it would be protected and backed up. Carefully balance the need for security with the security procedure.

For any security plan to work, the employees must take it seriously. The most effective action you can take is to educate your users and administrators on why your security plan is important. When people understand why controls are necessary, they are more likely to cooperate. Make it clear to prospective and current employees that everyone is expected to cooperate. Establish clear consequences for failure to cooperate. Be specific about policies and procedures. Write them down and give everyone a copy. Make sure each individual knows what to do. Don't overdo it. Insofar as possible, make it easy to cooperate. Enlisting the support of employees is probably the single most cost-effective security precaution a company can take.

Finally, natural threats, such as power failures, earthquakes, and other such disasters are a rare but real part of life. Develop a disaster recovery plan to deal with natural disasters and follow it. Archive important data and emergency backup hardware offsite in a secure facility. Keep enough in the archive for you to get your business up and running (and relatively current) should your primary facility get flattened—it could happen!

The Virus Threat

By most accounts, in October 1988, only three DOS computer viruses were known. By October 1991, McAfee Associates identified some 900 computer virus strains. At the 18th Computer Security Institute Conference, Scott Charney from the U.S. Justice Department indicated that the government expected to see an additional 600 viruses and mutant strains introduced during 1992.

Peter Tippett, president of Certus, reported a new virus was discovered about every six days in January 1990; by June 1990, a new virus was discovered about every four days; and in September, 1990, one was found every three days. According to Charney's prediction, we would have discovered 1.6 new viruses daily in 1992.

THE COST OF A VIRUS

Although many viruses are labeled benign (more annoying than actually causing damage to the system and/or data), a virus usually causes at least some inconvenience, some loss of system-access time and, at the worst, loss of data.

Recent virus cleanup figures at a large corporation found an average of one hour of technician time was required to locate and remove a virus from each computer. Data from Certus support staff suggests that a reasonable figure for direct technician time to resolve a disastrous computer virus is approximately $250 per computer or LAN workstation.

WHAT IS A VIRUS?

A virus is a program that has the ability to reproduce by modifying other programs to include a copy of itself. It may contain destructive code that moves into multiple programs, data files, or devices on a system and spreads through multiple systems in a network. Viral code may execute immediately or wait for a specific set of circumstances. Viruses are not distinct programs; they need a host program executed to activate their code.

Many distinct programmed threats have been lumped together as viruses; however, most are not actually viruses at all. To better understand the threat, we will identify and define these other techniques.

Bacteria, also known as rabbits, are programs that do not explicitly damage any files. Their sole purpose is to reproduce themselves. A typical bacteria program does nothing more than reproduce itself exponentially, eventually eating up all the processor capacity, memory, or disk space, denying the user access to those resources. This kind of programming attack is one of the oldest forms of programmed threat.

A *logic bomb* is a program or a section of code built into a program that lies dormant until a predefined condition is met. When that condition occurs, the bomb goes off with a result that is neither expected nor desired. Time bombs explode frequently. Depending on who authored the bomb and how many generations of backups it contaminated, the recovery effort ranges from mildly inconvenient to nearly impossible.

A *password catcher* is a program that mimics the actions of a normal sign-on screen but stores supplied ID and password combinations, usually in a hidden file accessible only to the author. The collected ID/password combinations are later used to attack the system. Running for three or four days will generally yield more than 90 percent of a site's active system users. Truly clever ones cause no perceptible delay and force no repeated sign-ons.

A *repeat dialer* is a program that continually calls the same number, thus placing it virtually out of service for any other caller. This technique has been used against TV preachers during fund drives to stop pledge calls. As would-be donors keep receiving busy signals, they tend to get frustrated and stop trying.

Trapdoors, also known as backdoors, are undocumented entry points into an otherwise secure system. During software development, programmers often create entry points into "their" programs to aid in debugging and adding final enhancements. These trapdoors are supposed to be closed before the program goes through the promotion to production process. Many times, however, they are not. This breach leaves an unadvertised but very real hole in the system's security.

A *Trojan horse* is a program that appears to perform a useful function, and sometimes does so quite well, but also includes an unadvertised feature that is usually malicious in nature. Viruses and logic bombs can be hidden in Trojan horses. The code in a well-constructed Trojan horse can perform its apparent function long and admirably before encountering the triggering condition that prompts it to let loose its secret agenda.

A *war* or *demon dialer* is a program run from outside an organization's environment and control, usually by hackers, to find dial-up ports into computer systems. Such a program identifies numbers in a given range that connect to a computer. From a modem-equipped PC, the hacker enters a starting phone number and an ending value to the resident dialer program. The program then sequentially dials each number in the range, seeking a computer tone. Copies of this type of program are found on bulletin boards everywhere.

A *worm* is a program that scans a system or an entire network for available, unused disk space in which to run. Originally, worms were developed by systems programmers searching for fragments of core in which to run segments of large programs. They tend to tie up all computing resources in a system or on a network and effectively shut it down. Worms can be activated at boot-up or submitted separately. Probably the most well-known worm was the November 2, 1988, Internet incident. In two days, an estimated 6,200 Unix-based computer systems on the network were infected.

HOW DOES A VIRUS SPREAD?

A computer virus, like its human counterpart, does not spread through the air. Humans become infected by a virus by coming in contact with someone who is infected. So it is with computers. They must come in contact with some contaminated source. The virus infects any form of writable storage, including hard drives, diskettes, magnetic tapes and cartridges, optical media, and memory. The most frequent sources of contamination include:

- physical or communication contact with an infected computer,
- copying an unknown disk containing a carrier program,
- downloading a file from a bulletin board system,
- running an infected LAN program,

- booting with an infected disk,
- infected software from a vendor, and
- overt action by individuals.

VIRUS PROTECTION

A number of clues can indicate that a virus has infected or attempted to infect a system, even before any damage is done. Unexplained system crashes, programs that suddenly don't seem to work properly, data files or programs mysteriously erased, disks becoming unreadable—all could be caused by a virus.

Here are some indicators that may confirm the presence of a virus. Most viruses use information provided by the command DIR, which lists a disk's directory, and CHKDSK, which snapshots disk and memory usage.

File size increase. A file's size may increase when a virus attaches itself to the file.

Change in update timestamp. When a virus modifies another program— even one such as COMMAND.COM (which is part of the operating system)— the "last-update" date and time are often changed. Since most programs are normally never modified (except when they're upgraded), periodically checking the last-update timestamp, with the DIR command, can alert the user to the presence of a virus. Another danger sign is when many programs list the same date and/or time in their last-update field. This occurrence indicates that all have been modified together, possibly by a virus.

Sudden decrease of free space. When running a new program, particularly if it is freeware or shareware, be alert for a sudden, unexpected decrease in disk space or memory.

Numerous unexpected disk accesses. Unless a program is exceptionally large or uses huge data files, it should not conduct a high number of disk accesses. Unexpected disk activity might signal a virus.

PREVENTING INFECTION

Preventing a virus infection is the best way to protect your organization against damage. If a virus cannot establish itself within your systems, then it cannot damage your programs or data. The following steps can help keep a clean system from becoming infected with a virus.

Awareness training. All employees having access to computer systems should be required to attend a training session on the virus threat. It is crucial that employees realize how much damage a virus can inflict.

Policies and procedures. The organization should prepare a policy on virus control to address the following issues: tight control of freeware and shareware; a control process that includes running anti-virus software regularly by each department; a virus response team and methods for contacting the team; control of the infection once it is detected; and recovery from the virus, including backup and dump policies.

For two very important reasons, the user community should be made aware of the risks of sharing software. The primary cause of the spread of virus infections is through the uncontrolled use of diskettes being introduced into computer systems. The other reason is the possibility of the illegal use of copyrighted software.

If your organization lets employees transport diskettes out of the work facility, a quarantined system to test diskettes and software before their introduction into the system should be in effect. This quarantine system should test all diskettes for the possibility of virus contamination.

In the LAN environment, avoid placing shareware in a common file server directory, thereby making it accessible to any PC in the network. Only allow the network administrator to sign on to the file server node.

The most prudent precaution is to carefully make, store, and routinely check backup copies of files and programs—all on an established schedule. And control access to backups to guarantee integrity.

VIRUS-PROTECTION PACKAGES

Several commercially available programs can now help detect viruses and provide some degree of protection against them. However, if you use such programs, be careful that they don't cause greater problems than they solve. Some anti-virus programs interfere with the normal operations of programs they are supposed to protect (such as blocking a disk formatting utility).

Also, an anti-virus program may warn of a suspected infection when none has actually taken place. Because of the differences in anti-virus packages, it's important to standardize testing procedures and analytical tools, so results can be compared on a consistent basis.

Unfortunately, malicious code is now a fact of life. Computer viruses appear to be a long-term threat. Systems and data will continue to be vulnerable until a proactive preventive and corrective action is established. In the short term, caution in testing and using unfamiliar software, as well as carefully made backups, are your best safeguards. Your slogan should be, "Don't accept software from strangers."

Wireless Network Security

Remember when you cruised into your driveway one evening, touched your Genie garage door opener, and the neighbor's garage door opened along with yours? Then you went inside, made a phone call on your cordless phone to a business associate, and much to your dismay, heard the cries of your little two-month-old baby coming in via the shared signals of your phone and nursery monitor.

Herein lies the skepticism that is deeply embedded in the realm of wireless communication. This kind of doubt and worry among users is one of the biggest hurdles facing wireless network vendors and has contributed to the slow growth of the market. Potential buyers equate wireless with broadcasting and worry that private data can—and therefore will—be easily picked off by eavesdroppers.

But there's irony here. Wireless communications, specifically spread spectrum technology, was developed during World War II for military applications. The goal of that transmission technique was to provide reliable and secure voice communications in the field. One of the early patents for spread spectrum defines a frequency hopping radio for guiding torpedoes to their targets. Logic dictates that transmission for this mission would be extremely secure.

Market statistics compiled about those who use wireless network devices also testify to a reliable level of security. Government installations, generally accepted as needing the highest level of security, account for almost 10 percent of all wireless users (see figure).

AIM AND SHOOT

There are three camps in the in-building wireless world: infrared, 18GHz microwave, and spread spectrum. While sharing some of the same security features, each technology and vendor-specific implementation employ specialized methods of security.

372

SHARE OF WIRELESS NETWORKS BY BUSINESS SEGMENT

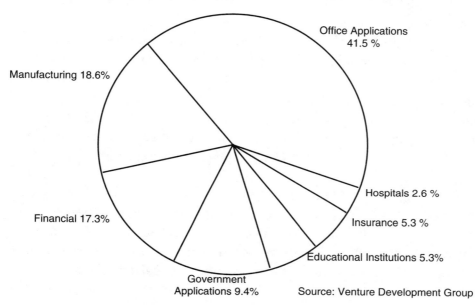

Office Applications
41.5 %

Manufacturing 18.6%

Hospitals 2.6 %

Insurance 5.3 %

Educational Institutions 5.3%

Financial 17.3%

Government
Applications 9.4%

Source: Venture Development Group

SEALED AIRTIGHT: Wireless networks are trusted in environments that require very high security, including government and finance.

Currently no standards are in place for wireless transmissions or data security. The committees responsible for developing and influencing these matters include the IEEE 802.11 and 802.10, with the first group devoted to access methods and the physical medium and the latter group focusing on interoperable LAN security.

With no available standards, network administrators should compare the three technologies in terms of data rate, speed, price, and even security. Infrared technology, while not as commonplace as spread spectrum among wireless network products, is considered to be highly site-secure. Unlike spread spectrum, infrared cannot penetrate solid objects, and the signal does not propagate beyond a room. Additionally, infrared is immune to electromagnetic and radio frequency interference, making it unlikely that someone with common radio-based jamming equipment could interfere with the data.

Infrared does not rely on scrambling or encryption. Rather, it has security features inherent to transmission. The two methods of infrared transmission are line-of-sight and diffuse propagation. Line-of-sight requires units in the same room to be aimed directly at each other; this technology is used by BICC (Auburn, MA) in InfraLAN.

Diffuse propagation products employ a slightly different technique. Transmitters bounce light beams off a reflective surface and onto PCs and peripherals. Diffused infrared signals bounce off all passive surfaces, including walls, ceilings, and floors. The whole room reflects the signal, eliminating the need to aim the devices. This technology is used by Photonics (San Jose, CA). A diffused propagation device is slightly more susceptible to breeches, since a partially concealed sensor can pick up a signal bouncing off a common wall or ceiling.

Line-of-sight infrared products have optical nodes that must be placed no more than 80 feet apart. For intruders to bust into one of these networks, they would have to install a base unit and adjust all the sensors on each device to point to each other. Because of these requirements, security breaches would be more than obvious to anyone in the room during actual data transfer. Lehman Brothers in New York uses a line-of-sight infrared network on the trading floor.

TUNING IN

Another transmission method, 18GHz radio, is currently used in the network world only in Motorola's (Arlington Heights, IL) Altair products. Although this licensed, radio-based transmission method varies greatly from spread spectrum, Motorola and most spread spectrum vendors approach wireless security with somewhat similar methodologies.

Fundamental WIN technology used in Altair addresses both ways information could be stolen or compromised: a receiver outside of the network capturing data, or an unauthorized capture of data by someone within the network.

Preventing reception of Altair network data by someone outside is an inherent benefit of a system that allows spectrum reuse within a short distance. First, Altair uses the very lowest possible levels of transmitted power. Second, the licensed, low-power 18GHz radio signals used provide coverage within a microcell but are blocked by continuous barriers (such as floors and exterior walls) and dissipate with distance. As a result, the Altair network is invisible to others operating on the same channel as close as 200 feet away.

To capture Altair signals, expensive, sensitive, and hard-to-hide receiving systems with large, high-gain parabolic antennas adjacent to the network would be required. The only possible way to tap into the network would be through the use of Altair hardware within the microcell.

INTRUDERS FROM WITHIN

To prevent capture of data by unauthorized hardware, the Altair network scrambles data sent between the Control Modules (CM) and User Modules (UM). Scrambling is controlled by a system-wide key and polynomial that are assigned when a unit is manufactured. Also, each time data is sent out on the microcell, a unique identifier (one of 1,024 possibilities) is assigned and combined in the scrambling process, which makes scrambling unique for every piece of data sent on the Altair microcell.

Also, a restricted address feature is built into the network's time division multiplexing architecture. This feature allows the network administrator to configure a unique registration of each of the 32 UMs controlled by a CM. It allows only those UMs whose l2-digit IEEE 802.3 Ethernet addresses have been entered into the CMs table to have access to, and communicate with, the CM.

An unauthorized UM could neither transmit nor receive data in the microcell. The key to understanding this security concept is that reception is not a passive function, such as in traditional radio receivers. Receiving and transmitting is specifically enabled, not automatic.

NO FREE DATA

Spread spectrum, the de facto wireless network technology, relies on many of the same security strongholds as Altair. Nonlicensed spread spectrum radios "spread" the bandwidth of the data stream far beyond the minimum required for transmission. The main security goal in spread spectrum is to guard against unauthorized reception and interference of the signal, intentional or otherwise.

The FCC has allocated three separate bands for low powered systems:

902MHz to 928MHz, 2.4GHz to 2.5GHz, and 5.8GHz to 5.9GHz. The two most widely used forms of spread spectrum in these bands are *direct sequence* and *frequency hopping*. In direct sequence, signals are spread over a continuous band of frequencies. Frequency hopping is just that—signals hop from frequency to frequency. In either case, the receiver must know the spreading code in advance to retrieve the flying information.

Most spread spectrum products have four basic modes of security. First, they use low power levels, which allows transmission to remain safely in the desired area. Second, they use some form of scrambling. Spread spectrum transmission effectively scrambles the data by sending it over multiple radio frequencies. Third, like Motorola, spread spectrum Ethernet products use specific and unique IEEE 802.3 addresses assigned to each user.

Lastly, most products, such as Windata's (Northboro, MA) FreePort, use spread spectrum encoding. The controller selects a unique spread spectrum code, and the hub and devices operate on that code. The hub next door would have a different code and therefore could not communicate (or steal) data.

TOO BIG TO CARRY

In addition, most casual eavesdroppers can't go out and buy a scanner or radio receiver that can pick up a product-specific signal. Nor could a hacker carry a wireless reception device into a building as easily as he could a nutcracker, the small wizard that allows intruders illegal entry into a wired Ethernet LAN. Most wireless transmitters and receivers are sizable pieces of hardware.

These measures and physical limitations, combined with the network operating system security, should prove sufficient for most applications. Intruders of any sort would face a very difficult problem scaling what appears to be an invisible wall leading to the network.

If a bigger fortress is needed, some products such as NCR's (Dayton, OH) WaveLAN, offer DES encryption at the hardware level. For a premium, users can buy a plug-in chip that automatically encrypts all data. Solectek's (San Diego, CA) AirLAN parallel port wireless adapter also offers an optional DES encryption chip. AirLAN and the emerging genre of wireless portable adapters and PCMCIA cards possess a greater danger for intrusion due to their smaller size and ease of use.

Telecommuting

Mention telecommuting, and visions of doing twice the work in half the time dance in many people's heads, while nightmares of employees watching "Oprah" pop into managers' heads. Corporations have some very legitimate reasons to examine telecommuting.

This tutorial discusses telecommuting's applications and its business hurdles. Next month's tutorial will cover the technology issues, including how to equip telecommuters and how to prepare the corporate network for telecommuters.

WHY TELECOMMUTE?

Telecommuting has different manifestations. People may telecommute full time; their only office is at home and they rarely go into the corporate office. People may telecommute part time; they may work from a home office one or two days a week and travel to the office the rest of the time. Or a company may set up a regional telecommuting site, where employees travel only a short distance to work.

By permitting telecommuting, a company can recruit employees outside its main geographic locations. Instead of relocating employees to corporate offices, employees remain where they are. By locating workers at home, the company reduces its office space requirements.

Corporations may want to consider telecommuting for some in-your-face reasons. States are enacting air-quality legislation that requires a reduction in air pollution. Every commuter off the road is that much less pollution. Natural disasters (and there's no shortage of examples from East Coast to West) have taken their toll. If a building becomes unfit for occupation, a telecommuting site can serve the office function.

Telecommuting can change the nature of how work is accomplished. "We will end up in a highly distributed work force. We must learn how to restructure work, so we can impact the unemployment crisis," says Eric Benhamou, president and CEO of 3Com (Santa Clara, CA) and a director of Smart Valley (Palo Alto, CA), which is sponsoring a telecommuting pilot project.

WORKERS BENEFIT

For employees, telecommuting has benefits, too. Jobs can come to them; they don't have to go to the job—whether travel means permanent relocation or a daily commute. Productivity can increase when workers are freed from many of the daily interruptions. Released from long hours in the office, people can spend more time with their families or pets, making them more satisfied with their jobs. They can set up a more flexible schedule, which enables students or parents to participate more fully in the work force.

Telecommuting may be particularly handy to people who have long-term illnesses or disabilities. Whereas they may have difficulty commuting to an office or face prejudice when they arrive, telecommuting allows them to be a part of the work force. "Disabled people can use telecommuting to provide access. You can sit in bed with a keyboard and a screen, and you can type," says Harry Saal, president and CEO of Smart Valley.

WHO'S TELECOMMUTING?

In February, Smart Valley launched a telecommuting pilot project in the San Francisco Bay Area involving a dozen companies, including 3Com, Silicon Graphics (Mountain View, CA), Hewlett-Packard (HP, Palo Alto, CA), Stanford University (Stanford, CA), and Gray Cary Ware and Freidenrich (Palo Alto).

3Com is testing telecommuting to provide additional flexibility for employees, to attract and retain employees, to improve productivity, and to test networking solutions. "We're at the adventurous edge of the scale of companies trying telecommuting," says Benhamou. "We'll evolve the organization at a pace it can move." 3Com's telecommuting program involves 50 employees in human resources, finance, engineering, marketing, MIS, and manufacturing departments. Employees perform a diversity of tasks from recruiting to financial analysis.

Silicon Graphics plans to be progressive using telecommuting to restructure its organization. It has 26 telecommuters from engineering, MIS, and technical education departments.

HP has been practicing telecommuting since 1990. It has 300 technical support, technical-documentation, and product-development personnel working from a central engineering and technical call center.

Ten employees in the communications department at Stanford have been telecommuting since 1993, as they experiment with Integrated Services Digital Network (ISDN).

Gray Cary Ware and Friedenrich, a law firm, will test telecommuting over the next nine months in an effort to comply with air-quality legislation and to provide quality-of-life options. Thirty employees will write and edit legal documents from home.

Smart Valley's Telecommuting project's goal is to have 1,000 active telecommuters by June. The final phase, set for June and beyond, is a wider deployment throughout the Bay Area.

THE BUSINESS OF MANAGING

Telecommuting waters are uncharted from a management and an employee standpoint. Management must understand what it wants to learn from a telecommuting pilot. It must define its goals, identify the participants, set the project in motion, and measure the results against the objectives (see sidebar "From Plan to Action").

Organizations should choose their telecommuters carefully. Not everyone will make a good telecommuter. Candidates should be good performers, familiar with their jobs, and self-motivated. They will have to hone their time-management skills, since the normal Pavlovian triggers of arriving at work, eating lunch, and going home will be missing.

Telecommuters should not view working from home as a day off. If the cobwebs on your ceiling fan distract you enough to make you clean the entire house when you should be working, then perhaps you need to improve your self-discipline. Nor should you expect to both work from home and take care of children—that's two full-time jobs.

Telecommuters need a clearly defined work space, whether it's a spacious, sun-drenched room or a dark but cozy corner next to the hot water heater. Workers need to define "at work" rules to keep family members from encroaching on work time and to keep coworkers from intruding on personal time. Just because a coworker labors at home does not mean she should receive calls at 9 p.m.

Managers will have to undergo adjustments in a telecommuting world. If a group of workers telecommutes, a supervisor may feel he has no control over his employees. Managers will have to sharpen their skills for managing people remotely. They can set up regular telephone conference calls with their workers.

Although toiling from home, telecommuting employees should be subject to the same performance metrics as office-bound workers. Telecommuters need a well-defined list of objectives and checkpoints and a timetable that's regularly reviewed. Managers will have to define the employees' objectives both individually and as a group.

A CAPITAL IDEA

A company must tackle issues of office space, equipment, tax requirements, workers' compensation, security, insurance, and union considerations.

One reason to permit telecommuting is to reduce corporate overhead. But what about the worker's rent or mortgage? If he lives in a place without a suitable work space for telecommuting, does the company rent him a larger living space?

Corporations generally buy the workers the capital equipment they need to telecommute. If a worker uses her own computer and a part fails, who pays for the repair? How does the telecommuter differentiate business and personal phone calls on the bill?

Workers should contact their accountants or tax consultants to see how working at home affects their income taxes. Part of their rent or mortgage may be tax-deductible.

How will the company handle worker injuries? If the employee is hurt using office-related equipment or if the injury occurs at home, then workers' compensation will probably cover the costs. But what happens if the employee is hurt while mowing his lawn at 3 p.m. on a Tuesday?

Assess the security issues. What sort of work will the employee have at home, and how can you ensure its security? Who has access to the data in the worker's home or telecommuting site? Will sensitive data travel over the phone lines? Physical security issues will also arise. What happens if company-owned equipment is stolen from the employee's residence?

Unions may be opposed to telecommuting, fearing that corporations will create electronic sweatshops. If you are involving union employees in a telecommuting project, get the union involved.

FROM PLAN TO ACTION: SMART VALLEY'S 26 STEPS TO TELECOMMUTING

Smart Valley (Palo Alto, CA), an advocacy group for a San Francisco Bay Area electronic community, launched its telecommuting pilot project in February, 1994. From its *Telecommuting Guide*, here are Smart Valley's 26 steps to implementing a telecommuting program.

1. Prepare and present a telecommuting proposal.
2. Obtain support from top management.
3. Establish a telecommuting implementation committee.
4. Define pilot program parameters.
5. Present telecommuting orientation sessions.
6. Develop a telecommuting policy for your organization.
7. Develop a telecommuting agreement between the employees and the managers.
8. Develop criteria to select participants.
9. Develop evaluation criteria for the program.
10. Determine equipment and technology needs.
11. Develop resource and reference materials.
12. Recruit participants.
13. Implement managing by objectives.
14. Select the telecommuters and supervisors.
15. Select the control group.
16. Train the telecommuters and supervisors.
17. Administer the pretelecommuting evaluation.
18. Begin telecommuting.
19. Conduct focus groups.
20. Administer telecommuting evaluations.
21. Analyze and prepare the results of the evaluation.
22. Present the results to senior management.
23. Obtain concurrence from senior management to expand and formalize the program.
24. Begin implementation of the program throughout the organization.
25. Monitor the program.
26. Make adjustments where necessary.

The *Smart Valley Telecommuting Guide* is available for $7 by calling (415) 328-4575 or sending e-mail to *svi.org* on the Internet.

Telecommuting Technology

The technology for telecommuting is rather low-tech. There's nothing awe-inspiring about a desk, a chair, and a phone. The telecommuter will also need a computer, probably a printer, and maybe even a fax machine. The most high-tech part of telecommuting may be the phone line, which rarely surges above Integrated Services Digital Network (ISDN) speeds. Considering the nascent technology MIS shops deploy into production networks every day, the technology used for telecommuting is fairly straightforward. It's the social and corporate aspects that are tricky. This tutorial covers the technology issues of telecommuting; the previous tutorial discussed the corporate aspects.

WHAT THEY NEED AT HOME

The first step to setting up a telecommuting nest in your house is to define your workspace. Your workspace can be a grand three-room suite or a freshly cleaned-out junk room. You'll need a desk, a chair, and a phone line with a different number than your home phone (so you can distinguish the late-night personal calls from the late-night work calls). You may want a separate line for the modem and fax.

• **You'll need a desktop computer.** You may already have a computer that you own, or your company may provide you one for use at home. Evaluate the computing power you'll need—the workstation speed, monitor quality and size, and disk space. If you will frequently access information from the corporate network or from on-line services, you will need a larger disk than the one you have in the office.

You may be able to use a notebook computer for at home and in the office, so you'll always have the same computing environment. Notebooks offer the same speed as desktop computers but usually sacrifice screen quality, disk space, and expansion slots. A docking station equipped with extra slots and storage space may alleviate the problem.

Don't be locked into thinking that you need the same type of workstation at home as you do in the office (this may be the way to get the Mac you've been wanting). Many applications are cross-platform, so you may be able to run familiar applications on a different machine.

• **You'll need application software.** You'll need applications similar to those you use in the office, but you may only need a subset. How you run applications from the home office will be as important as which applications you run. Remote versions of some packages are available. Others must be coupled with some type of remote-access software, whether file-transfer, remote-control, or remote-node software.

You can use file-transfer software to transfer small- and medium-size files rather successfully, but large files often prove difficult. Most times, you'll find yourself attempting several uploads. Compressing the files before you send will reduce the transfer time.

The remote control vs. remote node debate is akin to the "tastes great, less filling" promo of lite beer companies. In its wake is the understanding that remote control vs. remote node is not an either/or proposition. You need both.

With remote-control software, your machine at home literally takes control of a machine at work. The applications execute at the machine in the office, and every keystroke, mouse click, and screen update is transferred to the home machine.

With remote-node software, your home machine becomes a node on the network. It runs its own software, and network requests are sent back to the server, as if you were local. With remote-node software, you execute programs locally—loading any significant program over the phone line will be slow.

If you're using the same software suites at home as you do at work, check the vendors' licensing agreements. Most licenses allow you to use your office copy at home, under the premise that the home machine is an extension of the office machine, as long as they are used by the same person. These two copies cannot be active simultaneously.

• **You may need a printer and a fax.** If you print occasionally, you may be able to get by with an inexpensive printer or without a printer at all. A big fast printer can cost as much as several workstations. Multiplied across a host of telecommuters, that cost escalates rapidly.

If you do a lot of faxing, consider a fax modem or a standalone fax machine.

Fax modems are great for sending out electronic files, but unless you have a dedicated fax server, receiving a fax from someone else is rather clumsy. If you want to fax something that's already on paper, a fax modem or server is useless without a separate scanner.

• **You'll need a communications link.** What type of information you access, how often you need it, and how far you are from the office will determine what type of telecom link you'll need. Table 1 shows the different applications and their telecom needs, as outlined by Smart Valley, a sponsor of a telecommuting pilot project in the San Francisco Bay Area.

If you are using a terminal to access a host computer or if you are transferring less than 500KB of files a day, a standard telephone line and modem will suffice. 28.8Kbps V.34 modems are standard fare nowadays, and a 500KB file transfer may take as little as three to five minutes, or even less if compression is used. Evaluate how much data you really need to send between the office and home. If you're primarily doing e-mail or transferring occasional files, a standard phone line is probably sufficient.

To sate a more hearty appetite for bandwidth, you'll need more sophisticated telecom services. If you need all-day access to file servers or database servers, consider an ISDN or Switched 56 link. Switched 56 provides 56Kbps of bandwidth; ISDN can provide 128Kbps. ISDN and Switched 56 are also handy if you're using X Window to access Unix workstations or servers back in the office. Both WAN services will provide sufficient bandwidth for shared whiteboard applications as well as for low-end videoconferencing.

READY THE CORPORATE NETWORK

The most difficult issue of setting up a telecommunications hub on the corporate network is security and scalability. Most likely, you currently have some facility for remote access, whether you're using comm servers or dial-up routers. You have to make sure that your network remains uncompromised and that your remote-access facilities can accommodate a growing number of telecommuters.

Any modem is a potential security breach, but you can take a number of preventive steps, including the use of call-back modems, user authentication, and encryption. Don't forget the anti-viral software; you never know where those telecommuters' computers have been.

TABLE 1. CHOOSING YOUR TELECOM LINK

Type of Access	Typical Application	Volume of Data	Distance	Hours of Daily Use	Type of Link
Terminal access using terminal or workstation and terminal emulator	• Access to central applications running on corporate computing facilities	Not applicable	<30 miles	All day	Standard telephone line and modem
	• E-mail		>30 miles	<3 hours	Standard telephone line and modem
				>3 hours	Dedicated line and modem
File transfer and terminal access	• Accessing files and documents stored on computing facilities at office	<500KB per day	<30 miles	All day	Standard telephone line and modem
	• Sharing documents with colleagues		>30 miles	<3 hours	Standard telephone line and modem
	• Archiving files on computing facilities at office			>3 hours	Dedicated line and modem.
	• Workstation-based e-mail	>500KB per day	<30 miles	All day	ISDN line and terminal adapter or Switched 56 and DSU
				<3 hours	ISDN line and terminal adapter or Switched 56 and DSU
				>3 hours	Dedicated high-speed line and DSU
File sharing using NetWare AppleTalk, and so forth	• Regular access to file server at office	Not applicable	<30 miles	All day	ISDN line and terminal adapter or Switched 56 and DSU
	• Distributed client-server or distributed database application		>30 miles	<3 hours	ISDN line and terminal adapter or Switched 56 and DSU
				>3 hours	Dedicated high-speed line and DSU
Remote access to workstation at office	• Client-server applications	Not applicable	<30 miles	All day	Standard telephone line and modem
Client-server applications with server and client located at office	• Access to files, applications, and corporate computing resource identical to those at office		>30 miles	<3 hours	Standard telephone line and modem
				>3 hours	Dedicated line and modem
X-terminal access to workstation at office	• Transparent access to Unix workstations and Unix-based applications	Not applicable	<30 miles	All day	ISDN line and terminal adapter or Switched 56 and DSU
Extending corporate LAN	• Real-time distributed meetings		>30 miles	<3 hours	ISDN line and terminal adapter or Switched 56 and DSU
Shared whiteboard	• Transparent access to corporate network and associated resources			>3 hours	Dedicated high-speed line and DSU
Limited videoconferencing with reduced video quality	• NFS file sharing				

Managing hardware and software assets will be challenging. After all, you can't send a technician with a clipboard to everyone's satellite office. Software to perform inventory checks is becoming more sophisticated but still needs development. Also consider how to perform software updates on the telecommuters' machines.

Managing the Desktop

A "black box" means you don't have to concern yourself with a device's inner workings. Don't worry yourself with details, just let the product engineers take care of what's going on inside. The problem: Network managers have many black boxes attached to their networks, but users expect them to know what's inside. Except you can't tell your user, who's complaining that he can't print and the network doesn't work, that the manufacturers of these black boxes—workstations, printers, and software—assumed that the network managers didn't need to be concerned with the magic inside.

Network management has largely been focused on managing network devices, not the devices attached to the network. Administrators savvy to the Simple Network Management Protocol (SNMP) can tinker with the internals of routers, bridges, and hubs, deftly setting device parameters and diagnosing problems. But networks have far more workstations, adapter cards, and printers than internetworking devices. And those are mystical entities, mostly without SNMP agents.

The Desktop Management Interface (DMI) could help bring those dark corners of the network into broad daylight. Products, including servers, desktop computers, and adapter cards, implementing DMI for management will begin to ship this fall. The Desktop Management Task Force (DMTF, Hillsboro, OR) has finalized its DMI specification, and in July it will provide a DMI software development kit for DOS, Windows, and OS/2. Product makers can use this kit to write DMI agents for their products, which ideally will make them easier to manage.

Five product types can benefit from DMI: PC platforms, such as desktops

DESKTOP MANAGEMENT INTERFACE ARCHITECTURE

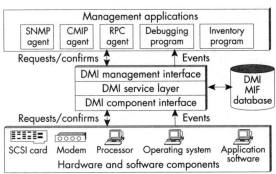

Figure 1. A management application can access and configure the managed components via the DMI Management Interface (MI). It can also respond to events occurring in its managed components. The local agent provides the services for managing the individual components. The Management Information Format (MIF) file describes the components' manageable aspects.

and servers; hardware and software components, such as operating systems, application software, video cards, fax modems, and network adapters; network and local management applications; peripherals, such as printers and mass storage devices; and management consoles.

For every DMI-managed device, the network manager will be able to determine what the device is, who made it, where it's installed, and other relevant information. With those capabilities alone, taking inventory of network devices might be less of a nightmare than it currently is. Network managers will be able to glean this information from their desks, using management software, rather than having to physically go to the site and unscrew the device cover to look inside. Beyond that, manufacturers can use DMI to configure and diagnose their products. Now that's a real boon to productivity.

HOW DMI WORKS

Implementing DMI-based management involves the management application, the local agent, which runs on the desktop computer, and the hardware and software components being managed. These parts utilize the three elements of DMI: the Management Interface (MI), the Service Layer, and the Component Interface (CI). Figure 1 shows the DMI architecture and its relation to devices.

The management application can retrieve a list of managed components, access the specific components, and configure the components via the DMI

Management Interface. The management application can also respond to events that occur in its managed components.

Each DMI-managed desktop has a local agent, which provides the services for managing the individual components. The local agent presents a common interface to management applications. It is also responsible for coordinating requests from management agents with actions to be executed by the components. The local agent is the embodiment of the DMI Service Layer. The Service Layer must be tuned to a specific operating system, and the first implementations are for DOS, Windows, and OS/2. Implementations for Unix and Windows NT are on the drawing board.

Because the Service Layer runs directly on the desktop computer, its memory footprint is crucial. Efficiently running on existing systems, including low-end PCs, is essential for the success of DMI. One reason SNMP is not widely used on desktop computers and their internal components is because of heavy memory and processing requirements. For the DOS Service Layer, the DMTF targets the TSR to be 14KB and loadable into high memory. In Windows, the Service Layer will be a Dynamic-Linked Library (DLL). For memory-constrained systems, the local agent can also operate as a network proxy, just as in SNMP.

The local agent communicates with the managed components via the DMI Component Interface. The Component Interface gets and sets the component devices' attributes. Component categories include PCs and servers, network adapters, printers, operating system software, application software, and modems.

But the DMI isn't only about the network manager initiating actions. DMI-managed components may initiate events when some undesirable action has occurred, such as discovering a virus or exceeding a pre-set limit for disk space. The component notifies the Service Layer, which in turn communicates the event to the management application. From there, the network manager can be notified or an action may be taken automatically, depending on the management application itself.

The DMI relies on a Management Information Format (MIF) file to describe the manageable aspects of a particular component. The MIF, which is an ASCII file, guarantees a basic level of information, called the standard component ID group, that even existing equipment can provide. In the standard component ID group, the product name, version, serial number, and the time and date of last installation are mandatory. The ID number is assigned on the basis of a device's order of installation relative to the other system components.

Each group also contains a component name, ID, and class. A management application can use the class identifier to find groups of a certain type, such as LAN adapters.

Each component typically has one or more groups in the MIF, and each group contains one or more attributes that describe the component. The product manufacturer chooses to include either DMTF-specified groups or private groups. For example, a fax modem manufacturer might write MIFs for the standard fax group, the standard modem group, and a private MIF for their own product.

DEVICES GET MIFFED

With the release of the DMTF developer's kit, three classes of products will be manageable: desktop and server systems, adapter cards, and printers. Future classes include software, mass storage, and servers. Let's get an understanding of what parameters the DMI lets you see and control.

The systems group accesses information relative to a PC motherboard. With a DMI-instrumented PC, the network manager will be able to find out the system name, location, primary user name, user phone number, system uptime, system date and time, bus architecture, and slot count. The system's MIF also defines another group of attributes that relate to plug-in cards, such as video cards. For those, the network manager will be able to find out the model, part number, revision level, warranty start date, warranty revision, warranty duration, and support phone number.

For the adapter card MIF, the network manager can discern the driver type (Open Data-Link Interface, Network Driver Interface Specification, NetWare 3.x, NetWare 4.x, LANtastic, and so on), topology type (Ethernet, Token Ring, LocalTalk, T-1, and so on), connector type (RJ-45, BNC, DB-9, for example), bus width, version and size, board number, permanent and current network addresses, data rate, buffer memory size, total number of bytes and packets both transmitted and received, and the total number of errors transmitted and received.

For printers, the network manager will be able to determine whether the printer is a part of the IEEE 1284 or Network Printer Alliance (NPA) group. For NPA printers, administrators can discover how much memory the printer has, whether it's duplex, and its speed, for example.

WHAT ABOUT SNMP?

If you're thinking the DMI sounds remarkably like SNMP, then you're on track. The difference is that DMI was designed to run on desktop systems, which typically don't have the extra horsepower to run resource-intensive SNMP code. The DMI MIF is sufficiently akin to the SNMP MIB that if the management-application vendor so desires, MIFs can be mapped to MIBs. Standard SNMP network management platforms, such as Sun's SunNet Manager, will be able to communicate with DMI applications. The DMI can also be mapped to use the IEEE 802.1B LAN Management protocol, which is Common Management Information Protocol (CMIP) over Logical Link Control (LLC) or CMOL.

BEHIND THE DMI CURTAIN

The DMTF was started by Intel in 1992, and critics viewed it as an Intel-centric specification. The DMTF now operates independently of Intel and is a non-profit organization. It has three levels of membership, depending on the level of involvement your company prefers, from defining the specifications to implementing them.

Few people would be surprised to find out that Intel plans to incorporate DMI into all of its networking products, and in fact, its 10/100Mbps Ethernet cards, the EtherExpress Pro/100 includes DMI agents. Intel also talks of incorporating DMI directly into its CPUs.

DMI also has some big-league support. For example, Microsoft will implement DMI in Windows 95—at least in some form, according to Chris Thomas, the DMTF evangelist. The LAN Adapter Working Group includes 3Com, IBM,

Intel, Hewlett-Packard, IBM/Pennant, Lexmark, QMS, Tektronix, and Xerox. The PC Platform Working Group includes AST, Compaq, Dell, and HP.

WHAT DOES IT ALL MEAN?

To say networks are heterogeneous is nearly a cliché, but as many different vendors' hardware and software products sit inside desktop computers as make up the physical network. Peering into desktop devices is largely a manual labor. But DMI provides a vendor-independent, software-based means of managing desktop pods of heterogeneity.

DMI applications will debut this fall, first for PCs, LAN adapter cards, and printers, but eventually DMI will worm its way into operating systems, applications software, and SNMP management platforms, giving network managers a way to see and control most things that reside on the network.

Tape Backup

Installing and testing a tape backup system is one of those tasks that is either a breeze or a nightmare. If you don't run into any surprises, the process will take a few stress-free hours—not including, of course, the time spent carefully planning the system before even ordering the hardware. Installations don't always go smoothly, however. At the first device unavailable message, you might as well call home to say you'll be working late.

At first glance, you wouldn't expect a tape drive installation to be any more fraught with pitfalls than installation of a hard drive. However, because the tape drive is often added to a fully configured system—usually as something of an afterthought—you're more likely to bring any hidden problems to the forefront. Also, given the different nature of tape drives and the fact that you're more likely to disconnect and reconnect them, the devices can strain a SCSI chain that's already marginal.

In this tutorial, we'll look at some of the dangers lurking in the back of the SCSI bus (or channel), and in the process, get an overview of SCSI fundamentals.

THE SCUZZY SPEC

The Small Computer Systems Interface (SCSI, pronounced SKUH-zee) specification started as an attempt to provide a device-independent way to connect multiple devices to a computer, without requiring a separate device driver customized for each type of hard disk or tape device. While the goal of eliminating separate drivers remains elusive, SCSI does promote the use of much more intelligent devices that handle many of the details of data writing and reading and defect management. Thus, the software on the computer doesn't have to include separate logic to handle each different type of drive.

A SCSI bus can address up to eight devices, each of which can be classified as initiator (a device giving commands to other devices) or target (a device carrying out those commands). Most often, the host adapter will take the role of initiator and the attached drives will be the targets. But, some SCSI devices can alternate between being initiators and targets.

Total SCSI cable length should be less than 6 meters, or about 19.7 feet. When measuring cable length, include cables inside the computer and within external devices, such as autoloaders. Cables with different impedance values should not be used in the same chain or the signal may tend to be reflected at the junction. You'll save yourself trouble by using high-quality cables and keeping the total length of the SCSI chain as short as possible—much shorter than the 6 meters specified in the standard.

TERMINATORS

Each end of the SCSI chain should be terminated. Terminating resistors keep the signal from reflecting back into the cable. Some of the hardest-to-find problems spring from improper termination; having too many, too few, or incorrect placement of terminators can cause unreliable operation. Also, bear in mind that improperly terminated SCSI chains may work fine for a time, but then fail when you add another device to the chain or use applications that stress the limits of the SCSI data transfer rate.

A SCSI bus with no termination isn't likely to work at all. A bus that's missing just one terminator will work in most cases, but it won't be as reliable with long cables or in an environment with a lot of electrical noise. The same holds true for a SCSI bus in which the terminators aren't at the very ends of the chain.

Remember that for proper termination, only the devices (drives or host adapter) at the ends of the daisy chain must have terminators installed. Note that many drives come with terminating resistor packs installed. If you use drives in external cabinets, make sure that the drives installed in those cabinets are properly configured. Usually, it's easiest to remove the termination from the drive itself and install a plug-type terminator on the external box.

If the host adapter controls one SCSI channel and both internal and external SCSI devices are installed, the devices at each end of the chain need to be terminated and the host adapter itself should not be terminated. Some SCSI host adapters simplify configuration by including separate internal and external SCSI channels. With these cards, the adapter and the last drive in each chain should be terminated.

The original SCSI specification called for passive terminators—a pair of resistors for each signal line on the SCSI bus. With its faster data transfer rates and tighter timings, the SCSI-2 specification introduced an alternate, more reliable form of termination called active termination. Incorporating one or more voltage regulators, active terminators provide much more consistent termination and are less susceptible to noise. Active terminators will work with SCSI or SCSI-2 channels. So, if you are experiencing hard-to-trace problems with SCSI devices, you may want to try replacing your passive terminators with active ones.

Improper termination isn't always the culprit when SCSI channels exhibit intermittent problems. The power supplies of some external SCSI cabinets can occasionally malfunction, causing unreliable operation of the drive and mimicking termination or SCSI ID problems with the SCSI channel. Other problems can arise from incorrect settings on the drives themselves.

Sometimes, adding a tape drive to a SCSI bus can suddenly cause the entire chain to operate more slowly. If you have a tape unit, CD-ROM, or other device attached to the SCSI bus, you should enable the disconnect feature on those devices. This allows the host-based adapter (HBA) to issue a command or series of commands to that device and then disconnect and return to servicing disk requests. If the disconnect feature is not enabled, the SCSI bus must wait for the device to return with a completion code, which may make the bus unable to fulfill other requests to talk to the drive.

SCSI IDS

Up to eight devices, including the host adapter, can attach to one SCSI channel. The SCSI ID must be different for each device on the same channel. The controller itself usually has ID 7. A bootable hard drive is usually set to ID 0. Other devices on the chain should have IDs that correspond to their priority; 0 has the lowest priority, and 7 has the highest.

This makes intuitive sense in the case of the controller, because it would obviously need the highest priority. However, with bootable hard drives, device priority may be confusing. The BIOS on many controllers will only make a drive with SCSI ID 0 bootable; this seems problematic because the device needing the highest priority is assigned the lowest. But, it turns out that SCSI priority isn't very important in normal operation. Most devices cooperate to keep the bus as free as possible, so arbitration priority is needed only as a last resort during device contention. In addition, arbitration is needed only at the beginning of a transaction between two devices, usually the host adapter and another SCSI device. While the two devices communicate, no other devices can access the SCSI bus.

SCSI ID is very important, even if arbitration priority isn't always a serious issue. Remember that each device, even internal drives, must have a unique ID. The ID also serves as the device address, a three-bit sequence that's included with each command issued to a device. Duplicate device IDs are a very common source of errors, and the problems they cause can be intermittent and hard to track down. This is especially true if you install drive mechanisms into do-it-yourself external SCSI cabinets and have incomplete information about the drive-select jumpers.

Installing a SCSI host adapter with multiple channels may ease the process of selecting unique IDs. Some SCSI cards use different channels, each supporting up to seven devices, for the internal and external connectors. Thus, you wouldn't need to worry about the IDs of internal devices when you install external SCSI devices. Separate channels can also help you segregate fast hard drives from slower devices, such as CD-ROMs and tape drives.

It's a good idea to keep tape drives on a different SCSI channel than your hard drives. This keeps fast hard drives from becoming burdened by slower devices. It's also a much safer configuration for emergency surgery on a tape drive. Although disconnecting a tape drive from the SCSI chain with the server power on is never recommended, in an emergency, you may have to. Having the tape drive segregated from the hard drives will at least ensure that you don't bring the whole file system down when you replace a jammed tape drive. Better yet, get a server that actually supports hot-swapping of SCSI devices.

LAST WORDS

Some 8mm tape drives default to asynchronous transfer mode, while many host adapters default to synchronous transfer mode. If you power down the tape drive while the server is still running and then power it back on, the device will attempt to use its default asynchronous mode without renegotiating the transfer mode with the host controller. The next tape operation is then likely to lock up the workstation or server.

If there's no bootable hard disk on the SCSI bus, disable the SCSI adapter's BIOS and let the software driver control the SCSI devices.

Make sure that you are loading the latest version of the drivers for your host adapter. Tape backup programs will generally require ASPI (Advanced SCSI Programming Interface) drivers. The interface consists of two parts: a low-level, hardware-specific ASPI Manager that accepts ASPI commands and translates them into commands the adapter hardware understands; and an adapter-independent ASPI module. Although the ASPI module is adapter independent, it is generally customized to support a particular type of SCSI device, such as tape drives, CD-ROMs, or hard drives.

FEELING KIND OF SCSI: SCSI'S NEW GENERATION

In the face of increasing speeds offered by hard drives, the SCSI specification has been updated. The SCSI-2 specification included methods for faster and wider data transfer and for more robust termination. The SCSI-3 specification, which is currently being developed, is intended to solidify some of the improvements needed to handle even faster data transfer, such as support for fiber optic interfaces. It will also add support for other types of peripherals.

Here are some of the SCSI-related terms you're likely to hear:

- *Differential SCSI vs. single-ended SCSI.* These terms were defined by the original SCSI specification to support different types of SCSI interface cables. The most commonly encountered type is single-ended SCSI, which has one wire for each signal to be transmitted. Differential SCSI, in contrast, uses a pair of wires for each signal, providing greater immunity to electrical noise and supporting greater cable lengths.

A single SCSI bus supports either single-ended or differential devices; the host determines which type. You can't combine both types on the same chain. Most generic SCSI drives are single-ended SCSI devices.

- *Synchronous vs. asynchronous transfer.* Defined in the original SCSI specification, synchronous transfers allow data rates of up to 5MBps on SCSI devices by allowing devices to transmit without waiting for acknowledgment from the other device—the acknowledgments should eventually catch up, but the transmitting device doesn't have to wait for each one. SCSI-2 expanded this concept to support rates of up to 10MBps. This 10MBps rate is generally called Fast SCSI.

- *Fast SCSI.* By reducing some of the timing margins in the SCSI specification, SCSI-2 devices can transfer data faster than SCSI devices— 3MBps for asynchronous SCSI-2 transfers vs. 1.5MBps for SCSI, and up to 10MBps for SCSI-2 synchronous transfers. Fast SCSI generally refers to SCSI-2 devices capable of performing synchronous transfers faster than 5MBps.

- *Wide SCSI.* The original SCSI specification called for a single cable serving as the backbone of the SCSI bus. This cable supported a data width of eight bits, or one byte. SCSI-2 also allows for transfers using wider data paths of 16 bits or 32 bits. However, this wider path entails the use of an additional 68-pin cable called the B-Cable. Not surprisingly, the original SCSI cable is called the A-Cable. Because wide transfers are automatically negotiated between devices, you can mix devices using different data widths on the same SCSI bus.

Because the B-Cable carries only data signals, Wide SCSI devices conforming to the SCSI-2 standard still use only eight bits for command, status, message, and arbitration lines. SCSI-3 will add a specification for a new type of cable, the P-Cable, that supports 16-bit arbitration, as well as 16-bit data transfers.

Electrostatic Discharge

Electrostatic discharge (ESD) isn't an everyday topic of discussion, so it's easy to put it out of mind. However, careless work habits or the right—in this case, maybe the wrong—environmental factors can create a lot of trouble for you.

Recognize this experience? You walk across a carpeted room on a day when the humidity is very low, reach for a doorknob, and get zapped. Here's how it happens. Electrostatic charges, also known as static electricity, build up when two insulating materials are rubbed together. Electrons are rubbed off of one surface and onto another. So, one surface will now have an excess of electrons and thus be negatively charged, while the other will have a relative deficiency of electrons and be positively charged.

The magnitude of these charges is impressive—as much as tens of thousands of volts. The quantity of electron flow, or current, expressed in amperes, poses an electrocution hazard to people. Fortunately, the current in the situation just mentioned is very low. Although the shock that we get when we touch a doorknob or other conductive material is startling, it doesn't do any damage.

Even though people aren't harmed by such ESD incidents, transistors and the integrated circuits built from them are extremely sensitive to minute currents and any voltages that exceed the 5 volts to 12 volts from which they typically are powered.

THE UNSEEN THREAT

Manufacturers of computers and other electronic devices, such as telephones, copiers, fax machines, and so on, take great pains to design their systems so they're armored against ESD hazards. In general, they're mostly successful in that regard. Most computers are enclosed in a grounded metal chassis that will shield the internal electronics from any discharge. The chassis is further surrounded by an insulating plastic outer casing. About the only vulnerable points of most computers are serial and parallel ports, and users are unlikely to be touching these in everyday use.

The part of a computer most likely to get zapped is the one you come into contact with most frequently: the keyboard. 3M (St. Paul, MN) has come up with a self-adhesive static dissipative strip that you can apply to a keyboard, just below the space bar. It includes a ground wire that you connect to a known electrical ground—the screw on the faceplate of a grounded AC wall outlet, for example).

By touching the grounding strip before touching anything else on your computer, you'll dissipate any electrostatic charge that you may have built up by walking across the carpet. I've also seen other types of keyboard wrist rests and related devices that incorporate some type of anti-static feature.

Perhaps the situation where you must take the most precautions against ESD is when you're servicing a computer or handling circuit boards. Electronics manufacturers are keenly aware that unmounted integrated circuits (ICs) and circuit boards are extremely vulnerable to ESD hazards, and they take elaborate precautions in their manufacturing operations.

Most do not install carpeting on shop floors, preferring linoleum or other floor tiles, polished with electrically conductive floor waxes. Assembly tables are covered with conductive laminates. Workers wear cotton anti-static shop coats and eschew nylon or other nonconductive synthetic textiles. Parts bins and trays are molded from special conductive plastics. And finished circuit boards are shipped in anti-static plastic bags.

MINDING THE SHOP

A completed circuit board—a network adapter or modem, for example—is most vulnerable to ESD right when it arrives in your shop, ready for installation in a computer. But you eliminate ESD hazards by taking a few simple precautions and investing in a couple of low-cost anti-static components.

A good start is to obtain conductive anti-static table mats for your service bench. These have a ground wire for connection to a reliable ground point. It's a good idea to place any computer that you're going to service on such a mat *before* opening it up. You can also get anti-static wrist straps. These come with a coiled cord that connects to ground through a 1-megohm resistor. The resistance is for personal safety, in the event you should come into contact with 110-volt power. The coiled cord shouldn't interfere with your work. And, most use a snap attachment to the wrist strap, so if you need to walk away from the bench to fetch something, it's a simple matter to unsnap the coiled cord, then quickly snap it back onto the wrist strap when you return.

If you refuse to be chained to your workbench, you can get elastic grounding straps that go around your ankle and under your shoe. (Perhaps the pinnacle in geek attire, they could make a great conversation starter if you wear one out to lunch. Maybe you'd like to rethink that wrist strap now.) For the grounding straps to work, you need to be standing on a grounded, conductive surface. A grounded anti-static mat is best.

For those times when you need to work on a computer at the user's site rather than in the shop, you can get static dissipative field service kits that consist of a wrist strap and a roll-up flexible plastic mat.

If you need to work on a computer, but don't have an anti-static mat and wrist strap, there are still some precautions you can take. For example, before opening up the computer, make sure the power is turned off, but leave the power cord plugged in. This will ensure that the computer's chassis is grounded through the power cord.

Alternatively, use a wire terminated with alligator clips to connect the chassis to an earth ground. Touch some point on the metal chassis, the back panel, for example, before opening the computer. This will drain off any static charge that may have been on your body. When you've opened up the system—and before you reach in to remove any circuit boards—touch the chassis again.

Before opening the anti-static bag on any new board you're installing, hold the board in its protective bag in one hand while you touch the chassis with your other hand. By doing this, you'll drain off any static charge that may exist on the outside of the bag. You can then open the bag and remove the board. It's good practice to handle circuit boards by their edges or mounting brackets, and avoid touching ICs or circuit traces. Obviously, if the board has jumpers that need to be set, you're going to have to touch the board. But it's still a good idea to avoid handling circuit boards to the extent that you can.

Walking around is a good way to build a static charge, so if you need to step away from the system, make sure you again ground yourself by touching the chassis upon your return.

By using these techniques, you can work on a system with very little likelihood of doing any ESD damage. Clearly, though, using an anti-static wrist strap is a far more positive way to guarantee that you aren't harboring a static charge.

BE SENSITIVE

If a circuit board arrives in an anti-static plastic bag, you should probably conclude that the component is static-sensitive. So, don't pull it out of the bag until you're ready to install it in a computer. First, place the computer and all the boards you're going to install (still in their conductive plastic bags) on the grounded anti-static mat. Then, put on your wrist strap before pulling any circuit boards out of their bags. Any boards you remove should be put into conductive anti-static bags. (It's a good idea to hang onto anti-static bags that come with new boards.)

Handling polystyrene cups, polystyrene peanuts and packing material, and the plastic shrink-wrap film that new software comes in can expose you to a high-voltage static field that can zap components, so keep these things out of your server rooms, wiring closets, and service shop.

To understand why nonconductive plastics are such an ESD hazard, consider the polystyrene cup. Let's assume it has a high-voltage static charge on its surface. Touching the cup to a grounded electrical conductor will drain off the charge only at the point of contact. Because the plastic in the cup acts as an insulator, the charge that exists over the rest of the cup's surface remains in place.

Ionized-air blowers are available for service benches. These produce a stream of ionized air (both positive and negative ions) that neutralizes any static field that may exist on nonconductive plastic surfaces. The blowers can be a nice insurance policy, in case nonconductive materials come into contact with sensitive electronic components. Even if you take this precaution, however, it's still good practice to have a policy of keeping plastic cups and other materials away from the service bench.

ON THE CARPET

You'll also want to give some attention to the type of floor covering that's being used in your offices. Many synthetic carpets are complete insulators and promote static build-up. If you're outfitting a new office or putting new carpet into an existing one, look for carpets that are conductive—either by nature of the material they're made of, or from some coating that's been applied. You can also treat existing carpeting with anti-static sprays. (Repeated carpet cleaning tends to remove anti-static treatments and sprays, so you'll need to periodically reapply them.)

Many people have trouble rolling their office chairs across carpeting (especially if it's deep pile), so they put a hard plastic or rubber chair mat on top of the carpet, to get a nice, smooth rolling surface. The only problem with this is that most of these mats are electrical insulators, which again means there's potential for static charges to build up. An alternative is to buy special static-dissipative chair mats. These are made of conductive plastic and come with a ground wire that you can connect in the same fashion as the keyboard anti-static strip mentioned previously.

Also, avoid low relative humidities. Humid air conducts electricity, to a certain extent. By contrast, very dry air is an insulator. Heaters and furnaces not only heat air, they reduce the relative humidity as they do so. You may want to add a humidifier to your heating system to add moisture back into the air. Obviously, you don't want to go overboard with this—relative humidities in excess of 90 percent can result in condensation that can short-circuit electronics. It's ultra-low relative humidities (15 percent or less) that you want to avoid.

HOW BAD CAN IT BE?

Am I going overboard with this ESD stuff? Somewhere between paranoia and oblivion lies a happy medium. Some organizations don't have much of an ESD problem. Others, particularly those in dry or cold climates, can have severe problems. What's so insidious about ESD is that an organization may have a problem and not even know it. It takes fairly high voltages (up in the thousands of volts) to produce a noticeable spark when you touch a metallic object. You can be carrying a static charge of a few hundred volts, which is enough to damage a circuit board, and not know it, because you don't feel the discharge when you touch metal.

One way to determine whether hazardous ESD levels exist in your environment is to use a static field meter. These devices, which typically sell for $300 to $500, can measure the static charge on a surface, when placed within a few inches of the surface.

Making changes to your office building's heating and air conditioning equipment is not a trivial expense. If you're not willing to take that plunge, there are still a number of easy, inexpensive steps you can take. The logical move is to eliminate the points of greatest vulnerability. So, focus your efforts on those areas where computers are being worked on and circuit boards are being handled.

For the most part, it doesn't cost a fortune to purchase the equipment and supplies needed for ESD protection. Anti-static wrist straps cost $25 or less. Most table mats are priced at less than $100. Wrist strap resistance testers are in the $100 to $300 range. The cost of all of this probably adds up to less than that of a single computer. (I can hear it now: "If it saves even one computer's life, it's worth it." But it's true.)

For anti-static materials and equipment, check out suppliers of electronic assembly equipment and computer furniture. If you don't know of any sources, here are a couple you can use as a starting point. This is by no means an exhaustive list, however.

Contact East, a distributor of test, repair, and electronic assembly products has a catalog that lists numerous static protection products, including anti-static mats, wrist straps, parts trays, static-shielding bags, anti-static sprays and floor waxes, and ionized-air blowers. It even carries a few videotapes and books on ESD awareness and techniques. (I haven't reviewed the tapes or the books, so I can't vouch for their merit. But they may well prove to be quite informative).

Misco, a distributor of computer peripherals, supplies, and furniture, carries anti-static chair mats and the 3M keyboard strip previously mentioned. Jensen Tools, which distributes a broad range of electronics toolkits, carries anti-static wrist straps, floor mats, table mats, and roll-up field service kits.

SOURCES OF SUPPLY

Here are some vendors of anti-static equipment and supplies:

Contact East
335 Willow St.
North Andover, MA 01845
(508) 682-2000
Fax: (508) 688-7829

Jensen Tools
7815 S. 46th St.
Phoenix, AZ 85044
(800) 426-1194
(602) 968-6231
Fax: (800) 366-9662

Misco
1 Misco Plaza
Holmdel, NJ 07733
(800) 876-4726
Fax: (908) 264-5955

Fault-Tolerant Systems

Network downtime is not only frustrating to users and network administrators, it can become downright expensive. A nonoperational network can cost an organization upwards of $50,000 per hour, depending on the application and marketplace (according to the findings of a downtime cost survey performed by market research firm The Yankee Group). Take the case of a reservation system—an airline or theater-ticket agency. During a two-hour period in which such a system is down, an agency dependent on such a LAN could lose thousands or—in the case of an airline—millions of dollars in revenue.

As a result, there is a strong demand among end users for products that protect their network systems against loss of data; these include magnetic tape-based backup-and-recording systems, uninterruptible power supplies, and fault-tolerant systems.

Most network managers rely on some form of regular backup procedures, which create archival files, and uninterruptable power sources, which provide battery-supplied electricity that takes over operation of the network automatically when regular electrical service fails. As a result, these are fairly well-understood and implemented technologies.

Fault-tolerant products such as Novell's System Fault Tolerant (SFT) NetWare are not so well understood and, as a consequence, there are relatively few in use. Because they are based on hardware redundancy that provides two identical copies of data and program files—fault-tolerant systems also go by the nickname of *mirroring* devices.

The term mirroring is apt in one sense: Fault-tolerant products rely on two mass-storage devices—usually, a server or hard disk—that work in tandem to support a mirror image of each other. That is, they contain identical formatting, applications, and data files. The analogy isn't exact, however—a true mirrored image is backward from its original, while the formatting and files on fault-tolerant systems, as one might expect, are identical, not backward.

Still, the mirroring analogy is helpful in describing and understanding the concept of fault-tolerant systems. Fault-tolerant products offer a measure of security that goes beyond the backup-and-recovery process, which provides a static, or time-specific, record of the data stored on a network's hard disk drives.

IDENTICAL DATA STORES

Fault-tolerant systems prevent data loss and network downtime by giving the network operating system real-time, immediate access to two identical and dynamically changing copies of the information stored on the networks. A fault-tolerant system thus relies on hardware redundancy, either with two identical hard disks or servers.

In a fault-tolerant system, the failure of one mirrored component—for example, a hard disk—doesn't bring on a catastrophic collapse of the network: The duplicate, or secondary, device, which is running concurrently with the primary device, merely takes over the operation of the tasks the primary component was handling, and the user isn't aware that his or her network has experienced trouble.

In a disk-mirroring system, a network server contains hard disks in shadowed pairs of primary and secondary drives. When network users store data to the network, the server writes it to both drives, thus creating mirrored images on the separate devices. Should either hard disk fail, net work operation can continue uninterrupted, since the NOS automatically makes all reads and writes to and from the remaining hard disk.

Some disk-mirroring packages offer specific options to fine tune a system. Novell's SFT NetWare, for example, lets network administrators duplicate directories and file-allocation tables while providing a read-after-write verification process. And if a NetWare SFT server fails to read a block of data from one mirrored disk, the server automatically looks to the secondary disk to fetch the data. Moreover, SFT NetWare marks that bad area on the disk unusable, then repairs the file by copying the valid data from the secondary disk to a known-usable area on the primary disk.

MIRRORING SERVERS

Similarly, a server-mirroring system, composed of primary and secondary servers, operates with the two servers running in parallel. The primary server

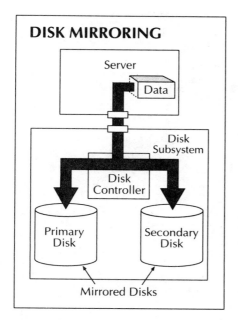

DISK MIRRORING

Server

Data

Disk
Subsystem

Disk
Controller

Primary
Disk

Secondary
Disk

Mirrored Disks

In disk mirroring, a server stores data to both a primary and a secondary hard disk. Should either disk fail, the server can access the remaining disk, without loss of network uptime or data.

handles all network activity while the secondary server operates concurrently—in the background, as it were.

Mirrored servers generally are linked via a special cable and dedicated interface adapters, one of which must be plugged into each server's internal bus. Depending on vendor, these links can be made via RS-232, parallel, or SCSI connections.

Each server continuously monitors the operation of the other, so when the primary server fails, the secondary server automatically takes control of the network. Because the secondary server's hard disks contain mirrored images of those on the primary server, users don't lose data in the exchange. Should the primary server failure be limited to just a hard-disk crash, then the primary server automatically switches disk I/O to the secondary server's mass-storage system.

DISK DUPLEXING

Another form of fault tolerance is *disk duplexing*, in which two disk controllers

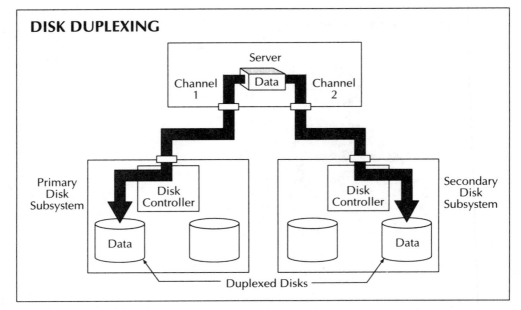

Disk duplexing allows a server to store data to two disk channels—one leading to the server's primary disk subsystem and the other to a secondary drive. Duplexing allows the server to retrieve data from either channel, providing both fault-tolerance and better performance since the server can communicate with whichever drive responds more quickly.

rather than one are used within a server. This provides nonstop operation should a disk controller, disk interface or disk power supply fail. Duplexing can improve a system's performance by creating two data channels. If any component within one channel fails, the second channel takes over automatically, again without loss of data.

In this type of system, the server's processor can receive data from whichever disk channel responds first. This often improves performance because the majority of requests across a network are disk reads. In addition, a server with duplexed disk drives can read from one disk drive, write to a second, then, when the process is completed, create a mirror image of the most-recently stored data.

After a disk or server has been taken out of operation and is ready to be put back online, a fault-tolerant system must provide a synchronization process that puts the redundant components back in sync with each other.

COSTLY OVERHEAD?

All fault-tolerant products offer drawbacks, the most obvious of which are costs of the redundant hardware and the software to run the hardware. Another factor is overhead from the executable code that controls the mirroring or duplexing process.

Monetary costs are easy to figure out. You'll pay for two of the most expensive components on a network—a server or hard disk (or, in duplexing, a disk controller)—not just one.

Determining whether such hardware and software costs are justifiable in any particular installation is a much more complex matter. This risk analysis process involves evaluating the loss potential, determining the equipment necessary to reduce the risk, and forming effective management procedures. (Numerous network vendors can provide worksheets and formulas that help in determining whether a particular installation would benefit from the installation of fault-tolerant products.)

Software overhead is a key issue in server and disk mirroring. Not only must the fault-tolerant product provide the code to handle reads and writes to and from redundant disks or servers, it must also be capable of determining when one of the disks or servers has failed, then put the secondary component in charge. This, of course, can consume quite a bit of RAM and CPU cycles on the server and traffic on the wire.

In the final analysis, however, many network managers believe that the security that fault-tolerant products provide is well worth the costs.

Glossary

Professionals ostensibly use jargon to communicate with their peers, but the plethora of obscure terms, invented words, and acronyms in the networked world often confuse not only the uninitiated, but the initiated as well. Here is a glossary of networking terms to help dispel the mystery of network argot.

3+. 3+ was 3Com's network operating system that implemented Microsoft MS-Net file sharing and Xerox's XNS transport protocols. 3Com no longer sells 3+.

3+Open. 3+Open was 3Com's network operating system based on Microsoft's OS/2 LAN Manager. 3Com no longer sells 3+Open.

1Base5. 1Base5 is the implementation of 1Mbps Starlan, which is wired in a star topology.

10Base2. 10Base2 is the implementation of the IEEE 802.3 Ethernet standard on thin coaxial cable. Thin Ethernet or thinnet, as its commonly called because the cable is half the diameter of 10Base5 Ethernet cable, runs at 10Mbps. Stations are daisy-chained along a terminated bus topology and the maximum segment length is 185 meters.

10Base5. 10Base5 is the implementation of the IEEE 802.3 Ethernet standard on thick coaxial cable. Thick, or standard Ethernet, as its commonly called, runs at 10Mbps. It uses a bus topology and the maximum segment length is 500 meters.

10BaseF. This is the specification for running IEEE 802.3 Ethernet over fiber-optic cable. It specifies a point-to-point link.

10BaseT. 10BaseT is the implementation of the IEEE 802.3 Ethernet standard on unshielded twisted-pair wiring. It uses a star topology, with stations directly connected to a multi-port hub. It runs at 10Mbps, and it has a maximum segment length of 100 meters.

100BaseT. The 100Mbps Ethernet standard, 100BaseT, is defined by the IEEE 802.3 committee for two pairs of unshielded twisted pair (100BaseTX), for four pairs of unshielded twisted pair (100BaseT4), and for fiber optic cable (100BaseFX).

802.1. This is the IEEE standard for hardware-level network management. It includes the spanning tree algorithm for Ethernet MAC-layer bridges and the Heterogeneous LAN Management (HLM) specification for managing Ethernet and Token Ring wiring hubs.

802.2. This IEEE standard specifies Logical Link Control (LLC), which defines services for the transmission of data between two stations at the data-link layer of the OSI model.

802.3 This IEEE standard governs the Carrier Sense Multiple Access/Collision Detection (CSMA/CD) networks, which are more commonly called Ethernet. 802.3

networks operate at varying speeds and over different cable types. See 1Base5, 10Base2, 10Base5, 10BaseF, 100BaseT, and 10BaseT.

802.4. This IEEE standard defines the use of the token bus network access method. Token bus networks are sometimes used in manufacturing networks, but are rarely used in office-automation networks.

802.5. This IEEE specification standard defines a logical ring network that uses a token passing access method. It is commonly called Token Ring. It comes in 4Mbps and 16Mbps speeds. It is physically wired in a star topology, with multistation access units, or hubs, as the center, to which workstations, servers, and other network devices are attached. Token Ring runs over shielded twisted-pair, unshielded twisted-pair, and fiber-optic cabling.

802.6. This IEEE specification standard defines metropolitan area networks (MANs). The MAN standard implements a distributed queue, dual-bus access method over a fiber-optic cable plant. Switched Multimegabit Data Services, an emerging high-speed WAN service, can run over a MAN physical network.

802.7. Defined by the IEEE, the 802.7 standard defines broadband LANs. They can carry video, data, and voice traffic. Broadband LANs are constructed of cable television-like components and use RF to transmit information in separate channels in a single cable. They are built using a tree topology. Broadband LANs are rarely used anymore. Do not confuse with Broadband ISDN or wideband networking, which is a term used to denote a wide-area network service with substantial bandwidth, usually in the hundreds of megabits per second.

802.9 The IEEE 802.9 standard defines integrated digital and video networking.

802.11 When finalized by the IEEE, the 802.11 standard will define wireless networking. The standard will encompass many different methods of wireless transmission, including infrared and spread spectrum radio. Many data communications, computer, and telephone vendors are involved in the wireless LAN committee.

A

access method. An access method is the set of rules by which the network arbitrates access among the nodes. Collision Sense Multiple Access with Collision Detection and token passing are two access methods commonly used in LANs.

address. An address is a unique identification code that is assigned to a network device, so it can independently send and receive messages.

Address Resolution Protocol (ARP). Within TCP/IP, ARP is the protocol that determines whether a packet's source and destination addresses are in the Data-Link Control (DLC) or Internet Protocol (IP) format. ARP is necessary for proper packet routing on a TCP/IP network.

Advanced Program-to-Program Communications (APPC). APPC is the protocol suite within IBM's Systems Application Architecture that provides peer-to-peer access, enabling PCs and midrange hosts to communicate directly with mainframes. APPC is key for distributed computing within an IBM environment. APPC can be used over an SNA, Token Ring, Ethernet, or X.25 network.

Advanced Peer-to-Peer Networking (APPN). APPN is the network architecture within IBM's Systems Application Architecture that provides for peer-to-peer access among computers. Under APPN, a mainframe host is not required. It also implements concepts such as dynamic network directories and routing in SNA.

American National Standards Institute (ANSI). ANSI is the principal group in the United States for defining standards. ANSI represents the U.S. in ISO, the international standards-making body. Fiber Distributed Data Interface, a 100Mbps network, is one network standard developed by ANSI.

analog. An analog signal or representation continuously indicates some value or quantity, while a digital signal or representation indicates a limited number of discrete values, most commonly the binary distinction between on and off or 0 and 1.

AppleShare. Apple Computer's network operating system is designed to run primarily with Macintoshes, but also accommodates DOS and Windows PCs. AppleShare Pro runs under A/UX, Apple's version of Unix, and is a high-performance version of the network operating system.

AppleTalk. AppleTalk is the name of Apple Computer's networking specification. AppleTalk includes such physical layer specifications as LocalTalk, EtherTalk, and TokenTalk; network and transport functions such as Datagram Delivery Protocol and AppleTalk Session Protocol; addressing such as Name Binding Protocol; file sharing such as AppleShare; and remote access such as AppleTalk Remote Access.

application programming interface (API). An API is a set of programming functions, calls, and interfaces that provide access to services, such as messaging, text formatting, or the functions of a particular network layer.

application layer. The seventh and uppermost layer of the OSI model, the application layer allows users to transfer files, send mail, and perform other functions where they interact with the network components and services. It is the only layer that users communicate with directly, though many application layer services are provided to programs or processes, and are not intended for direct consumption by people.

Arcnet. Datapoint designed this 2.5Mbps token-passing, star-wired network in the 1970s. Its low cost and high reliability has made it attractive to companies on a tight network budget. ArcnetPlus is a proprietary product of Datapoint that runs at 20Mbps. TCNS is a 100Mbps version of Arcnet over fiber optic cabling developed by the Thomas Conrad Corporation.

Asynchronous Transfer Mode (ATM). ATM is a method of data transmission used by Broadband ISDN. It is specified as 53-octet fixed length packets that are transmitted over a cell-switched network. Speeds up to 2.2 gigabits per second and higher are possible, and it is capable of carrying voice, video, and data. ATM has been embraced by the LAN and WAN industries, who have proclaimed it as the solution to integrating disparate networks across a large geographic distance. It is also called cell relay.

ASCII (American Standard Code for Information Interchange). The ASCII schema represents 128 characters-the upper and lower case alphabetical characters, 10 numerals, common punctuation marks, and certain printer commands—using the numbers that can be formed with seven binary digits. Other representation codes are in use, such as EBCDIC in the IBM mainframe world, and it is the responsibility of layer 6 of the OSI model, the presentation layer, to handle character code conversions if necessary.

asynchronous communication server (ACS). An asynchronous communication server is some combination of a computer motherboard, asynchronous modems, and software that enable multiple people to dial out of a LAN. ACSs also provide dial-in service, where users not in the office can use modems to call up their network services in the office. ACSs are also called dial-in/dial-out servers or modem servers.

attenuation. Attenuation is the amount of power that is lost as a signal moves over a medium from the transmitter to the receiver. It is a measured in decibels (dBs).

B

backbone. A backbone is the main "spine" or segment of a building or campus network. Departmental networks are attached as "ribs" to the central backbone.

bandwidth. Bandwidth is the difference between the highest and lowest frequency a channel can conduct, measured in MHz. The bandwidth of a voice-grade telephone line is 4KHz, while the bandwidth of a broadcast TV channel is 6MHz. The term bandwidth is often used informally to refer to a channel's throughput, which is typically measured in Kbps or Mbps. All other things being equal, a channel with twice the bandwidth of another channel can carry twice as much traffic—that is, it can have twice the throughput. See throughput.

bandwidth on demand. A concept in wide area networking that allows a user or application can agglomerate additional WAN bandwidth as the application warrants. It enables users to pay only for bandwidth that they use, when they use it. Implementing bandwidth on demand requires switched services, such as ISDN or Switched 56 lines.

Basic Rate Interface (BRI). BRI is an ISDN service that offers two "bearer" (B) channels with 64Kbps throughput that can be used for bulk data transfer plus a "data link" (D) 16Kbps channel for control and signaling information.

blackout. A blackout or power outage is an interruption or total loss of commercial electrical power. Uninterruptible power supplies provide battery-backed up power that will supply electricity during a blackout (while their batteries last).

bridge. A bridge connects two networks of the same access method, for example, Ethernet to Ethernet or Token Ring to Token Ring. A bridge works at the OSI's Media Access Control layer, and is transparent to upper-layer devices and protocols. Bridges operate by filtering or forwarding packets according to their destination addresses. Most bridges automatically learn where these addresses are located, and thus are called learning bridges.

Broadband ISDN (B-ISDN). A class of emerging high speed data and voice services for the wide-area network. Switched Multimegabit Data Services and Asynchronous Transfer Mode are two emerging B-ISDN services that will provide megabits and gigabits of bandwidth across a wide-area network.

broadcast. A broadcast message is addressed to all stations on a network.

broadcast storm. In a broadcast storm, network congestion occurs when excessive numbers of frames are broadcast.

brownout. A brownout is an abnormally low voltage on commercial power distribution lines. Power utilities may intentionally produce a brownout when there is near over-load demand for power, or natural conditions, such as storms, fires, or accidents, may cause a brownout.

brouter. A brouter is a device that can transparently bridge protocols as well as route them. It is a hybrid of a bridge and a router.

bus topology. A bus topology is a network architecture in which all of the nodes are con-nected to a single cable.

C

campus network. A campus network connects LANs from multiple departments within a single building or campus. Campus networks are typically local area networks; that is, they don't include wire-area network services, though they may span several miles.

campus wiring system. A campus wiring system is the part of a structured wiring system that connects multiple buildings to a centralized main distribution facility, local exchange carrier, or other point of demarcation. It is also referred to as a backbone.

Carrier Sense, Multiple Access with Collision Detection (CSMA/CD). Ethernet and 802.3 LANs use the CSMA/CD access method. In CSMA/CD, each network device waits for a time when the network is not busy before transmitting—they detect transmissions already on the wire from other stations.

cascaded star. A cascaded star topology is a network configuration in which multiple data centers or hubs are constructed for the purposes of redundancy. It is also called a tree topology.

Category 1. The Electronics Industry Association/ Telecommunications Industry Assoc-iation (EIA/TIA) specifies a five-level standard for commercial building telecommun-cations wiring. Category 1 wiring is old-style unshielded twisted-pair telephone cable and it is not suitable for data transmission.

Category 2. The EIA/TIA 568 standard certifies Category 2 UTP for use up to 4MHz. Category 2 UTP is similar to the IBM Cabling System Type 3 cable.

Category 3. The EIA/TIA 568 standard specifies Category 3 UTP for speeds up to 10MHz, and it is the minimum-performance cable required for 10BaseT. The wire pairs should have at least three twists per foot, but no two pairs should have the same twist pattern.

Category 4. The EIA/TIA 568 standard specifies Category 4 as the lowest grade UTP acceptable for 16Mbps Token Ring.

Category 5. The EIA/TIA 568 standard specifies that Category 5 is certified up to 100MHz. It is suitable for FDDI over copper, 100BaseT and other high-speed networks.

cell. A fixed-length packet. For example, Asynchronous Transfer Mode (ATM) uses 53-octet cells.

cell relay. Cell relay is a form of packet transmission used by Broadband ISDN networks. Also called ATM, cell relay transmits 53-octet fixed-length packets over a packet-switched network. ATM is important because it makes it possible to use a single transmission scheme for voice, data, and video traffic on LANs and WANs.

client. A client is a computer that requests network or application services from a server. A client has only one user; a server is shared by many users.

coaxial cable. Coaxial cable has a inner conductor made of a solid wire that is surrounded by insulation and wrapped in metal screen. Its axis of curvature coincides with the inner conductors, hence the name coaxial. Ethernet and Arcnet can use coaxial cable. It is commonly called coax.

concentrator. A concentrator is a multiport repeater or hub that brings together the connections from multiple network nodes. Concentrators have moved past their origins as wire concentration centers, and often include bridging, routing, and management devices.

Connectionless Network Protocol (CLNP). Of the two OSI transport protocols—CLNP and Connection-Oriented Network Service (CONS)—CLNP is more efficient for LANs. Like TCP/IP, it uses datagrams to route network messages by including addressing information in each.

Connection-Oriented Network Service (CONS). Of the two OSI transport protocols—CLNP and CONS—CONS is more efficient for WANs. CONS allows the transport layer to bypass CLNP when a single logical X.25 network is used.

Consultative Committee for International Telegraphy and Telephony (CCITT). The CCITT defines international telecommunications and data communication standards. In March of 1993, the group changed its name to ITU-TS.

Controlled Access Unit (CAU). A CAU is a managed Multistation Access Unit (MAU), or a managed multiport wiring hub for Token Ring networks. Management features include turning ports on and off.

common carrier. A common carrier is a licensed, private utility company that provides data and voice communication services for a fee. For example, Sprint and MCI are common carriers.

Common Management Information Protocol (CMIP). CMIP is the OSI management information protocol for network management. It is not widely implemented.

compression. A technique to "squash" files, making them smaller as to optimize bandwidth utilization. Compression is important for WAN transmission and disk and tape storage.

D

Data Access Language (DAL). DAL is Apple's database query language that is based upon SQL, but it provides far greater functionality.

data dictionary. In a distributed database, a data dictionary keeps track of where the data is located and stores the necessary information for determining the best way to retrieve the data.

Data Encryption Standard (DES). DES is the United States government's standard for encryption, in which data is scrambled and security codes called keys are added, so data cannot be deciphered by unauthorized users.

data-link layer. The data-link layer is the second layer of the OSI model. It defines how data is framed and transmitted to and from each network device. It is divided into two sublayers: medium access control and logical link control.

database server. A database server is a database application that follows the client-server model, dividing an application into a front end and a back end. The front end, running on the user's computer, displays the data and interacts with the user. The back end, running on a server, preserves data integrity and handles most of the processor-intensive work, such as data storage and manipulation.

DECnet. Digital Equipment Corporation's network system for networking personal computers and host computers. DECnet can use TCP/IP and OSI, as well as its proprietary protocols.

departmental LAN. A departmental LAN is a network that's used by a small group of people laboring toward a similar goal. Its primary goal is to share local resources, such as applications, data, and printers.

directory services. Directory services provide a white pages-like directory of the users and resources that are located on an enterprise network. Instead of having to know a device or user's specific network address, a directory service provides an English-like listing for a user. The OSI's X.500, Novell's NetWare Directory Services (NDS), and Banyan's StreetTalk are examples of directory services.

distributed computing. In a distributed computing architecture, portions of the applications and the data are broken up and distributed among server and client computers. In the older model, all applications and data resided on the same computer.

distributed database. A database application where there are multiple clients as well as multiple servers. All databases at remote and local sites are treated as if they were one database. The data dictionary is crucial in mapping where the data resides.

Distributed Queue Dual Bus (DQDB). The medium access method of the IEEE 802.6 standard for metropolitan area networks.

downsizing. Downsizing or rightsizing is the process of porting mission-critical applications from a mainframe to a minicomputer or PC LAN or from a minicomputer to a PC LAN.

Dual-Attached Station (DAS). In FDDI, a DAS connects to both of the dual, counter-rotating rings. Concentrators, bridges, and routers often use DAS connections for fault tolerance. In contrast, a single-attached station is connected to only one ring.

dual homing. In FDDI, dual homing is a method of cabling concentrators and stations in a tree configuration that permits an alternate path to the FDDI network in case the primary connection fails.

Dynamic Data Exchange (DDE). DDE is Microsoft's specification for Windows 3.1 and earlier versions that enables applications to communicate without human intervention.

E

E-1. In Europe, E-1 is the basic telecommunications carrier, and it operates at 2.048Mbps. In the U.S., the basic carrier is T-1, which operates at 1.544Mbps.

electromagnetic interference/radio frequency interference (EMI/RFI). EMI and RFI are forms noise on data transmission lines that reduces data integrity. EMI is caused by motors, machines, and other generators of electromagnetic radiation. RFI is caused by radio waves.

Electronic Data Interchange (EDI). EDI is a method of electronically exchanging business documents, such as purchase orders, bills of lading, and invoices. Customers and their suppliers can set up EDI networks. EDI can be accomplished through OSI standards or through proprietary products.

electronic mail. E-mail is an application that enables users to send messages and files over their computer networks. E-mail can range from a simple text-based system to a messaging system that accommodates graphics, faxes, forms-processing, workflow, and more.

encapsulation. Encapsulation or tunnelling is the process of encasing one protocol into another protocol's format. For example, AppleTalk is often encapsulated into TCP/IP for transmission over a WAN because TCP/IP is more efficient over a WAN.

end system. In Internet terminology, an end system is a host computer.

End System To Intermediate System (ES-IS). ES-IS is an OSI routing protocol that provides the capabilities for hosts (or end systems) and routers (or intermediate systems) to find each other. ES-IS does not handle the router-to-router protocols; the Intermediate System to Intermediate System protocol does.

Enterprise Management Architecture (EMA). EMA once was Digital Equipment Corp.'s umbrella architecture for managing enterprise networks. EMA is a distributed approach.

enterprise network. An enterprise network is one that connects every computer in every location of a company, and runs the company's mission-critical applications.

Ethernet. Ethernet is a CSMA/CD network that runs over thick coax, thin coax, twisted-pair, and fiber-optic cable. A thick coax Ethernet and a thin coax Ethernet use a bus topology. Twisted-pair Ethernet uses a star topology. A fiber Ethernet is point-to-point. DIX or Blue Book Ethernet is the name of the Digital Equipment Corp., Intel, and Xerox

specification; 802.3 is the IEEE's specification; 8802/3 is the ISO's specification.
EtherTalk. EtherTalk is Apple Computer's implementation of Ethernet.

F

fault management. Fault management, one of the five categories of network management defined by ISO, is the detection, isolation, and correction of network faults.
fault tolerance. Fault tolerance is the ability of a system to continue operating in the event of a fault. You can implement fault tolerance in many places in a network, including in file servers with Novell's NetWare SFT III, in disks with RAID, and in bridges with the spanning-tree algorithm.
fast packet. Fast packet is a technique for asynchronously transferring data across the network.
fiber-optic cable. Fiber-optic cable can be used to transmit signals in the form of light. Glass fiber is composed of an outer protective sheath, cladding, and the optical fiber. It comes in single mode and multimode varieties. Single-mode fiber is more often used in the public-switched telephone network; multimode fiber is more often used in local and metropolitan area networks. Single-mode fiber uses lasers to transmit the light; multimode uses light-emitting diodes.
Fiber Distributed Data Interface (FDDI). FDDI is the ANSI X3T9.5 specification for a 100Mbps network that is logically implemented as dual, counter-rotating rings. A fiber FDDI network can support up to 500 stations over 2 kilometers. FDDI, originally specified to run over fiber, can also operate over shielded and unshielded twisted-pair, although the distances are greatly shortened.
File Transfer, Access, and Management (FTAM). FTAM is the OSI protocol for transferring and remotely accessing files on other hosts also running FTAM.
File Transfer Protocol (FTP). FTP is the TCP/IP protocol for file transfer.
filtering. Filtering is the process by which particular source or destination addresses can be prevented from crossing a bridge or router onto another portion of the network.
firewall. A firewall is an impermeable barrier through which broadcast or other types of packets cannot pass. Routers, not bridges, are used to set up firewalls.
flow control. A router controls the progress of data through the network in a process called flow control. It ensures that other routers are not being congested by a heavy traffic flow, and it will route around congestion points.
forwarding. Forwarding is the process by which a bridge copies a packet from one segment or ring to another.
fractional T-1. In fractional T-1, the 1.544Mbps T-1 capacity is divided into 64Kbps increments. Users can order as many channels as they need, but they are not required to purchase the entire 1.544Mbps from the service provider.
fragmentation. Fragmentation is the process in which large frames from one network

are broken up into smaller frames compatible with the network to which they'll be forwarded.

frame relay. Frame relay is the CCITT standard for a low-overhead packet-switching protocol that provides dynamic bandwidth allocation at speeds up to 2Mbps or more. It is considered a second generation X.25 in that it is more efficient.

front-end application. Users present, manipulate, and display data via front-end or client applications. These applications work with back-end applications, such as a mail or database engines.

G

gateway. In OSI terminology, a gateway is a device or process that connects two dissimilar systems, such as a PC on a LAN and a mainframe. It operates on all seven layers of the OSI model. In Internet terminology, a gateway is another name for a router.

global network. A global network spans all departments, campuses, branch offices, and subsidiaries of a corporation. Global networks are international, and bring with them the problems of dealing with multiple languages, cultures, standards, and telephone companies.

Government OSI Profile (GOSIP). GOSIP is the U.S. government's specification for OSI conformance. Some level of GOSIP support has been required for all bids made on government projects, though it is unclear that it will be required in the future.

H

heterogeneous network. A heterogeneous network is made up of a multitude of workstations, operating systems, and applications of different types from different vendors. For example, a heterogeneous network may contain 3Com Ethernet adapter cards, Dell 486 PCs, Compaq SystemPros, Novell NetWare, FTP TCP/IP, and an HP 9000 Unix host.

Heterogeneous LAN Management (HLM). HLM is an IEEE 802.1 specification for jointly managing mixed Ethernet and Token Ring networks with the same objects.

High-level Data Link Control (HDLC). HDLC is an ISO standard for a bit-oriented, link-layer protocol that specifies how data is encapsulated on synchronous networks.

High Level Language API (HLLAPI). HLLAPI is a set of tools developed by IBM to help developers write applications that conform to its Systems Application Architecture.

High-Speed Serial Interface (HSSI). HSSI is a standard for a serial link up to 52Mbps in speed over WAN links.

homogeneous network. A homogeneous network is made up of identical or similar components-hardware, operating systems, protocols, databases, and applications.

horizontal wiring subsystem. This part of a structured wiring system connects the users' computers in the departments. It is attached to the vertical wiring system. The horizontal wiring system is often copper cable, such as twisted-pair or coax.

hub. A hub or concentrator is a multiport repeater that brings together the connections from multiple network nodes. Modular concentrators have moved beyond their origins as wire concentration centers, and often house bridges, routers, and network-management devices. Some hubs are stackable, which usually implies that they have an external backplane that permits multiple units to be connected together without taking up a "repeater hop" or using one of the ports.

I

impedance. Impedance is the resistance equivalent for AC, and it affects a network's propagation delay and attenuation. Each protocol and topology has its own impedance standards. For example, 10BaseT UTP cable has an impedance of 100 ohms to 105 ohms, while 10Base2 coaxial cable has an impedance of 50 ohms.

infrared. Infrared electromagnetic waves have frequencies higher than microwaves but lower than the visible spectrum. Infrared transmission is used for wireless LANs, as well as for point-to-point communications with portable devices.

intermediate system. In Internet terminology, an intermediate system is a router.

Institute of Electronics and Electrical Engineers (IEEE). The IEEE is a professional society of electrical engineers. One of its functions is to coordinate, develop, and publish data communications standards for use in the United States.

Integrated Services Digital Network (ISDN). ISDN is the ITU standard for carrying voice and data to the same destination. Although ISDN has not been popular in the United States, it is commonly available in Europe (especially in the U.K., Germany, and France) and in Japan.

Intermediate System-to-Intermediate System (IS-IS). IS-IS is an OSI routing protocol that provides dynamic routing between routers or intermediate systems.

International Standards Organization (ISO). ISO is a multinational standards-setting organization that formulates computer and communication standards, among others. ISO defined the OSI reference model, which divides computer communications into seven layers: physical, data-link, network, transport, session, presentation, and application.

Internet. The Internet is a collection of more than 2,000 packet-switched networks located principally in the United States, but also in other parts of the world, all linked using the TCP/IP protocol. It links many university, government, and research sites.

Internet Activities Board (IAB). The IAB is the coordinating committee for the design, engineering, and management of the Internet. The IAB has two main committees: the Internet Engineering Task Force (IETF) and the Internet Research Task Force (IRTF). The IETF specifies protocols and recommends Internet standards. The IRTF researches technologies and refers them to the IETF.

Internet Protocol (IP). IP is part of the TCP/IP suite. It is a network-layer protocol that governs packet forwarding.

internetwork. An internetwork is collection of several networks that are connected by bridges, switches, or routers, so all users and devices can communicate, regardless of the network segment to which they are attached.

Internetwork Packet Exchange (IPX). IPX is the part of Novell's NetWare stack that governs packet forwarding. This network protocol is based on the Xerox Network System (XNS).

interoperability. Interoperability is the ability of one manufacturer's computer equipment to operate alongside, communicate with, and exchange information with another vendor's dissimilar computer equipment.

inverted backbone. An inverted backbone is a network architecture in which the wiring hub and routers become the center of the network, and all subnetworks connect to this hub. In a backbone network, the cable is the main venue of the network, to which many bridges and routers attach.

isochronous transmission. An isochronous service transmits asynchronous data over a synchronous data link. An isochronous service must be able to deliver bandwidth at specific, regular intervals. It is required when time-dependent data, such as video or voice, is to be transmitted. For example, Asynchronous Transfer Mode can provide isochronous service.

J

jitter. Jitter is a kind of distortion of digital signals that takes the form of phase shifts over a transmission medium.

L

LAN Manager. LAN Manager is Microsoft's early model of a network operating system based on OS/2. It uses NetBEUI or TCP/IP network protocols. LAN Manager supports DOS, Windows, OS/2, and Macintosh clients. Through LAN Manager for Unix, it offered connections to various Unix hosts.

LAN Server. LAN Server is IBM's network operating system that is based on the OS/2 operating system and the NetBIOS network protocol. LAN Server supports DOS, Windows, OS/2, and Macintosh clients.

LANtastic. LANtastic is Artisoft's peer-to-peer, NetBIOS-based network operating system. It supports DOS, Windows, OS/2, Macintosh, and Unix clients.

leased line. A leased line is a transmission line reserved by a communications carrier for the private use of a customer. Examples of leased-line services are 56Kbps or T-1 lines.

line of sight. Laser, microwave, and some infrared transmission systems require that no obstructions exist in the path between the transmitter and receiver. This direct path is called the line of sight.

local area network (LAN). A LAN is a group of computers, each equipped with the appropriate network adapter and software and connected by cable (or wireless links), that share applications, data, and peripherals. It typically spans a single building or campus.

Local Area Transport (LAT). LAT is Digital Equipment's protocol suite for connecting terminals to an Ethernet network. Because LAT lacks a network layer, it must be bridged in an enterprise network, not routed.

LocalTalk. LocalTalk is one of Apple's physical-layer standards. It transmits data at 230Kbps using Carrier Sense Multiple Action with Collision Avoidance (CSMA/CA) over unshielded twisted-pair wire.

Logical Link Control (LLC). OSI Layer 2, the data-link layer, is divided into the Logical Link Control and the Media Access Control sublayers. LLC, which is the upper portion, handles error control, flow control and framing of the transmission between two stations. The most widely implemented LLC protocol is the IEEE 802.2 standard.

Logical Unit (LU). IBM's LU suite of protocols govern session communication in an SNA network. LU1, LU2, and LU3 provide control of host sessions. LU4 supports host-to-device and peer-to-peer communication between peripheral nodes. LU6.2 is the peer-to-peer protocol of APPC. LU7 is similar to LU2.

M

mail-enabled applications. Mail-enabled applications are a class of software that incorporates e-mail's functionality, but provides additional services, such as workflow automation, intelligent mail handling, or contact management software.

main distribution facility. In a structured wiring system, the main distribution facility is the portion of the wiring that's located in the computer room. From the main distribution facility extends the campus wiring subsystem, which runs to each building.

management information base (MIB). A MIB is a repository of the characteristics and parameters that are managed in a device. Simple Network Management Protocol (SNMP) and Common Management Information Protocol (CMIP) use MIBs to identify the attributes of their managed systems.

Manufacturing Automation Protocol (MAP). MAP is an ISO protocol for communicating among different pieces of manufacturing equipment.

Media Access Control (MAC). The MAC is the lower sublayer of the data-link layer (Logical Link Control is the upper sublayer), and it governs access to the transmission media.

mesh topology. In a mesh network topology, any site can communicate directly with any other site.

Message Handling System (MHS). MHS is Novell's protocol for electronic mail and other message management, storage, and exchange.

Message Handling Service (MHS). MHS is another name for ISO's X.400 protocols for store-and-forward messaging.

Message Transfer Agent (MTA). In ISO's X.400 electronic messaging protocols, the MTA is responsible for storing messages then forwarding them to their destinations. The MTA is commonly implemented as the mail server.

metropolitan area network (MAN). A MAN covers a limited geographic region, such as a city. The IEEE specifies a MAN standard, 802.6, which uses the Dual Queue, Dual Bus access method and transmits data at high speeds over distances up to 80 kilometers.

Messaging API (MAPI). Using Microsoft's MAPI, application developers can add messaging to any Windows application and the program can gain access to the message storage, transport, and directory services of any MAPI server.

mission-critical application. A mission-critical application is one that is crucial to a company's continued operation. As corporations downsize from mainframes, many mission-critical applications are moved to networks.

multicast. Multicast packets are single packets that are copied to a specific subset of network addresses. In contrast, broadcast packets are sent to all stations in a network.

multimedia. Multimedia is the incorporation of graphics, text, and sound into a single application.

multimode fiber. Multimode fiber-optic cable uses light-emitting diodes (LEDs) to generate the light to transmit signals. Multimode fiber is prevalent in data transmission.

multiplexing. Multiplexing is putting multiple signals on a single channel.

Multipurpose Internet Mail Extensions (MIME). MIME is an Internet specification for sending multiple part and multimedia messages. With a MIME-enabled e-mail application, users can send PostScript images, binary files, audio messages, and digital video over the Internet.

multistation access unit (MAU). A MAU is a multiport wiring hub for Token Ring networks. IBM calls MAUs that can be managed remotely Controlled Access Units, or CAUs.

N

Narrowband ISDN. Narrowband ISDN is another name for ISDN. Narrowband ISDN offers a smaller bandwidth than the Broadband ISDN services, such as Asynchronous Transfer Mode (ATM) and Switched Multimegabit Data Services (SMDS).

NetBIOS (Network Basic Input Output System). NetBIOS is a networking API developed by IBM that allows programs to access the network and exchange data. Because NetBIOS does not provide network-layer services, it cannot be routed in a network, which makes building large internetworks of NetBIOS-based networks difficult. Examples of NetBIOS-based NOSs include IBM LAN Server and Artisoft LANtastic.

NetBEUI (NetBIOS Extended User Interface). Microsoft's extended version of NetBIOS is called NetBEUI. It is a protocol that governs data exchange and network access. Because NetBEUI does not provide a network-layer, it cannot be routed in a network, which makes building large internetworks of NetBEUI-based networks difficult.

NetWare. NetWare is Novell's network operating system. NetWare uses IPX/SPX, NetBIOS, or TCP/IP network protocols. It supports DOS, Windows, OS/2, Macintosh, and Unix clients. NetWare versions 4.x and 3.x are 32-bit operating systems; NetWare 2.2 is a 16-bit operating system.

NetWare Loadable Module (NLM). An NLM is an application that resides in the NetWare server and coexists with the core NetWare operating system. NLMs provide better performance than applications that run outside the core.

network. A network is a system of computers, hardware, and software that is connected over which data, files, and messages can be transmitted and end users communicate. Networks may be local or wide area.

network layer. The third layer of the OSI model is the network layer, and it governs data routing. Examples of network-layer protocols are IP and IPX.

Network Driver Interface Specification (NDIS). NDIS is a specification, developed by Microsoft and 3Com, for generic device drivers for adapter cards used by LAN Manager and subsequent Microsoft network operating systems.

Network File System (NFS). NFS is Sun Microsystems' file-sharing protocol that works over TCP/IP.

network interface card (NIC). A network interface card is the adapter card that plugs into computers and includes the electronics and software so the station can communicate over the network.

network operating system (NOS). A network operating system is the software that runs on a file server that governs access to the files and resources of the network by multiple users. Examples of NOSs include Banyan's VINES, Novell's NetWare, and IBM's LAN Server.

network-aware application. A network-aware application knows that it is running on a network and has file- and record-locking features.

network-ignorant application. A network-ignorant application has no knowledge that it is running on a network. It lacks file and record locking, and cannot guarantee data integrity in a multiuser environment.

network-intrinsic application. A network-intrinsic application knows it is running on a network and takes advantage of a network's distributed intelligence. For example, a client-server database is a LAN-intrinsic application.

noise. Noise is sporadic, irregular, or multifrequency electrical signals that are superimposed on a desired signal.

O

Object Linking and Embedding (OLE). OLE is Microsoft's specification for application-to-application exchange and communication. It is more powerful and easier to use than Microsoft's older Dynamic Data Exchange (DDE) API.

octet. An eight-bit byte. Internet RFCs refer to octets rather than bytes, presumably because some mainframes and minicomputers have 16-bit or 32-bit bytes.

Open Data-Link Interface (ODI). ODI is Novell's specification for generic network interface card device drivers. ODI enables you to simultaneously load multiple protocol stacks, such as IPX and IP.

Open Shortest Path First (OSPF). The OSPF routing protocol for TCP/IP routers takes into account network loading and bandwidth when moving packets from their sources to their destinations. OSPF improves on the Routing Information Protocol (RIP), but it is not as widely implemented.

open systems. In open systems, no single manufacturer controls the specifications for the architecture. The specifications are in the public domain, and developers can legally write to them. Open systems is crucial for interoperability.

Open Systems Interconnection (OSI). The OSI model is the seven-layer, modular protocol stack defined by ISO for data communications between computers. Its layers are: Physical, Data Link, Network, Transport, Session, Presentation, and Application.

optical drives. Optical drives use lasers to read and write information from their surface. Because of their slow access times, optical drives are used for archiving and other activities that are not particularly time-sensitive. Several types of optical drives are available. CD-ROMs, or compact disk read-only memory, can be remastered. Information can be written to WORM, or write once, read many, disks only once; they cannot be erased. Data can be written to and removed from erasable optical disks.

OS/2. OS/2 is IBM's 32-bit multithreaded, multitasking, single-user operating system that can run applications created for it, DOS, and Windows.

outsourcing. Outsourcing is the process of subcontracting network operations and support to an organization outside your company.

P

packet. A packet is a collection of bits that includes data and control information, which is sent from one node to another.

packet switching. In packet switching, data is segmented into packets and sent across a circuit shared by multiple subscribers. As the packet travels over the network, switches read the address and route the packet to its proper destination. X.25 and frame relay are examples of packet-switching services.

peer-to-peer. In a peer-to-peer architecture, two or more nodes can directly initiate communication with each other; they do not need an intermediary. A device can be both the client and the server.

personal communications services (PCS). PCS is a category of applications that includes wireless local and personal area communications for portable and desktop computers, wireless notepad and messaging devices, and wireless office and home telephone systems. The FCC is in the process of allotting both licensed and unlicensed frequency ranges for PCS-based devices.

Physical Layer. The lowest layer of the OSI model is the Physical Layer, and it defines the signalling and interface used for transmission media.

point-to-point. A point-to-point link is a direct connection between two locations.

Point-to-Point Protocol (PPP). PPP provides router-to-router and host-to-network connections over asynchronous and synchronous connections. It is considered a second-generation Serial Line Internet Protocol (SLIP).

Presentation Layer. The sixth, or Presentation Layer, of the OSI model is responsible for data encoding and conversion.

Primary Rate Interface (PRI). PRI ISDN is a T-1 service that supports 23 64Kbps B channels plus one 64Kbps D channel.

propagation delay. Propagation delay is the time it takes for a bit to travel across the network from its transmission point to its destination.

protocol. A protocol is a standardized set of rules that specify how a conversation is to take place, including the format, timing, sequencing and/or error checking.

proxy agent. A proxy agent is software that translates between an agent and a device that uses a different management information protocol. The proxy agent communicates the data to the network manager.

public data network (PDN). A PDN is a network operated by a government or service provider that offers wide area services for a fee. Examples are networks from British Telecom and Infonet.

Q

query language. A query language enables users to retrieve information. Structured Query Language (SQL) is a standardized, vendor-independent query language, though most database vendors have proprietary extensions to SQL.

R

Redundant Array of Inexpensive Disks (RAID). RAID 1 is disk mirroring, in which all data is written to two drives. In RAID 2, bit-interleaved data is written across multiple disks; additional disks perform error detection. A RAID 3 disk drive has one parity drive plus an even number of data drives. Data is transferred one byte at a time, and reads and writes are performed in parallel. Like RAID 3, RAID 4 has a dedicated parity drive, but the data is written to the disks one sector at a time. Also reads and writes occur independently. In RAID 5, the controllers write data a segment at a time and interleave parity among them. (A segment is a selectable number of blocks.) RAID 5 does not use a dedicated parity desk. It offers good read performance, but suffers a write penalty. RAID 1, 3, and 5 are appropriate for networks.

Remote Monitor (RMON). The RMON MIB defines the standard network monitoring functions for communication between SNMP-based management consoles and remote monitors, which are often called probes. RMON extends SNMP by looking at traffic between devices instead of at individual devices. It also facilitates local capture of statistics, history, and even traffic, so that polling activity by the management console can be minimized.

Remote Procedure Call (RPC). An RPC is part of an application that activates a process on another node on the network and retrieves the results.

repeater. A repeater is a Physical Layer device that regenerates, retimes, and amplifies electrical signals.

requirements analysis. A requirements analysis is the process through which you define and evaluate the business needs of your network system.

request for proposal (RFP). An end-user company issues an RFP document that asks systems integrators and manufacturers to bid on their network designs and specifications.

request for information (RFI). An end-user company issues an RFI document to ask systems integrators and manufacturers to propose and design a system that will fulfill the corporation's business requirements.

Request For Comment (RFC). An RFC is the Internet's notation for draft, experimental, and final standards.

return on investment (ROI). Calculating the ROI enables MIS shops to gauge the network's success from a business profit-and-loss standpoint. The savings or benefits of networking projects ought to represent a return on invested capital as good or better than that of the business as a whole.

ring topology. In a ring topology, packets travel in a closed loop. Packets pass sequentially between active stations, and each station examines them and copies any that are intended for it. The packets finally return to the originating station, which removes them from the network.

risk analysis. A risk analysis is the process by which a company analyzes the business and technology risks of installing a new system.

RJ-11. An RJ-11 connector is a four-wire modular connector that is used by the telephone system.

RJ-45. An RJ-45 is an eight-wire modular connector that is used by telephone systems. The eight-pin modular connectors used for 10BaseT UTP cable resemble RJ-45 connectors, but they have substantially different electrical properties.

roll back. A database application's ability to abort a transaction before it has been committed is called a roll back.

roll forward. A database's ability to recover from disasters is called a roll forward. The database reads the transaction log and re-executes all of the readable and complete transactions.

router. A router is a network-layer device that connects networks that use the same Network-Layer protocol, for example TCP/IP or IPX. A router uses a standardized protocol, such as RIP, to move packets efficiently to their destination over an internetwork. A router provides greater control over paths and greater security than a bridge; however, it is more difficult to set up and maintain.

Routing Information Protocol (RIP). RIP is the routing protocol used by most TCP/IP routers. It is a distance-vector routing protocol, and it calculates the shortest distance between the source and destination addresses based on the lowest "hop" count.

S

sag. A sag is a short-term drop (up to 30 seconds) in power-line voltage that typically is in the region of 70 percent to 90 percent of the nominal line voltage.

server. A server is a computer that provides shared resources to network users. A server typically has greater CPU power, number of CPUs, memory, cache, disk storage, and power supplies than a computer that is used as a single-user workstation.

Serial Line Internet Protocol (SLIP). SLIP is used to run IP over serial lines, such as telephone lines.

Sequential Packet Exchange (SPX). SPX is Novell's transport protocol, which supports end-to-end connections for IPX networks.

session. A session is an end-to-end, online communications connection between two nodes.

session layer. The fifth OSI layer, the Session Layer, defines the protocols governing online communication between applications.

shielded twisted-pair (STP). STP is a pair of foil-encased copper wires that are twisted around each other and wrapped in a flexible metallic sheath to improves the cable's resistance to electromagnetic interference.

Simple Mail Transfer Protocol (SMTP). SMTP is TCP/IP's protocol for exchanging electronic mail.

Simple Network Management Protocol (SNMP). SNMP is a request-response type protocol that gathers management information from network devices. SNMP is a de facto standard protocol for network management. Two versions exist: SNMP 1 and 2. It provides a means to monitor and set configuration parameters.

single-attachment station (SAS). In FDDI, a single-attachment station is one that is connected to only one of the dual counter-rotating rings. Workstations and other non-critical devices are normally connected using SAS, which is less expensive than dual-attached stations.

single-mode fiber. Single-mode fiber uses lasers, not light-emitting diodes, to transmit signals over the cable. Because single-mode fiber can transmit signals over great distances, it is primarily used in the telephone network, and not for LANs.

SNA mainframe gateways. An SNA mainframe gateway is hardware and software that connects a LAN to an SNA mainframe. It translates between the different systems, making the PC look like a 3270 terminal to the SNA host, so the PC user can access mainframe applications, files, and printers.

source-explicit forwarding. Source-explicit forwarding is a feature of MAC-layer bridges that enables them to forward packets from only those source addresses specified by the administrator.

source routing. Source routing is normally used with Token Ring LANs. In source routing, the sending and receiving devices help determine the route the packet should traverse through the internetwork. The route is discovered via broadcast packets sent between these two points.

source-routing transparent (SRT). Source-routing transparent addresses the coexistence of Ethernet, Token Ring, and FDDI. A SRT bridge passes both source routing and transparently bridged data. The bridge uses source-routing to pass packets with the appropriate embedded routing information, and transparently bridge those packets that lack this information.

spanning-tree algorithm. The spanning-tree algorithm is an IEEE 802.1D technique for configuring parallel MAC-layer Ethernet bridges to provide redundancy. The spanning-tree algorithm manages illegal loops created by multiple parallel bridges.

star topology. In a star topology network, the nodes are connected in a hub and spoke configuration to a central device or location. The "hub" is a central point of failure.

standby power supply (SPS). A standby power supply is a backup power device that is designed to provide battery power to a computer during a power failure. A SPS experiences small interrupts during switch-over to battery operation.

Station Management (SMT). SMT is part of the FDDI specification, and it defines how to manage nodes on FDDI networks.

StreetTalk. StreetTalk is Banyan's distributed global naming and directory service for its network operating system, VINES.

Structured Query Language (SQL). SQL is an ANSI standard query language for extracting information from relational databases. It was originally developed by IBM.

structured wiring. Structured wiring is a planned cabling system which systematically lays out the wiring necessary for enterprise communications, including voice and data. IBM's Cabling System and AT&T Premises Distribution System are two such structured wiring designs. A structured wiring system is made up of horizontal, vertical, and campus subsystems. A horizontal subsystem is the system between the wiring closets and the users' systems. A vertical subsystem or backbone includes the wiring and equipment from the wiring closets to the central equipment room. The campus subsystem interconnects the buildings to a central distribution facility, local exchange carrier, or other point of demarcation.

superserver. A superserver is a computer that is designed specifically to serve as a network server. It typically has multiple CPUs, error-correcting memory, large amounts of cache, large amounts of redundant disk storage, and redundant power supplies. It is designed to provide high speed, high capacities, and fault tolerance.

surge. A surge is a short term (up to 30 seconds) rise in power-line voltage level.

Switched 56. A Switched 56 service is a dial-up connection that uses throughput in 56Kbps increments.

Switched Multi-Megabit Data Service (SMDS). SMDS is a high-speed metropolitan area network service for use over T-1 and T-3 lines. SMDS' deployment is being stalled by the enthusiasm for Asynchronous Transfer Mode, although SMDS can run in conjunction with ATM.

Synchronous Data Link Control (SDLC). SLDC is IBM's bit-synchronous link-layer protocol. It is similar to HDLC.

Synchronous Optical Network (SONET). SONET will establish a digital hierarchical network throughout the world that will enable you to send data anywhere and be guaranteed that the message will be carried over a consistent transport scheme. The existing telephone infrastructure is digital but is designed for copper lines; SONET is digital and has been designed to take advantage of fiber. SONET offers speeds up to 2.5Gbps.

synchronous transmission. A transmission where events occur based on precise clocking, rather than on delimiters whose timing may vary.

Systems Application Architecture (SAA). SAA is IBM's set of rules for computer communications and application development. SAA was designed to help create programs that will run on a wide variety of IBM computing equipment, but it is no longer held out as a panacea for developers who desire universal interoperability.

Systems Network Architecture (SNA). IBM's protocols for governing communications between terminals, intermediate devices, and mainframes. It was IBM's architecture prior to SAA.

systems integrator. A systems integrator is a company who is paid to combine disparate pieces of technology into a unified, working system for an end-user company.

T

T-1. The CCITT specifies a four-level, time-division multiplexing hierarchy for the telephone system in North America. T-1 provides 24 channels of 64Kbps bandwidth, for a total bandwidth of 1.544Mbps. A T-1 circuit can transport voice, video, data, and fax. T-1 service sold in 64Kbps increments is called fractional T-1.

T-2. T-2 is the equivalent of four T-1s, and it offers 6.3Mbps of bandwidth. Each T-2 link can carry at least 96 64Kbps circuits. T-2 is not a commercially available service, but it is used within the telephone company's hierarchy.

T-3. A T-3 circuit carries in one multiplexed signal stream the equivalent of 28 T-1 circuits. It provides 44.736Mbps of bandwidth. T-3 is not widely used for LANs.

Technical Office Protocol (TOP). TOP is the OSI protocol stack for office automation; it is not widely implemented.

Telnet. Telnet is the TCP/IP protocol for terminal emulation.

terminal emulation. A terminal emulator converts a perfectly capable computer into an enslaved screen and keyboard combination, capable only of raw input and output.

throughput. Throughput is a measure, in bits per second (bps) or bytes per second (Bps), of the traffic carrying capacity of a channel. LAN and telephone throughput is generally expressed in bps, while computer-based throughput, such as bus capacity and drive I/O rates, are generally expressed in Bps. One Bps is usually equal to 8bps. Given a particular signaling scheme, a channel's throughput is proportional to its bandwidth (expressed in Hz). Despite common usage, maintaining the distinction between bandwidth and throughput is essential to a full understanding of how networks function. (See bandwidth.)

time domain reflectometer (TDR). A TDR is a troubleshooting device that is capable of sending radar-like signals through a cable to check continuity, length, and other attributes.

token. A token is a pattern of bytes that mediates access on a Token Ring or Token Bus network.

token passing. Token passing is a network access method that requires nodes to possess an electronic token before transmitting frames onto the shared network medium. Token Ring, Token Bus, and FDDI use token-passing schemes.

Token Ring. Token Ring is the IEEE 802.5 specification for a 4Mbps or 16Mbps network that uses a logical ring topology, a physical star topology, and a token-passing access method. It works with UTP, STP, and fiber optic cable. Each ring can have up to 256 stations.

transceiver. A transceiver is a device for transmitting and receiving packets between the computer and the wire. The transceiver is usually integrated directly onto the network adapter card.

Transmission Control Protocol/Internet Protocol (TCP/IP). TCP/IP is the protocol suite developed by the Advanced Research Projects Agency (ARPA), and is almost exclusively used on the Internet. It is also widely used in corporate internetworks because of its superior design for WANs. TCP governs how packets are sequenced for transmission on the network. IP provides a connectionless datagram service. The term "TCP/IP" is often used to generically refer to the entire suite of related protocols.

transparent bridging. Transparent bridging connects similar LANs and is usually used with Ethernet. In transparent bridging, when the station transmits a frame, that frame does not know what path it will take. Instead, the bridges determine the best path at the time the frame is sent. In contrast, in source routing, the path is determined at the start of the transmission, rather than frame by frame.

transport layer. The transport layer is the fourth layer of the OSI model, and it provides reliable end-to-end data transport, including error detection between two end user devices. Examples of transport protocols are the Internet Protocol (IP), Sequenced Packet Exchange (SPX), and Transport Protocol Class 0 (TP0).

Transport Protocol Class 0, Class 4 (TP0, TP4). These protocols are OSI transport protocols. Transport Protocol Class 0 is a connectionless transport protocol for use over reliable networks. Transport Protocol Class 4 is a connection-based transport.

Trivial File Transfer Protocol (TFTP). TFTP is a simplified version of FTP, the TCP/IP file transfer protocol.

tunneling. The process of encasing one protocol in another's format is called tunneling. For example, AppleTalk packets are often enveloped in TCP/IP packet formats for transmission on an enterprise network. Tunneling is also called encapsulation.

twisted-pair. Twisted pair is a type of copper wiring in which two wires are twisted around one another to reduce noise absorbtion and signal loss. The Electronics Industry Association/Telecommunications Industry Association (EIA/TIA) specifies a five-level standard for commercial building telecommunications wiring. Category 1 wiring is old-style unshielded twisted-pair telephone cable and is not suitable for data transmission. Category 2 is for use up to 4Mbps; it resembles IBM Cabling System Type 3 cable. Category 3 UTP is specified for speeds up to 10Mbps, and it is the minimum cable required for 10BaseT Ethernet. Category 4 is the lowest grade UTP acceptable for 16Mbps Token Ring. Category 5 is certified for speeds up to 100Mbps, but it can handle speeds of up to 155Mbps. Category 5 cable is suitable for FDDI and other high-speed networks.

two-phase commit. In a distributed database, a two-phase commit ensures data integrity by confirming the successful completion of every step in a transaction before committing any of the steps.

Type 1. The IBM Cabling System specifies different types of wire. Type 1 is a dual-pair, 22 American Wire Gauge (AWG) cable with solid conductors and a braided shield. It is a type of shielded twisted-pair.

Type 2. Type 2 is the IBM Cabling System's specification for a six-pair, shielded, 22 AWG wire used for voice transmission. It is the same wire as Type 1, but has an additional four-pair wire.

Type 3. Type 3 is the IBM Cabling System's specification for a single-pair, 22 or 24 AWG, unshielded twisted-pair wire. It is common telephone wire.

Type 5. Type 5 is 100/140 micron fiber; IBM now recommends 125 micron fiber.

Type 6. Type 6 wire is two-pair, stranded 26 AWG wire used for patch cables.

Type 8. Type 8 wire is a two-pair, 26 AWG, shielded cable without any twists; it is commonly used under carpet.

U

undervoltage. In an undervoltage condition, a lower-than-usual power-line voltage lasts from several seconds to several hours.

uninterruptible power supply (UPS). A UPS is a power conditioning and supply system that affords protection against short-term power outages. A UPS rectifies the incoming AC line voltage to DC, which is then applied to batteries. An inverter, driven by DC power, supplies AC voltage for equipment that requires conditioned power. During outages, the converter is driven by battery power.

Unix. Unix is a 32-bit multitasking, multiuser operating system. Versions of Unix are available for nearly every type of computer platform. Unix was initially popular in universities and research labs, but it is now the basis of many corporate applications.

unshielded twisted-pair (UTP). UTP is a pair of foil-encased copper wires, twisted around each other. UTP is classified into several levels of wire quality suitable for different transmission speeds (see "Category").

user agent (UA). In X.400 mail systems, the user agent is the client component that provides the X.400 envelope, headers, and addressing. The user agent sends the messages to the X.400 mail server, or Message Transfer Agent, which then routes the messages to their destinations.

User Datagram Protocol (UDP). UDP is the connectionless transport protocol within the TCP/IP suite. Because it does not add overhead, as the connection-oriented TCP does, UDP is typically used with network-management applications and SNMP.

V

value-added reseller (VAR). Also called an integrator, a VAR is a company that resells manufacturers' products and adds value by installing or customizing the system.

VAX. Digital Equipment's brand name for its line of minicomputer and workstation hardware is VAX.

vertical wiring subsystem. The vertical wiring subsystem is the part of the structured wiring system that connects the campus wiring system to the departmental wiring system. It runs in a building's risers.

VINES. Banyan's NOS based on a Unix core and TCP/IP protocols. VINES supports DOS, Windows, Mac, and OS/2 clients and is especially popular in large enterprise networks. Its crowning feature is StreetTalk, its distributed directory service.

virtual circuit. A virtual circuit is a shared communications link that appears to the customer as a dedicated circuit. A virtual circuit passes packets sequentially between devices.

Virtual Terminal (VT). VT is the OSI terminal-emulation protocol.

virus. A virus has the ability to reproduce by modifying other programs to include a copy of itself. Several types of viruses exist. Bacteria or rabbits do not explicitly damage files but do reproduce and eat up disk space or RAM. A logic bomb lies dormant in a piece of code or program until a predefined condition is met, at which time some undesirable effect occurs. A password catcher mimics the actions of a normal log on but catches user IDs and passwords for later use. A Trojan horse is a program that appears to function but also includes an unadvertised and malicious feature. A worm scans a system for available disk space in which to run, thereby tying up all available space.

V.21. V.21 is the modem standard for the trunk interface between a network access device and a packet network. It defines signalling data rates greater than 19.2Kbps.

V.22, V.22 bis. V.22 is a 1,200-bps duplex modem for use in the public-switched telephone network and on leased circuits. V.22bis is a 2,400-bit modem that uses frequency division multiplexing for use on the public telephone network and on point-to-point leased lines. (The CCITT uses "bis" to denote the second in a series of related standards and "ter" to denote the third in a family.)

V.32, V.32 bis. V.32 are two-wire duplex modems operating at rates up to 9,600bps (with fallback to 4,800bps) for use in the public telephone network and on leased lines. V.32 bis offers speeds in increments of 4800bps, 7200bps, 9,600bps, 12,000bps, and 14,400bps.

V.34. Modems that comply with the V.34 standard can operate at rates as high as 28,800bps.

V.35. Prior to 1988, V.35 was a modem specification that provided data transmission speeds up to 48Kbps. V.35 was then deleted from the V-Series Recommendations.

V.42 error correction, V.42 bis data compression. The V.42 error-correction standard for modems specifies the use of both MNP4 and LAP-M protocols. V.22, V.22 bis, V.26 ter, and V.32 bis may be used with V.42. With V.42 bis compression, data is compressed at ratio of about 3.5 to 1, which can yield file-transfer speeds of up to 9,600bps on a 2,400-bps modem. Manufacturers can provide an option that will allow a V.42 bis modem to monitor its compression performance and adjust the ratio accordingly.

VMS. VMS is Digital Equipment's proprietary operating system for the VAX.

vulnerability analysis. A vulnerability analysis is a type of risk analysis in which you calculate the effects of a project's success or failure on your overall business.

W

wide area network (WAN). A WAN consists of multiple LANs that are tied together via telephone services and/or fiber optic cabling. WANs may span a city, state, a country, or even the world.

Windows. Microsoft's popular 16-bit GUI that runs on top of DOS. Windows 95, previously known as Windows 4.0 and code-named Chicago, is a 32-bit OS that integrates DOS and Windows. Windows for Workgroups is Microsoft's peer-to-peer network that uses a Windows interface and NetBIOS communications.

Windows NT. Microsoft's "New Technology" is the company's 32-bit, multitasking operating system that includes peer-to-peer file sharing. Windows NT Server provides high-end networking services. Cairo is Microsoft's code name for its next generation Windows NT.

wireless LANs. A wireless LAN does not use cable to transmit signals, but rather uses radio or infrared to transmit packets. Radio frequency (RF) and infrared are the most commonly used types of wireless transmission. Spread spectrum is used in the Industrial, Scientific, and Medical (ISM) bands. Most wireless LANs use spread spectrum transmission. It offers limited bandwidth, usually under 1Mbps, and users share the bandwidth with other devices in the spectrum; however, users can operate a spread spectrum device without licensing from the Federal Communications Commission (FCC). High-frequency RF offers greater throughput, but it is used less often because it requires an FCC license for the right to transmit.

Infrared may also be used as a wireless medium, and has greatest applicability for mobile applications due to its low cost. Infrared allows for higher throughput-measured in megabits per second-than spread spectrum, but it offers more limited distances. Infrared beams cannot pass through walls.

wiring closet. A wiring closet is a room or closet that is centrally located and contains operating data-communications and voice equipment, such as network hubs, routers, cross connects, and PBXs.

workflow software. Workflow software is a class of applications that helps information workers manage and route their work. It is a special class of groupware or workgroup software.

X

X Window System (X). X Window System, developed by MIT, is a graphical user system most often implemented on Unix systems. The Open Software Foundation's implementation of X Window is Motif. Sun and HP use a version called OpenLook.

X.25. X.25 is the CCITT and OSI standard for packet-switching networks that provide channels up to 64Kbps. Public and private X.25 networks can be built. In the United States, common X.25 networks are British Telecom, AT&T, CompuServe, and Infonet.

X.400. X.400 is the OSI and CCITT standard for store-and-forward electronic messaging. It is used for large enterprise networks or for interconnecting heterogeneous e-mail systems. X.400 divides an electronic mail system into a client, called a User Agent, and a server, called a Message Transfer Agent. Message Stores provide a place to store messages, submit them, and retrieve them. Access Units provide communication with other device types, such as telex and fax. Distribution Lists are routing lists.

X.500. X.500 is the OSI and CCITT specification for directory services. For computer users, a directory service provides a function similar to the function the telephone company's white pages provides telephone users. Using a directory service, computer users can look up easily the location of resources and other users.

Xerox Network System (XNS). XNS is Xerox's data-communication protocol; it is the basis for the IPX/SPX network protocols used in NetWare.

Index